REPRESEN CHAPTERS IN ANCIENT HISTORY

---

*An Introduction to the West's
Classical Experience*

Volume I I

From Romulus to Justinian

Richard W. Hooper

University Press of America,® Inc.
Lanham · New York · Oxford

Copyright © 2000 by
University Press of America,® Inc.
4720 Boston Way
Lanham, Maryland 20706

12 Hid's Copse Rd.
Cumnor Hill, Oxford OX2 9JJ

Library of Congress Cataloging-in-Publication Data

Hooper, Richard W. (Richard Walter)
Representative chapters in ancient history : an introduction
to the West's classical experience / Richard W. Hooper.
p.   cm.
Includes bibliographical references and index.
Contents: V. l. From australopithecus to Alexander —
v. 2. From Romulus to Justinian.
1.   History, Ancient. 2. Civilization, Ancient. 3. Mythology,
Classical 4. Human evolution. I. Title
D57.H66   2000   938—dc21   00-061582 CIP

ISBN 0-7618-1819-7 (pbk: alk. ppr.)

⊖™ The paper used in this publication meets the minimum
requirements of American National Standard for Information
Sciences—Permanence of Paper for Printed Library Materials,
ANSI Z39.48—1984

Contents

Maps and Table

23 The Rape of Lucrece

Meanwhile back at Italy, the next victim of the inexorably westward move of civilization was turning into a country. It will take us a few chapters to bring these Latins up to the point at which they absorbed the Greeks and then went on, reversing the tide of their origins, to conquer their cultural ancestors as well. This time, myth will be less of a help, for the Romans, as anyone who has studied Latin knows, were a rough and practical people; in the old days they cared nothing for books and pretty stories, so that by the time exposure to Greek culture told them that they needed an early history, they discovered that they hadn't bothered to keep track of one.

Romans of the 4th century were frankly embarrassed by the cultural riches of the snooty Greeks. Their pride demanded something similar, something indeed which could show the Greeks that they had taken part in the Trojan war too. The Romans therefore took Prince Aeneas, one of the minor Trojan heroes of the great war, and told how he escaped the burning city and sailed westward to found a new race in Italy.[1] Aeneas' son founded Alba Longa, the mother city of Rome, and it was his descendants, the twins Romulus and Remus, who founded Rome itself.

There is, as we'll see, some truth behind all this, but not much. This is all manufactured myth, and the story of how the divine twins Romulus and Remus were floated down the Tiber river in baskets, only to be suckled by a she-wolf (rationalized by Livy as a shepherdess called "She-Wolf" because of her promiscuity) sounds painfully like stories of Sargon and Cyrus that we've already examined.[2]

Once again, however, archaeology does help. The Italian layer cake is especially complex, and demonstrates that the Italian people are as much hybrids as anyone else. It will suffice for our purposes to point out that, as was the case in Greece, the first Indo-European peoples arrived between 2000-1000 BC. The Latins were only one of them and were hemmed into the narrow area

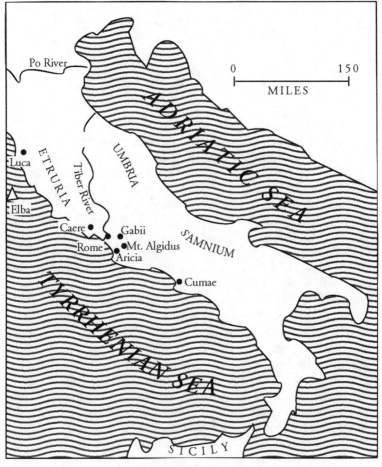

Early Italy

called after them Latium in the center of Italy; in the mountains to
the west were the Umbro-Sabellians, and to the south were the
Samnites, all three speaking related Indo-European languages
related to Celtic. During the 8th century the south of Italy was
overrun with Greeks—so much so that South Italy and Sicily came
to be nicknamed Magna Graecia (Big Greece)—and in the 6th
century the savage, blue-eyed Gauls seized the Po valley to the
north. Northern Italians have been blonde ever since.[3]

If, however, there is any truth in the story about Aeneas's

immigration from Asia Minor, it is to be found in the misty history of still another set of invaders, the Etruscans, who seem to have arrived in Italy during the late 9th century BC. In the legend, Aeneas was a Greek and even fought against the Etruscan King Mezentius, but if we imagine Aeneas' Trojan invasion as a politically inspired variant of the Etruscan conquest, it won't be the first time that national pride has turned a victim into a conqueror.

Etruscan history is misty because we can't understand their language. We're rather in the same position with the Etruscans as we are with the mysterious people who wrote in Linear A. We can read the sounds of Etruscan, for they adapted the Greek alphabet, but as their language is pre-Indo-European and has left no descendants, it is impossible to make much sense of it. We can read names and, employing Grotefend's methods, puzzle out some obvious patterns from the inscriptions, but for all intents and purposes the Etruscan language has remained undeciphered.[4] Herodotus tells us that the Etruscans came from Asia Minor. He says that they were led out of Lydia by King Atys' son Tyrrhenus in order to escape a famine. They sailed off to Umbria and took their name (Tyrrhenians) from their leader.[5]

The Etruscans arrived (as did Aeneas) on the west coast of Italy about 800 BC. They occupied the coastal area still called Tuscany today and gradually spread out to form a league of allied cities, each ruled by its own king–like Mezentius in the legend[6] or the very real Lars Porsenna of Clusium. Sometime during the 6th century they swallowed up Rome as well. Etruscan expansion was stopped by the power of the Greeks and Samnites in the south, the savage Gauls of the Po Valley to the north, and eventually, as we'll see, by the revolt of the Romans.

The city of Rome was created within this patchwork quilt of Latins, Greeks, Samnites, Gauls, and Etruscans. The words "Latin" and "Roman" sometimes cause confusion, and the influence both of the New Testament and Hollywood has so mystified these people that it's sometimes difficult to remember that they're basically old Italians. "Latin" is first of all the language of the Indo-European peoples who settled in the center of Italy. The people themselves are consequently called "Latins," and their area was known as "Latium." Latium contained many important cities, such as Tusculum, Praeneste, Ardea, Tibur–and Rome. So when we say "Romans" we mean those Latins who lived in the city of

Rome. The name Roman spread in meaning as the Romans proceeded to conquer all of Italy.

According to legend, therefore, the first Roman—in the broadest sense of the term—was Prince Aeneas, a son-in-law of King Priam of Troy and a son of the goddess Venus, who escaped from the burning city in the 12th century BC and made his way west to Italy. Landing at Cumae, which in reality would be the first Greek colony on Italian soil some 400 years later, Aeneas proceeded northwards along the coast to the Tiber river and then inland where he had a long and difficult war with the aboriginal Latins and (anachronistically) their evil allies the Etruscans. Aeneas founded the city of Lavinium and then ascended into heaven. His son Ascanius built the city of Alba Longa on the west bank of take Albano, which is about 13 miles south of the Tiber. The 13 kings of Alba Longa then conveniently fill up the time from the fall of Troy to the traditional date of the founding of Rome: April 21, 753 BC.[7]

Things went smoothly in Alba until King Proca gave birth to two sons, the elder of whom, good Prince Numitor, was overturned by his evil brother Amulius. Amulius killed his nephews and forced his niece Rhea Silvia to become a Vestal Virgin, which is to say a nun of the pagan Roman religion. She was, however, meant for greater things and was raped by Mars, the god of war. The result was the twins Romulus and Remus. As we've seen, they were floated down the Tiber river Sargon-and-Moses-style by their evil uncle, but were rescued Cyrus-style by a kindly she-wolf and a sympathetic shepherd.

The myth then follows the pattern of the story of King Cyrus: Recognized through their royal deportment by their uncle Numitor (for royal blood will always out), the twins led a successful revolt against their evil uncle and put Numitor back on the throne. It was now 753 BC. The boys set out to found a new city of their own, but unfortunately got into a fight over where it should be located. Romulus had chosen the Palatine hill, one of the famous 7 hills of Rome. He was busily building his brick walls when his brother, as brothers will do, hopped over the knee-high structure to poke fun at his brother's efforts. Romulus, who had little sense of humor, killed his brother on the spot—which is a good way to establish mythologically the sacredness of Rome's city limits.[8] That's why the present capital of Italy is called Rome instead of Reme.[9]

Looking for the truth behind this legend is a complex business. Even the connection between Rome and Alba Longa is problematical, for archaeology can't grant primacy to any of the many settlements scattered among the Alban and Roman hills. Indeed, these settlements were so disconnected that we can probably dismiss the city of Alba Longa itself as a simplification designed to explain the ancient pan-Latin festival of the *Feriae Latinae,* which was held on Monte Cavo. It was easier for the Romans to invent the destruction of Alba by Rome's third king Tullus Hostilius than to explain the origin of the *Feriae Latinae* without an urban center.

Settlements in what we could call pre-urban Rome go back to the 11th or 10th centuries near the island in the Tiber which controlled an easy ford across the river. These clusters of wooden huts spread up the Capital, Palatine, Velia, and Quirinal hills to escape both floods and mosquitoes.[10] The settlement on the Palatine by Romulus–and indeed traces of a mid eighth century wall were discovered in 1985 by Andrea Carandini–would have established a center for a scattered community already in existence.[11] By the early 7th century Rome was the most powerful city in Latium and the only place where the Latins still had access to the sea. It was inevitable that the Etruscans would try to move in and take over.

Two of Rome legendary kings have Etruscan names: Tarquinius Priscus and his son Tarquinius Superbus. Livy paints the first Tarquin as a powerful immigrant originally named Lucumo who ingratiated himself to the Roman people and was freely chosen as their king. He was later assassinated by the jealous sons of his predecessor King Ancus. The details are impossible to verify and of course Roman pride would avoid solidifying a story of conquest into myth, but nonetheless as we reach the Tarquins Roman legend seems slowly to merge into Roman history. Most interestingly a 4th century Etruscan tomb from Vulci contains a fresco in which one Oneve Tarchu Rumach (clearly "Gnaeus Tarquinius Romanus") is shown being killed by someone labeled Marce Camitlnas. The Tarquins were certainly historical and, as we'll see, Lucius Tarquinius Superbus was probably, just as the legends say, the last King of Rome.[12]

Etruscan rule at Rome would have conformed to the pattern they set up throughout their empire. The Etruscan landowners and merchants (though there was little to distinguish between an

Etruscan merchant and an Etruscan pirate in those days) would have formed the upper class and intermarried with the local Latin aristocracy. They alone would have comprised the cavalry and the major striking force of the army, relegating Latin farmers to the chores of foot soldier and camp follower. In Rome, however, the Etruscans never succeeded in imposing their language or the bulk of their culture upon the Latins. The Romans and even their Etruscan kings the Tarquins certainly spoke Latin and continued to worship the Latin gods.

Nonetheless, Etruscan influence was pervasive and long lasting. The Etruscans had traded with the Greeks for centuries, and Etruscan tomb paintings show that they lived in much the same high style as the civilized Greeks of Asia Minor. Rome's first exposure to Greek culture would have come from these Etruscans rather than from the hostile Greek and Samnite cities of the South. The Etruscans first paved the streets of Rome and regularized the city plan. They also introduced the symbol of Roman political power, the fascis. A fascis is an iron ax (symbolizing the power held by the king of life and death) surrounded by a bunch of wooden rods (symbolizing his power to inflict corporal punishment). Twelve of these fearsome bundles were always borne before the king by twelve state functionaries called lictors. The special curule chair on which the king sat as well as his purple robe were also Etruscan. Most charming was the Etruscan custom of having slaves fight to the death at funerals of great men as a blood sacrifice to the shades of the dead; this was the origin of Rome's gladiatorial combats.[13]

The next chapter will be devoted to describing the Roman republican government, but it might be a good idea to look briefly here at how Rome was governed at the time of her last kings. As might be expected, the typically Indo-European 3 part division between king, council of elders, aid Assembly of Adult Male Citizens prevailed. The citizens were, first and foremost, organized along family lines. That's why Romans traditionally have 3 names. Julius Caesar, for example, was actually named Gaius Iulius Caesar. Gaius was his given name, what his friends called him. There were only about a dozen of these *praenomina* in use for boys, while girls were invariably named after their fathers so that the name of Caesar's daughter was Julia. The middle name was the gens or clan name, and the Iulii were an old and honored, though in Caesar's time impoverished, clan. The last name could be a nickname (such as Calvus "Baldy," Flavus "Whitey," or even Magnus "Great"), but it usually, as in Caesar's case, denoted the family group of the clan to which he belonged.

The people as a whole were divided into three great tribes with obviously Etruscan names: Ramnes, Tities, and Luceres. These, much like the Athenian phratries, were subdivided into 10 curiae each. These were the basis of a typical assembly of all adult males, called the Comitia Curiata. It met to hear the king's decrees but also had the power to ratify a new king's appointment and to vote yes or no on questions of peace and war. Voting was by individual curia, so that in all only 30 actual votes were counted. Under the great King Servius Tullius, the predecessor to Tarquin the Proud, another military assembly called the Comitia Centuriata was formed. It eventually superseded the Comitia Curiata, but that is another story.[14]

The Council of Elders was called *Senatus*, the original of our word Senate. The Romans believed that Romulus originally had appointed 100 advisors for life and that the number was doubled by Tarquinius Priscus. It reached 300 by the end of the monarchy.[15] Senators were basically a source of advice and tradition to the kings, but they also were responsible for appointing a new king when the old one died.

Senators were addressed by the honorific title *patres*, "fathers," and their descendants came to be called *patricians*. The patrician class became increasingly exclusive as time went on until the Senate became virtually a closed club. The common folks were called *plebeians*. They were barred from most governmental service, and were completely barred from all of the priesthoods.

The origin of the gulf that came to separate the patricians from the plebeians is now difficult to trace. There is no evidence that it was either based on race or that it was defined by source of income, which in the fifth century would mean land for the aristocrats and lowly trade for the plebs. The safest bet is that the distinction was largely political in origin, for as the ruling families became progressively exclusive, their dependents were systematically squeezed out of both governmental and religious sources of power. Of course the more exclusive the patriciate became, the more explosive grew the frustration of the plebs.[16]

The seven kings who tradition says followed Romulus may well

be the names of real people, though it is of course impossible to say
how much truth there is in the stories Livy tells about them.[17] The
kings were absolute rulers who served for life, though they had to
be appointed by the Senate and confirmed by the people. They
were the chief generals of the state, as well as the chief judges and
priests.[18] Livy tells how the monarchy was driven out of Rome
forever in 509 BC. It's a story all Romans knew, and as such it can
tell us even more about the Roman character than it can about the
development of their constitution.

Luke "the proud" Tarquin was not a popular king. His wife
Tullia had helped him seize the throne literally over the body of
her father, good king Servius Tullius; driven by greed and envy,
Luke had even murdered his own nephew, so that the boy's
younger brother, Lucius Junius, was forced to act like an idiot to
escape his uncle's temper and had consequently earned the
nickname Brutus ("The Dummy").

Tarquin had even attacked the rich Latin city of Ardea in order
to finance his grandiose building schemes at Rome and to buy his
popularity from the Roman people, but the attack failed and
turned into a long and tedious siege. One evening around the
camp fire, Tarquin's son, Prince Sextus Tarquin, and his royal
friends, among whom was another nephew of the king named
Collatinus Tarquinius, were passing the time by bragging about
their wives. Despite what you might expect, the men bragged
about their wives' virtue as much as about their beauty. The
common picture of Rome as a place of wild and exotic orgies was
never really true except during the later empire, and then only in
the palaces of the rich and the nobles. The Romans were, at heart,
rather close to the Calvinist Puritans, and this was truest in the
centuries before the great Punic Wars. Even the Tarquins gloried
in the good old double standard, and expected their women (at
least the ones to whom they were married) to be modest, retiring,
and devoted.

Collatinus especially praised his wife Lucretia, and to prove his
point he suggested that all the princes pay a surprise visit to their
wives. The results were especially disappointing: all of the wives
were found throwing parties with their friends—except, of course,
the virtuous Lucretia, who was surprised in her living room
weaving wool yarn before the family hearth with her slaves, which
was precisely how a virtuous Roman matron was supposed to

spend her time. At the sight of all that beauty and virtue, the evil heart of Sextus Tarquin, as they say in novels, took flame. Several days later he secretly rode back to Collatinus's house in the town of Collatia where he was, of course, duly welcomed and given a guest room for the night.

Having waited for everyone to fall asleep, Sextus took his sword and sneaked into Lucretia's bedchamber. He woke her up and protested his love. That didn't work, so he put his sword to her throat. Good Roman matron that she was, Lucretia chose death before dishonor and refused to give in to the handsome young prince. Irritated at her obstinacy, Sextus then told her that if she didn't consent, he would kill her, butcher a slave boy, and put the two bodies in bed together so that he could tell Collatinus he had found his wife committing adultery with a slave–a sin to an ancient Roman just above doing it with a dog. Lucretia was forced to choose dishonor above disgrace, and Sextus rode back to camp with a smug smile upon his face.

Next morning Lucretia sent a message to her husband at Ardea and to her father at Rome that they each come with a single faithful friend, for "a terrible thing had happened." Her father and husband arrived that evening, Lucretius having brought a friend named Valerius, and Collatinus the goodhearted Lucius Junius Brutus whom, as we have pointed out, everyone took to be something of a dim-witted idiot. Lucretia announced what had happened and refused to be consoled even though everyone assured her that the outrage had obviously not been her fault. Lucretia demanded that her honor be avenged, but nonetheless refused to live on as a possible excuse or precedent to loose-living Roman ladies of the future. With that she took out a concealed dagger, stabbed herself, and fell dead at the feet of her stunned relations and friends.

Just like Zorro or the Scarlet Pimpernel, Brutus now threw away his mask and made an impassioned speech: The hated royal family had gone too far, and it was now time to cast them out of Rome. Under Brutus's leadership the men ran to the forum of Collatia where Brutus spoke again to the people. Apparently, Brutus understood what Marx, Engels, and Trotsky called "the art of insurrection," for he had chosen the right moment to strike. The populace, fed up at last with the Tarquins in particular and with monarchy in general, sped on to Rome, where the scene was repeated. The city gates were closed to the royal family while Brutus and his forces rushed to the army encamped before Ardea. The sight of Lucretia's bloody dagger whipped the sentimental Roman soldiers into a frenzy, and Tarquin and his son Sextus found themselves out in the cold. Sextus fled to Gabii, a town he had earlier infiltrated as a spy and taken over through treachery in his father's name. He was there assassinated in return for previous murders and outrages. Tarquin and two of his other sons fled to the town of Caere in Etruria,

The Roman people were so fed up with kings that from this point on, the very name of king (*rex*) became a dirty word in Roman politics.[19] To make sure that Rome would never be oppressed by tyrants again, the people in assembly elected two executive officers, whom they called consuls, to rule together with equal power for a term of one year, the idea being that each consul would prevent the other from becoming too powerful. As might be expected, the first consuls chosen were Lucius Tarquinius Collatinus and Lucius Junius Brutus.[20]

Of course King Tarquin fought back hard. He induced his fellow monarch, Lars Porsenna of Clusium, to avenge Etruscan honor and attack the rebel city. As the Etruscans swarmed over the Janiculum and swooped down on the central city itself, only Horatius Cocles held his position single handedly at the Sublician Bridge. There he stood hacking away like a one man Thermopylae while his men tore down the bridge behind him. Calling out to Father Tiber for protection, Horatius then flung himself into the river and swam to safety.[21]

Prevented from taking the city by Horatius at the bridge, Porsenna settled down for a tedious siege. At last courageous Gaius Mucius, having first been careful to get the Senate's permission, swam to the enemy's camp where he almost managed to assassinate King Porsenna. When brought before the king for interrogation, Mucius thrust his right hand into a flaming brazier and held it there, impervious to the pain, to show his contempt for torture. Three hundred similarly determined assassins, he warned the king, were waiting to take his place. Taking the hint, Porsenna concluded a peace treaty with Rome, and Mucius got the nickname *Scaevola* ("Lefty"). Meanwhile Porsenna's son Arruns was sent by his father to conquer the Latin town of Aricia. There the Latins, thanks to help from King Aristodemus of Cumae, cut the

Etruscans to ribbons.[22]

This is all very exciting, but how much of it is true? Ultimately of course such a question is impossible to answer, but we should start by allowing Livy himself to explain why he wanted his fellow Romans to know these stories:

> I shall not dwell upon how this ad similar tales are to be interpreted. Rather, let each one notice for himself the biographies, the morals, the men, and the means by which both at home and in the field empire was acquired and increased. Let him then follow how, when discipline slipped just a little, morality fell, then tumbled more and more, and finally went down head-long until we have arrived at these present times, when we can endure neither our vices nor their remedies.[23]

When Livy wrote his history, right at the moment when the Republic, which he was so eloquently describing, was turning into the Empire, he didn't care about "what happened." He wanted to explain why his generation, which had seen the horrors of civil war, had descended into chaos. The reason, as he explained above, was lack of discipline. The way the death of Lucretia illustrated that historical process was more important to him than the fate of the woman herself. In making that choice, Livy tells us a lot about the Romans and about himself.[24]

Lucretia's story is simply too neat to be "true." Brutus and Sextus are drawn as complete opposites. Sextus's sin is not merely that he's a heel and a rapist, but that, unlike the true Roman Brutus, he has no self control. He is, indeed, such a focus of chaos that he is actually seduced by Lucretia's virtue. Brutus, on the other hand, has so kept his emotions under control that he has been able to play his role of dummy for years. Later on in Livy's story (2.5) he would even order and watch the execution of his own sons because they had betrayed the state. He represents the virtues that Livy hopes will give a new birth to Roman glory; Sextus represents the vices that nearly destroyed it.

Most depressingly unrealistic, however, is poor Lucretia, who is allowed no personality of her own. Locked permanently within her house (which she never leaves during the whole story![25]) she is only a possession and extension of her husband. Her rape is a violation of his property rights, and her death the only expiation allowed.

We saw this pattern before in the deaths of Harmodius and Aristogeiton. The fact that these characters are supposed to have been "real" doesn't change the symbolism of their deaths. In the young boy Harmodius especially we meet the fateful worm in society's rose. It was beauty, both his and Lucretia's, which tempted evil tyranny to its destruction. Although as moral members of society we are allowed to share the lesson, we cannot be allowed to succumb to the same seduction. We are not supposed to lust after the beauty of Lucretia and Harmodius, nor are we permitted to admit that we feel any attraction. But we can enjoy the lurid and bloody tales of their deaths. Even as we weep for their tragedies we are supposed to realize that they have served their countries best as corpses, and that they probably deserved what they got for showing off anyway.

Once Lars Porsenna enters the scene, further contradictions in our sources throw everything into confusion. Livy reports, for instance, that the remnants of Arruns' hated army fled back to Rome for protection, where they were not only welcomed, but even given their own ward, the *vicus Tuscus*.[26] There is also a rival version, preserved casually by Tacitus and more fully by the encyhclopaedist Pliny the Elder[27] that Lars Porsenna took Rome and subjected it to harsh terms!

We are once again the victims of Roman propaganda. Not only did Porsenna take Rome; it is probable that he was the one actually to overturn the Tarquins and so make the Republic possible. The Roman analysts were undoubtedly unhappy with this shameful fact, as well as with the humiliation of having been rescued from Porsenna's control by their Latin allies under the leadership of Aristodemus the Effeminate, tyrant of the Greek city of Cumae.[28] How much more uplifting to read about the noble Brutus and the bleeding but still noble Lucretia, about Horatius at the bridge and the indomitable Mucius Scaevola!

> He left the name, at which the world grew pale,
> To point a moral, or adorn a tale.[29]

24 S.P.Q.R.

The revolution of Brutus and Collatinus was less revolutionary than it might at first seem. The kings were out, but the two consuls who took their place ruled much like their predecessors. True, they were restricted to a one year term, could veto each other's acts, and were forced to alternate their display of lictors and *fasces*,[1] but it's significant that consuls were always chosen from the same small group of patrician families. Indeed, the Fabii ruled Rome in an unbroken stretch from 485-479.[2]

Like the kings before them, consuls introduced foreign ambassadors to the Senate, brought bills before it, and carried out its decrees. They convened the assemblies, levied both native and allied troops (over whom they had the power of life and death), and served as their chief generals. Consuls sat on the throne-like *sella curialis* and wore the *toga praetexta*, a white robe bordered with a purple stripe. When commanding the army they were dressed fully in royal purple. The start of the revolution was not so much the expulsion of the Tarquins as the establishment of an oligarchy controlled by a system of checks and balances.

The mutual veto was taken very seriously. If events became so chaotic that a single strong hand was needed, rather than pervert the built-in balance of the dual consulship, a whole new officer called a *dictator* was appointed by one of the consuls.[3] The first dictator was appointed in the year 500, but the most famous of them all was Lucius Quinctius Cincinnatus. A deputation from the Senate went to his farm in 458 to ask for his help: the consul Lucius Minucius had gotten himself and his army trapped in a valley below Mt. Algidus by a fierce northern tribe called the Aequi, and everyone was convinced that only the wily old Cincinnatus could save the day.

The senatorial commission found him plowing his fields. Lucius had his wife bring him his toga so that he could face his fellow senators in a dignified fashion. He listened to their appeal, nodded gravely, and then rode off to do his deed. The Aequi routed,

Cincinnatus laid down his command and returned to his farm. It was this kind of selfless devotion (as little Latin boys were told in school) that made the Roman republic work.[4]

The patricians further weakened the consulship by introducing two new officers called censors, the first being appointed in 443. Censors eventually came to be appointed every five years: they drew up the list of qualified senators, divided the citizens into property classes to determine their voting rights and military service (as we'll see shortly), and in the end even supervised public morals—hence the meaning of the modern word *censorship*. The most famous censor of all was Marcus Porcius Cato (the Elder), who was elected censor in 184. Cato once expelled a man from the senate because the fellow had shown the bad taste to kiss his own wife in public.[5]

It was the gradual evolution of this system of checks and balances over the next two hundred years which created the Roman Republic. The actors were not only the typical members of the Indo-European troika we've seen so often already, but the social classes of patricians and plebeians and, later when those terms ceased to have any real meaning, of rich and poor as well.

Having examined the consuls, who had taken over the old job of the kings, we should glance at the Council of Elders and the Assembly as well. That done, we can stand back and watch them slug it out.

We've already met the Senate, which by the time of Tarquin's expulsion had grown to 300 members.[6] The Senate controlled the purse strings of the state. Neither the *quaestors*, who were state and military treasurers, nor the censors, who besides their above mentioned duties were also in charge of public works, could expend funds without a senatorial decree. The Senate handled all disputes among the Italian allies, received all foreign ambassadors, and directed international relations.[7] In the early 3rd century BC when Cineas, the ambassador from Pyrrhus, King of Epirus, visited the Senate, he reported back to his master that it "seemed to him an assembly of kings."[8] With the real kings gone, the consuls at first took on the job of filling vacancies in the Senate. Once the censors absorbed that power, they tended to restrict their choice to the pool of ex-magistrates.[9]

It is considerably more difficult to explain the Roman Assembly, for unlike the Sumerians, Spartans, and Athenians whom we've already looked at, the Romans weren't content with a single Assembly of adult males. They had four: The *Concilium Plebis* (Assembly of the Plebs), The *Comitia Tributa* (The Assembly by Tribes), The *Comitia Centuriata* (The Assembly by Centuries), and the *Comitia Curiata* (The Assembly by *Curiae*). The royal assembly, the *Comitia Curiata*, which appeared in the last chapter, fortunately faded into an ornament whose only important job was to confirm the election of the consuls. Only plebeians belonged to the *Concilium Plebis*; all Roman citizens belonged to the *Comitia Tributa*, but the poorer folks, by dint of their numbers, usually controlled it.

The most important of the republican assemblies was the *Comitia Centuriata*. This was the assembly which elected the important magistrates—the consuls, praetors (judges), and censors—and was thought of as the nation under arms. It's therefore closest to the concept of an assembly of adult males that we've been studying ever since Gilgamesh overruled the old men of Erech. Since this was a military unit, it could not assemble within the walls of Rome, where no army was allowed. The *Comitia Centuriata* was organized by centuries, or companies of the Roman army[10], and was assembled by trumpet call to meet on the Field of Mars (*Campus Martius*) north east of the Forum, where the Tiber bends abruptly to the west. The Romans assigned its invention to King Servius Tullius, who saw it as an opportunity both to reorganize the army and perhaps to regularize the distinction between patricians and plebeians. As such, the invention of the *Comitia Centuriata* can be looked upon as similar to the reforms of Solon and Cleisthenes. Indeed, from a military standpoint it reflects a general tendency throughout the Mediterranean world during the 7th-6th centuries to modernize the old fashioned citizen militia into a disciplined, heavily armored hoplite mass.

Good King Servius Tullius[11] divided the entire population into five classes or property divisions. In those days it was an honor to serve in the army and—exactly opposite to us—it was an honor jealously guarded by the rich. Soldiers weren't paid in old Rome; they even had to buy their own armor and equipment. Thus the poor were not allowed to serve and were, in consequence of their lack of risk in battle, virtually disenfranchised. In the *Comitia Centuriata*, the richer you were, the more your vote counted.

It worked like this. The richest men in Rome were those who

could afford to keep a horse in the garage. They were divided up into 18 centuries of Knights (*Equites*)[12] and were originally given the privilege of voting first. Next to vote were the first class infantry—those who could afford to buy a full suit of armor. They were divided into 70 centuries. After the First Punic War the right to vote first was transferred to one of these 70 centuries of the first class infantry. This lucky century was chosen by lot and got the name *praerogativa.* Its vote was highly sought after, for it gave the citizenry a usually irresistible hint of the intentions of their betters.

There were five infantry classes in all, as well as additional centuries of carpenters, armorers, musicians, blacksmiths, and camp followers. All in all they made up 192 centuries, to which was added a final century, the *proletarii* (which word is the origin of Marx's *proletariat*) of all the poor devils who were too poor to serve in the army. As in the case of the *Comitia Curiata* it was not one man one vote; a straw vote was taken century by century, and each century was granted one vote.

As will be noted, the Knights and the First Class together held 88 votes. It was thus seldom necessary to extend the voting down further than the third infantry class in order to secure a majority. The *proletarii* at the bottom would only be called upon to vote if there were a dead tie through the 192 centuries of the rest of the population. The poorest folk, therefore, didn't vote at all.[13]

At first, in the old days, that might have seemed fair, since after all it was the rich who took the risks. Besides, in primitive Rome someone without a farm or a small business would, if he wasn't a slave, in all probability starve to death. This gradually changed, however, until by the time of Augustus the *proletarii* outnumbered the other five classes put together! Nonetheless, throughout the history of the Roman Republic, even as their numbers shrank in proportion to the rest of the population, the rich controlled the election process.[14]

The *Comitia Centuriata* was, however, a clumsy assembly. People had to traipse all the way out to the Campus Martius to vote in it, and a consul usually had to be dug up to be the chairman. It soon became easier, especially in cases of poor men's business, to assemble the plebeians by tribes in the *Concilium Plebis,* which didn't need a big-wig politician to run it, could be quickly assembled within the city walls, and didn't vote in the complicated century system. Servius Tullius had dumped Rome's three old tribes with their quaint rustic names and, much like Lycurgus and Cleisthenes, had redivided Rome into residential tribes: four for the city limits, and sixteen (later expanded to thirty-one) for the countryside. If both patricians and plebeians had to be consulted, the consul could assemble the other tribal assembly, the *Comitia Tributa.*

The tribal assemblies were still rigged, of course. The disproportionate number of country and suburban tribes can be attributed to the fact that the rich landowners had their estates in the country. Voting was still according to the group system (one tribe, one vote), so the country districts always had the advantage.

As Rome grew, however, first over Latium and then over Italy itself, it became harder and harder for the rural tribe members to make it to Rome for meetings of the tribal assembly. In consequence, the four urban tribes, who were always about and willing to vote, grew in importance. Officials inevitably got careless, and if suburbanites weren't available to vote in the thirty-one rural tribes, city dwellers were appointed to vote in their place. Thus, as we'll see, the tribal assembly gradually became more and more important in Roman politics.[15]

It should be obvious that this was by no means a representative government. That idea never occurred to the ancients, who felt that citizens could only conduct their government in person, and who thus condemned themselves to trying to control increasingly cosmopolitan states with a system suitable only for the business of a small town.[16]

At the start of our story, only the *Comitia Centuriata* could pass laws. The best the tribal assemblies could do was to pass resolutions called *plebiscita*, which were only binding upon the *plebs* if they were ratified by the Senate. As long as this distinction stayed intact, Rome was thoroughly in the hands of the rich.

As is usually the case, the rich were not worthy of their trust. Without a king to turn to as Big Brother, the plebeians were at the complete mercy of the upper classes. Like their colleagues in Athens, many of Rome's poor put themselves up as collateral and so, upon default, were sold off into slavery. Although there had been 12 plebeian consuls between 590 and 486, there were no more for 25 years. An aristocratic clique was gradually, through custom, tightening its grip on power.[17]

Within only 15 years after the expulsion of Tarquin, the plebs

were so hard pressed that they decided to go on strike: Upon returning from a campaign against the Volsci, the entire army withdrew to the Aventine hill and told the patricians to try to run the
country without them. The Senate sent the praetor Menenius
Agrippa to talk them back, and he apparently did so with a fable
about a body which, he said, once went on strike to force its lazy
belly to go to work. The strike, Agrippa went on, seemed like a
good idea until the body noticed itself wasting away—the moral
being, of course, that all parts of the body politic were essential,
even (as he apparently meant) the fat paunch of the nobility.[18]

A positive concession, however, was also necessary, so the Senate, after swallowing hard, coughed up a new officer called the
tribune. Two were elected by the plebs in 493, and by 448 the
number had been raised to ten. Tribunes were meant to be the
Big Brother that the plebeians needed. No patrician could hold
the office. Nobody could strike a tribune and escape with his life.
For his part, the tribune, who was required to stay in the city during his year of office and keep his door open at night, was supposed to step in on a plebeian's side whenever the need arose. By
simply saying *veto* ("I forbid!") he could cancel any decree, and
indeed even prevent the Senate from holding a meeting. He was
elected by and could summon the *Concilium Plebis*, once at the
head of which he could, of course, propose *plebescita* to his heart's
content. The only drawback to the great power of the *veto* was that
senators could generally talk one tribune into canceling the acts
of another.[19]

The strike which led to the creation of the tribunes was, however, only the beginning. For the next two hundred years the patricians and plebeians fought it out until they achieved political
equality. The next important step was in 451 when the tribunes
forced the patricians to write down the laws. This sounds perhaps
like a small thing, but going to court without knowing the law is
rather like trying to play cards with a five-year-old: you can't
possibly win if you don't know all the rules. Ten patricians were
appointed for the job. They produced ten large wooden tablets,
and a second commission of five patricians and five plebeians was
then elected the next year to add on two more. The idea of a commission of decemvirs unfortunately misfired, for they became
tyrannical and weren't driven out of office until the plebs went
on strike again in 449, but the result was the Law of the Twelve

Tablets, which as Livy pointed out, "even now, in this immense pile of laws heaped one upon another, is the fountain of all public and private law."[20]

The picture which emerges from these laws isn't of an especially enlightened society, and it certainly doesn't make Rome compare well with Athens which, at this time, was busily building up the Delian League. The opening passage apparently ran as follows:

> If he is summoned into court, let him go. If he doesn't go, summon witnesses against him, then seize him. If he stalls or runs away, lay hands upon him. If he is sick or old, provide a pack animal; if he is unwilling, do not provide a covered wagon.

The father's absolute authority within the family is evident from this law from Tablet 4: "If a father has sold his son three times, let the son be free from the father." If this sounds like Hammurabi's Code, the similarity seems even stronger from this law in Tablet 8: "If he has broken a limb, nor has made an agreement with him, let it be tit for tat." There is even a fragmentary reference to witches in Tablet Eight.[21] Rough though they were, however, the Twelve Tablets at least made the laws the common property of all Romans.

The next logical step was to make the Romans the common property of each other. That perfectly natural desire had been thwarted by a law inserted into the 11th of the Twelve Tables by the aristocrats, who were becoming increasingly unwilling to share their power with their former plebeian colleagues. In 445 the Tribune Gaius Canuleius introduced a bill to legalize marriage between plebeians and patricians. The patrician consuls understandably railed against this, saying in the Senate:

> For what other effect will promiscuous marriages have except that the intercourse of patricians and plebeians will be commingled almost like that of wild beasts? No one will know his patrimony, his bloodline, nor his proper place in the sacred rites! Half patrician, half plebeian, no one will even be at peace with himself![22]

The opposition of the upper crust was doomed to failure, however, because the patrician clans, considerably diminished in number already thanks to the constant blood-letting of foreign wars, needed the new money of the plebeians to shore up their own tottering aristocratic houses. As usual, Canuleius and the other tribunes wouldn't allow a levy for a foreign war until the right of intermarriage was granted.

Feeling puffed up from this victory, Canuleius's colleagues then proposed that one of the two yearly consulships be set aside by law for a plebeian. This ancient quota system seems to have been approved, but again only after a compromise: a new office called "military tribune" was created. These were military officers with all the power of the consuls, and by their very presence they undermined the consuls' authority until their eventual replacement in 367. So the patricians were still unwilling to entrust to the lower classes a consulship with its powers undiminished. The plebeians themselves, creatures of habit like the rest of us, tended to elect their patrician "betters" to the rank of military tribune and so undercut their own throats.

By 377 Rome was beginning to look like pre-Solon Athens. Many plebeians had been enslaved for debt (an evil practice which wasn't officially outlawed until the *lex Poetalia* of 326), and the presence of the military tribunes had obliterated the promised plebeian consulship. Two tribunes names Gaius Licinius Stolo and Lucius Sextius struck back with three outrageous proposals: First, they proposed that all debts be reduced by the amount of interest that had already been paid, and that any remaining amount be paid off in three easy installments. Given the high rate of interest and the age of many of the poor folks' inherited debts, that would have the effect of almost canceling all debts—just like Solon.

Second, the tribunes proposed a new land distribution scheme. As Rome had expanded over Italy, she had taken over large tracks of land from her conquered neighbors and opened up these territories to homesteading. Unfortunately, the rich senators had largely moved in on this "public land" and turned it into large plantations for their own use. Licinius and Sextius proposed that these illegally held plantations be split up into 300 acre (500 *iugera*) plots and redistributed among the common people. Thus the spirit of Lycurgus lived on.

Third, they proposed to revive the Canuleian dead letter and see to it that the consulship be restored and that one of the consuls be a plebeian.

For ten years the patricians bought off tribunes to veto these provisions, and during the same period the plebeians kept reëlecting Licinius and Sextius to their posts. For five of those years the two popular tribunes shut down the executive branch of the government with their vetoes. The stand-off was finally broken in 367 with—you guessed it!—another compromise. The consulship was restored, and Lucius Sextius was elected as the first plebeian consul since the early days of the Republic. That was to make the plebeians happy. For the patricians, two new officers were created, the praetorship and the "curule" aedileship.

The praetors were, as Livy put it, "colleagues to the consuls" (7. 1), and even had the power to command an army. For the most part, however, they took over the legal duties of the consul, duties which had originally, of course, been part of the king's job. There were two praetors: the urban praetor, who handled cases between Roman citizens, and the peregrine praetor, who dealt with foreigners. Their yearly edicts, by directing procedure—i.e. the formulas under which an action could or could not take place— had a profound influence on how Roman law developed. As the Roman Empire grew and the number of provinces increased, more praetorships were created so that ex-praetors could serve as governors. Six eventually became the standard number until Sulla raised it to eight in the first century. Augustus was forced to double the number. Nonetheless the private law still remained the exclusive responsibility of the original urban and peregrine praetors.

The two new curule aediles, who at first were patrician, more prestigious than their colleagues, and elected by the *Comitia Tributa*, joined the original plebeian aediles, who were elected by the *Concilium Plebis*. The distinction is not clear and gradually faded. Cicero conveniently summarized the aediles' duties as "curators of the city, of the markets, and of the customary games."[23] Their care of the city involved the general supervision of streets, baths, bordellos, and graveyards. From their supervision of markets evolved their general direction of the capital's grain supply. From their supervision of the "customary games" came their politically most useful function: their ability to bribe future voters with the production of bloody gladiatorial spectacles. Indeed, Livy tells us (6. 42) that the curule aediles were created because the plebeian aediles couldn't afford the lavish butchery scheduled to celebrate the end of the Licinian-Sextian conflict.[24]

The final reform was passed 80 years later when the plebs, still complaining about debt, tramped off to the Janiculum Hill and again went on strike. To calm them down a plebeian named Quintus Hortensius was appointed dictator and saw to it that an old dream was finally realized. The *Concilium Plebis* was, in effect, made equal to the *Comitia Centuriata*, for its *plebescita* became binding upon the whole Roman state. There were now two ways to pass legislation in Rome. It should be remembered that both assemblies were (theoretically) made up of the same people, but because of the way they were organized, the rich controlled the *Comitia Centuriata* while the smaller landowners controlled the *Concilium Plebis.* So now the rich and the poor could frame and pass their own bills—subject, of course, to the vetoes of the tribunes and the oversight of the conservative Senate.[25]

By tradition and habit the offices that we've described were arranged into a sequence, the *cursus honorum,* which was established in law in 180 BC. Its graduates turned into a new noble class which did away with the distinction of patrician and plebeian. As the patricians and the plebs could now intermarry, their identity blurred, but these rich patrician-plebeians saw to it that only their families were allowed into the closed club of the offices. No official in Rome was paid, so you had to be rich to serve anyway.[26]

By the third century, therefore, a young nobleman (and, again, notice that I didn't say patrician or plebeian) would begin his career at the age of 30 by standing before the tribal assembly for one of the eight quaestorships. As quaestor he would administer the financial affairs of an army and, if he were lucky, even see military service under the provincial governor who would be his commanding officer. The quaestorship would also qualify him for life-long membership in the Senate.

He then had to wait nine years until he was allowed to face the *Comitia Centuriata,* so he might pass the time by running for the aedileship, where he would see to it that the sewers remained unclogged, the public buildings were kept clean, and the populace, who would one day vote for him as consul, were kept happily entertained with gladiatorial shows. If this young nobleman were of plebeian stock, he might run for the tribuneship. Tribunes were not only elected by, they presided over the *Concilium Plebis.* Thanks to the *Lex Hortensia,* they could initiate legislation and play up to the voters even more effectively than could the aediles with their action-packed public spectacles.

Finally, on the ninth year following his quaestorship, the nobleman could stand before the *Comitia Centuriata* for one of the eight praetorships. Only the most successful politicians could advance to the consulship, and only after they were 43 years old.

Note that the *Comitia Centuriata* elected the praetors, consuls, and (every 5 years) the censors. It's no coincidence that the three most powerful offices in the state were elected by the "rich man's assembly." The consulship was glorious, but the censorship was kept as the crown of a noble's political career.[27]

Elections were held at Rome in late July, just after the games to Apollo, which acted as a considerable draw to get the yokels into the big city. Remember that there was no such thing as an absentee ballot: You had to vote in Rome, in person, and (until 139) out loud. The nobles were very careful to keep in close contact with the upper class land owners of the Italian countryside. Since they made up the first class in the *Comitia Centuriata*, they controlled who would be elected to the positions of consul and praetor.

Thus when this Roman gentry streamed into the capitol each summer for the shows and the elections, they found the roadside plastered (actually, painted) with election posters for the favorites of the political big wigs. First century AD examples of these posters have survived in Pompeii, where they have become so standardized that recommendations are reduced to abbreviations.[28]

There were neither parties, party platforms, nor party tickets in Roman elections. Each nobleman ran on his own influence and by means of whatever deals he could make with his political cronies and family connections. Candidates went down to the Campus Martius or the Forum to kiss babies, shake hands, and beg humbly for votes. They were called "candidate" (*candidatus*) because they wore a toga specially whitened with chalk–the Roman equivalent of a red, white, and blue campaign button. Just as in American elections, there was a lot of politicking and then a formal announcement of candidacy–in the Roman instance just 25 days before the election.[29]

Our concept of a balance of power comes from the Roman Republic–or at least from the Greek historian Polybius's description of it.[30] As he put it, if you looked at the Roman Senate, you'd call the government an aristocracy; if you looked at the consuls, you'd call it a tyranny; if at the people, a democracy. Each segment acted as a brake upon the ambitions of the others.

The Roman republican government sounds impossibly complex and cumbersome, but that's because it evolved slowly and organically. Clumsy though it was, it was still flexible and adaptive enough to lead Rome through its years of growth and greatness. We think of Rome as the city of the Empire, but in so doing we forget that she was, at least in name, a democratic republic for 500 years.

25 The Purple People

So long as Rome confined herself to expanding in Italy, she was free to engage in what, from the modern standpoint at least, could be called internal politics. But once her merchants expanded outside of Italy, she slammed into the interests of the ancient city of Carthage, the greatest commercial power of the western Mediterranean. We'll be looking at a lot of immediate causes for the war, but this basic commercial rivalry was always a big part of it.

There was racial hatred too. Carthage, actually *Qart Chadascht* (The New City)[1], was not Indo-European: it had been founded back in 814 by the Semitic Phoenicians, those alphabet inventing merchants from modern Lebanon.[2] As often happens, the outpost ended up being much more durable than the mother city Tyre, for Carthage built up an empire stretching from the Gulf of Gabès westward to Algeria and even beyond the Pillars of Hercules to her allies the Lilyphoenicians.

The Romans did such a commendable job of wiping Carthage off the face of the earth that no Punic literary works have survived. There is a tantalizing fragment in Greek translation called *The Periplus of Hanno,* which supposedly recounts a Carthaginian circumnavigation of Africa some 2,000 years before Vasco da Gamma. It appears, unfortunately, to be a forgery,[3] and thus leaves us with a very one sided view of the people we are about to describe. There is another suspicious story that at the final destruction of Carthage in 146 BC the Romans handed over to "the petty kings of Africa" Carthage's great libraries so that the cultural heritage of their enemy could be preserved. The scene is very difficult to imagine and perhaps only shows that a small minority of literate Romans felt some twinge of remorse if not for the murder of people, then at least for the loss of books.[4]

Both Polybius and Aristotle compare Carthage's government with Sparta's, for both were ruled by two "kings" riding herd over a boisterous Assembly and the predictable Council of Elders. These kings were actually annually elected officials called *suffetes* who, like the Roman consuls, came from a select group of upper class families. Aristotle complains that wealth was such a factor in the selection of the suffetes that the office was virtually for sale. Although open debate was allowed in the Assembly, a narrow oligarchy seems to have kept pretty strict control both of the legislative and the judicial branches of the Carthaginian government. Polybius complains that by the time of the Second Punic War the balance of power in Carthage was shifting to the public assembly, a "democratization" which he saw as a sign of weakness.[5]

Plutarch seems to have been correct in his assessment of the Carthaginians as "bitter, sullen, subservient to their magistrates, harsh to their subjects, most abject when afraid, most savage when enraged, stubborn in adhering to their decisions, disagreeable and hard in their attitude towards playfulness and urbanity." Modern excavations of the Tophet, or sacrificial enclosure, of Carthage have proven that their priests regularly sacrificed human infants to Baal Hamon, just as the prophet Jeremiah thundered in the Old Testament:

> For the children of Judah have done evil in my sight, saith the Lord: they have sent their abominations in the house which is called by my name, to pollute it. And they have built the high places of Tophet, which is in the valley of the son of Hinnom, to burn their sons and their daughters in the fire...

More than two hundred urns containing their charred bones have been uncovered in the ruins of the city.[6]

Rome fought three wars with the Carthaginians. They're always called "The Punic Wars," which is to say "The Purple Wars," after the purple dye for which the Phoenician traders were famous.[7] The first war (264-241 BC) was fought over the possession of Sicily. It went on for so long because the two cities were so evenly but oppositely matched: Carthage, the merchant power, was at first unbeatable on the sea, while Rome's citizen militia of farmers was far superior to the mercenary armies employed by Carthage. At the conclusion of the first war Rome seized Sicily and then stuck Carthage with a huge fine. The fine so drained the Carthaginians of cash that they couldn't pay off their mercenaries, who promptly revolted and nearly captured the city of Carthage itself. Taking advantage of this distraction, Rome seized the Carthaginian colonies of Sardinia and Corsica and calmly offered to restart the war

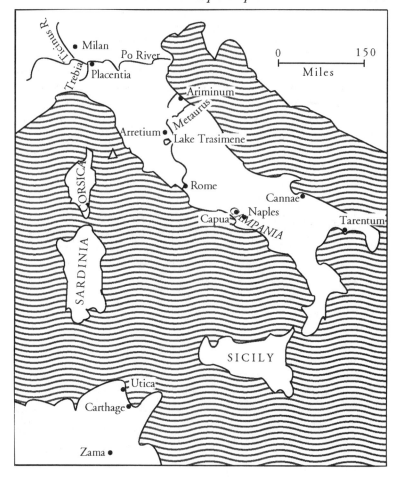

Africa, Sicily, and Italy during the Punic Wars

if Carthage dared complain.

To complete our picture of the Roman constitution, I should point out that Sicily and Corsica-Sardinia were organized into the first two Roman provinces so that we have here the official beginning of the Roman Empire. Each year the Senate appointed ex-consuls or ex-praetors to serve as governors, and as the number of provinces increased it became necessary to raise the number of praetors to take up the slack. After the Second Punic War the number of praetors was doubled to four; by the reign of the first emperor Augustus it varied between ten and sixteen. As we'll see, the scramble for choice provinces became one of the major focuses of a Roman political career.[8]

The defeat of the First Punic War left a particularly bitter taste in the mouths of the Carthaginians. This was especially the case for Carthage's general Hamilcar Barca (Hamilcar "the Lightning Bolt"), who had negotiated the unfavorable treaty, but whose own troops had never been defeated in Sicily. The wily Hamilcar decided to make up for the loss of Sicily and Sardinia-Corsica by conquering the interior of the then Celtic Iberian peninsula. He died in Spain trying to accomplish that goal. Before leaving on his last campaign, however, he brought his young son Hannibal up the steps of the altar of Baal-Moloch. As Hannibal later told the Seleucid King Antiochus of Syria, "He took me by the right hand and led me up to the altar and bade me lay my hand upon the victim and swear that I would never be friends with Rome."[9]

In 229 the Carthaginian army elected the twenty-five year old Hannibal as its general, a choice which was subsequently confirmed by the Assembly back home. For expediency's sake Hannibal honored a treaty his brother-in-law Hasdrubal had made with Rome not to march north of the Ebro River; it suited his purpose and conformed to his father's advice not to get into

Punic Spain

war with Rome until he had secured Spain as a base of operations. Hannibal conquered all of Spain south of the Ebro except the semi-Greek city of Saguntum, which was a recent ally of Rome.

By the winter of 220-219 the people of Saguntum were very nervous and were sending to Rome for help. Further north the people of Massilia were getting nervous too. Massilia (which name the modern French have slurred into "Marseilles") had been founded by Phocaea way back in 600 and had been at odds with Carthage ever since. Some time before 218 Massilia signed a formal alliance with Rome, who was probably more concerned with the Gallic threat on her northern frontier than with Carthaginian expansion into Spain or dominance over the markets of the Western Mediterranean.[10]

In response to this pressure from her allies, Rome sent a senatorial commission to Hannibal in Spain. He was furious: Pointing out that Rome had recently put down a political uprising in Saguntum and executed its ringleaders, he not only accused Rome of meddling in Saguntum's affairs, but even threatened to come to her aid! The Romans sailed off in a huff, Hannibal forthwith attacked Saguntum, and the city fell after an 8 month siege. Hannibal used loot from Saguntum to consolidate his political position back home.[11]

The Roman Senate sent an embassy to Carthage with a choice: Hannibal's head on a platter, or war with Rome. Rome cited a clause in the First Punic War Treaty which stated, "The allies of neither of the parties to the treaty shall be attacked by the other." Carthage countered by pointing out that at the time of the treaty, Saguntum was not yet an ally of Rome. The Romans called that quibbling; of course the treaty had implied "all subsequent allies too." Carthage retorted that the language wasn't in the treaty. The Romans turned to Hasdrubal's treaty which stated, "The Carthaginians shall not cross the Ebro with arms." Carthage replied cleverly that the treaty in question had not been ratified and so was invalid.

If we join Polybius and look behind this bickering, it's clear that neither side was innocent in this war. Carthage clearly had no right to attack Saguntum—especially since Hannibal didn't come as a liberator, but rather as a looter—but by the same token Rome had had no right to seize Sardinia-Corsica during the Mercenary War and then slap Carthage with an additional fine to boot.

The precise cause for such a war, however, is incidental. Given the hopelessly contrasting commercial interests and the deep seated cultural hostility of the two great cities, war was inevitable. So the Roman ambassador told the Carthaginians that he carried in the folds of his toga both peace and war. The suffete told him to bring out whichever he chose. He chose war and the Carthaginian Senate shouted back that they accepted it.[12]

Like any good general, Hannibal proceeded to do the unexpected. Since the Romans had expected to fight the war in Spain, Hannibal decided to invade Italy by marching across the Riviera and then onward through the Alps. He cleverly sent agents into North Italy to encourage the Gauls, only recently conquered by Rome, to join with him in a revolt against their hated conquerors. He then set out from Spain with 50,000 infantry, 9,000 cavalry, and 32 elephants equipped with Indian mahouts. Meanwhile the Romans, thinking that they were well prepared, had dispatched the consul Tiberius Sempronius Longus to Africa with a fleet of 160 ships to terrify the Carthaginians. The other consul, Publius Cornelius Scipio, was sent off to Spain.

Scipio made a stop-over in Marseilles and received the shock of his life: Hannibal, rather than cowering in Spain and awaiting his arrival, had already crossed the Rhône River and was proceeding on to Italy. Scipio tried to force a battle, but Hannibal thumbed his nose, put his cavalry and elephants to the rear for protection, and marched on to Italy. Scipio had no choice. He dispatched his brother Gnaeus to Spain, sent word to Tiberius to get back to Italy, and hastened himself to Etruria, where he could await Hannibal's descent into the Po valley.[13]

From New Carthage, the Carthaginian base in South Spain, to the Po Valley is a distance of 1,125 miles. Hannibal made the trip in 5 months. The passage of the Alps took 15 days. He lost a lot of men from native attacks and bad footing on the treacherous mountain passes, but as a monument he left behind stated, he survived with 12,000 Libyan troops, 8,000 Spaniards, and 6,000 cavalry.[14]

Hannibal first met the waiting consul Scipio at the Ticinus River, a northern tributary of the Po, in November 219 BC. Hannibal's cavalry was always his strong point, and even in this first engagement he used it to outflank the unwary consul. Scipio was severely wounded himself and, as Polybius swears was the case, was only rescued by the heroic actions of his 17 year old son Scipio Jr., a lad who was destined to meet Hannibal again.[15]

Scipio limped off to Placentia, where all his Gallic cavalry revolted to Hannibal, bringing with them the heads of their Roman guards as an initiation fee. The following month the other consul

Tiberius joined up with Scipio at the Trebia River, a southern tributary to the Po. Tiberius had marched up from Rome with a good
deal of ballyhoo. The consular elections were at hand, and he was
anxious to knock off Hannibal on his watch. He was, unfortunately, too anxious: Hannibal set up an ambush on his side of the
Trebia and then enticed Tiberius across the icy river before his
soldiers had eaten breakfast. As the tired and numb Roman soldiers tried to advance out of the river and through a sleet storm,
Hannibal sprung his trap and won a great victory. There was, to
put it mildly, consternation at Rome.[16]

When the new consuls took office in 217, the story was repeated.
The two consuls marched through Etruria to Ariminum and
Arretium, where they could block the two major roads leading
south. Of course Hannibal left the roads and marched 4 days
through the swamps towards Arretium where Gaius Flaminius was
stationed. Hannibal chose Arretium because his intelligence
sources had told him that Flaminius was "a mere mob-orator and
demagogue with no ability for the actual conduct of military affairs."[17] By this time, after the rigors of the Alpine crossing and
the icy battle at the Trebia, Hannibal had only one elephant left.
He rode this through the swamps himself and eventually lost an
eye from a bothersome swamp infection.

Hannibal laid waste the territory around Arretium to dare
Flaminius to come out and attack; the consul's colleagues told him
to wait for Gnaeus Servilius, the other consul, who was coming
with cavalry reinforcements, but Flaminius wouldn't listen. On the
misty morning of June 22, 217 he chased Hannibal into a narrow
valley bordering Lake Trasimene. Shielded by the mists, the
Carthaginians had occupied all the hills overlooking the valley.
As soon as Flaminius was inside, they sprang the trap and rushed
down upon him. 15,000 Romans, including Flaminius, were killed
and 6,000 captured. When Servilius later arrived with his reinforcements, that column was cut apart too.[18]

All of these battles show a fundamental flaw in the executive
branch of the Roman government. If the two consuls didn't agree
on tactics, the army was rendered completely ineffective. Worse,
if one of the consuls was an idiot, the only possible outcome was
disaster. Of course, the Roman constitution had a provision for
just such an emergency, and in the panic following Lake Trasimene
the people took that option and replaced the surviving consul with

a dictator. They chose a respected but cautious soldier named Quintus Fabius.

Fabius, realizing that he had neither trained troops nor sufficient cavalry to defeat Hannibal in a pitched battle, resorted to guerrilla tactics. He consistently kept the high ground above Hannibal's army. Carthaginian scouting parties started to disappear. Fabius, however, refused to fight a pitched battle. Unfortunately, he could not simultaneously stop Hannibal from looting. The Carthaginians passed into Campania, the richest farmland of Italy and uncomfortably close to Rome, but still Fabius, remembering Flaminius's mistake, wouldn't engage.

When an ambush set up by the dictator failed and Hannibal escaped into winter quarters with plenty of loot and food, popular opinion started turning against Fabius and his methods. He picked up the nickname *Cunctator*, "the Delayer," and Roman citizens started to speak of his cowardice.[19] When his six-month term ran out and it was time for new consular elections, the electorate was fed up with caution.[20]

The elections of 216 were ugly. The common people supported Gaius Terrentius Varro, a demagogue of the Cleon type who bragged in his electioneering speeches that he would end the war the day he caught sight of the enemy. He was elected along with an experienced soldier of the upper classes named Lucius Aemilius Paulus, who had served as consul before, but whose former term in office had been tainted by an economic scandal involving his colleague. These two consuls from opposite sides of the tracks seem to have hated each other on sight, and their disagreements paved the way for a disaster even worse than Lake Trasimene. It had been precisely to avoid this sort of foolishness that Fabius had been appointed dictator in the first place.[21]

During the harvest season of 216 BC Hannibal seized an important grain distribution center named Cannae in Apulia, near his winter quarters. The Senate decreed that an immediate confrontation was necessary, and most uncharacteristically dispatched both of the consular armies, totaling some 80,000 men, to attack. Since both consuls would be present with the army, the unfortunate custom was in force that the two consuls would alternate command on opposite days. That's no war to run a horse race, never mind a war.

Varro and Aemilius disagreed at once. Though the Romans had

nearly double the number of Hannibal's infantry, they were out-numbered in cavalry by almost as much. Aemilius didn't want to fight in the open land before Cannae where Hannibal would have all the room he needed to deploy his cavalry and his infantry. Varro disagreed and seemed vindicated when his troops won a minor cavalry skirmish. When his day of command came up he brought the army forward; Aemilius could do nothing except follow along and help dig in along the Aufidus River.[22]

The battle, which is still studied at West Point as a masterful example of encircling tactics, was fought on August 2, 216. Hannibal arranged his line in the shape of a crescent with the bulge facing the Romans. That bulge consisted of his weaker Gallic and Spanish allies; he placed his crack Carthaginian troops on either wing of the crescent. When the too eager Romans attacked the tempting bulge, it broke and fell back, putting the pursuing Romans between the two wings of Carthaginian infantry. Hannibal's cavalry then attacked the Romans from the rear as the wings suddenly engaged.[23] In one bloody, skull-crunching afternoon, Rome lost 70,000 troops, among whom were the consul Aemilius Paulus, two quaestors, 29 military tribunes, and 80 Roman senators. As the fates would have it, Varro managed to get clean away.[24]

With the debacle of Cannae, everything seemed to go wrong at once. Rome's Greek allies in Italy, such as Capua and Tarentum, went over to Hannibal, and many of the cities of Campania even opened their gates. King Philip of Macedon, smelling blood and dreaming of Alexander, concluded an alliance with Hannibal,[25] as did King Hieronymus of Syracuse. It's not surprising that right after Cannae Maharbal, Hannibal's cavalry commander, told him that he would be dining at the Capitol in five days.[26]

Well, Hannibal missed that dinner, and Carthage lost the war. To understand why, it's important to remember that Hannibal was still in hostile territory, and that he hadn't received any reinforcements. The Greeks and the Gauls might go over to Carthage, but Rome's Latin allies never would. Rome had granted those allies full citizenship—a trick that Solon had trouble pulling off for even a few immigrant tradesmen—and she didn't assess them tribute. The allies certainly preferred fellow Latins to foreign invaders. These Latin cities and Rome were strongly walled and much fortified. Hannibal had neither leisure nor equipment for long sieges.

Rome was also at her best. The peak of Roman civilization didn't come later under the empire, when Rome stretched from Scotland to Iraq and became the richest city in the history of the world; we've already pointed out that conquest invariably marks the beginning of decline for a culture. Rome was at her best now, when she refused to give an inch to her would-be conquerors.

For instance, though in desperate need of troops, Rome refused Hannibal's offer of ransom for the 8,000 soldiers he had captured at Cannae. The senators who voted against ransom even had relatives among those hostages, but they still wouldn't give in. Of the 10 ambassadors who had been sent by the captives to the Roman senate, 9 fulfilled their oaths to Hannibal and returned voluntarily to captivity. The tenth, a clever fellow who had rushed back into the Carthaginian camp pretending to have forgotten something and had thus hoped to fulfill his vow to return, was sent back to Hannibal in chains. Romans didn't like cheaters. The few hundred soldiers who had escaped from Cannae were branded as traitors and were sent into exile in Sicily for the duration. It was this spirit more than anything else that kept Rome afloat.[27]

The Senate returned to Fabius's strategy at home, while abroad the army isolated Hannibal's allies and conquered them one by one. The praetor Marcus Valerius Laevinus was sent to Greece virtually as a secret agent to stir up trouble for Philip. In 211 he concluded an alliance with the Aetolian League, promising them land after their victory and ships to help them win it. Philip was so busy fighting his own social war that he never did send help to Hannibal. The Aetolian League, disgruntled when Rome proved too preoccupied to keep her promises, signed a separate treaty with Philip in 206. The following year the Romans went along and also signed a hasty agreement recognizing the status quo. Philip could be dealt with later.[28]

Marcus Claudius Marcellus was elected consul for the third time in 214 and was dispatched to reconquer Sicily. The siege of Syracuse took him two and a half years. Part of the problem was the Greek scientist Archimedes, the same genius who is reputed to have shouted "Eureka!" (εὕρηκα—"I've found it!") when, sitting in his bathtub, he suddenly figured out the principle of specific gravity. He's also reported to have said that he could move the earth if he could find a place to stand and a lever long enough. At any rate, this same scientist, like Leonardo, also turned his genius to siege mechanics, causing no end of problems for the Romans.

He had constructed graduated catapults to keep up a barrage of stones on the enemy's ships regardless of the distance; he built cranes to drop rocks on Roman ships that got too close to the walls of Syracuse; and, most dangerous, he developed a "crane's beak" which could reach down from the walls, grab the prow of a Roman ship, lift it into the air, and then drop it suddenly, either swamping or capsizing the boat.

When Marcellus finally did breach the walls of Syracuse it was because a deserter told him that everyone in the city was drunk following a three day festival to Artemis. The party ended abruptly and, much to Marcellus's regret, Archimedes was killed during the assault. A Roman soldier cut the scientist down when he was too absorbed in a geometry problem to realize what was going on![29]

Further successes followed: Capua was retaken in 212, and Tarentum in 209. The real turning point, however, came in Spain. This had been prepared as early as 217 when Gnaeus Scipio, brother to the consul wounded at the Ticinus, had sunk a Carthaginian fleet at the mouth of the Ebro River. Later, with the help of his brother Publius, he inflicted on Hannibal's brother Hasdrubal the first defeat of a Carthaginian army in a pitched battle. It provided a vital boost in morale after Cannae. Most important, it kept Hasdrubal from sending reinforcements to Hannibal in Italy, and this contributed to Hannibal's inability to administer the *coup de grace*. Unfortunately for Rome, the two Scipio brothers were killed in 211 while attempting to move on New Carthage in the south of Spain.[30]

It's fortunate that the death of these two commanders came after the fall of Capua, for the gradual turning of the tide gave the Senate enough breathing room to send reinforcements. As their commander the people would settle for no one else except the son of the martyred ex-consul, the same Publius Cornelius Scipio we saw rescue his father during the battle of the Ticinus. He was now only 24 and, having only held the aedileship, was technically too young to command an army. The people gave him the command anyway. In 210 he arrived in Spain with about 30,000 reinforcements.[31]

As it turned out, Scipio was the hero that Rome had been waiting for. Scipio completed his father's plans and took New Carthage in 209. He then defeated Hasdrubal in Baetica, and though he carelessly allowed Hasdrubal to escape across the Alps into Italy, in 206 Scipio faced the remaining Carthaginian commanders at Ilipa and, through his victory, destroyed Carthaginian rule in Spain forever. Meanwhile poor Hasdrubal, who had advanced down to the Metaurus River on the coast of Umbria, was stopped dead by the two consuls Gaius Claudius Nero and Marcus Linius Salinator. Showing the grim Roman sense of humor, Claudius cut off Hasdrubal's head and flung it before Hannibal's guard posts so the commander would realize that his reinforcements weren't showing up.[32]

After Scipio was elected consul for 205, he had a serious debate with Fabius, the now elderly "Delayer." Fabius was no imperialist: his cautious objective was to drive Hannibal out of Italy, and he wasn't really anxious to risk anything else. Scipio, however, was both an imperialist and as imaginative a general as Hannibal. Just as Hannibal had tricked the Romans at the start of the war by invading Italy, it was Scipio's plan to turn the tables on Carthage, invade Africa, and make Rome a Mediterranean power. Scipio won the debate and the invasion was on.[33]

Scipio fought for two years in Africa while Hannibal was gradually forced into the toe of Italy. While in Spain, Scipio had taken the trouble to recruit the Numidian prince Masinissa. With his help he besieged Utica and wiped out the army of another general Hasdrubal. He accomplished that trick by rather underhandedly setting fire to the enemy's camp at night. The camp went up like a tinder box, and Hasdrubal's army disappeared in a terrible night of fire, panic, and slaughter. It was at this point that the Carthaginians recalled Hannibal.[34]

Scipio managed to negotiate a truce with the peace party at Carthage, but they were wasting their time. Trusting in Hannibal, the Carthaginian nationalists restarted the war by seizing some Roman supply transports in the Bay of Carthage. Scipio sent three envoys to protest, but the Carthaginians ambushed and almost murdered them. Just as everyone apparently wanted, the two heavyweights met in a face-to-face contest.[35]

Scipio paid Hannibal the compliment of imitating his tactics. First he precipitated a battle by laying waste the countryside and forcing the Carthaginians to act before Hannibal was ready. He then made sure that his friend Laelius and King Masinissa were at hand with enough cavalry to equal the enemy's and so prevent any flanking moves. Hannibal finally pitched camp at Zama, a town about five days' march to the west of Carthage. Polybius (15. 6-8) and Livy (30. 30-31) have the two generals meet before the battle, but that may be just an historical excuse to write a couple of set speeches.

Hannibal led his attack with 80 elephants, but they went mad with wounds and the noise of battle; most ran off through breaks in Scipio's line left for that purpose. To make matters worse for Hannibal, his mercenaries broke and even turned on his own men. At the last minute the cavalry under Laelius and Masinissa hit the enemy in the rear, deciding the hard-fought infantry battle.[36] Hannibal managed to escape, but his army was destroyed. Back in Carthage for the first time in 36 years, he advised peace, and indeed Scipio didn't want to start on a siege of Carthage either.[37]

Rome drove a hard bargain: Carthage could keep all her towns in Libya and didn't have to accept Roman garrisons, but she had to hand over all but 10 of her warships, and all of the elephants. She could go to war with no people outside of Libya, and with none inside Libya without Rome's permission. This latter provision made it possible for Masinissa to raid her borders with impunity. Finally Carthage was forced to pay a fine of 10,000 talents of silver in installments over 50 years.[38] Some Carthaginian senators refused to sign, but Hannibal dragged one senator who opposed the treaty off the podium and then apologized for having forgotten his manners after being absent for so many years fighting for his country. The Carthaginian Senate ratified the treaty.[39]

The end of the war also ended the glory of its two famous generals, who shared strikingly similar fates. Scipio eventually fell prey to his political enemies, who indicted him for embezzlement of state funds in 189. Scipio would not condescend to defend himself against the charge. He only talked of his great achievements for the state. When that didn't work, he withdrew into voluntary exile on his estate at Liternum, where he died in 184 at the age of 48. At his request he was buried on his estate, "so that my funeral might not be held in my ungrateful native city."[40]

Although Livy doubts the legend, Hannibal was supposed to have died the same year as Scipio. When his own political enemies had driven him out of Carthage, he joined the court of the Seleucid king Antiochus III in Syria. When Lucius Scipio and big brother Publius defeated Antiochus, Hannibal fled to Prusias, the King of

Bithynia. He was followed there by Titus Quinctius Flamininus, the hero of our next chapter, who demanded his extradition to Rome. When Prusias gave in and Flamininus surrounded his house, Hannibal took poison.[41] Of course I can't resist quoting Juvenal's famous lines on the moral of all this:

> Weigh out Hannibal's dust. How many pounds does he come to,
> This greatest commander of all? Here was a leader, too mighty
> Even for Africa's reach, from the Moorish sea to the desert,
> From the steaming Nile to the elephant-teeming jungles.
> Spain is under his sway, he leaps the Pyrenees mountains;
> Nature bars his advance with the ice of the Alpine glaciers
> But he splits the rocks with his vinegar, cracks mountains open,
> Now he holds Italy, but still he intends to press onward.
> "Nothing is won," he says, "until the soldiers of Carthage
> Smash the gates of Rome and plant their flags in the forum."
> What a face he had! What a wonderful theme for a picture,
> A general with one eye riding an elephant—splendid!
> What is the end? Alas for glory! He also is conquered,
> Runs off to exile, and there, a truly magnificent client,
> Sits in the court of a king, awaits his Bithynian pleasure.
> What brought an end to the life that once confounded all nations?
> Not a sword, not a stone, not a spear. The avenger of Cannae,
> All those seas of blood, was a little ring that held poison.
> Run, then, over the Alps, behave like an absolute madman,
> To end up the schoolboys' delight, the theme of their declamations.[42]

26 "All Greece is Free!"

Imperialism is a disease which afflicts successful nationalist states, much as old age is a disease which afflicts youth. It inevitably stems from the fact that no successful state has ever existed except through exploitation, either (if it's lucky) of its own people, or else (most commonly) of somebody else. Rome stumbled into imperialism in an attempt to maintain the balance of power she found herself controlling after the war against Hannibal. If Rome made a mistake in all of this, it was in attempting to become the policeman of Europe.[1]

The Second Punic War left Rome with some unfinished business in the person of King Philip of Macedon. His former alliance with Hannibal still rankled, as did the unfavorable treaty Rome had rushed through in order to free her eastern flank for the invasion of Africa. To make matters worse, Philip had entered into a nasty alliance with Antiochus the Great of the old Seleucid Empire. These two would-be Alexanders were anxious to take advantage of the recent death of Ptolemy Philopater, the "pharaoh" of Alexander's successor state in Egypt. A child was now the king of Egypt, its princes were sleeping late in the morning, and Philip and Antiochus were moving in for the kill. So in 202 BC Antiochus seized southern Syria while Philip attacked some of Egypt's dependencies in Asia, an action which brought Rome's allies Rhodes and Pergamum against him.[2] It was only a few months after having completed the treaty with Carthage that Rome decided to act, doubtless prodded by the fact that the exiled Hannibal himself was staying with Antiochus and (as the Romans imagined) encouraging the Seleucid King to make war on Rome. So the new consul Publius Sulpicius went before the Comitia Centuriata and requested that the people declare war on Philip of Macedon. The people turned him down flat. They were tired of war, and a tribune named Quintus Baebius even accused the Senate of plotting against the lower classes.[3]

Not wishing to provoke yet another tiresome strike by the plebs,

the Senate resorted to intrigue. A commission was sent to provoke
Philip with an impossible demand: he was told to submit his disputes with Rome's allies to binding arbitration, and "to make no
war upon any Greek state."[4] The commission was in no hurry to
face Philip and traveled to Epirus, Aetolia, and Achaea to drum
up support.

Greece at the Time of the Roman Conquest

They had the most luck at Athens where, with the help of the
feeble but still eloquent old King Attalus of Pergamum, they were
able to convince the Athenians to declare war on Philip. The
Macedonian general Nicanor promptly attacked Athens, advancing all the way to the Academy. This brought new threats from
the Romans and a frantic cry of help to Rome from Athens itself.

Philip was meanwhile investing the city of Abydos in the Hellespont so as to have a permanent foothold in Asia. It was there that the commission finally caught up with him. The Roman ambassador Marcus Aemilius repeated the Senate's ultimatum, which must have given Philip something of a shock. First of all, Rome had no treaties with any Greek cities, and second, as Philip himself remarked to a later Senatorial embassy, "What is this Greece, pray, from which you bid me depart? How do you define it? Why, most of the Aetolians themselves are not Greeks!"[5]

Philip contemptuously ignored the ultimatum by taking the city. In despair, the citizens of Abydos then started committing suicide in such numbers that Philip allowed them a 3 day truce to kill themselves in peace.[6]

It was probably in July of 200 BC, when the panicky Athenian embassy appeared in Rome, that Sulpicius went before the Assembly again and called for war. He could now tell the people that Philip had already started the war himself, and that this was their last chance to confine the war to Macedonia and prevent Philip, like a second Hannibal, from crossing over into Italy. The fact that Philip wasn't strong enough to do that didn't matter; the Senate perceived him as a danger, and that very perception made him an enemy. The people gave in and voted for the war.[7]

Sulpicius then directed the heralds of the state formally to declare war on Philip. That meant that an ambassador, his head wound with a wool fillet, would have sailed over to Philip's nearest ally, jumped on shore, and then recited to the first person he saw: "Attend, Jupiter! Attend, territory of the Macedonians! Attend, righteousness! I am the public ambassador of the Roman people; I come justly and piously; hear me in good faith!" He would then make his formal demands. If no agreement was reached within 30 days, the ambassador would return with a bloodied spear and symbolically throw it across the enemy's border. It's amusing to think of the reaction of the unsuspecting Greek traveler who stumbled upon that first Roman messenger.[8]

Sulpicius frittered away two years of campaigning to the exasperation of the Roman people. As a result, the Senate gave a special dispensation to a talented young soldier named Titus Flamininus who, though only in his late 20's, was allowed to run for the consulship without having passed through the intermediary offices of the *cursus honorum*. Flamininus had already proven himself against Hannibal under the command of Marcellus, he had been governor of Tarentum, and he had founded the colonies of Narnia and Cossa. And now he got his big chance.[9]

Titus sailed to Epirus and disembarked his army at the river Apsus in modern Albania. Philip had already taken the pass, but Titus went after him; after some shepherds showed a way around Philip's rear and to the high ground above his position, Flamininus drove Philip into Thessaly with a loss of about 2,000 men. Philip burned everything in his path, but Titus was careful to keep his troops in good order and to win over as many friends to the Romans as he could. Philip had told everyone to expect a barbarian commander over a barbarian army, but instead Flamininus turned out to be "a man, in the flower of his age, of a gentle and humane aspect, a Greek in his voice and language, and a lover of honour."[10] Since the days of Alcibiades, it had never been a disadvantage to be good looking in Greece.

Flamininus wintered at Phocis, on the north shore of the Bay of Corinth. He kept his own men under control and convinced the Thebans to come over to Rome's side. This policy not only won friends for the Romans, it skillfully undercut the support Philip needed in Greece for supplies and maneuvering.[11] It was at this point that Philip had the meeting with Flamininus from which we quoted at the start of the chapter. When no agreement could be reached, Philip suggested, and Titus agreed, to submit the whole problem to Rome for arbitration. This took about 2 months, a period Titus used to consolidate his position with the Greeks and see to it that the Senate renewed his command as proconsul for the following year. The Senate, of course, threw Philip's ambassadors out.[12]

In the spring of 197 Flamininus invaded Thessaly. Philip, who had been in Larissa, moved south to meet him, and both armies camped near the village of Pherae. Flamininus had about 26,000 troops, out of which Rome's old allies the Aetolians supplied about 6,000 infantry and 4,000 cavalry. Philip had about the same number of men.[13] The two armies, however, had dramatically different ways of fighting.

In Macedon strategy as well as government had stiffened since Alexander's day. His 13-14 foot long spears had lengthened to 21 feet, and his fluid tactics had shifted to almost total reliance on the phalanx. This was a tightly compacted line of soldiers, 16 men deep, each holding one of those gruesome 21 foot long spears. Leaving room for a grip, the spears of the first rank stuck out 15 feet. The next four ranks of spears protruded proportionally until that of the 5th man back projected 3 feet beyond the front line. The men beyond the 5th rank held their spears above their shoulders so as to form a prickly protection for their heads against missiles. They also leaned against the men in front of them, thus giving the charge of the phalanx an irresistible momentum. The Roman line, on the other hand, was made up of individual units fighting with sword and shield.

Each side had its weaknesses. The Macedonian was in irresistible force, but it only worked on level ground, for once the phalanx was broken up, it lost its effectiveness: the spears were so long that they couldn't be used effectively in hand-to-hand combat, and the heavily armed Macedonian soldier had no way to protect his back. Roman soldiers were considerably more flexible. As we'll see, it was this flexibility that made them effective against the phalanx.[14]

The morning of the battle was foggy, so foggy that the two armies' foraging parties stumbled onto each other at a line of hills called Cynocephelae (Dog's heads). When Philip's party, which held the high ground, routed the Romans, the encouraging and heady reports of victory enticed him into a battle at once, even though he had rejected the ground earlier as being too uneven for the phalanx. The right wing of Philip's line was able to form a proper phalanx; it charged downhill into the Roman left and routed it. However, Philip's left was on uneven ground and was delayed getting into position. Realizing this Flamininus switched over to his right and attacked, sending in his elephants first. The Romans, apparently, had learned a few tricks from the Carthaginians. When Philip's left broke and fled, a clear-thinking tribune then shifted over to the Roman left, rushed further down hill, and hit the so far victorious Macedonian phalanx from behind. Philip's men were ham strung and finally routed. When the king finally saw what was happening, he fled too. Titus's losses were about 700 men; Philip had 8000 killed and 5000 captured.[15]

From Titus's standpoint, the biggest irritant in the battle was the Aetolians. By rushing into the enemy's camp after loot, they allowed Philip to get away. Titus's soldiers were angry when they were cheated of their share of the booty, and everyone was angry when the Aetolians went around afterwards bragging how they were the ones who had won the battle for the Romans. These bad feelings would cause real trouble later on.[16]

It cost Philip 200 talents and the surrender of his son Demetrius to the Romans as a hostage, but Titus granted him a 4 month truce. The Aetolians wanted Philip kicked out of office, and they demanded back all their cities which had gone over to Philip. Citing Rome's treatment of Carthage, Flamininus grandly pointed out that overturning governments wasn't Rome's style. He refused the Aetolians' demands for their cities, saying that during the war they had passed under Rome's protection. This treatment effectively turned the Aetolians against Rome, but Flamininus felt pressed to pacify Philip before he had a chance to link up with his old ally Antiochus and really become a threat to Rome. He may even have hoped to taunt Antiochus into doing something stupid.

As a final settlement, Flamininus got the Senate to ratify a treaty obligating Philip to withdraw all of his troops from Europe and Asia. He surrendered all but 3 of his decked ships and paid a fine of 2,000 talents, half at once and half in installments over 10 years. As a favor, Titus was able to cancel the original fine of 200 talents and to release Philip's son.[17]

Titus had a good deal of trouble maintaining his high ideals of Greek freedom, for a commission of 10 senators sent out "to confirm the freedom of the Greeks" had no intention of surrendering the strategic Greek cities of Corinth, Chalcis, and Demetrias, nicknamed by Philip "the shackles of Greece." It was only after a lot of arguing from Flamininus and taunting from the Aetolians that the senators agreed to liberate these cities along with the rest of Greece. Besides, with Corinth now restored to the Achaean League in the south, there was a real counterweight to the disgruntled Aetolians up north.[18]

Titus, who seems to have had a flair for the dramatic, went to the Isthmian Games at Corinth to make his formal announcement to the Greek people. The stadium was, of course, packed, and it took the trumpet call of a herald to get everyone quiet. The herald then announced that the Roman commander, Titus Quinctius Flamininus, having conquered King Philip and the Macedonians, rendered "free, autonomous, and exempt from all foreign taxation" all those states which had previously been subjugated to Philip. The Greeks either couldn't hear, or couldn't understand what the herald had said, so he repeated it. The crowd then, as they say, went wild, and it was only with difficulty that Titus got away without being mobbed by his new fans.[19]

To the Greeks, being declared "free" was nothing new. Such declarations were part and parcel of the ceaseless wars that had plagued the Balkans since the death of Alexander the Great. But no one had expected to hear the catchwords so appropriately and appealingly taken up by Roman barbarians. In the past, unfortunately, "freedom" and "autonomy" and "restored laws" had done nothing to stop anarchy and territorial aggrandizement.[20]

The first sign of diplomatic breakdown came from the Aetolians who, angered at what they thought was their unfair treatment by Rome, invited Antiochus to invade Europe as their champion. The Romans put a famous soldier named Manius Acilius in charge of the war, and made Flamininus his lieutenant. They defeated Antiochus at Thermopylae. He fled back to Asia, where he was decisively trounced at the city of Magnesia in 190 BC. The nominal commander was Lucius Scipio, acting as a front for his famous brother Publius, who in 190 was ineligible for another consulship. By the treaty of Apamea, the Greek cities of Asia that had been friendly to Rome were declared "free"; Greek enemies and all barbarian lands were divided between Rome's allies Pergamum and Rhodes, who now stood as bulwarks against the shrunk Seleucid Empire, driven out of all Asia beyond the Taurus mountains.[21]

Titus Flamininus would certainly have expected the praise which Livy put into the mouths of the grateful Greeks:

> There is indeed a people upon the earth who at their own expense, labor, and danger wage war for the liberty of others. Nor do they do this only for their close neighbors or in contiguous lands, but they cross the seas so that no unjust government might exist anywhere in the world, and so that everywhere there might be justice, right, and the power of law.[22]

The Greeks at the Isthmian Games might have talked like that—they had little choice—and the Senate certainly enjoyed the coincidence of altruism and political expediency. But Titus Flamininus and the Senate were both kidding themselves.

27 The Phony Philip

Macedon was down, but it wasn't yet out. Although all the smart money was now on Rome, it would be very premature to say that the victory at Cynocephelae had made her the mistress of the Western World. Macedon was only the strongest of the triplets born from Alexander's empire. There were still the Seleucids and the Ptolemies to reckon with. And of course to the West there was still Carthage.

For our purposes, however, we can look upon the Seleucid Empire as out of the picture. It had always been the least cohesive remnant of Alexander's dream, and since Antiochus had been chased out of Asia, we can let it fall out of our picture and abandon Israel and Syria to Pompey in a later chapter. Egypt and the Ptolemies can also wait for Caesar and Augustus. The Ptolemies in the first century were much like the Hapsburgs in the 19th: crumbling anachronisms looking desperately for diplomatic means to justify themselves.[1] That left Macedonia and Carthage, the subjects of the next two chapters.

The Greeks eventually became for the Romans not only a threat but, what is worse, a pain in the neck. All the Hellenistic States (which is what you call the Greek descendants of Alexander) tried to use Rome as the decisive factor in their constant squabbles. Everybody wanted to be Rome's buddy; everyone clamored for her protection. Cultural jealousy, aristocratic snobbery, and imperialistic greed consistently colored Roman reaction to Greece, a reaction which gradually gave way to a generalized disgust, best personified in the person of the stern old senator and censor Marcus Porcius Cato. This attitude hardened into prejudice, so that by the 2nd century AD our friend Juvenal could write:

> Citizens, I can't stand a Greekized Rome. Yet what portion
> of the dregs of our town comes from Achaia only?
> Into the Tiber pours the silt, the mud of Orontes,
> Bringing its babble and brawl, its dissonant harps and timbrels,
> Bringing also the tarts who display their wares at the Circus...

Desperate nerve, quick wit, as ready in speech as Isaeus,
Also a lot more long-winded. Look over there. See that fellow?
What do you take him for? He can be anybody he chooses,
Doctor of science or letters, a vet or a chiropractor,
Orator, painter, masseur, palmologist, tightrope walker.
If he is hungry enough, your little Greek stops at nothing...
Furthermore, nothing is safe from his lust, neither matron nor vir-
gin,
Not her affianced spouse, nor the boy too young for the razor.
If he can't get at these, he would just as soon lay his friend's
grandma.[2]

Plutarch tells us that King Philip, after losing to Titus
Flamininus, lived "like a slave that was pleased with ease,"[3] but
his campaigns in Thrace, which both gobbled up strategic loca-
tions and aroused suspicions in Rome, completely belie that
charge. Philip's old enemy King Eumenes of Pergamum along with
the ever beleaguered Greeks sent whining embassies to Rome
begging for help. Since the Roman senatorial commissions sent
to Philip believed none of his protestations of innocence, the king
finally decided in 184 to send his young son Demetrius as his
ambassador to Rome. As we saw in the last chapter, the boy had
been a hostage there after the last war, and he had managed to
leave behind a fine impression. This clever maneuver proved to
be the greatest mistake of Philip's life. The Senate thought the
charming young fellow to be too inexperienced to be taken seriously, but Titus Flamininus took him aside, buttered him up, and
even suggested the advisability of a return visit.

Demetrius's head was turned, people started to talk, and word
got back to Demetrius's older brother Perseus, the crown prince.
Perseus was not the self-possessed, confident sort. Fearful that his
younger brother might push him aside, he forged a letter from
Flamininus that implicated Demetrius in a treasonous plot with
Rome. Completely taken in, Philip ordered his younger son to be
executed. By the time he finally died in 179, Philip is supposed to
have learned the truth of the false accusation and died a bitter and
disillusioned man. Perhaps he did.[4]

Perseus, whether we think of him as Cain or as The Man in the
Iron Mask, seems to have begun his reign well. It was probably
his increasing popularity that got him into trouble with Rome. He
restored exiles, cancelled debts, recalled political prisoners, and

in imitation of his father began once again to expand Macedon's borders.[5] He married Laodice, the daughter of Seleucus IV (admittedly a typical diplomatic move for the period) and attracted further attention with a military progress through northern Greece to the Delphic oracle. As Eumenes of Pergamum warned his Roman protectors, hateful memories of Roman intervention were turning the fickle Greeks toward Perseus.[6]

Eumenes precipitated the crisis when the appeared before the Senate in 172. He read off a list of Perseus's crimes, the Macedonian denial of which seemed much less convincing when Eumenes on his way back home was almost killed by a falling rock at Delphi. As they had done at the start of the Second Macedonian War, the Senate dispatched a commission to drum up support around Greece. The commissioners got most of the Boeotian cities, including of course Thebes, to abandon Perseus and join them; Rome then broke up the old Boeotian League. She similarly got Rhodes to join her side while the Achaean League, led by the pro-Roman collaborator Callicrates, had already dropped Perseus in 175.

Perseus requested an interview with Quintus Marcius Philippus, the head of the senatorial commission, but the senator had no authority to negotiate and could only offer further delay–a diplomatic necessity he later portrayed as a clever ploy. When Perseus's own embassy finally got to Rome in the spring of 171 the Senate was too suspicious to bargain. The embassy was told to depart from Rome, and all other Macedonians were given 30 days to get out of Italy. The war was on.[7]

The first three years of the war were disastrous for Rome. The consul Publius Licinius Crassus was defeated by Perseus at Larissa, which is below the Vale of Tempe in Thessaly, along the same route Xerxes had used in the old days. Licinius's only contribution to the war effort was his stubborn insistence upon unconditional surrender from the Greeks. Since he had lost, the Macedonians didn't think this made much sense. Perseus, however, kept sending the consul so many embassies that his advisors finally told him to stop acting like the loser. The next two consuls in charge, Hostilius Mancinus and the former ambassador Quintus Marcius Philippus, so frittered away their commands and permitted such outrages by their troops that the folks at home started looking for a hero to bring the war to an end.[8]

That hero was the old soldier Lucius Aemilius Paulus, son of the smart consul who fell at Cannae. Paulus was already famous for his conquests in Spain during his praetorship and for his victories against the Ligurians, an Alpine tribe, during his consulship. He had tried unsuccessfully to run for a second consulship once before, but this time the Roman populace came right up to his door and begged him to stand for office. When he won the consulship, the people wouldn't even allow the consuls' duties to be appointed by lot, but illegally gave the Macedonian command to Aemilius Paulus.[9]

Having done well against the Romans so far, Perseus stood pat on the east coast and waited for the new commander. He moved north into Macedon and stationed his 40,000 heavily armed troops and 4,000 cavalry at the foot of Mt. Olympus. Once Aemilius Paulus joined the army he found that he had a good deal of tightening up to do. As frequently happens on a losing team, discipline had gone lax and morale was low. Paulus broke a few heads and, just to keep them on their toes, made the guards stand duty without weapons so they would pay more careful attention! In a replay of the old battle of Thermopylae, informers told the Romans that there was an unguarded pass up Olympus around the Macedonian position. Paulus picked the son-in-law of the great Scipio, Scipio Nasica, to lead the raid; Nasica occupied the high ground and thus forced Perseus to move his troops northward, further into Macedon. Perseus took up position at a plain near the seashore called Pydna. The level ground was perfect for the phalanx and would, he thought, prevent a repeat of his father's disaster at Cynocephelae.[10]

The night before the battle there was a lunar eclipse, which has allowed astronomers to pinpoint the date at June 21, 168 BC. The superstitious Macedonian troops were convinced that the eclipse was an omen, portending that their king was fading just like the moon. Paulus knew quite well that eclipses were caused by the moon's passing through the earth's shadow, and he predicted the astronomical event to his troops the day before it occurred. When the moon turned off on schedule the Romans' faith in their commander increased dramatically. Just to play it safe, however (he was, after all, an official priest back at Rome), Paulus sacrificed heifers while his soldiers banged on pots to bring the moon back. To make sure the omens were favorable for the battle, Paulus slaughtered 21 heifers until he got a liver he liked.[11] Roman priests, you see, foretold the future by studying the shape of their sacrificial victim's liver, or by observing the position of birds in the sky, or by seeing whether or not the sacred chickens took their holy feed on the morning of an important day.

Perseus was sacrificing too, but in the nearby city of Pydna, so that he conveniently missed the battle. Paulus was in no hurry. He had made camp the afternoon before to allow his travel-weary troops to rest, and on the 21st he waited for the Macedonian army to force his hand. The phalanx came out in the afternoon and gradually forced the Roman advance guard to engage. Aemilius was at first stumped by the prickly-pear, seemingly impregnable Macedonian line. He noticed, however, that even gentle irregularities in the ground caused small gaps in the phalanx. Breaking his own line up into independent platoons, he told his men to attack not *en masse,* but in separate groups, and to hit the phalanx wherever there was a break. Once the Roman legionaries achieved close quarters the phalanx tottered and then broke. With the loss of only about 100 men, the Romans slaughtered 25,000 routed Macedonians.

Informed of what had happened to his army, Perseus ran to his capital Pella, where in a pique of temper he stabbed two of his treasurers. He then abandoned his country and fled to the island of Samothrace with his family and as much of his fortune as he could carry. A Roman fleet chased him and surrounded the island; his fortune was stolen, his family kidnapped, and Perseus himself at last surrendered to the Romans. When finally brought into Aemilius Paulus's presence, King Perseus only managed to inspire disgust when he grabbed Paulus's knees and blubbered for mercy. He begged not to be put on display in Paulus's victory parade, or triumph, and Paulus told him that he was free to kill himself to escape the disgrace. Perseus appeared in the triumph. He died some time later in a Roman prison and was survived by only one of his sons named (appropriately) Alexander, who spent his life as a minor clerk in the Roman imperial service.[12]

There now remained the problem of what to do with the Greeks. Annexation seemed out of the question, for as even the old Greek hater Cato the censor remarked, "Macedonia must be set free since we cannot guard her."[13] She could, however, be taught a lesson, so there was a massive purge of anti-Roman activists. Five hun-

dred troublemakers from the Aetolian League were executed after a mock trial. One thousand agitators were rounded up from
the Achaean League (including the historian Polybius, whose name
has taken over my footnotes for the past couple of chapters) and
sent to Rome, supposedly for trial. Instead, they were scattered
among Italian towns and held hostage until 151 BC. Epirus, which
is south west of Macedon, suffered the worst. The Senate told
Aemilius Paulus to hand it over to his soldiers. 70 cities were
sacked and 150,000 people sold into slavery.[14]

Macedon itself was chopped up into 4 independent republics
whose citizens were forbidden to trade or even to intermarry. They
were called republics, but as might be guessed only the upper
classes were allowed to vote in the Popular Assembly. A general
disarmament was imposed upon the country, as was a fine of 100
talents, an amount, however, which was only one half of what
Perseus used to demand. In order to cripple its economic recov-
ery, Macedon's gold and silver mines were shut down.[15]

Rome then, incredibly, withdrew all of her troops, figuring that
after such a kick in the pants Greece would be good. Rome was
still kidding herself. By turning Macedon into 4 little Roman
clones, all the Senate had done was to destroy the precarious balance of power in Greece without setting up anything effective in
its place. The democratically run Achaean League, stretching from
Corinth south over the Peloponnesus, would have liked the job,
but it was on that very suspicion that Rome had seized 1,000 of
its best and brightest as hostages.

Nonetheless, as the surviving Greek states squabbled for power,
each inevitably tried to drag Rome in as big brother. The final
straw came in 149 BC when a commoner named Andriscus, who
happened to bear a strong resemblance to King Philip, claimed
to be the son of Perseus and was used to stir up Macedon into a
general revolt. The Roman praetor Caecilius Metellus made short
work of this "Phony Philip" in 148 BC, and Macedonia was finally
made into a Roman province, with Metellus as its first governor.[16]
Rome was now a visible presence in Greece, and further complications were inevitable.

These complications arose from within the Achaean League
where, because of the hostages, hatred there against Rome was
great. They were now ruled by the pro-Roman flunky Callicrates,
whom even children in the street hooted as a traitor. When the

hostages were finally restored in 151—thanks largely to the influence of Polybius and his powerful young friend, Scipio Aemilianus, the son of Aemilius Paulus—the political temperature in the League rose considerably. Callicrates died in 150 and was replaced by an anti-Roman general named Diaeus.

As we've seen before, this kind of hatred inevitably leads to war as soon as an excuse presents itself. The excuse was presented by our old recalcitrant friend Sparta, who now makes her final appearance in our story. Sparta had broken away from the Achaean league back in 189, only to be reconquered by the League's famous general Philopoemen, and now Sparta revolted again. As the cycle started to repeat itself and Sparta was once again defeated, a Roman commission led by Lucius Aurelius Orestes arrived in 147 to tell the League to keep its hands off the Spartans. His announcement at the League Congress at Corinth in 147 set off a riot from which Orestes barely escaped with his life.[17]

Rome still didn't declare war. She sent more commissions. Such actions, however, only convinced the anti-Roman party, led by Diaeus and his colleague Critolaus, that Rome, preoccupied (as we'll see) with its new war against Carthage, was afraid to tangle with the Achaeans. This view was undoubtedly correct, but the Achaeans tragically underestimated their opponents. Critolaus spent the winter of 147-146 drumming up support for the cause by promising relief from the debt laws and suspension of all loans for the duration. "I am desirous of being a friend of the Romans," he told the Congress, "but I have no taste for them as my masters!" He accused his opponents of being traitors and got the Achaeans to declare a new war on Sparta, which in reality was a war against Rome.

In 146 the Senate put the consul Lucius Mummius in charge of the war. Hoping to beat him to the punch, the Macedonian governor Laetellus marched south and defeated Critolaus at Scarpheia, south of Thermopylae. Critolaus seems to have been drowned in the rout. This left Diaeus in charge, who felt that he had gone too far to listen to the conciliatory overtures that were coming from the Senate. The consul Lucius Mummius therefore came next.

Diaeus was reëlected *strategos* in 146. He declared a draft of all citizens of military age and even offered freedom to slaves who would join the army. Politicians who dared to speak against him were executed. Diaeus's actions caused panic in Greece, though Polybius probably exaggerates when he says that whole cities surrendered to the Romans, panic-stricken citizens jumped off cliffs or into wells, while the whole population of Thebes ran off, leaving the city deserted!

When Mummius arrived with 26,000 troops and 3,500 cavalry, Diaeus fled south to Megalopolis, where, rather like Dr. Goebbels, he first killed his wife and then himself. Corinth was viciously looted by Mummius's soldiers and then burned to the ground. The consul was at least thoughtful enough to confirm the tax-exempt status of the local actors' guild.[18]

There was no point in making Greece a province yet (though it would be about a century later), for it had no borders that needed protecting, but it was placed under the direct supervision of the Macedonian governor. It had cost them their liberty, but the Greeks were finally forced into unity.

28 The Last Punic War

In the fifty years of peace that followed the war with Hannibal, Carthage, even though she had no military power to speak of, made impressive commercial and agricultural gains. Her major trouble came from Rome's old ally to the south, the aged but wily King Masinissa of Numidia. Taking advantage of Carthage's treaty with Rome, which forbade her to make war without Rome's permission, Masinissa seized Carthaginian territory and carried off her cattle. Carthage sent no less than three commissions to Rome, only to be answered by a visiting committee of Roman senators with secret instruction to favor Masinissa. The most famous of these commissions was in 157 BC, and that because it contained the famous, eighty-one year old, and very conservative senator Marcus Porcius Cato. Cato was appalled: not with the injustice of Masinissa, but with the fact that Carthage was once again a bustling, prosperous city.

When he got back to the Senate, Cato brought along some Carthaginian figs which he allowed nonchalantly to fall from his toga. When the senators remarked that they were indeed pretty good figs, Cato reminded them that the city which had produced them was only 3 days' sailing from Rome. Consequently, it was Cato's opinion that the city of Carthage should cease to exist. Scipio Nasica, whom we met at the battle of Pydna, countered with the argument that success was making Rome soft; the city needed the fear of a powerful enemy to keep her at her best. Cato, however, always had the last word. From that point on, he ended each of his speeches with the friendly thought, *Karthago delenda es!* ("Carthage must be destroyed.")[1]

Cato's views about Carthaginian prosperity do not seem to have been misplaced. In 191 Carthage made the surprising offer to pay off her tribute in one lump sum—an offer which the Senate, anxious to keep her enemy as subservient as possible—pointedly refused. Instead Carthage flooded the Roman market with hundreds of thousands of bushels of grain during the first half of the second century. Large amounts of Carthaginian pottery found at Rome and corresponding amounts of fine Campanian ware unearthed at Carthage attest to the bustling trade that grew up between the two enemies. The Roman playwright Plautus even produced in the 190's a comedy called *The Phoenician*. Hanno, the crafty Carthaginian *gugga,* must have struck a familiar chord with Plautus's audience; when he first enters he is even given thirty lines of Carthaginian gobbledy gook to raise a cheap laugh.[2]

It would, however, be a mistake for us to look upon the approaching Punic War as a trade war in the modern sense. Rome in the second century BC didn't have a politically powerful commercial class. By the *Lex Claudia* of 218 Roman senators were forbidden to engage in large scale commerce. The class of knights, or *equites,* who did control trade, were generally looked down upon a vulgar *nouveaux riches*. It is difficult to pin down any specific diplomatic or military move made by the Senate, either in the eastern or the western theater, which was clearly motivated by commercial considerations.[3]

But the motives behind the Third Punic War were complex and, as in any war, subject to indirect pressures. Glorious military victories remained the only sure-fire way for ambitious senators to climb the *cursus honorum* to fame, glory, and of course increased earning potential. And though it might be *déclassé* for a senator to dirty his fingernails in the marketplace,[4] there was nothing wrong with making money or being rich.

This brings us back to Cato, whose surviving monograph on farming provides us with the best contemporary picture we have of a Roman senator from that period. This is how Cato describes the ideal estate owner:

> Let him sell oil, if he can find a good price; let him sell whatever wine and grain he has left over: old cattle, defective plow animals, blemished sheep, wool, hides, old wagons, old iron tools, aged slaves, sickly slaves—whatever he has left over , let him sell. The father of a family should be fond of selling, not fond of buying.[5]

As I pointed out earlier in dealing with Akhnaton, nothing is more powerful than a moral or patriotic imperative incidentally connected to financial reward.

An honorable looking pretext was of course needed to declare war, and that was provided once again by Masinissa in 152. In that year the Carthaginians, long fed up with Numidians' shenanigans, at last declared war on Masinissa who, at 88 years of age, could still ride a horse and was quite capable of defending himself. In fact, he and his sons outmaneuvered the army of a Carthaginian general named (as usual) Hasdrubal, surrounded it, and slaughtered 58,000 men. Carthage, however, had broken her treaty, and in 149 Rome felt that she could finally declare war.

Carthage's response, after kicking out Hasdrubal, was to surrender at once. Unfortunately, the African city of Utica beat her to the punch and surrendered first. Robbed of her dramatic effect, Carthage sent an embassy to Rome instead to offer unconditional surrender. Having delivered their message, the only reply they could get out of the senators was, "You have been well advised." When they asked what they had to do to insure peace, the Romans told them to hand over as hostages 300 boys from their ruling families. This seemed a harsh blow, but the commissioners agreed and, once back at Carthage, convinced their people, though nervous that no guarantees had been given about the city, to hand over the boys. The hostages ended up confined to their ship in a dockyard in Rome.

An army of 80,000 infantry and 4,000 cavalry under the consuls Marcus Manilius and Lucius Marcius Censorinus then landed at the obliging port of Utica. When a commission of Carthaginian ambassadors approached the Roman force, they were told by Censorinus that, as a further condition of peace, they would be obliged to agree to complete disarmament. Only too anxious to please, the Carthaginians handed over 200,000 complete suits of armor, 2,000 catapults, and a large number of javelins, darts, and swords. Censorinus then dropped the second shoe: the people of Carthage would be required to abandon their city and move ten miles inland! Ten miles inland would put them in the Sahara desert; it was obvious that the Romans would not take peace for an answer.

The Carthaginian ambassadors went berserk. They howled and ranted, beat their heads on the ground, and screamed that the Romans were breakers of oaths, perjurers before the gods. With 80,000 troops at his back, Censorinus was unmoved. The ambassadors could do nothing but go back home, where they were of course killed as the bearers of bad news. The Carthaginian Senate declared war that same day. As their general they chose

Hasdrubal, the same fellow who had lost his army to Masinissa and been condemned to death for his trouble. He had raised an army of 30,000 men outside the walls of Carthage for his own defense, and the Carthaginians now had no one else to whom they could turn.[6]

He was not a happy choice. Polybius describes him as "a vain, ostentatious person, very far from possessing real strategic ability." He was also obscenely fat, "so that he seemed to be living like fat oxen at a fair and not at all like a man to be in command at a time of such terrible miseries as cannot easily be described in words."[7]

Although Carthage was down, although it had a fat ox for a commander, it was not about to roll over and play dead. It was still a heavily fortified city whose walls, 30 feet thick and 65 feet high, ran for a circumference of 20 miles. Although the Romans controlled the useful port of Utica, they were not in possession of the countryside, which was still controlled by the army of Hasdrubal. The Carthaginian people showed considerable spunk as well: They turned their temples and public squares into workshops for the manufacture of weapons, the women even cutting off their hair to make ropes for the newly constructed catapults. So when Manilius attacked by land up the isthmus on which the city was located and Censorinus by sea, they were surprised to discover that the city was no longer, as they had expected, defenseless.[8]

Censorinus brought up battering rams and made a breach in the wall. Shouting for victory, he and his men rushed inside where they were quickly surrounded and cut off. They would have been destroyed had not a young military tribune named Scipio Aemilianus foreseen the trap and kept his troops outside the breach in reserve. He rode to the rescue of Censorinus, a deed which greatly increased his reputation and got the soldiers muttering that he had "shown himself wiser than the general."[9]

In all fairness to Censorinus, when someone is rich, handsome, brilliant, and well connected, people are bound to talk about him anyway. Since Scipio is the hero of this chapter (assuming, of course, that you're rooting for the Romans), I should explain who he was. We've already met him as the friend of the exiled Greek historian Polybius. His full name was Publius Cornelius Scipio Aemilianus. He was the son of Aemilius Paulus, the hero of the last chapter. Paulus had, however, divorced Scipio's mother, and when he remarried he had the boy adopted by the son of Scipio Africanus, the man who had defeated Hannibal. This wasn't simply done to get the kid out of the house. In Latin the word for friendship, *amicitia*, originally means "political alliance," and the two best ways to cement a political alliance were *(1)* to arrange a marriage, between either yourself or your children with a member of your prospective friend's family, or *(2)* to have one of your sons adopted into said family.

This didn't mean that you abandoned your son, for Scipio and Aemilius Paulus seem to have remained close. Indeed, Livy recounts that young Scipio served under his father at Pydna, and gave him quite a scare when he couldn't be located immediately after the battle.[10] A link-up with as powerful a family as the Scipiones, however, would have literally doubled young Scipio's power and influence, giving him twice as many powerful relatives, friends, and clients.[11] The relationship of these people is a bit confusing, so I've included a chart of the important members of the two families. They will dominate Roman politics right into our next chapter.

Appian recounts three further military successes of Scipio against the Carthaginians, all of which greatly increased his reputation both among the soldiers and the people back home. There's a hint of the jealousy this must have aroused too: When it was observed that only Scipio's foraging parties went unattacked by the Carthaginians, his enemies attributed his success to a deal with the old Carthaginian friends of the Scipio family. Appian reports, I think correctly, that the real reason was the good order in which Scipio kept his men.[12] By the time of the consular elections of 148, everyone, even the consul Manilius, was convinced that Scipio was the logical leader for the war. Old Cato, who had died only the year before, had himself been spreading the good news: "What have you heard? He alone has the breath of wisdom in him. The rest are but flitting phantoms."[13] King Masinissa, who finally died at the age of 90, made Scipio the executor of his will. Similarly, a Carthaginian traitor named Phaneas deserted to Scipio with about 2,200 cavalry.[14]

There was, however, still a year to wait. Lucius Calpurnius Piso was elected consul in 148 and given the command. Scipio himself escorted him back to the African camp. Piso unfortunately so frittered away his command that the people of Rome became impatient. In the elections for 147 they insisted that Scipio be chosen consul, even though, like his adoptive grandfather, he was running only for the aedileship and was legally too young for the top job. The people got so loud that the Senate permitted the tribunes to repeal the elections laws for one year and then reenact them later.[15]

Scipio began his command just as his father had done in Greece. He tightened up discipline, in his case by stopping indiscriminate looting and throwing out the mob of camp followers who were dissipating the energy and morale of his soldiers. His first major move was a night attack on a district of Carthage named Megara. Hasdrubal countered by hauling his Roman prisoners to the wall and butchering them in the sight of Scipio's troops. Disgusted, Scipio then fortified the isthmus connecting Carthage to the shore in order to begin a systematic starvation of the city. The Carthaginians' countermove was to build a new harbor, out of which they sailed with an armada put together from spare parts. But they hesitated just long enough (3 days) for Scipio to regroup, and he defeated their last-chance fleet in a great sea battle.

These events occupied the entire summer of 147. During the winter campaign Scipio moved in on Carthage's suburbs. He took the town of Nepharis, slaughtering more than 70,000 citizens during the final assault on the fortifications. In the spring of 146 he took the harbor of Cothon, and then moved in on Byrsa, the strongest part of Carthage. It was a citadel, to which 3 streets led up from an open square. The streets were lined with houses 6 stories high, and from these the Carthaginians rained down missiles upon the Romans. So there was a two-level attack—on the streets below and on the roofs, where planks were placed like bridges across the narrow alleys. After spending 6 days to clear the houses, Scipio set fire to all 3 streets.[16]

50,000 survivors surrendered to Scipio, leaving only the citadel of the city, in which Hasdrubal, his wife, his two children, and about 900 Roman deserters were holed up. To save himself, Hasdrubal abandoned his family and surrendered to Scipio. In return he was obligated to lie down at Scipio's feet in full sight of the citadel. The deserters got the message: They fired the citadel and committed suicide, as did Hasdrubal's wife and two boys.[17] Scipio then allowed his soldiers to loot whatever was left and finally set the ruins on fire.

Polybius was standing by Scipio as Carthage was burning. Scipio, believe it or not, was weeping, not only because of the many innocent Carthaginians who were dying and being led off into slavery, but also because of these lines of Homer, which he quoted to his friend:

> For I know this thing well in my heart, and my mind knows it:
> there will come a day when sacred Ilion shall perish,
> and Priam, and the people of Priam of the strong ash spear.[18]

He was thinking of Rome.

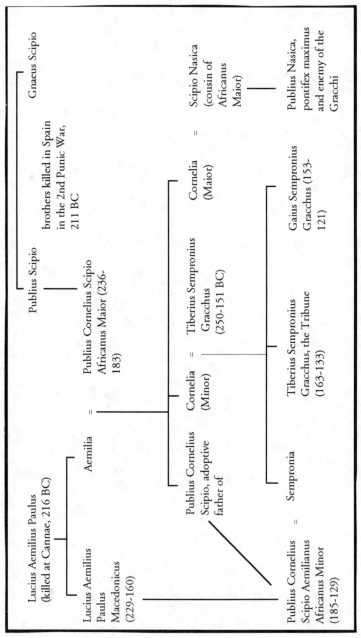

Family Nexus of the Aemilii Pauli, Sempronii Gracchi, and Scipiones

29 The First Communist

Not everybody in Rome benefited from the wars described in the last three chapters. Hannibal had most visibly devastated the farms of southern Italy, but the forced absence of farmers on extended military service was devastating too; only the rich could afford to keep up or rebuild their farms. Roman farmers even suffered from Rome's success: By the end of the second century cheap grain from the provinces of Sicily and Sardinia depressed grain prices around the capital; it was only the prohibitive cost of overland transport that kept rural grain markets alive.[1]

As farmers went bankrupt, cheap land became an object of speculation for war profiteers with money to dabble. Although this process intensified in the second century BC, it wasn't new. Deforestation relentlessly impoverished Italy's already poor soil, and the rich had been hogging land ever since the fourth century. We saw evidence for this in chapter 24 during our discussion of the Licinian-Sextian laws of 367. To refresh your memory, one of the provisions of that omnibus bill involved Rome's so-called "public land."

Ager publicus was land seized by Rome during her wars of expansion in Italy. Typically, the Senate would take over $\frac{1}{3}$ of the land of a conquered Italian enemy and rent it out to Roman citizens at a modest rate—$\frac{1}{10}$ of the grain produced and $\frac{1}{5}$ of the fruit, or a set toll on the animals. The Licinian-Sextian Laws had attempted to stop the upper classes from turning all the homesteading land into open pasturage by putting a cap of 500 *iugera* (330 acres) on the amount that any individual could hold.[2]

Low population and aggressive colonization prevented social unrest during the 4th and 3rd centuries, as did the wrenching distraction of the Second Punic War. In the early 3rd century the censor's bureau, who should have been the guardian of the law, tended to wink at pasturage blight in order to get ruined land back into production. Invariably this caused trouble once the population rose, but who was going to guard the guardians? The senatorial class either ignored the law as a quaint anachronism or, if they felt hedged in by duty, used their relations as dummy owners.

Thus by the 2nd century much of Rome's *ager publicus* was no longer in the hands of the small peasant farmers for whom it had originally been intended. It is too early to imagine Italy covered over with large plantations (*latifundia*) manned exclusively by imported slaves—that pattern being more characteristic of the imperial period—but since slaves were cheap after the wars in Africa and Greece their availability drove down the wages of hired help. All sorts of people became entrepreneurs, not just the senatorial aristocracy, but the equestrian or business class as well along with the occasional centurion who had managed both to stay alive and to resist squandering his plunder. The average peasant, however, back after a staggering hitch of sixteen years in the ranks, fell into tenancy if he was lucky, and into seasonal part time labor if he was not.

Although there were extensive estates given over to pasturage, olives, and wine—especially in the south—the countryside was mostly chopped up into modest estates of between 100 and 250 acres. These depended on hired help and tenants as much as on slaves. There is a tendency to project the conditions of the industrial revolution onto late Republican Italy and thus to imagine a vast migration of farmers into urban slums,[3] but unlike Paris and London, ancient Rome had no jobs to offer the rural poor. Construction work and small scale, labor intensive industry were more suitable for trained slave gangs than for free workers. We should envision the countryside as a complex mosaic of small scale agribusiness, tenants, sharecroppers, slaves, and tenacious old time dirt farmers. The traditional patterns were still holding together, but the quality of life for average country folk was falling dangerously low. In 104 the tribune Marcius Philippus would declare, "There are not two thousand men of real wealth in the state."[4] The chasm between rich and poor was greater than at any time since the struggle between the orders.[5]

There were enlightened reform measures to repair this mess. The philosopher Gaius Laelius, a close friend of Scipio Aemilianus, dared to propose a land bill, but he was faced with such vicious opposition from the upper classes that he withdrew his suggestions, earning for himself the nick name *Sapiens* ("The Wise.").[6] It will be recalled that the original reform bill of the tribunes Licinius and Sextius had taken 10 years of demonstrations, vetoes, and strikes to get passed. By far the most important of the land reformers was a young nobleman named Tiberius Sempronius Gracchus, who introduced his land bill in 133 BC. This chapter is really about him.

It is an interesting historical phenomenon that most revolutionary leaders are from the upper classes. Motives are always difficult to disentangle, for the more successfully reformers labor against injustice, the more their liberal platforms propel them into power. Gracchus will, I think, provide a good illustration.

A glance at the family tree of the Aemilii Pauli and the Scipiones will show that Tiberius Gracchus was certainly from the upper classes. He was, through his mother Cornelia, the grandson of Scipio Africanus. His father, the elder Tiberius Gracchus, had been twice consul and once censor. After his death the king of Egypt proposed marriage to Cornelia, who modestly refused. She and the elder Gracchus had had 12 children, only 3 of whom survived: Tiberius and a brother Gaius, ten years his junior, and a sister Sempronia, who was unfortunately deformed and rather ugly, but whose high birth got her married to Scipio Aemilianus. Tiberius himself married the daughter of Appius Claudius, a famous lawyer and the ranking member of the Senate. Young Tiberius was all set for a brilliant career.[7]

He began that career conventionally enough, serving first on the staff of his brother-in-law against Carthage. Plutarch quotes an early annalistic historian named Gaius Fannius as saying that Tiberius was the first up the wall when Carthage fell (with Fannius right behind him!). Tiberius then served as quaestor in Spain under the consul Gaius Mancinus, where his brilliant career hit a snag. Mancinus's army was cut off during a retreat from the Numantines and captured. The Spanish barbarians insisted on using Tiberius as their go-between, for they had dealt profitably with his father and respected his memory. Tiberius negotiated a treaty that saved the life of 20,000 Roman soldiers. When he got home, however, the Senate turned on him, accusing him and the consul of cowardice since they had not fought to defend Rome's honor to the death. The Scipio family's enemies gleefully suggested that all of the officers be handed over in chains to the Numantines, who would do the-gods-know-what to them. Tiberius was saved from this fate, not only thanks to the help of his brother-in-law Scipio,

but also because of support from the relatives of the 20,000 soldiers he had saved.

This incident seems to have been the turning point in his life.
We can't know of course, but Plutarch hints, and common sense
rather suggests, that such treatment from the senators would have
embittered the young quaestor—especially since Scipio did noth
ing for the consul Mancinus, whom Tiberius saw shipped off to
the Numantines as a scape-goat. Brother Gaius Gracchus also
wrote that when Tiberius first had set out to Spain on his
quaestorship, he noted in passing through Tuscany that there were
no native Italians working the farms—only barbarian slaves. That
was an exaggeration, of course, but it must have contained enough
truth to work as political rhetoric.

Practical career choices came into play as well. Tiberius had a
rival named Spurius Postumius, who had achieved great advancement while Tiberius was away serving in Spain. After his fiasco
with the Senate, a straight run through the *cursus honorum* to the
consulship would have been a long shot at best. Tiberius opted
for the tack of standing for the tribuneship of the people and out-
flanking his rivals with a great popular measure. This by no means
implies that his motives were not sincere. But with 20,000 happy
veterans at his back, he could afford to turn to the people as his
power base.[8]

What Tiberius had to offer the people was land. Despite the
provocative title I've given this chapter, it's important to realize
that Tiberius was not playing Lycurgus and suggesting that all the
land in the state be evenly divided up among the citizens. His bill
only called for a redistribution of the *ager publicus* we've already
talked about. In other words, he was demanding that the Licinian-
Sextian Laws be obeyed. He proposed that a commission of three
men be set up to seize all *ager publicus* held in excess of the legal
limit and divide it up in 30 *iugera* plots among the landless poor
of Rome.

The bill also contained major concessions to the rich. The beautiful farm land of Campania, where most of the large estates were
located, would be exempt from confiscation. Families already in
possession of their legal limit of *ager publicus* would own the land
free and clear (with an extra 250 *iugera* for each son up to a total
of 1000 *iugera*), while the new comers would have to pay rent on
theirs and be forbidden to sell it. Always aware of potential sena-

torial opposition, Tiberius was also careful to play up the conservative argument that disenfranchised farmers would fall off the census rolls and, as landless *proletarii,* become ineligible for military service. As Rome's population of farms shrank, so would her draft pool.[9]

Tradition demanded that Tiberius submit so sweeping a bill to the Senate, and he had support there: Let's not forget that his father-in-law Appius Claudius was the *princeps senatus,* which meant that he got to speak first. Appius Claudius was behind him, as was Mucius Scaevola, a famous lawyer and the consul for that year, and Scaevola's brother Publius Licinius Crassus Mucianus, the father-in-law of Tiberius's brother Gaius. Tiberius, however, didn't think that liberal support and generous concessions were enough. We've already looked at his relation with the Senate. Besides, how could the very people who were breaking the Licinian-Sextian Laws be expected to pass a bill that would cost many of them, individually, a fortune? Turning instead to the powers granted to the Popular Assembly by the *Lex Hortensia,* Tiberius chose to use the tribuneship of 133 BC to submit his bill there, completely by-passing the Senators.[10]

Both Appian and Plutarch tell us that Tiberius was a powerful speaker. Plutarch has preserved a fragment of what he said to the Popular Assembly:

> The savage beasts in Italy have their particular dens, they have their places of repose and refuge; but the men who bear arms, and expose their lives for the safety of their country, enjoy in the meantime nothing more in it but the air and light; and, having no houses or settlements of their own, are constrained to wander from place to place with their wives and children.[11]

That's powerful, revolutionary stuff, and the Senate was furious. Senators had, after all, long considered the land that Tiberius was appropriating as their own. Many had taken out loans on it, or used it as their daughters' dowries, or even buried their parents and grandparents on it. Equally outrageous was Tiberius's attempt to turn the Popular Assembly into a law making body in opposition to the Senate. As we've seen, this wasn't illegal, but Roman conservatives resented it as an attack on their power, just as American conservatives today resent the use of our courts to declare legislation unconstitutional and thus bring about social change.

The senators had a solution. They convinced another tribune named Marcus Octavius, a friend of Tiberius with, however, considerable holdings of public land himself, to veto Tiberius's land bill. Gracchus was flabbergasted. When repeated entreaties to his friend got him nowhere, he even agreed to submit the bill to the Senate for prior approval. But it was too late for conciliation, and the Senate threw his bill out. Having been completely outmaneuvered, Tiberius had no legal recourse. He therefore (though he probably wasn't completely aware of it himself) began The Roman Revolution. Standing before the Assembly, Gracchus told the people that any tribune who violated the trust and undermined the clear will of the people had betrayed his office and should be deposed. Taking up his cry, the 35 tribes of the people began to vote, one after the other, to impeach the tribune Octavius.

This was without precedent and illegal. As we've already seen, it was death even to punch a tribune, never mind to kick him out of office! After the 17th tribe had voted for impeachment, Tiberius stopped the proceedings, embraced Octavius, and tearfully begged him to withdraw his veto so that so fatal a step as impeachment wouldn't have to be taken. Octavius wavered, but the sight of his rich supporters standing in a group and glaring at him settled the issue. He told Gracchus to do his worst, and the 18th tribe voted him out of office. Not wishing to use public officers for so illegal a move, Tiberius had one of his former slaves drag Octavius off the speaker's platform. Tiberius then had a flunky named Quintus Mummius (or Mucius) appointed tribune in Octavius's place. The land bill was then easily passed.[12]

The Assembly appointed three commissioners to implement the bill: Tiberius, his brother Gaius Gracchus (who at that time was off killing Spaniards with brother-in-law Scipio), and his father-in-law Appius Claudius. As we've seen repeatedly, Roman politics was very much a family affair.[13]

Not having thought very far ahead, Tiberius forgot that fledgling farmers need money to buy seed, stock, and equipment, and that even land commissioners need funds to do their job. The Senate, of course, controlled all money. With a grim sense of humor the Senate voted the land commission a *per diem* expense account of 9 obols—say 50 cents. When Tiberius put in the standard request for a tent to shield the commissioners from the sun as they did their work, the Senate refused. Without money there would be no surveying, no redistributing, and no stocking—only sunstroke.

At that point news reached Rome that crazy King Attalus III of Pergamum, probably terrified at the threat of a rebel leader named Aristonicus, had died and in his will made the Roman people his heirs. Tiberius claimed that the Senate, therefore, had no jurisdiction in this case, and so passed a bill that the money from Attalus (by which he probably meant the money from the king's private estates) should be distributed among the poor who were being set up on farms by the land commission. Not only was this move of Tiberius illegal, but it struck directly at the sacred prerogatives of the Roman Senate. Even worse, Tiberius went so far as to claim that the Senate had no authority over the cities listed in Attalus's will, and that the Roman People would decide their fate. There can be no doubt that this move more than any other destroyed Tiberius's relationship with the senatorial class, who were now eagerly awaiting his year of office to run out. Once Tiberius was no longer a sacrosanct tribune, he could be prosecuted in open court for malfeasance, misappropriation of state funds, and treason. As the Senators put it, he would learn to regret what he'd done.[14]

To protect himself, Gracchus decided to run for tribune a second time. This wasn't exactly illegal, but it hadn't happened in over 200 years, since which time the nature of the tribunate had changed. We've seen that the office had originally been created to protect the plebeians from the patricians. Now that the struggle between the orders was long since over, that was no longer necessary, and the tribunate had become instead a useful tool for controlling the popular assembly, as indeed the Senate had attempted to do with Octavius.[15] By threatening to make the tribuneship a life-long job, Tiberius seemed to the senators to be upsetting the balance of power. A tribune who acted as a mouthpiece for the Popular Assembly would be a direct threat to the power of the Senate and a potential dictator. This was even worse than stealing Attalus's legacy.[16]

On election day Tiberius and his supporters took over the temple on the Capitoline Hill, where the polls had been set up. There was trouble at once, for the senators' and Tiberius's thugs scuffled at the outskirts of the crowd, preventing voting from taking place. As the confusion got worse, Tiberius gave a prearranged signal,[17] his supporters surrounded him, broke the *fasces* of the lictors, and violently drove off the rich. Rumors started flying: Tiberius had deposed all of the tribunes by violence, he had declared himself tribune without an election, or perhaps he had even asked the people to make him a king.

Meanwhile, back at the Temple of Fides where they were meeting, the senators were dumbfounded. Publius Cornelius Scipio Nasica, a cousin of Tiberius and the Pontifex Maximus of Rome (the Chief Priest or, in Christian terminology, the Pope), demanded that the consul Mucius Scaevola do something. Mucius had been a supporter of Gracchus; he blandly replied that the consul would not be the first to use violence. At that Nasica lost control. "Let those who would save our country follow me!" he shouted, storming out of the temple. By the time he reached the Capitoline hill he was trailing a mob of red faced, white haired senators waving clubs and pieces of broken furniture they had picked up along the way. Naturally the crowd parted before them. These good old boys from the Senate then swarmed over Tiberius Gracchus and his supporters and clubbed them to death, to the number of about 300. The bodies were tossed into the Tiber River.[18]

More followers of Gracchus were rounded up and slain, but the Senate already felt it had gone too far. This was, indeed, the first blood shed in civil unrest since the expulsion of the Tarquins way back in 509 BC.[19] Unfortunately, this was also the first clear indication that the republican form of government at Rome was breaking down. Times were changing, but the Senate was too self-interested to go along. Gracchus had tried to pass some of the Senate's power onto the Roman plebs, but they were no longer the citizen militia of farmers who had defeated Hannibal. Many of those in the capital were now freed slaves trained in crafts rather than agriculture, and in order to carry on his brother's work, Gaius Gracchus would have to bribe them with cheap grain[20]—a first step towards the welfare on which the Roman mob would live for the next several centuries. Having learned the trick of political murder, both demagogues and senatorial conservatives would continue to use it for the next 100 years.

For now, though, as we said the Senate had gone too far. To get him out of the way, Nasica was sent off on a wild goose chase to

Asia, where he had the good sense to die. The Land Commission was allowed to continue its work, Publius Licinius Crassus, Gaius Gracchus's father-in-law, being elected in Tiberius's place. They must have been busy, for the census figures supplied to us by Livy show that between 131 and 125 BC, 75,000 citizens were added to the census rolls.[21] A former rival of Gracchus even set up a milestone in Lucania bragging, "I first compelled the grazers to give back the public land to the tillers."[22]

But there were problems. Many boundaries were difficult to trace, so it was often impossible to tell where the *ager publicus* left off and private land began. This was particularly troublesome for Rome's Italian allies who, when bumped off their land by the commissioners, lacked the protection afforded by Roman citizenship.[23] They turned to Scipio Aemilianus, who as a soldier understood the value of the Italian allies to Rome's war effort. He took up their cause, but the Romans were too jealous of their privileges to listen to him. Instead, Scipio dissipated his popularity by defending "foreigners," and the Roman people set themselves up for the terrible Social War of 90-88 BC, at the end of which the Italians achieved citizenship anyway. Scipio was found dead one morning in his house just before he was going to make another speech on the Italian question. As he was in his late 50's the death was never formally investigated, but there have always been suspicions that his political enemies had him murdered. Scratch another hero.

After the murder of brother Gaius Gracchus in 121, the agrarian law became pretty much a dead letter. First a law was passed in 111 allowing the new landowners to sell their 30 *iugera* plots. This allowed the rich once again to gobble up land and force out squatters. A tribune named Spurius Thorius did pass a law stopping redistribution of the land and allowing for a single rent on the property, but even this rent was quickly abolished by another tribune, so the law broke down completely.[24]

Tiberius Gracchus failed because like many reformers he saw only the end results of the problems he hoped to redress. He thought that he could reverse an historical trend by tinkering with one of its symptoms. One hundred years later the assassins of Julius Caesar would make the same mistake.

30 «Tous pour un, un pour tous»

The murder of Tiberius Gracchus—and subsequently of his brother Gaius—established a bad precedent. In any society, the rule of law and order rests ultimately on a voluntary agreement between the citizens and their government. Even if the state is oppressive, it will survive so long as the citizens figure that anything is better than the dog-eat-dog uncertainty of anarchy. Once the citizen body accustoms itself to violence, however, the government falls. After the Gracchi, violence became increasingly the rule.

The Roman civil war didn't begin with street riots and barricades, but rather with a gradual and cancerous spread of the army into daily life. To get the people's mind off the Gracchus brothers and to increase its own reputation, the Senate initiated a series of foreign wars, the continuous presence of which gradually tipped the balance of power away from the Senate to the very generals it thought it was appointing. The first of these was a military genius of the equestrian class named Gaius Marius. Employing the rabble-rousing techniques of the Gracchi, he got himself elected consul in 107 BC to fight a sticky little war against one of King Masinissa's grandsons, the Numidian King Jugurtha. Jugurtha had been leading Roman politicians and generals around by the nose for years, and had once said of Rome that it was "a city for sale and ripe for lopping, if only it could find a buyer."[1]

Even more important than his eventual victory over Jugurtha was the nature of the army Marius used to accomplish it. For the first time, Marius openly recruited volunteers without regard to the property class (remember the *Comitia Centuriata*?) to which they belonged. That is to say, he drafted the landless ones, the *proletarii*.[2] As we've seen, this was the one solution to unemployment that Tiberius Gracchus had resisted. He had tried to raise the property class of Rome's lowest citizens until they could qualify for military service. Marius abandoned that attempt and with it the old idea that Rome's army must be a citizen militia, fighting for hearth and home.

Of course it hadn't really been that for a long time. Slaves had been enrolled during the dark days of the Hannibalic War, and even Gaius Gracchus had had to give the poorer soldiers some help in buying their equipment.[3] Nonetheless, so long as there had been a large proportion of citizen draftees present in the army, there had been constant pressure on every commander to get his campaign over with so that his soldier-farmers could get back home to plow the back forty. An army made up of impoverished volunteers would, however, completely reverse that picture. A slum dweller had nothing to go back to; the longer the campaign went on, the more money he would make. Furthermore, the only way one of these new soldiers could get a pension would be if his general forced through a land bill to set him aside a farm for his old age. So these armies of *proletarii* gradually hardened into professional soldiers whose first loyalty was not to the Roman state, but rather to the successful general who was leading them. It was this fundamental and, unfortunately, necessary change by Marius that made the civil wars possible, eventually overthrowing the Republic and establishing the Roman Empire.[4]

Marius came back a hero, and just in time to tackle a dangerous invasion of two Celtic tribes called the Cimbri and the Teutones. Thanks to his victories and the enthusiastic support of the Roman mob, Marius was, quite unconstitutionally and without precedent, elected to the office of consul 6 times between 107 and 100 BC. The inevitable aristocratic backlash came in the person of a young noble named Lucius Cornelius Sulla.

Sulla and Marius are the originals copied by Pompey and Caesar, to whom most of this chapter will be devoted. Sulla became famous in the terrible Social War (90-88 BC) fought between the Romans and their Italian allies who were demanding full citizenship rights. We saw this war foreshadowed in the death of Scipio Aemilianus. It was slugged out to a draw, by which time the Eastern provinces, talking advantage of the distraction, rose up in revolt under a barbarian, Greek-aping king named Mithradates of Pontus (along the southeast shore of the Black Sea). On a single day in 88 BC, Mithradates massacred all the foreigners who lived and did business in the eastern provinces he had overrun. That came to 80,000 men, women, and children, mostly from South Italy.

Both Sulla and the aging, now overweight Marius wanted the

command against Mithradates. When their squabbling escalated into street riots, Sulla fled to his soldiers in fear of his life. He then invaded Rome itself, drove Marius into exile in Africa, set the city to rights, and finally, fearing that his own soldiers might get itchy, set out after Mithradates. That gave Marius the opportunity to limp back to Rome and stand for his seventh consulship.

Marius died shortly thereafter, but not before he had initiated a new technique in the civil wars called "proscription." It involved posting lists of enemies who could then be killed by anyone for a reward. Meanwhile Sulla, after striking a hurried and rather unfavorable deal with Mithradates, returned to Rome in 85 and put up his own proscription list. It was not a happy time. In a famous story, Plutarch tells how Sulla had gathered 6,000 of his enemies in the circus with promises of mercy. He then ordered their execution, and when their screams of agony startled the senators who were meeting nearby in the Temple of Bellona, Sulla, "continuing his speech with a calm and unconcerned countenance bade them listen to what he had to say, and not busy themselves with what was doing out of doors; he had given directions for the chastisement of some offenders."[5]

Gaius Iulius Caesar was one of the lucky survivors who escaped Sulla. He was a teen-ager during the proscriptions and was doubly in danger: his young wife, Cornelia, was the daughter of Cinna, Marius's last partner in the consulship, and Caesar refused to divorce her on Sulla's orders; secondly, Marius himself had been the husband of Caesar's Aunt Julia. Young Caesar had powerful friends, though, who convinced Sulla that there was no point in murdering a boy. Sulla therefore contented himself with seizing Cornelia's dowry and Caesar's inheritance, meanwhile allowing the boy to do some traveling. He's supposed to have mumbled, however, that "there are many Mariuses in Caesar."[6]

While Caesar was off getting his first military experience in Asia, the brightest star on the horizon was a nobleman named Gnaeus Pompeius, whom we'll follow English tradition in calling Pompey. When he was only 23 he had raised 3 legions at his own expense and joined Sulla. He was so successful that Sulla not only gave him the nickname *Magnus* "The Great," but even allowed him to hold a triumph when he was still too young to serve in the Senate.

In the year 78 Sulla surprised everyone by retiring from public life. Rather like the emperor Charles V, he went off to the country and died in happy obscurity. He had, as he believed, put the senatorial aristocracy back in power, but he apparently failed to realize that, by his own example, he had demonstrated that the real power in the state was with its successful generals. Thus when difficulties arose, both Senate and people out of habit turned to the most successful general around to bail them out—Pompey the Great.

Pompey was sent to Spain to finish off the rest of the Marians, even though he had not gone through the *cursus honorum* and so had no right to a military command. He returned in 71 just as another commander, Marcus Crassus, was killing 12,300 of the gladiators fighting in Spartacus's famous slave revolt. Pompey tracked down the 5,000 who escaped and then reported blithely to the Senate "that Crassus had overthrown the slaves in battle, but that he had plucked up the war by the roots."[7]

Such bragging would hardly endear Pompey to Crassus, a former lieutenant of Sulla who had grown rich on the proscriptions.[8] As we'll see, the two men never did trust one another, but since they both had armies outside Rome, it was a simple matter to get themselves elected as consuls for the year 70.

But it was pirates, even more than the consulship, that brought Pompey his greatest fame. When I say pirates, you shouldn't think of buccaneer ships, peg legs, parrots and such; these pirates, whose bases were in Cilicia in Asia Minor, were really private armies on the prowl. They had amassed a fleet of over 1,000 ships and, during the confusion of the civil wars, had become bold enough to seize 400 cities throughout the Roman empire. Something obviously had to be done, and at the suggestion of the tribune Gabinius, a friend of Pompey, that something was to offer an extraordinary command to everyone's favorite general. The command was more than extraordinary; it was illegal. It violated the Senate's authority just as much as Tiberius Gracchus's appropriation of the Kingdom of Pergamum. For three years Pompey was to be given absolute command over the Mediterranean Sea and was to outrank every governor for 50 miles inland. He would have 200 ships at his disposal and the authority to raise as many men as he needed.

Pompey finished the war in 3 months. He took 20,000 prisoners, finally even besieging the pirates in their strongholds in Cilicia.

That left him with the problem of what to do with the rest of his command. The solution was offered by another tribune named Manlius: Pompey was to mop up Mithradates. That would involve bumping a brilliant but unpopular general named Lucullus and giving Pompey more power than a lot of senators would have liked, but the tribes insisted and Pompey got the job. Mithradates was defeated in a midnight battle near the Euphrates; he escaped, only to commit suicide later when his own son Pharnaces revolted against him. Caesar's career will bring us back to Pharnaces later. Pompey meanwhile, for want of anything better to do, conquered the East, almost as an afterthought overthrowing the last of the Seleucid kings, the pathetic Antiochus the Asiatic.

To borrow Plutarch's list, he triumphed over "Pontus, Armenia, Cappadocia, Paphlagonia, Media, Colchis, the Iberians, the Albanians, Syria, Cilicia, and Mesopotamia, together with Phoenicia and Palestine, Judaea, Arabia, and all the power of the pirates subdued by sea and land."[9] There was considerable nervousness in Rome as to what would happen when Pompey came home.

Julius Caesar was not idle during the years that Pompey achieved greatness. Sulla's death in 78 cleared the path for his return to Rome, where he could start a career in the usual fashion by prosecuting political enemies in the law courts. Cicero, Rome's greatest orator and worst politician, would later admit that Caesar was second to none as an orator.[10] His first prosecution against Cornelius Dolabella (for extortion, of course) was, however, a failure, so Caesar went off to the island of Rhodes to study oratory with Apollonius Milo.

In 75, while on his way, he managed to get himself captured by pirates—of the type whom Pompey, as we've seen, would stomp later. Caesar was insulted when the pirates demanded 20 talents ransom; he insisted on paying 50 and sent off his servants to raise the money. During the 40 days Caesar spent with the pirates he drank with them, read them his poems, called them idiots when they didn't applaud enthusiastically, and bragged that he would round the whole lot of them up after his release and crucify them. The pirates laughed, the ransom arrived, and Caesar was released. Caesar then gathered a fleet, rounded up the pirates, and had them crucified.[11]

Shortly after his return he was elected to a military tribuneship and then, in 69, began the *cursus honorum* with a successful bid for

the *quaestorship*. It was while he was quaestor that he lost his first
wife Cornelia, by whom he already had a daughter named Julia.
He subsequently married a woman named Pompeia, daughter of
Quintus Pompeius—not, of course, our friend Pompey the Great,
but, most ironically, a son-in-law of Sulla. Caesar served his
quaestorship in Spain, there gaining some more military experience.

Caesar achieved the aedileship in 65. As was pointed out earlier, one of the aedile's main functions was to put on the public
games—mostly at his own expense. This was a fledgling politician's
big chance to make a memorable splash with the electorate, and
Caesar spared himself no expense. Before he even entered into
office he was 1,300 talents in debt. In order to demonstrate to the
mob his popular sympathies, he held a great funeral for his Aunt
Julia, who had died many years before, and during that funeral
brought out the wax death mask and the statues of his Uncle
Marius. This was clearly telling the Senate where he stood. Caesar similarly put back in the forum (at night, for he was no fool,
and at his own expense, for no one else would do it) the old trophies awarded to Marius for his victories over the Cimbri and
Teutones. The actual games and hunting shows that Caesar put
on were especially magnificent, featuring (count 'em!) 320 single
gladiatorial combats! The popularity stirred up by all this borrowed magnificence put the nose of Marcus Bibulus, his colleague
in the aedileship, considerably out of joint.[12]

Deciding, as always, that he might as well go for broke, Caesar
determined to capitalize on his popularity and bribe his way into
the office of *pontifex maximus*, or pope of the Roman pagan religion. This sounds particularly shocking to us, but priesthoods in
Rome were valuable political offices. A soothsayer could, for instance, shut down an Assembly if he insisted that the oracles were
unfavorable. Caesar is supposed to have borrowed so much for
this election that as he went off to the polls he told his mother
Aurelia, "Mom, I won't come back unless I'm the pope!" Even
though his 2 competitors were much older than he was, he polled
more votes in their tribes than they could manage in all the other
tribes put together.[13]

In 62 Caesar advanced to the praetorship and obtained Spain
as his province. Before he could get away, however, he paid a
heavy price for his pontificate. Since Caesar was the pope, the

festival of the Bona Dea (The Good Goddess), which was for women only, was held at his house under the supervision of his wife Pompeia. Now Pompeia at this time was carrying on a hot and heavy affair with a disreputable young nobleman named Publius Clodius Pulcher (*i.e.* Publius "Pretty Boy"[14] Clodius), whom she had a good deal of trouble seeing because Caesar's mother watched her like a hawk. It was therefore agreed that Clodius would disguise himself as a girl and sneak into the Bona Dea festival.

The plan backfired. Clodius certainly looked enough like a girl, but while he was waiting for Pompeia one of the other young celebrants "met him, and invited him to play with her, as the women did among themselves."[15] He was quickly found out and chased out into the night. A terrible scandal resulted, and the Senate ordered a trial for sacrilege.

The trial itself became a scandal. Everyone knew that Clodius was guilty; indeed, the prosecutor Hortensius remarked that the evidence was so overwhelming that "his throat could be cut with a lead sword." Still, "Pretty Boy" was determined to get off. He hired thugs. His lawyers, as Cicero tells us, challenged every honest juror who was summoned. There was so much threatened violence that the jury, once impaneled, requested guards for their protection.

Caesar was no help. When called as a witness, he said calmly that he knew nothing about the affair at all. Why then, Hortensius asked him, had he bothered to divorce his wife Pompeia? "Because," Caesar replied, "it is necessary that the members of my household be as free from suspicion as from blame."[16]

Old moneybags Crassus, a political ally of Clodius, was even less help. For 2 days he bribed the jury openly, offering them money, women, or boys depending on their tastes. When the vote was finally taken, it was 31 to 25 for acquittal. Rome was shocked, and Quintus Catulus, a prominent senator, quipped to one of the jurors, "Why did you ask us for a guard? Were you afraid somebody would steal your money?"[17]

The divorce behind him, Caesar was ready to leave for his province in 61. His creditors wouldn't let him leave though, for he still had to pay back the enormous debts left over from his aedileship, his run for the pontificate, and his election to the praetorship. It was again Marcus Crassus to the rescue, who lent Caesar 830 talents so he could leave for Spain and military glory.[18] About the same time Pompey returned from the East.

Since the smart money was on Pompey's imitating his old master Sulla and marching on the city to take over, his arrival at Brundisium produced a lot of breast beating in the upper circles. To everyone's surprise, however, Pompey dismissed his army, "every man to his country and place of habitation," and returned to Rome with only enough soldiers to decorate his triumph.[19] The people went wild, the senators breathed a sigh of relief, and Pompey in his victory parade put on one of the greatest shows Rome had ever seen.

His motives are not too hard to guess. Though he was only 45 years old, he had already had a long and busy career, a career which had showed him first hand the ravages of civil war. Since he already was, especially in his own estimation, Rome's greatest general, Pompey saw no need to resort to force of arms to maintain his own *dignitas*. Besides, he had few requests. He wanted to be treated with respect, he wanted the land that all generals owed their veterans as a pension for their labors, and he wanted the acts and treaties he had set up in the East ratified by the Senate. He expected that his personal authority was enough to carry these modest demands.

He was mistaken. Marcus Cicero looked up to Pompey as, *faute de mieux*, the charismatic politician to unite the warring factions of the state into a good old fashioned republic, but in general the senatorial aristocracy did not. Pompey had enemies in the Senate, such as Lucius Lucullus the successful but unpopular general whom the *lex Manilia* had bumped from the Mithradatic War, and especially Marcus Porcius Cato, the great-grandson of old "Carthage must be destroyed" Cato, and the ultra of ultras. Cicero summed Cato up best: "For you love our Cato no more than I do; nonetheless, despite his great intelligence and good faith he sometimes harms the government. He speaks as though he were living in Plato's *Republic*, not in the crap of Romulus."[20] Cato and his cronies didn't trust Pompey.

Ever since the time of his extraordinary commands they had felt that too much power was being concentrated unconstitutionally in his hands,[21] and now that he had voluntarily declawed himself, they decided that it was time to put him in his place.

Thus when Pompey made his first speech to the people on his

return, he was surprised to see it fall flat. As Cicero put it, the speech was "unpleasing to the rabble, empty for the 'wrong side,' unwelcome to the rich, not serious enough for 'the good men.'"[22] Moreover, when Pompey presented a land bill for his 40,000 veterans before the Senate, his opponents filibustered and kept the bill from a final vote; when he brought it instead before the *comitia*, the consul Metellus Celer talked the people out of it. It seemed that Pompey had no place to turn.

But Pompey was not alone is his disaffection with the Senate; our old friend Marcus Crassus was having trouble too. To explain this I'll have to point out the surprising fact that the Roman government of the 1st century BC had nothing which would correspond exactly to our idea of a civil service. There was, for instance, no Internal Revenue Service. About one third of the government's tax revenue was collected by private firms who bid for tax collecting contracts. Thus Company A would submit a bid, saying that it could collect 100,000,000 sesterces from the province of Asia. If Company B submitted another bid for 150,000,000 sesterces it would win the contract. Of course Company B expected to be able to collect 200,000,000 sesterces in taxes; the difference of 50 million would be its profit. These blood-sucking speculators were called *publicani* and are the hated *publicans* of the New Testament.

Now, at the end of 61 BC the *publicani* who had contracted to collect taxes in Asia were in big trouble. The devastation caused by the Mithradatic war along with the usual feeding frenzy associated with competitive bidding had so reduced the revenues of the province that even the publicans' stone-squeezing methods couldn't raise enough money to cover their contract. They asked the Senate to let them off the hook. Crassus, a speculator himself, naturally supported the request. Cato, however, was shocked that the *publicani* should want to welsh on a deal, and the request was turned down. Crassus was furious.[23]

Finally, in 60 BC, Caesar returned from his praetorship in Spain. He had done a wonderful job killing Spanish barbarians[24] and felt that he deserved both a triumph and the consulship for 59. This was a problem, for if he entered the city to canvass for the consulship as the law required, he automatically lost his command and so was disqualified from a triumph. Caesar asked the Senate for a special dispensation so he could run for the consulship *in absentia*, but the Senate, given its current mood and under the leadership of Cato, turned him down. Caesar was not one to care more for ceremony than power, so he entered the city, gave up the triumph, and presented himself to the people for the consulship.

There was no chance that he would lose. Caesar by this time was a proven politician who was now backed up by lots of money from Spain. Besides, he only had two rivals for the job: Lucius Lucceius, who had little influence but a lot of money, and Marcus Bibulus, his old nose-out-of-joint colleague from the aedileship and, unfortunately, Cato's son-in-law. Forced to choose between the two, Caesar of course won over Lucceius, who proceeded to buy votes for both of them. The senators, who had no intention of facing a year with Caesar in complete control of the consulship—especially when they had just put Pompey in his place—started buying votes for Bibulus, who would be a good boy and do whatever he was told.

The senators realized that what Caesar really wanted was a rich province for his proconsulship. Since it was the Senate who handed out provinces at the end of a consul's term, the senators voted that the proconsular provinces for 59 would be the dreaded *silvae callesque*, which is to say "hills and dales." This was a studied insult, for far from being a rich and potentially glorious military province like Spain or Gaul, the "hills and dales" job involved the low level bureaucratic supervision of publicly owned pasture lands in Italy. Bibulus was resigned to his fate. Cato was delighted. Caesar was furious and, as everyone seemed to have forgotten, so were Pompey and Crassus, each for his own separate reasons.

By frustrating these three powerful men, the Senate literally forced them to team up for their own protection. They formed a deal which historians like to call "The First Triumvirate," although that incorrectly implies that there was something official and universally recognized about it. Actually, it was what we would call "smoke-filled room" politics, and was kept secret for as long as possible. Pompey, Caesar, and Crassus simply agreed that nothing should happen in the republic that displeased any of the three.[25]

Now came the pay-off. Caesar and Bibulus had, of course, been elected to the consulship, so Caesar, flexing his authority in the Senate house, introduced a land bill to provide farms for Pompey's soldiers. When the bill got nowhere in the Senate, Caesar stormed out and implemented plan B: He turned his consulship into a sort of tribuneship. Summoning the *Comitia Tributa*, Caesar had Pompey fill the forum with his soldiers, many of whom, in desperate straits by this time, had drifted to the capital in order to survive on welfare. In response to the inevitable opposition from pro-Senatorial tribunes, Caesar appeared on the speaker's platform flanked by Pompey and Crassus. In a rather high-flown speech, Pompey agreed to give assistance "with sword and buckler" against any who should offer violence to the will of the people—by which, of course, he meant anyone who opposed his land bill.

Bibulus immediately announced that he perceived unfavorable omens. Officially, if a consul saw that the gods were opposed to an assembly—if, for instance, he heard ominous rumbles of thunder—it was his duty to suspend proceedings. By law, once a consul announced that he was "watching the skies for omens," all business stopped. For his trouble, however, Bibulus had a chamber pot emptied on his head and was dragged by Pompey's thugs out of the forum. In the ensuing riot two tribunes were injured but, naturally, the land bill was passed.

After cleaning himself up, Bibulus appeared in the Senate the next day railing against such unconstitutional goings-on. No one, however, had the courage to stand up against the now open triumvirate and the very considerable muscle that stood behind it. Bibulus therefore announced that he would withdraw from the Senate chamber and lock himself up in his house watching the skies for omens. This legally should have closed down the government, but instead poor Bibulus was just ignored. As a joke, people who used to date documents with the official expression "in the consulship of Caesar and Bibulus" started dating them "in the consulship of Julius and Caesar."[26]

In such an atmosphere, Crassus's demands were easily satisfied: one third of the taxes due by the *publicani* were remitted while Caesar, for appearance's sake, scolded them to be more careful in the future.[27] He had a good deal more trouble, however, getting what he wanted: a decent proconsular province, the successful administration of which would complete the reputation he had been building so carefully since the days of his quaestorship. Still despairing of the Senate, Caesar had one of his friends, the tribune Publius Vatinius, pass a bill through the *Comitia Tributa* canceling the Senate's "hills and dales" legislation and giving him instead Cisalpine Gaul (i.e. the Po Valley in north Italy between the Alps and the Rubicon River) and Illyria (the coast of Yugoslavia) for 5 years. Later, when the projected governor of Transalpine Gaul died Pompey got the Senate to give that to Caesar too. The tricky thing about Transalpine Gaul (roughly modern France) was that it was unconquered territory. Most senators probably figured that once Caesar marched off into the unknown, barbarian-ridden forests of Gaul his problem would take care of itself. After all, Caesar had qualified for a triumph in Spain, but he hadn't done anything to suggest that he was a military genius. The only one who suspected that was Caesar himself.

Marcus Cato objected to Caesar's new governorship on constitutional grounds. He railed against it so consistently in the Senate that Caesar had him hauled off to jail. It will be important for us to remember the high-handed way that Caesar acted during his consulship when we discuss the actions of his dictatorship, for just as with Alexander, it's popular to see in Caesar a good man corrupted by power. We should also point out that he changed his mind about Cato and rescued him both from prison and a potentially irritating martyrdom. There were better ways to handle Cato.[28]

As it was characteristic of Caesar the general never to leave an enemy behind him, he started making plans in 59 to cover his Roman rear while he was away in Gaul in 58. That meant finding a replacement for his tribune Vatinius, and it's rather to Caesar's discredit that he settled for, of all people, "Pretty Boy" Clodius. It certainly fitted Clodius's political style to stand for the tribuneship, but since he was a patrician by birth, he could only become a tribune if he were first adopted into a plebeian family, a move the Senate had consistently blocked. As consul Caesar convened a rump session of the old *Comitia Curiata* and rammed through Clodius's adoption by a plebeian father who was considerably younger than Clodius himself.[29] It was no coincidence that Caesar had this done the same day that Cicero, Cato's friend, made a violent and ill-timed speech bemoaning the current state of affairs. Clodius, it seems, hated the great orator; Cicero had made him look foolish by blowing his best alibi during the Bona Dea trial, and Clodius was not the kind of man to forget an insult. As tribune he did both Caesar and himself a favor by having Cicero exiled on a charge of unconstitutional actions during his consulship of 63 BC. Caesar would have liked to dig up a similar charge against Cato, but that paragon of honesty was above reproach, so Clodius instead introduced a bill which kicked Cato upstairs into an emergency governorship of Cyprus. That at least got him out of the way. As a final hedge against the future, Clodius was given money by Crassus and Caesar to recruit gangs of thugs, guaranteed to keep politics at Rome advantageously chaotic while Caesar was away on campaign.[30]

But Caesar was too thorough to trust to violence alone. During his consulship he took as his third and final wife Calpurnia, the daughter of Lucius Piso, whom Caesar backed for the consulship of 58 BC . His best move, though, was to marry off his daughter Julia to Pompey. This involved some complications, for Julia was already engaged, and Pompey had earlier divorced his own wife because (it was said) she was having an affair with Caesar. But if Caesar could make up with Clodius, Pompey could cuddle up to "Aegisthus' daughter," and the marriage was arranged. To everyone's surprise Pompey, who was old enough to be Julia's father—indeed, he was 7 years older than her father—fell deeply in love, so that this marriage became one of the strongest links in the triumvirate.[31]

In 57 BC Caesar went off to his province. He was to stay there for 9 years. Since the next chapter will give us ample opportunity to see Caesar in his role as a general, we won't follow him now on his campaigns against the Celts and Germans. He tells the whole story himself in his *Commentaries on the Gallic War*, published in 51 BC as propaganda in his upcoming war with Pompey. They are devilishly clever books; Caesar writes throughout in the 3rd person, so that he never writes "I then attacked," but rather "Caesar then attacked." This gives the books a detached, scientific tone, but if you read them carefully it starts dawning on you that Caesar, cool, confident, and poised throughout, never makes a mistake and always wins in the end. As a matter of fact, that is true in the broadest sense. Not only was Caesar the first to bridge the Rhine and invade Germany, he was also the first to sail across the English Channel and attack England, though in the first century BC these countries had little that was worth a Roman's bother in stealing. Most important was his gradual and brutal conquest of the area we now call France. The Celtic culture there was systematically exterminated as were hundreds of thousands of Gallic men. Latin soldiers and businessmen moved in to take their place so that within only a few generations the entire province was speaking Latin. Julius Caesar is personally responsible for the French language and culture which should, I suppose, be considered an improvement over what the victims of Roman genocide had to offer. *Chacun à son goût.*

With Caesar away, Roman politics grew increasingly chaotic. That should have sent the Senate a message, but no one likes to be forced into virtue. Pretty Boy Clodius was the most visible symptom of the state disease. It was his job to keep an eye on Pompey for Caesar, but backed up as he was by a whole army of thugs, Clodius tended to act more and more for his own benefit. To protect himself, Pompey first went over Clodius's head to the *Comitia Centuriata* in order to recall Cicero. Since, however, the logic and rhetoric of a brilliant speaker are little proof against mob violence, Pompey eventually turned to the aid of another hot-head named Titus Annius Milo. Milo and his boys rioted for Pompey, while Clodius increasingly gravitated towards extreme conservatives like Bibulus. Milo even got himself arrested for rioting in February of 56; at the trial Clodius led his mob in chants against Pompey, and there was so much fighting that nothing was accomplished.[32]

Caesar's spies kept him informed of what was going on in the capital. The rioting he had expected, but two unexpected events forced him to intervene. First, Cicero was making speeches in the Senate to revoke the land bill Caesar needed to reward his own soldiers. Second, Cato was backing his brother-in-law Lucius Domitius Ahenobarbus as consul for 55, and Lucius was boasting how he would revoke Caesar's command and drag him back to Rome for trial. In April of 56 Caesar proceeded to Luca on the south-western boarder of his province. Pompey and Crassus dutifully reconvened the triumvirate there, followed by more than 200 senators and a crowd of 120 lictors. This was the Roman equivalent of 120 black Cadillacs pulling into Bangor, Maine. Everything was patched up: Cicero was told politely to shut up and, being no fool, from this point on ceases to play any important role in Roman politics; furthermore, plans were made to keep Lucius Domitius out of the picture by having Pompey and Crassus stand for the consulship instead. Caesar, it was agreed, would hold his command for 5 more years.

Back at Rome, Pompey and Crassus played it coy. When asked if he would run for the consulship, Pompey replied "maybe yes, maybe no." Crassus, sounding very much like a politician, said that he would do whatever benefited the republic. All doubt was removed, however, when Domitius and Cato proceeded in the early morning towards the forum for the consular elections. Caesar had furloughed troops from Gaul to back up his partners, and a contingent of these goons jumped Cato's party. Cato himself was wounded, two of Domitius's torch bearers were murdered, and the survivors were lucky to escape to a private house. As you've probably guessed, Pompey and Crassus were elected consuls for 55. When lots were drawn for their provinces, Pompey received Spain and Crassus Syria, where a war was brewing against the great Parthian Empire.[33]

Given the mood at Rome, no truce among the triumvirs could be considered permanent. It was apparent to the Senate, to Pompey, and to Crassus that Caesar was not making a fool of himself in Gaul; quite the opposite: He was building up a great reputation for himself and, more important, a crackerjack fighting force. Pompey was becoming jealous while Crassus, who had sat many years on his money since the days of Spartacus, was desperate. That explains his delight over his proconsular assignment to Syria. He marched off in 54, and in May of 53 at Carrhae in Mesopotamia 20,000 of his soldiers were killed, 10,000 were taken prisoner, and Crassus himself was killed in an ambush. His head was subsequently employed as a prop in a scene from Euripides' *Bacchae* presented at the wedding feast of the Parthian King Pacorus and the King of Armenia's daughter.[34]

This of course formally ended the triumvirate, but for a long time Crassus had been the 3rd wheel on a bicycle anyway. More ominous had been the death in September 54 of Pompey's wife Julia, who died giving birth to a daughter. The daughter died shortly thereafter, and the alliance really died with her.[35]

Yet a third death led to the final demise of the triumvirate. This set of troubles started out the year following Pompey and Crassus's second consulship, when so much money was taken out for bribery that interest rates rose from 4 to 8 percent, and when there was so much violence that elections couldn't even be held until

July of 53. It got worse throughout the terrible year of 52 BC, when Milo was running for the consulship and Clodius for the praetorship. The violence continued to escalate until our friend, Publius "Pretty Boy" Clodius, was murdered by Milo's mob. The rabble went wild at Clodius's funeral and burned down the Senate house as his funeral pyre; the shouting at Milo's trial was so intimidating that even Cicero was cowed into a mediocre performance, resulting in Milo's exile to Marseilles. Finally Bibulus, of all people, suggested that Pompey be made the sole consul. This was both illegal and unprecedented, but to everyone's surprise even Cato approved, saying "that any form of government was better than none at all." Pompey had clearly been chosen to be the Senate's champion, and he accepted the job.[36]

We've already seen how Caesar's *Commentaries* were published about this time as a propaganda blast against his enemies. It's important to realize just how much anti-Caesarian propaganda was in circulation too. Suetonius, who loves this sort of thing, has preserved a lot of it,[37] but most remarkable, I think, are the virulent attacks surviving among the works of Rome's greatest lyric poet, Caius Valerius Catullus. It tells something of Caesar's character that he was able to make up with Catullus in early 54, but the poet, in the tradition of Keats, Shelly, Mozart, and Schubert, died shortly thereafter and had little chance to change his song. Here's an English version of one of Catullus's lampoons of Caesar and his creature, the enterprising knight Mamurra:

> Can anybody handle it—unless
> a gambler, or a glutton, or a fop—
> To see Mamurra with the booty brought
> from long-haired Gaul and from the British Isles?
> Fag Romulus, can you put up with this?
> And now, I guess, all puffed up with himself,
> he'll leave his tracks in everybody's bed
> just like Adonis or some snow-white dove.
> Fag Romulus, you're taking it? Then you're
> a gambler, and a glutton, and a fop.
> Perhaps on this account, *mon général,*
> you passed into the West's most distant isle,
> just so that horny dickey-bird of yours
> could eat them up 300 at a time?
> Who needs left-handed openhandedness?
> It's just a little that he's eaten up?

He started with his own ancestral hoard,
moved on to Pontic loot, then gobbled up
whatever Spain' gold-bearing streams could spare.
Now Gaul and Britain wait and are afraid.
Why foster such a wastrel, what's he good
for—other than consuming fat bequests?
On this account, O Rome's most pious dad
and son-in-law, you've ruined everything?[38]

31 The Civil War

The closer it got to the Ides of November, 50 BC—the date agreed upon at Luca as the final extension of Caesar's command in Gaul[1]—the more nervous Caesar became. He knew that if he returned to Rome as a private citizen he would be a dead man. It was common practice to attack political enemies in the courts on trumped-up charges, and indeed it will be remembered that Caesar had begun his own political career in exactly that way. Without the immunity from prosecution offered by a consulship or proconsulship, Caesar in Rome would be, depending on your metaphor, a sitting duck or a cooked goose. To protect himself, Caesar proposed that he be allowed to run for the consulship *in absentia.* Back in 52 a law proposed by all the 10 tribunes had given Caesar precisely that right; Pompey later rescinded that law, but being reminded of his promise to Caesar, sent off engravers to carve Caesar's dispensation into the prematurely cast bronze tablets. Cato, however, refused to go along with this and told Caesar that he would have to enter Rome as a private citizen to canvass for the election, just as he had said under similar circumstances back in 60 BC. Cato was always consistent, and this time Pompey was quiet.[2]

A brilliant young friend of Cicero, the unlucky scapegrace Marcus Caelius, summed up the picture in a letter written from Rome in early August 50 BC:

> This is the problem that those in power are going to fight over. Pompey has decided not to allow Caesar to become consul unless he hands over his army and provinces first, but Caesar is persuaded that he can't be safe if he leaves the army. Still, he proposes that both hand over their armies. Thus their love affair and their hateful partnership have not simply degenerated into secret bickering, but have broken out into war.[3]

Caesar's counter-proposal may come as a surprise, but it seemed necessary to balance a motion passed in the Senate by Quintus

Metellus Scipio, Pompey's new father-in-law: "That before a certain day Caesar dismiss his army, and if he does not, that he be considered as acting against the Republic"—i.e. as an outlaw. When Pompey was asked what he would do if Caesar insisted on keeping his army and running for the consulship, he answered, "What if my son were to attack me with a cudgel?"[4]

On Jan. 8, 49, the new consul Lucius Cornelius Lentulus passed a decree of martial law (the *senatus consultum ultimum*), but when Caesar's pet tribune Marcus Antonius (Mark Antony, who now enters our story) made a formal presentation of Caesar's compromise calling for mutual disarmament, the Senate voted almost unanimously in its favor. That drove both Scipio and Lentulus into a fury. "Against a robber we don't need votes," they shouted, "we need arms!" Vetoes attempted by the pro-Caesarian tribunes Mark Antony and Gaius Scribonius Curio were ignored and the tribunes, taking the hint, fled to Caesar, who by now had moved to Ravenna in the south of his province.[5]

Pompey, at any rate, had plenty of reasons for confidence. "Whenever I stamp with my foot in any part of Italy," he said, "there will rise up forces enough in an instant, both horse and foot."[6] He was referring, of course, to all the settled veterans of his previous wars and to the clients and tenants on his own estates. Pompey was also the governor of Spain—though he had never gone there—and the province was filled with troops and experienced commanders loyal to him. Pompey had even stolen two legions from Caesar, for when the Senate had decreed that both generals hand over a legion for a proposed Parthian war to avenge Crassus, Pompey contributed a legion that had actually been raised in Caesar's province; he subsequently kept both legions for himself. Pompey was strongest of all in ships and cavalry. He had 500 war ships and 7,000 mounted troops, "the very flower of Rome and Italy, men of family, wealth, and high spirit." These denizens of the upper crust favored Pompey because they feared Caesar. As Cicero wrote to his friend Atticus on May 2, 49:

> For I foresee slaughter if he conquers and confiscation of private funds and exile and cancellation of debts and honor for the basest sort, and a kingdom intolerable not only to a Roman, but even for a Persian.[7]

Back in Cisalpine Gaul Caesar had his legions, raised for and

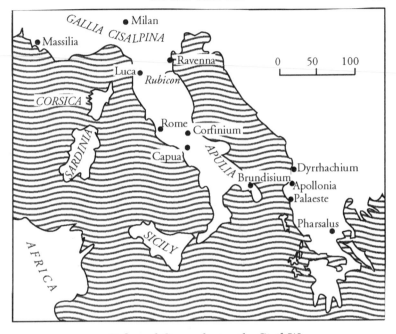

Italy and Greece during the Civil War

trained in 8 years of hard fighting. In infantry he was always superior to Pompey. At the time he was declared an outlaw, however, he had only one legion with him, the 13[th,] the others being in winter quarters. That didn't make his next step any easier. It was one thing to beat up a fool like Bibulus, but quite another illegally to march his army out of his province and, in effect, declare war upon the Senate. But when he heard that his tribunes had been interfered with and had left Rome, he sneaked out of Ravenna at night, using mules from a mill to pull his carriage, and joined his soldiers who had previously been sent ahead to the Rubicon River, the border of his province. Ever since, "crossing the Rubicon" has been a cliché for "passing the point of no return." Caesar simply paused for a moment, shouted "Roll the dice!" and galloped across.[8]

Inevitably the question arises as to whether Caesar had meant to take this step all along. Plutarch felt no doubt about it and even went so far as to say that the Gallic wars were nothing more than a training exercise. Cicero would have agreed, and reports that

Caesar liked to quote this line from Euripides: "If you have to use violence, do it for the sake of power. For the rest you might as well be holy." I think, however, that these judgments made after the fact ignore a consistent tendency throughout Caesar's career to roll with the punches. In this particular case, Caesar's lieutenant Hirtius tells us that the general was in Cisalpine Gaul to drum up votes for his upcoming consular election, which activity is hardly consistent with preparations for an armed attack on the constitution. Caesar seems almost to be composing a motto for his life when, in describing the construction of a siege tower, he remarks casually, "Experience is the master of all things."[9]

As Caesar proceeded south along the east coast of Italy, the Senate flocked to Pompey. Cicero would have preferred neutrality, but eventually joined the herd. So did Titus Atius Labienus, one of Caesar's best lieutenants, the consul Lentulus, who fled Rome in a panic, and Senator Marcus Brutus, a friend of Caesar who had previously never even talked to Pompey, the murderer of his father.[10] Pompey himself headed for Apulia, in the ankle of Italy, where the troops he had taken from Caesar were wintering. Caesar thus met with little resistance. While the Pompeians assembled in Capua, towns in the north opened their gates to Caesar's troops. One exception was the city of Corfinium, where Lucius Domitius, out recruiting for Pompey, was cut off by Caesar and besieged. He immediately sent word to Pompey to come to the rescue, saying that with two armies they could cut Caesar off from supplies and win the war. By a great stroke of luck, Pompey's reply has been preserved amid Cicero's correspondence. Since it's the one chance we have of hearing Pompey's voice, I'll print the letter:

> Your letter reached me on Feb. 17, in which you write that Caesar has pitched camp before Corfinium. Just as I expected and warned you, he refuses to join battle with you for the present, and with his massed troops he is hemming you in so you may not journey to me and join up your contingents of faithful citizens with these of mine, whose good faith we suspect. Therefore I am all the more upset by your letter. For neither do I sufficiently trust in the good will of these soldiers whom I have with me, nor yet have those who have been levied reported to the consuls.
>
> Therefore take care, if you can in any way extricate yourself, to come here as soon as possible, before all of the enemy's troops have

assembled. For neither can our levies of troops arrive here quickly, nor will it escape you how much troops who do not even know each other can be employed against veteran legions.[11]

I think it will be agreed that this is not the confident voice of a winner. Pompey certainly didn't help Domitius any, who after a siege of only 7 days was handed over to Caesar by his own troops. Caesar then initiated a pattern he maintained as much as possible towards senators in the Civil War: He released Domitius, even allowing him to carry off the considerable sums of money he had brought with him, and absorbed Domitius's troops into his own army. He then followed Pompey into Apulia.[12]

Pompey's next move is clearly foreshadowed in the above letter. He withdrew to Brundisium at the heel of Italy and dug in while the two consuls sailed off to Greece. Caesar followed and besieged Pompey for 9 days. There were exchanges of messengers and talk of a meeting, but nothing came of it. Finally, on March 17, Pompey loaded his troops onto transports and skillfully slipped out of the city, leaving behind booby-trapped streets filled with ditches and sharp spikes. Pompey and his army abandoned Italy.[13]

Pompey was off to Greece to imitate his master Sulla and retake Rome from the East; Caesar would have liked nothing better than to follow him, but he hadn't enough ships. Even more disturbing was Pompey's proconsular army in Spain, which Caesar could on no account allow either to move into Italy behind his back or to link up with his rival in Greece. He therefore decided to invade Spain himself and let Pompey stew for awhile in Greece. Caesar also sent lieutenants into the grain-producing provinces of Sicily, Sardinia, and Africa, for as Cicero has disclosed in a letter to Atticus, it was part of the Pompeians' plan to block grain shipments to Italy and starve the Caesarians into submission. Only Africa held out, and indeed Caesar's tribune Curio later lost his life and his army there to Pompey's ally, tricky King Juba of Numidia. Cato himself was in charge of Sicily, but he fled the island when it came under attack by the aforementioned Curio, complaining bitterly to the Sicilian assembly that Pompey had prepared nothing in advance. Cicero was similarly disgusted with Pompey: "I've always known him to be a crummy politician; now I know he's a crummy general too."[14]

Before setting off to Spain, Caesar proceeded to Rome and addressed what was left of the Senate. He had conquered Italy virtually without bloodshed in 60 days. Caesar asked the Senate for volunteers to treat with Pompey, but since Pompey had decreed that any senators who stayed behind in Italy would be treated as enemies, he didn't get any takers.

One pro-Pompeian tribune named Lucius Metellus had also stayed behind and kept trying to veto Caesar's appropriation of funds from the reserve treasury in the Temple of Saturn. Caesar told him, "If what I do displeases you, leave; war allows no free talking. When I have laid down my arms and made peace, come back and make what speeches you please." He then called for locksmiths to break into the treasury. When Metellus kept complaining, Caesar said he would kill him if he kept causing trouble. "And this you know, young man, is more disagreeable for me to say than to do."[15] At that Metellus ran away and Caesar, money in hand, made his final preparations to leave for Spain. "I'm going to an army without a leader," he said, "and then I return to a leader without an army."[16]

There's a tendency to think of the Civil War as a struggle between Pompey and Caesar. I think, however, that we've already seen that it was considerably more complex than that. There were two armies in Spain to deal with, one under Marcus Varro in Further Spain, and a closer one under Lucius Afranius and Marcus Petreius, which Caesar took on at once. That proved to be an extremely difficult campaign, so much so that rumors of Caesar's defeat prematurely boosted the morale of Pompey's followers. Simultaneously it was necessary to reduce the city of Massilia (Marseilles), for as we saw in the chapter on Hannibal, that port was an indispensable link between Italy and Spain, and no Spanish campaign could succeed if it were in enemy hands. Decimus Brutus and Gaius Trebonius besieged it for Caesar though Massilia didn't surrender until Caesar returned from Spain. By that time he had defeated and disbanded the army of Afranius and accepted the surrender of Marcus Varro. The next turn was Pompey's, "the leader without an army." [17]

During a stop-over at Marseilles, Caesar learned that the now obedient rump Senate, at the suggestion of the praetor Marcus Lepidus (remember that name!) had named him dictator. Caesar returned to Rome where in 11 days of frantic activity he got himself elected consul for the second time, resigned the dictatorship, passed economic laws to allay any fears that he might be planning to turn Solon and cancel all debts, and made the final plans to pass his army overseas to Greece. The problem was always ships. Caesar had 12 legions on paper, though they had been severely reduced by battle and disease, but he could only scrounge up enough ships to get 7 across the Adriatic. Even that was a risky venture, for Pompey had wintered his army and navy on the Greek coast and controlled the sea. Finally, on Jan 4, 48 BC, Caesar and 7 of his legions scurried across the sea to Palaeste, in northern Epirus.[18]

Pompey learned of Caesar's arrival from one of his own captured officers whom Caesar dispatched to him with offers of a truce. Pompey's reply, which Caesar only learned after the war, is characteristic. "What's the good of life or country to me if I seem to hold them as a kindness from Caesar? I could never bear the shame of seeming to have been led back into the Italy which I left."[19] Pompey had been wintering a bit inland up in the Candavii mountains; he now began a race to the sea, hoping to cut off Caesar from his reinforcements, left back at Brundisium under the charge of Mark Antony. The race ended in a tie, with the two armies facing each other across the Apsus river in the district of Apollonia (in modern Albania). Caesar then wintered through several frustrating months of stalemate. He had cut off Pompey's easy communication with the sea, but Pompey's fleet, under the command of Caesar's old friend Bibulus, effectively sank all attempts to communicate with Italy. When Bibulus finally died from the harsh conditions of the camp, Caesar decided to take a chance.[20] He must have been desperate, for he tried to cross to Brundisium himself, boarding a small ship in disguise in the dead of night. A storm forced him back,[21] but he got word to Mark Antony to sail over to Apollonia or to Dyrrhachium (modern Durrës) further north.

Antony made the crossing, but with a fleet from Rhodes hot on his tail. A storm obligingly came up to sink the enemy fleet and blow Antony safely into the harbor of Lissus. Although Caesar and Pompey both moved north to intercept, Antony was able to rendezvous with Caesar near Dyrrhachium. Pompey again took the sea coast, and another stalemate began.[22]

In this Dyrrhachium campaign Caesar made one of his few tactical errors. He attempted, by seizing the high ground along the coast, to besiege Pompey's greatly superior force. Caesar's forces were picked off with arrows as they went about their fortifications and were so hard up for provisions that they improvised a kind of bread out of a local wild root. When Pompey was shown a loaf of this stuff, he remarked, "We're dealing with animals!"[23] Still, Caesar had some success; by damming up the mountain streams he forced Pompey's men to live on swamp water, so that sickness spread through the camp. Deciding at last to take advantage of his numerical superiority, Pompey planned a break out. He was aided considerably by two Gallic turn-coats who deserted to him after Caesar had the effrontery to catch them skimming off the top of the cavalry's pay.

When Pompey successfully broke out of the encirclement and gained access to the sea, Caesar counter-attacked by seizing a former fort of his that was then occupied by Pompey's troops. The attack succeeded, but Caesar's men took a wrong turn while rushing through the fortification's walls and found themselves trapped by enemy reinforcements. 960 of Caesar's troops were slaughtered. Pompey's troops shouted that they had won the war, but their commander, fearing a trap, failed to order them onward against Caesar's main force. This blunder more than balanced Caesar's original mistake, and Pompey, like Jack Dempsey, lost on the long count. "Today," Caesar said, "the victory was the enemy's, had there been anyone among them to take it."[24]

Caesar blamed himself for the disaster and decided that a complete change of tactics was necessary. His major mistake, as he saw it, was to allow Pompey to choose the field of operations, near the sea where he could use his powerful navy for supply. So despite the protests of his humiliated soldiers, Caesar headed inland. He figured that if he were lucky, Pompey would be foolish enough to follow him; if not, he could at least attack Pompey's father-in-law Scipio, who was stationed in Macedonia.

Pompey was no fool, but he was not a free agent. The senators with him taunted him with cries of "Agamemnon!" Marcus Favonius called out, "Good friends, you must not expect to gather figs in Tusculum this year!" Only Cato supported Pompey in his plan for a war of attrition—the very tactic that Caesar feared. Most disturbing of all, however, were rumors reaching Pompey that the senators planned to dump him as soon as he had done them the favor of eliminating Caesar. Pompey pursued Caesar south-east-ward into Thessaly.[25]

The march into Thessaly was a race, with Caesar attempting to link up with his lieutenant Domitius and Pompey heading for Scipio. Caesar, by always breaking camp in the early morning before Pompey's soldiers were up, just managed to win. With his united forces Caesar advanced on the town of Gomphi, which is just on the boarder between Epirus and Thessaly (both of which are districts in modern Greece). Gomphi had been an ally of Caesar, but after Dyrrhachium it decided to go over to what appeared to be the winning side and so shut its gates. Caesar had carefully been building up a reputation for clemency, but there's a time and a place for everything. His soldiers needed supplies, and he needed an object lesson. Gomphi was taken in one day and handed over to his soldiers as a present. It would be best not to imagine what happened to its inhabitants. The object lesson worked; all the other towns of Thessaly except Larissa (called Lárisa today) surrendered to Caesar.[26]

Meanwhile in the camp of Pompey and Scipio there was little talk of strategy. Senators were arguing instead over who would be consul or praetor next year after Caesar's defeat; the hottest argument of all was over who would inherit Caesar's title of pontifex maximus. Many even wrote home to rent the choicest town houses in the forum. "Except for the leader and a few others—I mean of the officers," Cicero wrote, "the rest were not only grasping in war, but so crude in their speech that I trembled at the thought of victory."[27]

Caesar kept his army moving about Thessaly and skirmishing with Pompey's forces both to keep his enemy off guard and gradually to allow his soldiers to regain confidence. Pompey finally got fed up with this when both armies were near the town of Pharsalus (Fársala) and in the morning advanced his troops further beyond the rampart than usual so as to tempt Caesar to an attack. Pompey was convinced that he could turn Caesar's right wing with his cavalry and win the battle without even using his infantry. After all, Pompey had 45,000 troops—about twice as many as Caesar.[28]

Of course Caesar wasn't blind. When he saw the cavalry massing on his rival's left flank he guessed what he was up to and so posted his best legion—the 10th—on his right. Then, as an added surprise, he stationed 6 cohorts behind the 10th legion, ordering them not to move until he gave a signal with a flag. He told them that when Pompey's cavalry, that "very flower of Rome and Italy," attacked, they should not throw their javelins, as was usual, but rather run up and dart them into the faces of the riders, "that those fine young dancers would never endure the steel shining in their eyes, but would fly to save their handsome faces."[29]

Caesar's troops began the battle, for Pompey had ordered his to hold their ground and absorb the enemy's attack. Caesar was convinced that this was a major tactical error, and explains: "There is a certain ardor and spirit inborn in all men that is kindled by a battle; generals shouldn't repress, they should increase this spirit."[30] After this first shock, Pompey unleashed his cavalry, who slammed into Caesar's right flank, hoping to turn it and so hit the enemy from behind. Caesar raised his signal and the 6 cohorts rushed at the cavalry who quickly broke and fled, covering their eyes and faces. This completely uncovered Pompey's left wing, and the 6 cohorts, turning the tables, quickly executed a flanking maneuver. That allowed the still fresh 10th legion simultaneously to hit Pompey's left wing head-on. Pompey's whole line crumbled, and the battle turned into a rout.

Pompey, sad to report, fled the scene of battle and escaped to his camp. As this too fell to Caesar's troops, Pompey sneaked out the back with about 30 followers and rode off to Larissa. From there he made it to the sea and embarked on a grain ship. His soldiers followed suit, fleeing to the mountains where they were surrounded and forced to surrender the next morning. In all Caesar lost only 200 soldiers in the battle of Pharsalus—though that included 30 of his centurions. Pompey lost 15,000 killed and 24,000 captured. Looking at the mounds of bodies, Caesar said, "They wanted this. After all my great deeds, I, Julius Caesar, would have been condemned had I not asked for help from the army."[31]

Pompey was now an exile. He stopped off at Mytilene to pick up his wife and touched at southern Asia Minor, where he heard that his navy was still safe and that Cato and Scipio had taken many soldiers to Africa. But he also heard that his agents had been thrown out of Antioch and Rhodes, so not feeling safe in any Roman province, he set sail with about 2,000 soldiers to Pelusium in Egypt. That seemed like a good idea: Egypt was only 3 days' sailing away and besides, the 13-year-old pharaoh Ptolemy XIII held his throne only because his father, Ptolemy the Flute Player, had bribed the triumvirs for his support.

But alas for gratitude and honor, young Ptolemy was in the midst of a civil war with his sister-wife Cleopatra (yes, the famous one), and his three advisors, the eunuch Pothinus, the tutor Theodotus, and the royal prefect Achillas, couldn't decide which Roman dog would be safer to scratch behind the ears. It was finally decided to kill Pompey, for "a dead man cannot bite." A Roman mercenary named Lucius Septimius, who had served with Pompey in the pirate wars, was dispatched to welcome him to Egypt. Septimius convinced the general to leave his galley and accompany him in a dingy to shore. Then, as Pompey stepped from the dingy, in full view of his wife and followers on board the galley, Septimius stabbed him in the back, cut off his head, and carried it away to Ptolemy.[32]

32 "I am not king, but Caesar!"

Having guessed that Pompey would head for Egypt, Caesar gave chase with 2 legions, 800 cavalry, and 10 long boats. He arrived at Alexandria just in time to be presented with Pompey's head, pickled like a cabbage. He turned away in disgust and wept when he was shown his son-in-law's signet ring. Anyway, since Caesar was in Alexandria, and since the triumvirs had set Ptolemy the Flute Player on the throne, Caesar felt obligated to settle Egypt's raging civil war—and of course to collect the "1,750 myriads" of bribe money that Ptolemy owed him.[1] It was useless trying to talk to little King Ptolemy, who wasn't even old enough to play house with his sister. The trouble came from the eunuch Pothinus, who resented being bossed around by Roman barbarians and theatrically started dining on wooden vessels, complaining that Caesar had confiscated all his plate.

Fed up with court intrigues and hoping to act as mediator, Caesar sent word to Cleopatra to leave her army and come to the palace. Cleopatra, as we'll see even better in the next chapter, was a master of political intrigue. She needed significant foreign aid to seize the throne and was quite willing to take it from Rome, but she was afraid to put herself in the power of her hated kid brother or his eunuch. She therefore had herself smuggled into the palace by a Sicilian slave named Apollodorus, who wrapped her up in a carpet which he then presented as a gift to Caesar. When he unrolled it at Caesar's feet, out rolled Cleopatra, batting her eyelashes and changing the course of Roman history.[2]

It is always a mistake for a stranger to interfere in a family feud. During a banquet Caesar's barber overhead Pothinus plotting with Achillas, the royal prefect. Caesar executed Pothinus at once, but Achillas escaped, only to return later backed up by a huge force. When Achillas tried to seize all the ships in the harbor, by which means he could cut off all Caesar's supplies from the sea, Caesar boldly set fire to his own ships. The fire spread to the docks and thence to the city's great library, which burnt to the ground. Taking advantage of the diversion, Caesar seized Pharus island (site of the famous lighthouse, one of the seven wonders of the ancient world) fortified it, and thus maintained control of the sea.

Though the Alexandrians demanded the release of their king and Caesar had to stand a long siege of the royal palace, he was able to hold out until reinforcements reached him from the provinces. With these he easily dispatched the Egyptian army, its general Achillas, and young King Ptolemy, who seems to have drowned in the Nile during the rout. Caesar then dawdled for several months in Egypt, the final result of which being that Cleopatra and Caesar had a son named Caesarion or "Little Caesar." For appearances' sake Cleopatra was married to her surviving 12 year old brother Ptolemy XIV, and they were made joint rulers of Egypt. Caesar was unwilling to make Egypt a province because he feared that some governor, following his example, might use it as a power base to take over—which is precisely the trick Mark Antony will try in the next chapter.[3]

There was still a lot of work to do. Pharnaces, the son of the great Mithradates, was determined to reconquer his father's kingdom in the East, so Caesar at last left Alexandria for Syria and Pontus where, after a 5 day Blitzkrieg, Pharnaces went down at Zela (Spring, 49 BC). On a float in his Roman victory parade commemorating this campaign, Caesar set up a sign which became his trademark: *Veni, vidi, vici* ("I came, I saw, I conquered."). [4]

After Zela Caesar returned briefly to Rome, where he was elected dictator a second time and consul for the next year. He had to clear up trouble caused by the greediness of his appointed officials, one of whom was Mark Antony. As Caesar's *magister equitum* he had been put in charge of Rome and quickly earned a reputation as tyrant. Caesar dropped him for two years.[5]

His famous 10th legion also went on strike when it was clear that yet another war was brewing in Africa, but Caesar brought them around simply by addressing them as "citizens" instead of "soldiers." That African war was against Scipio, Cato, and King Juba. It was an extremely difficult war—at one point Caesar even had to feed his horses on washed sea weed!—but it ended when Scipio was defeated at Thapsus (Feb. 6, 46 BC) and Cato, good Samurai that he was, killed himself at Utica. "Cato," Caesar apostrophized, "I must grudge you your death, as you grudged me the honor of saving your life."

Caesar's last campaign was fought against Pompey's sons in Spain. Caesar called it his toughest battle, for at Munda he briefly contemplated imitating Cato. "I have often fought for victory," he told his friends, "but this was the first time that I ever fought for my life." Still, Pompey's younger son Sextus (whom we'll meet later) just managed to escape, and the head of his elder son was given Caesar to add to his collection. The battle at Munda was fought on March 17, 45 BC, and Caesar was finally free to return to Rome.[6]

Drawing on his experience as aedile, Caesar threw one whopping celebration for the Roman people. There were victory parades, banquets, sacrifices, gladiatorial contests, theatrical performances, elephant hunts, athletic contests, naval fights, and chariot races. So many people flocked to Rome that tent cities were built in the streets to shelter them; scores of spectators, including two senators, died in the press of the crowd!

No less important for his popularity were his relief measures. First off, 400 nummi along with presents of grain and oil were distributed to each citizen. 80,000 citizens were sent abroad as colonists to relieve congestion in the city. As he had done earlier in his career, Caesar ordered that the interest already paid be subtracted from all debts; to increase the number of jobs in the countryside, he ordered that no less than one third of all cowboys be freeborn. Great building projects were organized for temples, theatres, a public library, for the draining of swamps and the dredging of harbors. Soldiers would be kept busy too, for Caesar planned to succeed where Crassus had failed and to conquer the Parthian empire.

There were more visionary reforms as well. The most lasting was the calendar, which by the year 46 was 90 days ahead of the solar year. Caesar hired an Alexandrian mathematician named Sosigenes to fix the mess, and he set up our calendar of 365 days with an extra day added to February every 4 years. To put the year 45 back on track, Caesar made it 15 months long. That confused the conservatives who, as conservatives, preferred the old chaos to the new order. So when Cicero was told by a friend that the constellation Lyra would rise the next morning, he snapped back, "Yes, in accordance with Caesar's edict."

It should be no surprise that Caesar was a harsh but just judge, but it may be surprising that he anticipated his grandnephew

Augustus's puritan revolution by passing strict sumptuary laws. All Romans, apparently, had a strong conservative streak. Caesar's agents tramped through the markets confiscating objectionable goodies and even broke into private houses to snatch them off dinner tables.[7]

These puritanical tendencies did not, however, apply to himself. After returning to Rome he sent for Cleopatra, whom I regret to admit he kept in a suburban villa while continuing to live in the city with his wife Calpurnia. Cicero was greatly offended by "the haughtiness of that queen across the Tiber in her gardens" and also by her foreign ménage, which included not only her illegitimate son by Caesar but her new brother-husband as well. Little brother Ptolemy XIV was kept around until the fateful year 44 when Cleopatra had him murdered and replaced as regent by her son Caesarion—whose official name, by the way, was Ptolemy XV.[8]

However, "the haughty queen" was only one reason why Caesar's popularity did not extend to the upper classes. Like many geniuses, he had little patience with those who were too slow witted to share his vision. "The republic is nothing but a name without body or substance," he said.[9]

That was, unfortunately, true, but it was unwise to blurt it out in front of men whose sense of honor and self-worth were intimately bound up with the institutions of the republic. But by the time he returned from Spain, Caesar was 55 years old; I really wonder if he ever expected to return from his great Parthian campaign. He had a lot to do, he was running out of time, and fools kept getting in his way.

In order to get the job done, Caesar absorbed vast personal power. In all, he was elected consul 5 times and dictator 4—the last time in 44 BC for life. He controlled all elections, no longer by bribery as in the old days, but simply by endorsing half of the candidates to the comitia at each election.[10]

The consulship became so meaningless that Caesar broke up the year into segments so he could reward more of his cronies with the title. In an infamous example, he appointed Gaius Rebilius consul for one day when the consul Quintus Maximus died on the morning of Dec. 31, 45 BC. Cicero's jokes can be well imagined: "He was wonderfully watchful, not having seen sleep during his whole consulship!"[11] The Senate flattered him shamelessly with honors—one of which, by the way, we still obey, for the Senate renamed the month Quintilis as July in his honor–but their flattery only increased his contempt. Caesar unwisely showed that contempt too, as when a senatorial commission visited him in front of the Temple of Venus Genetrix. Though he watched the commission approach, he received it sitting down, and so insulted its dignity.[12]

Such open contempt was returned. As in the days of Tiberius Gracchus, the Senate's weapon was to spread rumors that Caesar was striving to become king. For someone as astute as Caesar, who had seen the bankruptcy of oriental kings like Ptolemy and Pharnaces, the accusation was ridiculous, but it stuck. Crowds greeted him with the title of "king," only to get thrown back in their faces the haughty and characteristic rebuke, "I am not king, but Caesar." After his statues appeared with crowns one morning–rather conveniently for his enemies, by the way–Caesar lost his temper. When two tribunes gleefully ran to take the crowns off, he had them dismissed and referred to them contemptuously as "Brutuses" during the proceedings. The newly reconciled Mark Antony, Caesar's co-consul for the year 44, appeared at the Lupercalian festival and presented Caesar with a crown, which he refused theatrically in front of the whole Roman mob. He did it several times. The mob cheered, and Caesar may have thought that he had finally made his point.[13]

If we remember Caesar's high-handed actions during his first consulship, there's no need to see him as drunk with power during his dictatorship. He had always been cocky; his fatal mistake was an inability to realize how power can transform a casual sneer into a blood insult. We can see the attitude that killed him in the following brief passage from the end of the *Civil War*. Caesar is explaining why he came to Egypt with so few troops, but he also shows why he walked about Rome in his last days without a bodyguard: "But Caesar, trusting in the glory of his great deeds, didn't hesitate to set out with a small force, believing that every place would be equally safe for him."[14]

At least 60 senators were determined to kill Caesar before he could do any more harm to their beloved republic. They were convinced that with Caesar out of the way, power would revert automatically to the Senate, and Rome would return to the good old days before the civil wars. In reality, the republic had died with Tiberius Gracchus, and the last chance for a senatorial dictatorship had passed with Pharsalus. Caesar died for shadows.

The leader of the conspiracy was Gaius Cassius, about whom Caesar actually said something like Shakespeare's "yond Cassius has a lean and hungry look." Caesar had not only pardoned him after Pharsalus, he had even made him a lieutenant in his war against Pharnaces. Even better known, however, was the conspiracy's front man, Marcus Brutus, who was descended on his father's side from Lucius Iunius Brutus, the Tarquin hater, whose story we told in chapter 23. He had, as we've seen, good reason to hate Pompey, but he fought for the Senate at Pharsalus out of loyalty to his class and to Cato, who was both his uncle and his father-in-law. Caesar not only pardoned Brutus, he put Cisalpine Gaul in his charge and later made him praetor of the city. Caesar, it seems, had been engaged in a long and notorious affair with Brutus's mother Servilia. It took Cassius (who was, to complete this amorous tangle, Brutus's brother-in-law) a good deal of trouble to woo Brutus back to the cause of "The Good Men," but he succeeded by playing up to his vanity. Graffiti saying things like "O that we had a Brutus now!" appeared on the bronze statue of the first Brutus on the Capitol, while notes reading "Awake Brutus!" or "You are no longer Brutus!" appeared under Brutus's chair of office. The great man, as he thought himself, eventually gave in.

It should be noted, and says something at least for his good name, that Cicero was not invited along, though the conspirators may simply have thought him too old and vacillating for the enterprise.[15] Caesar's imminent departure for the Parthian campaign probably hastened the conspiracy, as did Caesar's temptingly ironic decision to meet with the Senate on March 15 in the portico attached to Pompey's theatre and decorated with a statue of Pompey himself.[16]

Cassius and the other conspirators wanted to kill Mark Antony along with his colleague in the consulship, but Brutus objected. With the simple morality of an assassin, he said that a work of justice should not be sullied by injustice. Since, however, Antony was a strong man and a good fighter, it was agreed to delay him in conversation outside the Senate House while the deed was done.[17] We can pass over the usual stories of omens, premonitions, and "Beware the Ides of March!" soothsayers which always surface in the weeks following a violent death. It is, unfortunately, certain that Caesar was escorted to Pompey's complex in the Campus Martius by Decimus Brutus, his old companion in arms whom we saw do good service at the siege of Massilia, but who had joined the conspiracy for, as he saw it, the good of the Republic.

The plan was to surround Caesar in the Senate house while a conspirator named Cimber Tillius distracted his attention with a petition requesting the recall of his brother from exile. When Caesar waved him off, Cimber gave the signal by pulling Caesar's toga off his shoulder. "But this is violence!" Caesar shouted, only to be stabbed from behind by Senator Casca. He drove his pen through Casca's arm but was stabbed again when he tried to break away. Finally, seeing that he was surrounded by drawn daggers, he covered his head with his toga, pulling the lower part down over his knees so as to fall with some decency, and thus received in silence the 23 blows that killed him. He collapsed, with suitable Aristotelian pathos, at the base of Pompey's statue. In the frenzy to participate, several conspirators had even managed to wound each other.[18]

The murder was followed by so much running about and screaming in the Senate that no one stayed to hear the set speech Brutus was prepared to give. Mark Antony, for instance, changed into the dress of a servant and so was able to escape to his home. The whole crowd of conspirators marched out into the street, displaying their bloody daggers like banners, and filed up to the Capitol, where Brutus was finally able to give his speech.

When the Senate met the next day, Cicero and, to everyone's surprise, Antony made speeches suggesting that a general amnesty be passed, that all of Caesar's acts be ratified, and that the major conspirators be assigned honorable provinces. This being agreed, Brutus was assigned Crete, Cassius Africa, and Decimus Brutus Cisalpine Gaul. It appeared that Antony by his statesmanship had averted a new civil war and brought about a general reconciliation of the orders.

It was then that Antony made his move. He requested that Caesar's will be published and that an honorable funeral be arranged, at which he would be allowed to address the people. The conspirators had originally wanted to throw Caesar's corpse into the Tiber, but they had desisted out of fear of Antony; now they gave in to Brutus, who foolishly granted Antony's request. A funeral bier was erected in the Campus Martius, but it was never used, for the mob, hearing that Caesar had bequeathed 300 sesterces to each citizen and his beautiful gardens to the whole Roman people, went wild with gratitude. They thronged the funeral procession in the Forum and hung on every skillful word Antony delivered to them. When, as a climax, he displayed Caesar's bloody toga, they seized the body and, just as they had done at the death of Clodius, burned it on the spot. When a friend of Caesar named Helvius Cinna showed up at the funeral the maddened crowd, mistaking him for the conspirator Cornelius Cinna, tore the unfortunate name sake to pieces and then advanced, with his head stuck on the end of a spear, to the houses of the conspirators. Brutus and Cassius quite understandably left the city as, sometime before mid-April, did Cleopatra and "Little Caesar."[19]

Caesar's will was formally read in Antony's house on Sept, 13. The handsome and dashing Antony, who was now in his later thirties, had hoped to be named Caesar's heir, but he was disappointed. Up to the start of the Civil War Caesar had reserved that honor for Pompey. Later he hoped for a son by Calpurnia, and had even appointed several of his murderers as prospective guardians, should the boy be born. Caesarion, as a bastard and half-Egyptian to boot, was of course out of the picture. Since no child was born, the estate was divided among the three grandsons of Caesar's sister Julia: Lucius Pinarius and Quintus Pedius, in whom Caesar apparently didn't take much interest, divided ¼ of the estate. The remaining ¾ went to the 18 year-old Gaius Octavius. The boy had spent 4 months with Caesar in Spain; at the time of the assassination he was in Apollonia, getting ready for the projected Parthian campaign. At the bottom of the will Caesar added the formal adoption of the boy, so that his name was henceforth Gaius Julius Caesar Octavianus. The adoption was Caesar's last smart move; we'll never know what the shrewd old soldier saw in the sickly teenager, but in the next chapter we'll see the relentless wisdom of the choice.[20]

Though Alexander and Caesar immediately invite comparison, we'll have to wait until Napoleon for another personality to match. It's easy enough to think of other great names to add to the list, such as Constantine or Charlemagne or Thutmose III, but they won't do, really. Neither historical body counts nor imperial archives create a myth; an historical legend lives out of his own time, and perhaps what we think of him is more important than what he actually was. I believe, though, that Spengler is correct in associating Alexander with Napoleon as the two great "romantics" standing at the beginning of their eras, while putting Caesar apart as the hard-hearted realist who saw that his world was crumbling and made the best of it. As the formal start of Rome's imperialist stage, Caesar marks the proverbial beginning of the end.[21]

33 The Death of the Republic

Mark Antony used the two months following Caesar's death to take firm control of Rome. After all, as the surviving consul he was legally in charge, and the second-in-command, Caesar's "Master of the Horse" Marcus Lepidus, now owed his impressive, new title of Pontifex Maximus to Antony's intercession; they had both appeared before the mob shortly after Caesar's murder, and the people dutifully hailed Lepidus as the pope of their church.

Moreover, Antony's brother Gaius was praetor that year, and his younger brother Lucius was a tribune. Having seized all of Caesar's papers, Antony used them to appoint whomever he wished to office. People laughed and called those Officials *Orcini* ("dead man's freedmen"), but none dared oppose his will.[1]

Brutus and Cassius certainly didn't, for the assassins had been greatly disappointed in their hopes. As we've already seen, they had been forced to flee the city which they hoped to liberate. Hovering nearby at Antium, Brutus and Cassius kept looking for an opportunity to return. Instead, an offer came in June to inspect the Asian and Sardinian grain supplies—clearly a ruse to get them conveniently out of the way. "Should I accept an insult as a kindness?" railed Cassius to his friend Cicero. Brutus and Cassius's provincial appointments to Crete and Cyrene came in July. In August they both left Italy, but not to their inconsequential provinces: Brutus headed for Athens and Macedonia, where he recruited idealistic young Romans and disgruntled Pompeian veterans to fight for the Republican cause. Cassius headed to Syria to steal money.[2] We'll see them again in a moment.

Back in Rome, the balance of power had already been seriously upset in late April by the arrival of young Octavian, thanks to his inheritance now flaunting the powerful name Caesar.[3] The pushy teenager called immediately on Antony as his father's friend and requested his father's money so he could pay to every Roman soldier the behest provided in Caesar's will. Antony laughed at him, saying that the weight of being executor would rest uneasily on such young shoulders. Octavian kept insisting, and as his popularity rose, Antony stopped laughing. As a counter-measure he had the Popular Assembly in June appoint him to the governorship of Cisalpine and Transalpine Gaul, both securing for himself an important provincial command (the same one, indeed, that Caesar had used to rise to power) and insuring a war against the official governor, the assassin Decimus Brutus. He also opposed Octavian's bid for the tribuneship.

The final break came in October from rumors that Octavian had put out a contract on Antony. Both men then headed to the provinces to recruit veterans to their respective causes. At Brundisium Antony picked up four Macedonian legions owed him under the terms of his gubernatorial plebiscite. The troops, already corrupted by Octavian's bribe money and propaganda, booed their consul and asked why Caesar's murderers hadn't yet been punished. Antony was forced to execute the ringleaders in order to bring his army back in line.

Octavian, meanwhile, had raised 3,000 veterans in Campania. On November 10 he led them in a theatrical march on Rome. It was a risky gamble, and Octavian took it too soon; his speech before the Assembly fell flat, his soldiers melted away, the Senate waffled, and he was forced to retreat to Arretium.

Antony got back to Rome by late November. He fumed against Octavian but like his rival found the Senate nervous and uncoöperative. Even worse, reports reached him that Octavian was continuing to woo away his troops in the north. Antony was fed up with politics. If he couldn't get the Senate to outlaw Octavian, he could at least get himself sent off to Gaul against Decimus Brutus, who was holed up in Mutina (Moderna). This was Caesar's gamble all over again, and just like his mentor, Antony was leaving a powerful enemy behind him.[4]

With Antony out of the way, the old senator Cicero made his last play for influence. As we've already seen, he had not been part of the plot to kill Caesar, but he was a natural enemy to everything Caesar and Antony stood for.[5] Since he had lost faith in the efficacy of his old friends Brutus and Cassius, he now turned, with some misgiving ("Look at his name! Look at his age!"[6]), to Octavian as the savior of Senatorial law and order. In a series of brilliant speeches nicknamed *The Philippics* (after Demosthenes' attacks on King Philip, Alexander's father), Cicero convinced the

Senate to dump Antony. Decimus Brutus was once again recognized as the governor of Gaul, and Antony was told to leave him alone. When Antony refused, war was declared, and a consular army under Gaius Hirtius and Aulus Pansa was dispatched after him.[7] Octavian, who wasn't even old enough legally to be a member of the Senate, was sent along as a third wheel. As Octavian himself bragged many years later:

> The Senate enrolled me by honorific decree in its order, in the year that C. Pansa and A. Hirtius were consuls, granting me the ex-consul's right of speaking my opinion, and giving me a military command. The Senate ordered me as propraetor along with the consuls to see to it that no harm came to the Republic.[8]

The Senate hadn't learned its lesson. Once again it was turning to a strong man to solve its problems, for if the army were really under the command of Hirtius and Pansa, the legally elected consuls for the year 43, why was this illegally appointed, 19-year-old "propraetor" tagging along? He was there because the army was more loyal to his name and promise than to the laws of the Republic. Octavian himself was in a strange position: He was a general without portfolio going off to relieve Decimus Brutus, the Senate's legally recognized governor of Cisalpine Gaul and one of the assassins of his adoptive father.

The battle of Mutina was a disaster for Antony, but it nonetheless ended up quite differently than the Senate expected. The Republican armies had marched to relieve Decimus Brutus at Mutina in two columns; by the time Octavian and Hirtius were in place near Forum Corneli on the Via Aemilia, Pansa was just setting out from Rome. Pansa's relief force was ambushed by Antony at Forum Gallorum in April, during which skirmish the consul Pansa was seriously wounded. However, Hirtius intercepted Antony on his way back to camp and inflicted a crushing defeat, destroying "the greater part of his veteran legions."[9] The consuls forced a second battle with Antony on April 21 in which he was again defeated and compelled to raise the siege of Mutina. Antony retreated northwards in good order, for "Antony in misfortune was most nearly a virtuous man,"[10] but Hirtius had been killed in the battle and Pansa died shortly thereafter of his wounds.[11]

Decimus Brutus should have been delighted, but he soon had

much to complain about. Antony had escaped and linked up with his lieutenant, P. Ventidius Bassus (a former mule driver and later conqueror of the Parthians). Brutus guessed, as it proved correctly, that Antony would soon link up with his old war buddy Marcus Lepidus, now governor of southern France and the Nearer Spain. Most galling was the fact that although the Senate had transferred Hirtius and Pansa's troops to him, they obstinately refused to leave Octavian. Octavian, as Brutus complained, was doing nothing, "but it is neither possible for Caesar to be commanded, nor for him to command his own army."[12]

Decimus Brutus should have realized that reconciliation between him and Octavian was impossible. First off, he had been one of the murderers of Octavian's "father," and then after the defeat of Antony both Decimus and the Senatorial class to which he belonged made it painfully clear that young Octavian had become disposable. In a spurt of anti-Caesarian jubilation the Senate confirmed the assassins Marcus Brutus and Cassius in their eastern provinces, made the great Pompey's son Sextus the master of the sea, decorated Decimus Brutus, who had fought the war behind the walls of Mutina, with a triumph, and granted Octavian a measly "ovation." As Octavian later complained, he was addressed as "boy" and reminded that "he must be decorated and then gotten rid of."[13]

No legislature can control an ambitious general with appeals to morality or calls to patriotism. Octavian simply sent a delegation to the Senate and demanded the consulship. Cries of horror and appeals to morality went up everywhere. The Republican general Plancus (who later deserted to Antony) wrote to Cicero:

"What belief or whose advise turned him away from such glory (both necessary and, indeed, in his interest) to the consideration of a two-month long consulship acquired by means of terror and unadorned importunity, I certainly don't know."[14] The other senators couldn't figure it out either, but when the Senate spoke in such terms to Octavian's delegation, trying to put them off, the centurion Cornelius showed the hilt of his sword and said, "This will do it, if you don't."[15]

In early August Octavian crossed the Rubicon and marched a second time on Rome. The praetor Marcus Cornutus committed suicide, and the Senate capitulated. On August 19 he was elected consul with his uncle Quintus Pedius as his colleague. Octavian was 20 years old.[16]

Meanwhile, Antony had crossed the Alps and linked up with Lepidus. We don't have to believe Plutarch's romantic stories of how Antony, unshaven and disheveled, was reduced to begging for mercy across no-man's land. Lepidus knew which side of his bread had the olive oil on it.[17] I can't resist quoting the justification sent by Lepidus to the Senate; it's a wonderful example of proto-imperial double speak:

> Marcus Lepidus, twice imperator, pontifex maximus, to the praetors, tribunes, Senate, people and plebs of Rome, greetings. If you and your children are well, then I and the army are also well.
>
> I swear by both gods and men, senators, that I have always been well disposed to the Republic and have valued nothing more highly than the common safety and liberty—which I would quickly have proven to you, had not fortune preempted my plans. For the entire army, rising in sedition, has maintained its customary practice of preserving citizens and the common peace and has, to speak the truth, compelled me to take up the cause of the safety and well being of so great a multitude of Roman citizens. Wherefore, senators, I beg and beseech you to consult for the greatest good of the republic, laying aside private offenses, nor to interpret the mercy shown by us and our army as the crime of civil dissent. If you will but consider the safety and dignity of all, you will consult better both for yourselves and for the Republic.
>
> Given May 30 at Pons Argenteus.[18]

Octavian's consulship marks the final end of the Senate's political life. The legions still attached to Decimus Brutus melted away either to Octavian or to Antony. When the "triumphant general of Mutina" attempted to escape eastwards to Marcus Brutus and Cassius, he was captured by a Gallic chieftain who dutifully delivered his head to Antony.[19]

Now that Octavian himself had been forced to abandon the Senate as his road to power, the only thing left for him to do was to link up with Mark Antony. He proceeded north to Bononia where, on an island in a river, he met with Antony and Lepidus to form the Second Triumvirate. Unlike the first, this was no secret, back-room deal, but a formal commission "for restoring the Republic," passed in the Tribal Assembly on the motion of the tribune Publius Titius. The triumvirate was to last for 5 years and was empowered both to pass laws by decree and to appoint magistrates. In imitation of the First Triumvirate, a marriage was arranged between Antony's young step-daughter Clodia and Octavian; she was only a young girl, however, and after a quarrel with his head-strong mother-in-law Fulvia, Octavian dismissed his bride untouched.

Unlike the First Triumvirate, this one financed itself by a Sullan type proscription: 2,000 knights were killed along with 300 senators, the most famous being our old friend Cicero. Octavian argued for the old senator's life, we're told, but Antony couldn't forgive the biting criticism of Cicero's Philippics. There were also personal reasons: Antony's wife, the strong-will Fulvia we've just mentioned, had once been the grieving widow of Cicero's old enemy, Pretty Boy Clodius. So at Antony's orders the orator's head and right hand (with which he'd written the Philippics) were cut off and displayed on the speaker's platform in the Roman forum.

There's a good story about Octavian that many years later, by which time he had become the venerable emperor Augustus and could afford to be sentimental, he came upon one of his little grandsons reading a book by Cicero. Afraid to be caught reading treasonable, republican propaganda, the boy tried to hide the book, but Augustus picked it up and stood silently, winding through the scroll. "My child," he said finally, "this was a learned man, and a lover of his country."[20]

The Triumvirate's first task of necessity was to remove the threat of Brutus and Cassius in the East and simultaneously to avenge Caesar's murder. Both the bloody proscriptions at Rome and the assassins' depravations in the East—most notoriously Cassius's rape of Rhodes—were designed as fund-raisers for this great campaign. Once again the pattern of the First Triumvirate repeated itself, and because of its central position Greece was chosen as the battlefield.

Cassius and Brutus reunited their armies at Smyrna, on the coast of Asia Minor, and then crossing the Hellespont proceeded up the coast of Thrace towards Macedonia. They met their first opposition over against the island of Thasos and soon fell in with Antony's advance force. Octavian, who had been ill, tagged along 10 days later; Lepidus stayed back at Rome to guard the fort. The two armies faced off at a plain called Philippi.

This great battle is filled with "what-if's" and lost chances. On

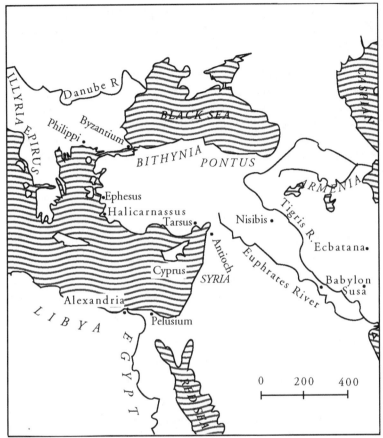

The East at the Time of the Second Triumvirate

the first day events seemed to fall out entirely in Brutus and
Cassius's favor: While Antony held his troops in reserve, Brutus,
who commanded his line's right, slammed into Octavian, over-
whelmed him, and rushed on to burn the young triumvir's camp.
Cassius on the left met with opposite luck, finding himself completely abandoned by Brutus's victorious advance. The lean and
hungry Cassius fell into despair, and mistaking a relief column
from Brutus as an attack force from Antony, he killed himself.
Brutus therefore held the high ground and seemed victorious, but
he had inherited a demoralized army.

The triumvirs were encamped in the mud which, it being

autumn, froze over that evening. A supply fleet from Rome was also sunk by Brutus's navy, but Brutus never learned of his good fortune. Had he, he probably would not have risked another battle, but would instead have starved Antony and Octavian into submission. Although cautious by nature, Brutus was heckled by his senatorial advisors into attacking the next day. His right wing was again victorious, but Cassius's troops wouldn't fight; the assassin's left wing collapsed, and Brutus, good Stoic that he was, begged a friend to hold out his sword, onto which he then, either heroically or stupidly (depending on your point of view) impaled himself.[21]

34 Too Many Caesars

It is always easier to win a victory than to write a peace. Antony and Octavian lived an uneasy peace for eleven years, but as the gunfighters used to say in B westerns, "This town ain't big enough for the both of us." It is difficult for us to trace their quarrel's gradual evolution since, thanks to Octavian's final victory, only his side of the story has survived. Still, I think it is possible to say something at the outset about Octavian's character to explain why he was the winner.

Octavian was a terrible general. We've already seen that at the Battle of Philippi; we'll see it again in the bungled Spanish campaign of 27-25 BC; and there is, I suspect, some truth in the humorously exaggerated picture Antony himself drew of Octavian's courage in the battle of Naulochus against Sextus Pompey:

> He wasn't able to look at the battle line standing up, but rather flat on his back, gazing at heaven. He lay in a stupor and neither rose nor came into his soldiers' sight until the enemy's ships had been put to flight by Marcus Agrippa.[1]

Unlike a lot of bad generals, however, Octavian knew his limitations and had enough command of his ego and sufficient ability to read the characters of other men so that he could appoint subordinates to run his armies for him—especially the above mentioned Marcus Agrippa, who later married Octavian's daughter to become himself the ancestor of kings. It was, I think, principally this touch of Socratic introspection that made Octavian the great manager and the amazing success machine that he became.

The first chore for the victorious triumvirs after Philippi was to divide up the Roman pie. Antony of course got Gaul back, though Octavian demanded that Cisalpine Gaul be detached and joined to Italy which, like the earth after the tripartite division of Jupiter, Neptune, and Hades, was to be common ground. Antony's immediate task, however, was to imitate Cassius and head East for money needed both to settle the veterans and to reorganize the Eastern provinces. For his own Octavian got Spain, Sardinia, and Africa, along with two seemingly unenviable tasks. He was to find (i.e. steal) land in Italy for their troops, and he was to deal with Sextus Pompey who, despite his great Republican name, had become little more than a powerful pirate king based in Sicily. Lepidus, who was suspected of dealing with Sextus, was put on the back burner, with a promise of Africa for himself if he was good. It was probably uncertainty about the army's loyalty which kept Antony and Octavian from turning the Triumvirate into a Duovirate.[2]

We'll deal with Octavian first, for he had troubles from the start. Nobody was happy with his land distribution, neither the settlers who were displaced, nor the soldiers who felt that they should have received more. Appian tells two almost unbelievable stories which are symptomatic of the growing unrest: first of a common soldier going berserk simply because Octavian had ordered him to vacate a reserved theater seat, and similarly of a riot in the Campus Marius when Octavian dared to show up late for a rally.[3]

Antony's brother Lucius (one of the consuls for the year 41) and his wife the hot-headed Fulvia seized upon this discontent and, thinking they were acting in Antony's interests, started a phony Republican uprising against Octavian. Driven into the Etruscan town of Perusia, the rebels were mercilessly starved into surrender. The town was plundered, but since Octavian couldn't yet afford to insult Antony, Lucius was shipped off to be governor of Spain, and Fulvia was set free; she died conveniently at Sicyon on the way to join her husband.[4]

Sextus Pompey wasn't so easy. Though in the long run Octavian could no more share power with him than he could with Antony, Sicily was needed as a source of grain for Rome. So for a while Octavian had to be accommodating. Pompey was no push-over either: He defeated Octavian in the Straits of Messana in 38, and was victorious again in August of 36. But Sextus finally fell in September to a joint invasion of Sicily by both Octavian and Lepidus; he fled east to a career of brigandage and piracy but was killed by Marcus Titius, the governor of Asia and a legate of Antony.

Lepidus was back in action not because he had been good, but because after the war in Perusia Octavian couldn't afford to drive him into the arms of Antony. Unfortunately, the Sicilian campaign went to his head. Having seized Messana and bribed Sextus

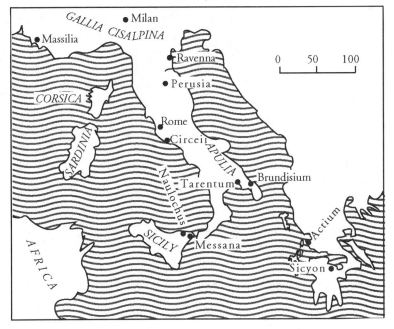

Italy and Greece during the Second Triumvirate

Pompey's troops by letting them plunder the city, Lepidus claimed that he was the master of Sicily. He and Octavian had an argument over this which escalated into a skirmish, but the troops were sick of civil war and especially doubtful of Lepidus's efficacy as a commander. They deserted wholesale to Octavian, leaving Lepidus on his knees to blubber for his life. Octavian chose to grant it, but he sent Lepidus off to Rome dressed as a private citizen and stripped of all rank save that of pontifex maximus. He lived with his title in the small Latin town of Circeii for the rest of his life, and so falls ingloriously out of our story.[5]

Meanwhile, back in the East, the other half of our tale evolved into the most famous love story of ancient times. After proceeding east in 41 following the battle of Philippi, Antony ordered Cleopatra to meet him at Tarsus in Asia Minor—ostensibly to accuse her of having helped Cassius, but actually to get as much money as he could out of Egypt. There's no need to be sentimental about Antony's motives at this stage of the game; anyone attempting to maintain troops in the East would eventually have to employ Egypt as his base of supply. In 41 Cleopatra was 29 years old, Antony about 42. Antony was still married to Fulvia, and Cleopatra had had a boy by Julius Caesar. Antony had probably met Cleopatra as a young woman when he was with Caesar in Egypt, and he must have seen her in Rome when she was Caesar's kept woman. However, in 41 he wasn't looking for romance; he needed funds.

Cleopatra also needed to be pragmatic. As we've already said, the Ptolemaic Empire was a tottering anachronism. Cleopatra only held her throne through the intercession of Julius Caesar, and now that he was dead she knew she would only hold onto it with the support of Rome. Circumstances forced her to choose a triumvir, and tragically (as it turned out) only Antony was available. She therefore went after him with everything she had. In a celebrated passage, Plutarch describes how Cleopatra sailed up the river Cydnus

> in a barge with gilded stern and outspread sails of purple, while oars of silver beat time to the music of flutes and fifes and harps. She herself lay all along under a canopy of cloth of gold, dressed as Venus in a picture, and beautiful young boys, like painted Cupids, stood on each side to fan her.[6]

Antony was enchanted, as one always is when duty and pleasure coincide. After dining sumptuously on the famous barge, he followed her to Alexandria where, if Plutarch is to be believed, they spent a winter of heroic debauchery. There was even time for a punitive expedition against the troublesome Parthians, but as this was also the time of Fulvia's ill-conceived rebellion against Octavian, Antony returned to Italy upon hearing of her escape. As we've remarked, Fulvia died before she could rejoin her philandering husband, and there then followed some trouble when Octavian's agents wouldn't let Antony land at Brundisium. But a peace conference having been arranged thanks to the intercession of Octavian's friends Asinius Pollio and Maecenas,[7] the Roman world was divided in half, with the Ionian Sea as the boundary. Antony got the Greek speaking East and Octavian the Latin speaking West. It was also at the Brundisian conference that Lepidus was confirmed in the province of Africa; we've already seen the final result of that decision.

The triumvirs were still slaves to the memory of the First Triumvirate, for another marriage bond was arranged, this time between Antony and Octavian's half-sister Octavia, to whom Octavian "was extremely attached, as indeed she was, it is said, quite a woman."[8] Indeed, Octavia emerges as one of the few really attractive characters in this story. Antony must have thought so too, for he didn't see Cleopatra for four years, even though he had left her in Alexandria with a set of twins.

Antony and Octavia settled down in Athens to rule the East, but events gradually drove the triumvirate apart. Antony became increasingly preoccupied with the great Parthian Empire, and undoubtedly felt jealous when his lieutenant Publius Ventidius Bessus scored a great victory there in 39 and then in 38 killed their king Pacorus in battle. The triumvirate officially lapsed in 38, so in October of 37 Antony and Octavian again met at Tarentum to renew the alliance for another 5 year term. It was an ugly meeting, and only the efforts of Octavia kept the alliance temporarily together. Antony supplied ships for Octavian's war against Sextus Pompey, and Octavian promised troops (which never were delivered) for Antony's proposed campaign against the Parthians.[9]

Then, suddenly, Antony deliberately destroyed the alliance. He sent Octavia back to Rome in order to have their child, he summoned Cleopatra to Antioch, and in a ceremony that was illegal by Roman law (for Cleopatra was a foreigner) he married her and publicly recognized their twins as his children. His motives in doing this are anybody's guess. W.W. Tarn sees the motives as basically personal:

> Antony's is a strange story. Two women had been devoted to him. Had he followed Fulvia, he might perhaps have been master of the Roman world; had he followed Octavia, he could have ruled his half in peace, too popular to be attacked; instead, he had broken Fulvia's heart and made Octavia homeless. Now he had married a woman whose only devotion to him was as the instrument of her ambition; and her he would follow, and follow to his ruin, because he loved her. That is what redeems his memory that at the end he did lose half the world for love.[10]

I like that a lot, but am perhaps a little too cynical to take it at face value. Antony and Cleopatra were lovers, but then so had been Antony and Octavia. It's no coincidence that the marriage with Cleopatra followed shortly on the highly unsatisfactory meeting at Tarentum. Antony knew that the triumvirate was drifting apart, and the exile of Lepidus the following year could only have confirmed him in his suspicions. He was not a man to play second fiddle, either to Octavian or to his virtuous sister Octavia, who indeed stayed on at Rome even after her husband's desertion, working in his home for his interests and raising high moral indignation against Antony by the humble performance of her matronly duties. Antony had decided that his only chance of survival was in the East. Cleopatra was as much a part of the East as the city of Alexandria.

By now Cleopatra was also pregnant with her third child by Antony, so he sent her back to Alexandria. Antony then determined to complete Julius Caesar's great plan and conquer the Parthian Empire, a feat that would give him vastly greater prestige than Octavian. As was typical of Antony, however, he acted too impetuously. Instead of wintering in Armenia and waiting for a spring campaign, he invaded that autumn, and didn't even slow down enough to let his siege train catch up with him. When his train was captured with a loss of 10,000 soldiers, Antony was unable to invest the great city of Phraaspa (near Zenjan in northwest Iran); when his Armenian allies deserted he was forced to retreat across the plains of Parthia, where his lack of cavalry removed all options from his army save those of defense. He lost in all 20,000 infantry and 4,000 cavalry troops.[11]

Still, Antony was able to bounce back. In 35 he conquered the kingdom of Armenia and made it a province. Characteristically, in 34 he held a great triumph in Alexandria for his Parthian disaster. In a ceremony always called "The Donations of Alexandria," Anthony erected two gold thrones for himself and Cleopatra on the Alexandrian parade grounds. Cleopatra was decked out as "The New Isis," while at their feet sat their three children on silver thrones. Acting in his capacity as triumvir (a title which Octavian was no longer using, the triumvirate's official term having expired), Antony then divided up the East among the members of his new family. Cleopatra, ruling jointly with her 13-year-old son Caesarion, was made Queen of Egypt, Cyprus, Libya, and Coele-Syria. The boys Alexander and Ptolemy, now addressed as "King of Kings," divided up the rest.[12]

Back in the Roman Senate, Octavian played the Donations for all they were worth. Antony was depicted as a slave of lust, a betrayer of his own people. Being more practical minded, Antony was busy complaining about the legions that had not been delivered to him and about the appropriation of Sicily. He even wrote Octavian to complain about his high moral tone:

> What's changed you? That I'm doing it with a queen? She's my wife. Have I just started, or haven't we been carrying on for nine years? Are you only doing it with Drusilla?[13] Come on, as you read this letter, haven't you done it with Tertulla or Terentilla or Rufilla or Salvia Titisenia or all the others? Or does it make a difference where and with whom you get horny?[14]

The invective flying between East and West almost seemed a return to the uncontrolled libel of the old days—or, as the Republicans would have said, to freedom of speech. But Octavian found himself in a different position when the year 33 came to an end. Although the Senate had conferred upon him the *sacrosanctity* of the tribuneship (quite apart from the office itself), this legal fiction gave him no clear constitutional status in Rome. Given the violence of the immediate past he didn't actually need an office, of course, but Antony in the East was still calling himself *triumvir* and was officially ruling over his provinces and dependant kingdoms as a promagistrate not yet replaced by the Senate. Octavian was rather trapped by his own propaganda: He wanted to portray himself as the champion of republican virtue and Antony as a tyrant propped up by corrupt foreigners. How could he pull it off?

In the end both Octavian's patience and his Roman location gave him the edge. In 32 the two consuls Gnaeus Domitius Ahenobarbus and Gaius Sosius were both followers of Antony. Wilting under Octavian's attacks in the Senate, over which he presided through the fiction of his tribunician sacrosanctity, the two consuls fled east to Antony and were followed by 300 senators, in effect giving Octavian a free hand at Rome.

This was still not war, however. For that Octavian needed a surefire propaganda theme which would help unite all of Rome behind him. It was dropped into his lap when Marcus Titius, the slayer of Sextus Pompey, and his uncle, the old Cesarean general Munatius Plancus, deserted Antony and fled to Rome. They told tales about Antony's will, which had been deposited with the Vestal Virgins at Rome.

Octavian seized the will. He may have doctored it a bit before he read it out in the Senate, but then the contents may simply have been too good to be true. The fact that Antony had not only named Cleopatra among his heirs but that he even desired to be buried in Egypt caused universal outrage. It seemed to confirm Octavian's charges that Antony had gone completely eastern, that he was contemplating moving the capital of the empire to Alexandria. War was no longer simply on the horizon; it had arrived.[15]

Despite a blustering challenge from Antony that he would fight Octavian in single combat and a similarly bombastic reply from Octavian that Antony could land his force in Italy for all he cared, poor Greece was still the obvious field of battle. Antony first gathered a large fleet and even larger land force at Ephesus, on the coast of Asia Minor, where he begrudgingly granted Cleopatra's demand that she tag along. From there they proceeded to Athens and then by ship into the Ionian Sea, while the army marched eastwards into Epirus. Octavian seized this moment to cross the sea himself, meeting Antony in the Bay of Actium.

Though the two sides were equal in cavalry, Antony had the larger land force—about 100,000 men to Octavian's 80,000. With his 500 warships Antony also had about twice as many ships as his opponent, but just as we saw way back in the battle of Salamis, the navies of the East depended more on numbers and pomp than on navigational skill; thanks to the training of his admiral, Marcus Agrippa, Octavian had by far the more efficient navy. We can only blame wholesale desertions from his land-based, native "allies"[16] for Antony's fatal decision to hazard all on a naval battle. Navies are, after all, best used for transport and bluster. With any kind of luck an army, even after a major defeat, can regroup and fight again. Once a navy loses, it's all over.

The battle was fought on September 2, 31 BC. Antony commanded the right wing of his line, where he was met by Agrippa on his own left. Octavian himself commanded his right wing, but once the battle started he did little more than back water. Antony's plan seems to have been to outflank Agrippa, but when his heavy, unmaneuvrable ships made no headway, his entire left wing deserted and headed back to camp.[17] At that Cleopatra panicked; hoisting her sails she hastened out to sea, where Antony joined her, deserting his troops. The army waited on shore for a week, not believing that Antony would not return to fight again. Finally, they surrendered to Octavian.[18]

No eyewitness accounts of this pivotal battle have survived, but in the 8th book of the *Aeneid* Virgil imagines that a representation of the fight was carved as the centerpiece of Aeneas' magic shield by his obliging step-father, the god Vulcan. His version clearly shows the anti-Eastern bias of our preserved tradition:

> Young Caesar, on the stern, in armor bright,
> Here leads the Romans and their gods to fight:
> His beamy temples shoot their flames afar,
> And o'er his head is hung the Julian star.
> Agrippa seconds him, with prosp'rous gales,
> And, with propitious gods, his foes assails...
> Rang'd on the line oppos'd, Antonius brings
> Barbarian aids, and troops of Eastern kings;
> Th' Arabians near, and Bactrians [!] from afar,
> Of tongues discordant, and a mingled war:
> And, rich in gaudy robes, amidst the strife,
> His ill fate follows him—th' Egyptian wife...
> The queen herself, amidst the loud alarms,
> With cymbals toss'd her fainting soldiers warms—
> Fool as she was! who had not yet devin'd
> Her cruel fate, nor saw the snakes behind.
> Her country gods, the monsters of the sky,
> Great Neptune, Pallas, and Love's Queen defy:
> The dog Anubis barks, but barks in vain,
> Nor longer dares oppose th' ethereal train...
> The trembling Indians and Egyptians yield,
> And soft Sabaeans quit the wat'ry field.
> The fatal mistress hoists her silken sails,
> And, shrinking from the fight, invokes the gales...
> Just opposite, sad Nilus opens wide
> His arms and ample bosom to the tide,
> And spreads his mantle o'er the winding coast,
> In which he wraps the queen, and hides the flying host.[19]

Octavian didn't advance on Antony immediately after the battle of Actium; he was delayed for 27 days at Brundisium by a revolt of his soldiers, who wanted bonuses and a dismissal from the service. Antony spent the time first sulking like a hermit on the island of Pharos, but then, after he learned of the surrender of his army in Greece, banqueting with Cleopatra in the palace at Alexandria along with a coterie of hangers-on who had dubbed themselves the "Diers-Together."

When Octavian finally landed at Pelusium, Antony did attempt to put on a last-ditch fight; however, having watched first his fleet, then his cavalry, and then his infantry go over to the enemy, he retreated to the palace. Cleopatra, reverting to the practices of her adopted country, had locked herself up in her tomb. When he was told that she was dead, Antony returned to his own apartments where, like Brutus and Cassius before him, he fell on his sword. He was bleeding badly all over the floor when a servant arrived to explain that he had misinterpreted the reason for Cleopatra's being in her tomb. Antony had himself carried there, but Cleopatra, still too terrified to open the door of the sepulcher, ordered her dying lover to be hoisted up through a second story window. Once inside the tomb, he died in her arms.[20]

Octavian would have liked to lead Cleopatra as his prize exhibit in a triumphal parade back at Rome, but the queen would not coöperate. She first had to be tricked out of her tomb, which was managed by talking to her through the tomb's main door while a soldier climbed up to the window through which the dying Antony had been hoisted. She tried to stab herself, but was disarmed. It would, of course, have been a waste of time for Cleopatra to try floating down the Nile on a barge to Octavian. She was now 39 years old, while Octavian, unlike Antony, didn't need a Queen in Egypt. Cleopatra therefore had a great banquet prepared, into which a servant smuggled, concealed in a basket of figs, a venomous snake called an asp. This is the Egyptian cobra, the same snake that appears, along with the vulture Nekhbet, on the golden death mask of Tutankhamen. Octavian's servants found the queen, decked out in her ceremonial robes, stone dead from the cobra's sting.[21]

Octavian killed Antyllus, the elder of Antony's sons by Fulvia and the brother of the girl he had briefly married, after pulling the boy off the statue of the divine Julius, to which he had fled. The three children of Antony and Cleopatra, who as half-breeds were no threat to Octavian, were well treated, and indeed were actually raised by the ever dutiful Octavia. However, Caesarion, Cleopatra's son by Julius Caesar, was a different story. The Donations of Alexandria had sealed his fate, for in that ceremony he had been opposed as the true son of Julius Caesar to the phony, adopted grand-nephew Octavian. Cleopatra had shipped him off to Ethiopia on his way to India, but his teacher Rhodon tricked him into going back, saying that Octavian would make him a king. Big brother Octavian, however, took the advice of the Alexandrian philosopher Areius that "too many Caesars are not well," and had the 17-year-old killed.[22]

35 The Great One

It is so easy to get lost in the romance of Antony and Cleopatra that some effort may be required to see the story from the Roman people's point of view. If reading the accounts of that bloody century seems dispiriting to us, how much more so must it have been to live through them and to watch the old Republic degenerate into factional strife and mob violence!

Octavian was not an inspiring personality like his great-uncle, but he accomplished what Caesar, Pompey, Marius, and Sulla had been unable to do: He ended the civil war. When he reentered the city of Rome in 29, the gates of the Temple of Janus were shut, symbolizing that there was peace throughout the Roman world. The last performance of that ceremony had been at the close of the First Punic War.[1] Interest rates dropped $\frac{2}{3}$,[2] and the whole Roman world broke into a frenzy of jubilation so intense that the rights of the senatorial aristocracy to the prerogatives they called "liberty" seemed little more than a quibble.

Dealing with that quibble was Octavian's first responsibility. Thanks to the wholesale appointments of Antony and his cronies, membership in the Senate had swelled to 1,000 members; Octavian whittled this down by making a list and checking it twice: He encouraged the Senate to trim itself, thanks to which hint 50 senators stepped down and so spared themselves the embarrassment of having their names posted. He and Agrippa made a second list and kicked 140 senators out of the body. He then forbade the Senate to meet more than twice a month, or at all during September and October, and created a steering committee of 6 months' duration consisting of the consuls, one each of the other officials, and 15 senators chosen by lot. To make sure there would be no more Brutuses and Cassiuses, he forbade all senators to leave Italy without his permission.[3]

The comitia also met as before, and indeed Octavian took care to vote himself in the Comitia Tributa, just like one of the guys. But Octavian selected and nominated all candidates for office. In the early days he would even bring his 3 approved candidates around to the hustings and solemnly ask for votes. And most important for the continuance of peace, he removed the army from the control of popular generals. He set up a special military treasury from new taxes so that funds would always be on hand to pay the army and so that soldiers would no longer look to a successful general to pass land bills through the Senate. This was, moreover, no longer the army of Caesar's day, raised among citizens, tenants, and recruits for a specific purpose. It was a standing army on permanent garrison duty, at the beck and call of the military dictator.[4]

In 27 BC Octavian entered upon his 7th consulship and made the final move to consolidate his power. He acted none too soon. Two descendants of former triumvirs had shown him all too clearly just how precarious his unofficial position in the now defunct Republic was. In the year 30 Marcus Aemilius Lepidus, the son of the disgraced triumvir, had planned an amateurish coup which was easily discovered by Agrippa. The execution of the young Lepidus (for which, by the way, his father was brought back to Rome) fixed that. Much more serious, however, was the career of Marcus Licinius Crassus, grandson to the martyr of Carrhae.

Crassus only came over to Octavian's side just before the battle of Actium. He was rewarded with the consulship in 30 and obtained Macedonia as his province. Left to his own devices out in the Balkans, he proved to be a brilliant general. When the Germanic Bastarnae broke across the Danube, Crassus not only defeated them, he even killed their king in battle with his own hand. Such a singular act of prowess entitled him to the *spolia opima,* a distinction which had been created first for King Romulus himself and had been achieved by only two other generals in Roman history. Since such fame and glory were of course exactly what grandfather Crassus had sought in Parthia, Octavian's consternation was extreme. Being no fool, Crassus declined the great honor and conveniently vanishes from history. But Octavian had been warned, and he now had a plan.[5]

Having first rehearsed his friends and supporters among the senators, he called the Senate to assembly and made a speech. His actual words have been lost, but Dio Cassius supplies us with a convincing version:

You see for yourselves, of course, that it is in my power to rule over you for life... However, I shall lead you no longer, and no one will be able to say that it was to win absolute power that I did whatever has hitherto been done. Nay, I give up my office completely, and restore to you absolutely everything–the army, the laws, and the provinces...Thus my very deeds also will prove to you that even at the outset I desired no position of power, but in very truth wished to avenge my father, cruelly murdered, and to extricate the city from great evils that came on unceasingly...

...Since, then, Fortune, by using me, has graciously restored to you peace without treachery and harmony without faction, receive back also your liberty and the republic; take over the army and the subject provinces, and govern yourselves as has been your wont.

Who could be found more magnanimous than I,–not to mention my deceased father–who more nearly divine?[6]

Octavian's rehearsed claque immediately broke into cries and protestations. How could he desert them? How could he turn his back on his own people? Senators who were not in the know cried out with equal desperation, imagining that Octavian was abandoning them once again to the horrors of civil war. Graciously allowing himself to be persuaded, Octavian hastened out of his brief retirement. With theatrical resignation he assumed, for 10 years, the governorship of northern Spain, Gaul, and Syria; Egypt, which Octavian ruled virtually as a private estate, was kept out of the picture. These were all, of course, precisely the powerful provinces which had been used to stage revolutions in the past. To the regular senatorial magistrates he left southern Spain, Africa, Asia, Greece, Crete, Cyrene, Bithynia, Pontus, Sicily, Sardinia-Corsica, Illyricum, and Macedonia.

Falling over each other with gratitude, the senators scrambled to reward Octavian with some impressive sounding title. "Romulus" was suggested but abandoned as too regal in tone. At the suggestion of Senator Lucius Munatius Plancus the title *Augustus* was adopted, an adjective originally ascribed to holy and consecrated places and rendered σεβαστός in Greek (hence our name "Sebastian."). From that day to this Octavian has been known as Augustus. So has the month *Sextilis*, which the Senate subsequently renamed in his honor.

Senatorial governors were to be appointed by lot in open Senate. They could not wear a sword or military uniform and could only serve for one year. Augustus had them called proconsuls since they went to the more peaceful provinces. To his provinces he himself appointed legates. They were called propraetors—a term associated in the Republic with military service—and they could wear a uniform and a sword, with which they even had the right to execute soldiers. They served as long as Augustus pleased. Both types of governors received direct orders from Augustus and were, for the first time in Roman history, assigned a fixed salary.[7]

The seriousness with which Augustus took these appointments is evident from the story of the great elegiac poet Cornelius Gallus, the first Prefect of Egypt. Gallus wasn't even a senator; he belonged rather to the equestrian order, but Augustus forbade senators even to set foot in Egypt—for obvious reasons. Apparently his extraordinary command of Egypt went to his head, for Gallus started spreading rumors about Augustus; he got so impressed with his own deeds that he set up monuments and carved his name on the pyramids. Distressed by such goings-on, Augustus dismissed him, and Gallus committed suicide.[8]

Even this arbitrary division between peaceful and powerful provinces wasn't strictly followed. Augustus either filled senatorial vacancies himself when the senators failed to do a good job, or else shifted provinces at will from one category to the other.[9] The transparency of the sham became amusingly obvious at the start of the reign of Augustus' successor, Tiberius. Imitating his step-father, Tiberius told the Senate that he could not rule the whole empire alone. When he paused for the expected howls of protestation, a senator named Asinius Gallus piped up, "Caesar, what part of the republic do you wish entrusted to you?"

Tiberius shot the fool a glance that taught him his mistake, so Asinius covered himself by saying that he had not meant to divide up what none wished separated, but rather to demonstrate that the republic had but one body and must be ruled by one mind. Placated, Tiberius spared the senator's life and went on with business. He made similarly short work of the comitia meetings, which were transferred without complaint from the Campus Martius to the Senate. By Tiberius's day the sham was no longer necessary.[10]

But shams in politics can be extremely important. Indeed, politics often seems to be made up of little else. In the year immediately after Actium, Augustus was in the same situation as his father Caesar had been after Pharsalus. If Caesar had been killed because of his impatience with the demands of fools, Augustus' genius lay precisely in the realization that injured fools are dangerous people. He took the trouble to deal with the Senate and to respect its traditions. Just as he declined the high-sounding epithet "Romulus," he preferred the old Republican title *princeps*, meaning simply the senior senator on the roll, so that his reign is often called the "principate." Here's how Augustus himself described his position in 27: "After that time I exceeded all in authority; however, I had no more power than the others who were my colleagues in the magistracy."[11]

That second clause is legally correct, but meaningless in the world of *Realpolitik*. However paternal and reassuring "authority" might have sounded, it rested upon the power of the Roman legions, who were loyal to Augustus. The most accurate picture, I think, is that drawn by the historian Tacitus:

> At home everything was tranquil; the traditional names of the magistracies remained; the younger men were born after the victory at Actium, even most of the older men had been born during the civil wars: who was left who had seen the Republic?[12]

In the later part of 28, Augusts went off to govern his province. He was determined to win military glory for himself in Spain, but his campaign was an unmitigated disaster, during which he was almost killed. He returned to Rome near the end of 25, only to be met with a conspiracy headed by a republican sympathizer named Fannius Caepio and Augustus's own co-consul Varro Murena, Maecenas' brother-in-law.[13] Some time after both men had been executed, Augustus happened to fall so dangerously ill that he must have been struck with this coincidental evidence, both of his own mortality and of the instability of his system. So after he was saved by the risky sounding, cold water shock treatments of his doctor Antonius Musa, he looked around for a permanent and plausible legislative basis for his authority.

In 23 Augustus entered his eleventh consulship. His holding of the office not only contradicted his propaganda of "restoring the republic," it threatened to turn *consulship* into a euphemism for *dictatorship*. Without it, however, he would have no legal fiction to cover his command over the Senate and the armies. His first suggestion was to serve as third consul with two other regularly appointed officers. Reaction to this idea was so negative that he allowed the Senate to talk him out of it. Finally, he hit on a much better plan.

He went to the Alban Mount and dramatically resigned his eleventh consulship. This both freed him from the various ceremonial duties associated with that office and automatically increased the number of proconsuls available for provincial duty. In return for his gesture the Senate dutifully granted him two new powers. First, by an interesting fiction in imitation of his vague "tribunician sacrosanctity," he was given the "tribunician power" without himself actually becoming a tribune. This was because, as a patrician, he couldn't hold an office reserved for plebeians. We saw earlier how Pretty Boy Clodius had to get himself adopted into a plebeian family to get over the same hurdle. But the tribunician power was better: It could be renewed each year (and in Augustus's case was—for 37 years!) and gave its holder the power to cancel the acts of any official, to bring whatever matter he wished before the Senate whenever he wished to do so, and even to condemn to death without trial for slander. It was this very power that Tiberius used to summon the Senate after Augustus's death.

Second, the Senate gave him the *maius imperium,* which is to say a proconsular authority outranking all governors in all the subject territories. Moreover, this *imperium* would not lapse once Augustus set foot within the walls of Rome; it was, it will be remembered, this very chink in his proconsular power that had forced Caesar to cross the Rubicon. It was in these two privileges of Augustus that all subsequent power of the Roman emperors resided.[14]

Augustus formally begins the Roman Empire, and the "principate" he established survived for 200 years though it became increasingly dictatorial with time. As we've already seen, even his step-son Tiberius dispensed with most of the Republican trappings that Augustus had felt so necessary. The Roman emperors were, of course, kings, most of whom tried very hard to establish their own dynasties. They imitated Augustus, however, in never employing that hated word, nor indeed even the old title "dictator," which Julius Caesar had rendered unlucky. *Princeps* died as a title with Augustus, and our own age remembers the Roman honorific *imperator* or emperor. In Republican times the term meant "victorious general," but the Roman emperors assumed it even if they never led troops in battle. To the end the Roman emperors based their authority on the legal fiction that, like

Augustus, they had taken over the titles, duties, and privileges of the old offices of the Republic.[15]

Augustus' style of ruling was determined by his memories of Julius Caesar, by the still (in his day) potent myths of the old Republic, and by his own personality, which, though it could stand no opposition, contained none of the mindless cruelty of Nero, Caligula, or Domitian. Once Octavian became Augustus, he settled into the role of a paternal, then of a grandfatherly figure. His actual life style would have seemed drab to those of us who have become accustomed to the trappings of the Imperial Presidency. Augustus dressed and lived simply, spending more than 40 years in the same small room in his house on the Palatine Hill. Access to the emperor was, by modern standards, easy. There's a story that he joked at a fellow very tentatively handing him a petition that he was offering it "like a peanut to an elephant!" The old emperor's principal hobby seems to have been collecting fossils.[16]

His style of foreign policy, though ambitious at first, grew similarly frugal, perhaps because of his one serious foreign military reversal, when Quintilius Varus with 3 legions, including all officers and auxiliaries, were wiped out in the Teutoburger Forest in Germany. Thus in his will Augustus advised the Senate to keep the empire within its present bounds. This proved in the future to be good advice.[17]

The city of Rome benefited greatly from Augustus' tenure, so much so that he could boast "I left marble what I found brick." He rebuilt temples, public works, fora, and aqueducts, being especially proud of the Greek and Latin libraries he erected in the Temple of Apollo on the Palatine. Augustus set up (believe it or not) the first organized police and fire departments the city of Rome had ever known, just as he took drastic steps to diminish the number of murders, muggings, and kidnappings for which the eternal city has always been notorious. He loved to give free gladiatorial and beast contests too, bragging in his official autobiography that he sponsored 8 gladiatorial shows in which fought 10,000 men; 26 wild animal hunts involving the slaughter of 3,500 beasts; and a spectacular naval regatta, held in a specially constructed artificial lake, in which 3,000 combatants (not counting rowers) hacked away at each other to the cheers of the ecstatic multitude. Unlike Uncle Julius, who was bored at such goings-on and frequently insulted aficionados by writing letters at the games, Augustus always cheered with the crowd and watched with rapt attention.[18]

But Augustus' greatest monument to the old Republic was his dogged attachment to the old time religion and to the strict morality of the days of the first two Punic Wars. In a series of laws passed between 18 and 9 BC, Augustus attempted to strengthen the Roman family and to encourage the institution of marriage. Divorce, which had been a rather informal and private affair under the Republic, was for the first time put under the strict supervision of state courts. Marriage was facilitated by removing the old prohibitions against marriage between the free born and the freed slave (though this prohibition remained for the senatorial aristocracy).

By the *Lex Julia de maritandis ordinibus* and its more moderate amendment the *Lex Papia Poppaea*, bachelors and spinsters were vigorously encouraged to marry. Those who didn't were not generally allowed to inherit property, while proud parents were given preferential treatment in elections. Until Constantine and the Christians started pushing the blessed joys of virginity, these laws formalized an on-going fight to tighten up the moral tone of the upper classes through the application of what we would call "family values."[19]

There is a temptation to call Augustus a moral hypocrite. As a young man he divorced his first wife Scribonia (immediately after she had given birth to their daughter!) and ran off with Livia Drusilla, a married woman pregnant with the son of one of his political enemies. But Augustus stayed married to Livia for 50 years, suffering in his own family a series of tragedies and scandals which, given his social legislation, seem more ironic than hypocritical. He had no surviving children by Livia and only that one daughter, Julia, by Scribonia. He married her off to Agrippa and they produced three grandsons, Gaius and Lucius Caesar (both of whom Augustus adopted and both of whom died as teenagers), and Agrippa Posthumus, who proved so mentally unbalanced that Augustus banished him in disgust to the island of Planasia. His nephew Marcellus, Octavia's boy by her first husband Gaius Claudius Marcellus, also died young, leaving Augustus with only Tiberius, his step-son by Livia, a fine and devoted soldier whom Augustus disliked intensely.

The two Julias, his daughter and granddaughter, seemed born to mock his *Lex Julia de adulteriis coercendis*. He had raised them both very strictly, teaching them to make yarn and to do or say nothing that couldn't be reported in the daily register, but as often happens his ambitions for them backfired. They became such notorious sluts that, rather than people Rome with illegitimate grandchildren born of the city's low-life, he condemned them to eternal exile. He forbade the use of wine, fine food, or companionship to his daughter on her island, only allowing her back on the mainland after five years. A child born to Julia his granddaughter was neither recognized nor allowed to be fed. Neither of the girls was ever forgiven, and in his will Augustus forbade their burial in his tomb. Immediately after his death his mad grandson Agrippa Posthumus was killed, apparently on his order.[20]

Only two of Augustus's direct descendants ruled as emperors. They were his great-grandson Gaius, known to history as the mad Caligula, and his great-great grandson Nero, famous for murdering his own mother (Augustus' great-granddaughter Agrippina), for starting the persecutions against the Christians, and (unjustly and anachronistically) for fiddling while Rome burned.

36 The Sermon on the Mount

The most influential person born during the reign of Augustus was the Jewish carpenter Jesus of Nazareth, son of Joseph, of the backwater province of Judaea. Before doing anything else, we should tell the basic story of his life. Here, therefore, is a drastically abridged, radically syncretized version of the four Gospels, adapted from the beautiful translation issued in 1611 by order of King James I of England:

The Angel Gabriel was sent from God unto a city of Galilee named Nazareth, to a virgin espoused to a man whose name was Joseph, of the house of David; and the virgin's name was Mary. And the angel came unto her and said, "Hail, thou that are highly favoured, the Lord is with thee: blessed art thou among women. The Holy Ghost shall come upon thee, and the power of the Highest shall overshadow thee. Therefore also that holy thing which shall be born of thee shall be called the Son of God."

And it came to pass in those days that there went out a decree from Caesar Augustus that all the world should be taxed. And all went to be taxed, every one into his own city. And Joseph also went up from Galilee, out of the city of Nazareth, into Judaea, unto the city of David, which is called Bethlehem. And so it was, that while they were there, the days were accomplished that Mary should be delivered. And she brought forth her first-born son, and wrapped him in swaddling clothes, and laid him in a manger because there was no room for them in the inn.

And there were in the same country shepherds abiding in the field keeping watch over their flock by night. And, lo, the angel of the Lord came upon them, and the glory of the Lord shone round about them, and they were sore afraid. And the angel said unto them, "Fear not: for, behold, I bring you good tidings of great joy, which shall be to all people. For unto you is born this day in the city of David a Saviour, which is Christ the Lord."

And behold, there came wise men from the East to Jerusalem, and the star, which they saw in the East, went before them, till it came and stood over where the young child was. And when they were come into the house, they saw the young child with Mary his mother, and fell down, and worshipped him, and presented unto him gifts: gold, frankincense, and myrrh.

And the child grew, and waxed strong in spirit, filled with wisdom: and the grace of God was upon him.

In those days came John the Baptist, preaching in the wilderness of Judaea and saying, "Repent ye: for the kingdom of Heaven is at hand. There cometh one mightier than I after me; I indeed have baptized you with water, but he shall baptize you with the Holy Ghost."

Then cometh Jesus from Galilee to Jordan unto John, to be baptized by him. And Jesus, when he was baptized, went up straightway out of the water: and lo, the heavens were opened up unto him. And lo, a voice from heaven saying, "This is my blessed son, in whom I am well pleased."

From that time Jesus began to preach and to say, "Repent: for the kingdom of Heaven is at hand." And Jesus, walking by the sea of Galilee, saw two brethren, Simon called Peter, and Andrew his brother, casting a net into the sea, for they were fishers. And he saith unto them, "Follow me, and I will make you fishers of men."

And Jesus went about all Galilee, teaching in their synagogues and preaching the gospel of the Kingdom, and healing all manner of sickness and all manner of disease among the people. And he ordained twelve, that they should be with him, and that he might send them forth to teach. And Simon he surnamed Peter, and James the son of Zebedee, and John the brother of James, and Andrew, and Philip, and Bartholomew, and Matthew, and Thomas, and James the son of Alphaeus, and Thaddaeus, and Simon the Canaanite, and Judas Iscariot, which also betrayed him.

And when they came nigh to Jerusalem, Jesus saith unto them, "Go your way into the village over against you. Ye shall find a colt tied, whereon never man sat; loose him, and bring him." And they brought the colt to Jesus and cast their garments on him; and he sat upon him. And many spread their garments in the way, and others cut down branches off the trees and strewed them in the way. And they that went before and they that followed cried, saying, "Hosanna; Blessed is he that cometh in the name of the Lord! Hosanna in the highest!"

And Jesus entered into Jerusalem, and into the temple and began to cast out them that sold and bought in the temple, and overthrew the tables of the money changers, and he taught them saying, "Is it not written 'My house shall be called of all nations the house of prayer'? But ye have made it a den of thieves!"

And the scribes and chief priests heard it, and sought how they might destroy him: for they feared him, because all the people was astonished at his doctrine.

And Judas Iscariot, one of the twelve, went unto the chief priests, to betray him unto them. And when they heard it, they were glad, and promised to give him money. And he sought how he might conveniently betray him.

And the first day of unleavened bread, when they killed the passover, his disciples made ready, and in the evening he cometh with the twelve. And as they sat and did eat, Jesus said, "Verily I say unto you, one of you which eateth with me shall betray me." And they were exceeding sorrowful, and began every one of them to cry out. Then Judas, which betrayed him, answered and said, "Rabbi, is it I?" He said unto him, "Thou hath said."

And as they did eat, Jesus took bread, and blessed, and brake it, and gave it to them, and said, "Take, eat: this is my body." And he took the cup, and when he had given thanks, he gave it to them, and they all drank of it. And he said unto them, "This is my blood of the new testament, which is shed for many. Verily I say unto you, I will drink no more of the fruit of the vine, until that day that I drink it new in the Kingdom of God."

And when they had sung an hymn, they went out into the Mount of Olives, and they came to a place which was named Gethsemane, and he saith to his disciples, "Sit ye here while I shall pray." And he went forward a little, and fell on the ground, and prayed that, if it were possible, the hour might pass from him.

And when he returned, he found the disciples asleep, and he saith unto them, "Sleep on now and take your rest. It is enough; the hour is come. Behold, the Son of Man is betrayed into the hands of sinners."

And immediately while he yet spoke, cometh Judas, one of the twelve, and with him a great multitude. And as soon as he was come, he goeth straightway to him and saith, "Rabbi," and kissed him. And they laid their hands on him, and took him.

And they led Jesus away to the high priest, which was Caiaphas that same year, and with him were assembled all the chief priests and the elders and the scribes. And the high priest asked him, "Art thou the Christ, the son of the Blessed?"

And Jesus said, "I am: and ye shall see the Son of Man sitting on the right hand of power, and coming in the clouds of heaven."

Then the high priest rent his clothes, and saith, "What need we of any further witness? Ye have heard the blasphemy: what think ye?" And they all condemned him to be guilty of death. And straightway in the morning the chief priests held a consultation and delivered Jesus to Pilate.

Pilate therefore said unto him, "Art thou a king then?"

Jesus answered, "Thou sayest that I am a king. To this end was I born, and for this cause came I into the world, that I should bear witness unto the truth. Every one that is of the truth heareth my voice."

Pilate saith unto him, "What is truth?" and when he had said this, he called together the chief priests and the rulers of the people, and said unto them, "I having examined him before you have found no fault in this man. I will therefore chastise him and release him." But they cried saying, "Crucify him, crucify him!" and the voices of them and of the chief priests prevailed.

Then Pilate therefore took Jesus, and scourged him, and the soldiers platted a crown of thorns, and put it on his head, and then put on him a purple robe and said, "Hail, King of the Jews!" And they smote him with their hands. Then delivered he him therefore unto them to be crucified, and they took Jesus and led him away.

And he bearing his cross went forth into a place called The Place of the Skull, which is called in Hebrew Golgotha, where they crucified him, and two others with him, on either side one, and Jesus in the midst. And about the ninth hour Jesus cried with a loud voice saying, "Eli, Eli, lama sabachthani?" that is to say, "My God, my God, why hast thou forsaken me?" Jesus, when he had cried again with a loud voice yielded up the ghost.

And now when the even was come, Joseph of Arimathaea, an honourable counsellor, went in boldly unto Pilate, and craved the body of Jesus. And he bought fine linen, and took him down, and wrapped him in the linen, and laid him in a sepulchre.

And when the sabbath was passed, Mary Magdalene, and Mary the mother of James, and Salome had bought sweet spices, that they might come and anoint him. And entering the sepulchre, they saw a young man sitting on the right side, clothed in a long white garment; and they were affrighted.

And he saith unto them, "Be not affrighted: Ye seek Jesus of Nazareth, which is crucified. He is risen; he is not here. Behold the place where they laid him. But go your way, tell his disciples and Peter that he goeth before you into Galilee. There shall ye see him, as he said unto you."

And they went out quickly and fled the sepulchre, for they trembled and were amazed. Neither said they any thing to any man, for they were afraid.[1]

The facts of Jesus' life will be of no use to us, however, unless we can come to some understanding as to what his actual message was. The solution to that problem is greatly complicated by the fact that no contemporary records of Jesus' life have survived.

Of the four Gospels mentioned above, it has been realized since the middle of the 19th century that Mark is the earliest,[2] and the prophecy after the fact of the destruction of the temple, which occurred in 70 AD, shows that Mark could not have been written any earlier than that date (Mark 13:1-2). Therefore the 4 gospels were not eyewitness accounts written by apostles (which, indeed, they themselves never claim to be), but rather different arrangements, by different hands, of some early, now lost collections of "the sayings of Jesus." The earliest historical reference to Jesus occurs in Tacitus Annals 15. 44. 2-3, concerning the great fire of 64 AD in Rome:

> But neither humanitarian aid, nor imperial largess, nor prayers to the gods could forestall the general belief that the fire had been ordered [by the emperor Nero]. Therefore to quell the rumor, Nero framed and most ingeniously punished those whom the crowd despised for their sins and used to call "Christians." Christ, the originator of the term, had been executed during the reign of Tiberius by the procurator Pontius Pilate; repressed for awhile, the fatal superstition was bursting forth again, not only throughout Judaea, the origin of the evil, but also in the capital city, where all horrors and revulsions flow and accumulate.

The most useful, and certainly the most elegant collection of Jesus' sayings occurs in the Sermon on the Mount (Matthew chapters 5-7). As the various sayings and parables comprising this sermon can be found scattered all over Mark and Luke, it's obvious that the speech could never have been delivered in the form imagined by the editor whom we call Matthew. Since, however, much of the content of this great speech is probably genuine and at least represents the fundamental beliefs of the historical Jesus, I'm going to quote the whole thing, this time in a modern translation.[3]

Many Christians who follow their religion from habit and have never bothered to read the Bible are shocked when first exposed to the radical, revolutionary tone of this document. In the next chapter we'll consider whether Jesus really meant what he seems to say.

When he saw the crowds he went up the mountain. And when he had sat down, his disciples gathered around him, and opening his mouth he taught them, saying:

    Happy are the poor in spirit
    because the Kingdom of Heaven is theirs.
    Happy are the mourners
    because they will be comforted.
    Happy are the timid
    because they will inherit the earth.
    Happy are those who hunger and thirst for justice
    because they will be fed.
    Happy are the merciful
    because they will receive mercy.
    Happy are the poor of heart
    because they will see God.
    Happy are the peacemakers
    because they will be called the sons of God.
    Happy are those who have been persecuted for the sake of justice
    because theirs is the Kingdom of Heaven.

Happy are you when they revile and persecute you and speak every evil about you for my sake. Rejoice and exalt because your reward will be great in heaven. For thus they persecuted the prophets before you.

You are the salt of the earth. But if the salt loses its taste, how will it be seasoned? It has no use except to be thrown out and trampled by men.

You are the light of the world. A city lying on top of a mountain cannot be hidden. Nor do men light a candle and place it under a basket, but rather upon a candlestick, and it gives light to all in the house. In the same way shine out your light before men so that they may see your good deeds and glorify your Father in heaven.

Don't think that I have come to destroy the Law or the Prophets. I have not come to destroy, but to fulfill. Truly I tell you, until heaven and earth pass away, neither one comma nor a single serif will pass from the law until all these things come to pass. Whoever destroys one of the lowliest commandments and so teaches others, he will be called the lowliest in the Kingdom of Heaven. But whoever will obey them and so teach, he will be called great in the Kingdom of Heaven. For I tell you that unless your justice is greater than that of the scribes and the Pharisees, you will not enter into the Kingdom of Heaven.

You have heard that it was said by the ancients: "Thou shalt not kill. Whosoever murders shall be brought to judgement." But I tell you that everyone who is angry with his brother will be brought to judgement. Whoever says "Fool!" to his brother will be brought before the Temple Council.

Whoever says "Stupid!" will be sent to the fires of hell.

For if you bring your offering before the altar and then remember that your brother has something against you, abandon your offering there before the altar and go first to make up with your brother, and only then come back to make your offering.

Make friends with your adversary whenever you meet with him on the road so that your adversary doesn't hand you over to the judge, and the judge to the officer, and you be thrown into prison. I tell you truly, you will not get out until you have paid your last penny.

You have heard that it was said, "Thou shalt not commit adultery." But I tell you that every man who has looked upon a woman with desire already has committed adultery with her in his heart.

If your right eye causes you to sin, tear it out and cast it from you. For it is better that you lose one of your parts than that your whole body be cast into hell. And if your right hand causes you to sin, cut it off and cast it from you. For it is better that you lose one of your parts than that your whole body go to hell.

It has been said, "Whenever a man would send his wife out of his house, then let him write her a bill of divorcement." But I tell you that every man who divorces his wife except on a charge of fornication turns her into an adulteress, and whoever marries a divorced woman commits adultery with her.

Again, you have heard that it was said by the ancients: "And ye shall not swear by my name falsely, and if a man vow a vow unto the Lord, he shall not break his word." But I tell you, don't swear at all, neither by heaven because it is the throne of God, nor by the earth because it is the footstool for His feet, not by Jerusalem because it is the city of the great king, nor by your own head because you cannot make even one hair white or black. Let your oath be "Yes, yes" or "No, no." Anything beyond this is evil.

You have heard that it has been said, "An eye for an eye, and a tooth for a tooth." But I tell you, do not stand up against evil. But whoever strikes you upon the right cheek, turn the other to him as well. And if someone wishes to sue you and take your shirt, give him your coat also. And if someone compels you to journey for a mile, go with him for two. Give to someone who asks of you, and do not turn away from one who wishes to borrow.

You have heard that it was said: "Thou shalt love thy neighbor and hate thine enemy." But I say to you: Love your enemies and pray for those who persecute you. Thus you will be the sons of your Father, who makes His sun rise over the evil and the good and sends rain upon the just and the unjust. For if you love those who love you, what reward will you have? Do not even the publicans do the same? And if you greet only your brother, what do you do more than others? Do not even the gentiles do the same? Therefore be perfect, as you father in heaven is perfect.

Beware showing off your righteousness before men or you will not have a reward from your Father in heaven.

Therefore, when you give charity, do not blow your own horn, as the hypocrites do in the synagogues and in the streets so that they might be honored by men. Truly I tell you, they have their reward. When you give charity, don't let your left hand know what your right hand is doing so that your charity may be in secret. And your Father, observing you in secret, will reward you.

And when you pray, don't be like the hypocrites. They love to pray standing in the synagogues and on street corners so that they might be seen by men. Truly I tell you, they have their reward. But when you pray, go into your cellar, shut the door, and pray to your Father in secret. And your Father, observing you in secret, will reward you.

When you pray, don't babble like the gentiles. For they imagine that in their wordiness they will be heard favorably. Do not imitate them! For your Father knows what you need before you ask him.

Therefore, pray as follows:
Our Father who are in heaven,
may your name be sanctified!
May your kingdom come,
may your will be accomplished
upon the earth, just as it is in heaven.
Give us the bread we need every day
and forgive us our sins
as we forgive those who have sinned against us.
And do not lead us into temptation,
but save us from evil.
For if you forgive men their wrongs, your Father in heaven will forgive you. But if you do not forgive men, neither will your Father pardon your sins.

And when you fast, don't put on a sad face like the hypocrites. For they disfigure their faces so that men might notice their fasting. Truly I tell you, they have their reward. But when you fast, anoint your head and wash your face so that your fasting may not be apparent to men, but rather to your Father secretly. And your Father, observing you secretly, will reward you.

Do not store up your treasures upon the earth, where moths and rust consume them and where thieves break in and steal. Store up your treasures in heaven, where neither moths nor rust consume them, and where thieves neither break in nor steal. For where your treasure is, there will your heart be also.

The lamp of the soul is the eye. If therefore your eye is sound, your whole body will be full of light. But if your eye is evil, your whole body will be full of darkness. And if the light within you is darkness, how great is that darkness?

No man can be slave to two masters. For either he will hate one and love the other, or he will be devoted to one and think little of the other. You cannot serve God and money.

Therefore I say to you: Do not let your soul worry about what you will eat or what you will drink, nor your body about what you will wear. Is not the soul worth more than food and the body more than clothes? Look at the birds of the sky, how they neither plant nor harvest nor store up in barns, but your heavenly Father feeds them. Are you not worth more than they are? Who of you by worrying can add one foot to his height? And why do you worry about your clothes? Consider the lilies of the field and how they grow! They neither toil away nor spin yarn. But I tell you that not even Solomon in all his glory was decked out like one of them. And if God so clothes the grass of the field, which is here today and cast into the oven tomorrow, will he not clothe you all the more, you people of little faith? Therefore don't worry and say, "What will we eat? What will we drink? What will we put on?" Those are all things that the gentiles crave. For your heavenly Father knows that you need them. Seek first the Kingdom of God and His righteousness, and all these things will be granted you. Therefore do not worry about tomorrow, for tomorrow will worry about itself. Each day's evil is evil enough.

Do not judge so that you will not be judged. For you will be judged by the judgement you make, and you will be measured by the measurement you take. Why do you look at the speck in your brother's eye but don't notice the two-by-four in your own eye? Or how can you say to your brother, "Remove the speck from your eye!" when—look!—there is a two-by-four in yours! Hypocrite! First take the two-by-four out of your own eye, and then you can see clearly enough to take out the speck from your brother's eye.

Do not give what is holy to dogs nor scatter your pearls before pigs lest they trample on them with their feet and turn to gore you.

Ask, and it will be given to you. Search, and you will find. Knock, and the door will be opened. For everyone who asks will receive, and everyone who seeks will find, and to everyone who knocks the door will be opened.

Is there a man among you who, when his son asks for bread, would give him a stone? Or when he asks for a fish would give him a snake? Therefore if you, evil as you are, know how to give good gifts to your children, how much more will your Father who is in heaven give good gifts to those who ask Him?

Treat men just as you would wish them to treat you. For that is the Law and the Prophets.

Enter through the narrow gate. For wide is the gate and easy the road leading to destruction, and many are those who proceed upon it. For narrow is the gate and tortuous is the road leading to life, and few are those who find it.

Turn away from false prophets, who come to you in sheep's clothing, but inside they are ravenous wolves. You will know them from their fruits. Do men gather grapes from thorns, or figs from thistles? Thus every good tree bears beautiful fruit, but the worthless tree bears evil fruits. The good tree cannot bring forth evil fruits, nor the worthless tree beautiful fruits. Every tree not bearing beautiful fruit is chopped down and cast into the fire. Thus from their fruits you will know them.

Not everyone saying to me, "Lord, Lord!" will enter into the Kingdom of Heaven, but rather whoever carries out the will of my Father in heaven. Many will say to me today, "Lord, Lord, have we not prophesied in your name, and have we not cast out demons in your name, and have we not performed miracles in your name?" And then I shall confess to them that "I have never known you. Get away from me, you sinners!"

Whoever hears these words of mine and acts upon them will be like the wise man who has built his house upon the rock. And the rains came down and the rivers rose and the winds blew and they fell upon that house. And it did not fall, for its foundations had been laid upon the rock. And whoever hears these words of mine and does not act upon them will be like the foolish man who has built his house upon the sand. And the rains came down and the rivers rose and the winds blew and they dashed against that house. And it fell, and its fall was great.

And when Jesus ended his speech, the crowds were amazed at his teaching. For he taught like someone with authority, and not like the scribes.

37 The Son of Man

Christianity fits uncomfortably into the pattern of ancient religiosity. At first glance we seem to be on familiar ground. Many of its details seem familiar enough—such as, for instance, the stories about Jesus' childhood. None of them occur in the Gospel of Mark, the oldest of the surviving biographies, and the tales in the other Gospels are pretty transparent inventions.

For the immaculate conception we can compare the last incarnation of the Bodhisatta (the future Buddha) upon the lady Maha Maya or the birth of the Winnebago's messiah, Hare, or the birth of Dionysus.[1] The star of Bethlehem is an example of what literary critics call "the pathetic fallacy," the belief that great human events must be mirrored in nature. The most common example of the pathetic fallacy is the thunderstorm that's always raging when the foul deed is done in a detective story. Just as with Jesus' birth, nature is supposed to have abounded in miracles at the births of Buddha and Alexander the Great,[2] and when Julius Caesar died a comet appeared in the sky.[3] I could also compare the story of the boy Jesus' impressing the elders in the Temple (Luke 2: 42-50) with the almost identical story of the boy Alexander impressing the ambassadors from Persia (Plutarch, *Alexander* 5 [pp. 803-804]). So far so good.

It would also be convenient to classify Christianity as a mystery religion. That's a cult based around a μυστήριον, a central myth whose true meaning, revealed only through initiation and divine revelation, would provide a union between the celebrant and his god. Although there were secret ceremonies made available only to the true believers, most "mysteries" weren't that mysterious at all, but were rather presented to large audiences in quasi-theatrical performances complete with dances, choruses, and music.[4] That would perhaps, make us think of the "mystery plays" of the Middle Ages. But we should look more closely.

Mystery religions were prevalent throughout classical antiquity, from the 6th century BC until the final victory of Christianity in the 4th century AD. There were many of them—Adonis, Attis, Dionysus, the Eleusinian Mysteries, the Great Mother—and in this book we've already examined one of the most important in some detail: the Egyptian cult of Isis-Osiris. Almost as popular was the strange god Mithra, a late arrival who didn't really take hold until the 2nd century AD, and whose origins have become increasingly problematical.[5]

Mithra's western followers (for the cult never took hold in Greece) were convinced that their religion was of Persian Origin and thus, it would seem, an offshoot of Zoroastrianism. Mithra was one of the three great Ahuras (or Lords) worshipped by the ancient Iranians. We've already met Ahura Mazda; the two other lesser Ahuras were Varuna, guardian of the oath, and Mithra, guardian of the covenant. Mithra was early associated with the sun, as is evident from the "Hymn to Mithra," one of the "great yashts," dating back to at least 2,000 BC:

> We worship Mithra of the wide pastures,..who travels the breadth of the earth, by the setting of the sun he has touched both edges of this wide, round earth with far borders. He sees all that is between earth and heaven..[6]

Just like the Zoroastrian Soshyant,[7] the western Mithra was depicted as having slain the great Bull, whose blood was transformed into bunches of grapes and from whose tail sprouted an ear of grain.[8] After this ritualistic slaying, Mithra and the Sun stretched out on the hide of the Bull to feast on its flesh, and Mithra is often shown mounting the Sun's flaming chariot. We can see these events portrayed with amazing regularity in surviving mithraic sanctuaries, just as we can see Mithra's miraculous birth from a rock. There is, however, neither temporal nor narrative consistency in the images, nor are there any surviving literary texts from within the cult. So the emotional and often even the literal meaning of the pictures is lost to us.[9]

Despite the superficial similarities, however, it is really impossible to link together the two mythologies. Neither do the Zoroastrians ever depict Mithra as having slain the Bull, nor is there anything in the Western monuments that reproduces the fundamental dualism of the Zoroastrian religion—i.e. the picture of the eternal struggle between the forces of Light and Darkness. Indeed, it's now a good bet that Mithraism was consciously invented in the West and that its Zoroastrian elements were introduced for exotic color.[10]

We can, however, link Mithra with Christianity, for both he and the Invincible Sun are responsible for the choice of December 25 as the birthday of Christ. There is, after all, nothing in the Gospels to hint at the date of Christ's birth, but in the Julian calendar December 25 was the date of the winter solstice, or the longest night of the year. After the solstice the days begin to get longer again, so the worshippers of Mithra celebrated that day as the sun's birthday. Unwilling to buck the competition of a popular festival, the early Church finally joined in.[11]

Astrology was also responsible for the gradual acceptance by the Roman people of the old Sumerian seven day lunar week, each day of which was sacred to one of the seven visible planets.[12] We have no way of knowing whether the primary influence for the change came from Mithra or any of the other mystery cults or merely from the perceived convenience of the lunar cycle.

Still, something is missing in our picture, for Christianity is more than a typical mystery religion. Mystery cults never developed the crusading, exclusive vision of Christianity. One could join as many mystery cults as he could afford, and although the experience was meant to be transforming, it did not impose an all embracing creed onto one's life the way Christianity did.[13] In this context it is instructive to contrast Plato's famous vision in the *Phaedrus:*

> For in heaven there are many blessed prospects and pathways upon which the race of blessed gods wanders. Each doing his own thing follows willingly and as he is able, for envy is situated apart from the divine choir.[14]

with the First Commandment:

> I am the Lord thy God, which have brought thee out of the land of Egypt, out of the home of bondage. Thou shalt have no other gods before me...for I the Lord thy God am a jealous God, visiting the iniquity of the fathers upon the children unto the third and fourth generation of them that hate me.[15]

Indeed, Christianity saw its influence as so fundamentally redemptive that it continued the experience into the afterlife, offering its followers resurrection and rebirth. The myths of Isis and Osiris, of Demeter and Persephone might make us suspect that the mystery religions did the same,[16] but there is no hard evidence to back up such an assumption. Persephone returns from Hades, but her initiates stay below without her, and indeed her liberation is eternally temporary. Osiris stays with the dead, as does Attis. Mithra never seems to die or suffer at all, but rather presents a story of conquest and victory. The ancient mysteries transformed the life of the here and now for their followers. Initiates were rewarded with a bird's eye view of the universe and an enlightening communion with their god, but they were meant to take that experience back into their daily lives. There were companionship, banquets, and magnificent public festivals to enjoy, right here on earth. This attitude was so frequently expressed on Roman tombstones that it was reduced to the initials *nf f ns nc (non fui, fui, non sum, non curo):* "I wasn't, I was, I'm not, don't care." Pagans felt that Christians were morbidly preoccupied with graves, death, and catacombs.[17]

The most important distinction between the ancient mysteries and Christianity, perhaps, is that the latter's founder, Jesus of Nazareth, was a real person and not a mythological fable. That in itself, though, raises some real problems, for people don't live, think, or talk in a vacuum. Since the historical Jesus was what we would call an orthodox Jew who was probably addressed by his followers as "rabbi,"[18] we cannot separate Christianity from Judaism—indeed, Christianity is a sect of Judaism. We cannot find Jesus in the hearts of 20th century Americans. He was a real man who lived in his own time, a time which we shall have to make some attempt to reproduce in order to understand who Jesus was and what he had to say. That means that we'll have to take a look at who the Jewish people were, and what they were up to in the 1st century AD.

We've already seen in chapter 5 that the Jews were first led out of the Sumerian city of Ur by the patriarch Abraham; they settled in the land of Canaan under Abraham's son Isaac and his grandson Jacob (or Israel). In chapter 8 we saw them enter Egypt, perhaps as part of the Hyksos invasion; tradition claims that having eventually fallen into slavery under the pharaohs, they were led back to Israel by Moses sometime in the 13th century BC. It was subsequent to their return to the Promised Land that the Jews enjoyed one of their two periods of political independence in antiquity. This was when King David (who ruled 1010-970) seized the city of Jerusalem to be their capital and set up an oriental style monarchy that was continued by his son Solomon (970-931). It was David who founded the great Temple in Jerusalem which subsequently became the center of Jewish religious and political life.

Upon Solomon's death the kingdom split into two parts, and the times of trouble began. In 732 the Assyrian king Tiglath Pileser III absorbed the Jews into the Assyrian Empire. When the Assyrian Empire fell in 612, they passed under the control of the Chaldaean king Nabopolasser, who ruled from Babylon. When they attempted to reassert their independence, King Nebuchadnezzar seized Jerusalem in 586 and carted the people off to a 50 year captivity in Babylon. Much of chapter 11 was devoted to explaining how King Cyrus the Great conquered Babylon, and finding the exiles more trouble than they were worth, shipped them back to Jerusalem to rebuild their Temple.

Alexander's defeat of the Persians brought no relief, for the Jewish nation passed first to the lazy command of the Ptolemies and then, in 200, to the Seleucid King Antiochus III (see the end of chapter 22). His son Antiochus IV "Epiphanes" stupidly accepted a huge bribe from Jason, brother to the high priest Onias, and so in 174 backed him in a temple coup. Jason was a philhellene. To the horror of the people, he proposed to build a gymnasium and train the youth of his country in Greek ways:

> Now such was the height of Greek fashions, and increase of heathenish manners, through the exceeding profaneness of Jason, that ungodly wretch, and not high priest; that the priests had no courage to serve any more at the altar, but despising the temple, and neglecting the sacrifices, hastened to be partakers of the unlawful allowance in the place of exercise, after the game of Discus called them forth; not setting by the honours of their fathers, but liking the glory of the Grecians best of all.[19]

Fighting between fundamentalists and assimilators became so intense that in 168 the vacillating Antiochus, reeling now from toleration to persecution, seized Jerusalem, slaughtered its defenders, and forbade the practice of the Jewish religion. In 167 BC the Jews began their one successful revolt. It was led by a priest named Mattathias and his five sons, the eldest of whom was the famous Judas Maccabaeus. The Maccabees drove out the Seleucids and rededicated the Temple in 165, this being the origin of the festival of Hanukkah.[20]

Thus began the second period of Jewish political independence, this time under a dynasty of high priests descended from Mattathias–the Hashmonean Dynasty, after the family name Hashmon. The Hashmonean Dynasty reached its greatest extent–almost equal to David's kingdom–under the two sons of the High Priest John Hyrcanus. The younger of these, Jannaeus (103-76 BC), whom the Greeks called Alexander, once crucified 800 rebels outside his palace so he could enjoy their death agonies during his victory party. His death led to civil war, which allowed one of his generals, named Antipater, to rise to power. Antipater came from Edom in the south, an area that had been forcibly converted to Judaism by John Hyrcanus only 50 years earlier. Antipater was being besieged on the Temple Hill when Pompey arrived on the scene in 64 (see chapter 30).

After Antipater was poisoned, his son Herod skillfully played off Octavian, Antony, and the Parthians against each other until the Senate named him King of the Jews in 40 BC. He was a strange man, consistently torn between his obligatory loyalty to Augustus and his desire to be a real leader of the Jewish people. As it turned out, Augustus never trusted him, and the Jewish people despised him as a mock-Jew and a foreign tyrant. He certainly never perpetrated the "massacre of the innocents" depicted in Matthew 2:16, but he did kill (among others) his Hashmonean wife, three of his sons, and about half the Sanhedrin, the ruling board of the Temple.

After Herod's death his kingdom was divided among his 3 sons Philip, Herod Antipas, and Archilaus. The Romans fired Archilaus from his province of Judaea in 6 AD, which explains why at Christ's trial the city of Jerusalem was under the command of the Roman procurator (actually prefect) Pontius Pilate. The Jewish kingdom was briefly revived by the emperor Claudius, who gave it to his friend Julius Agrippa I, one of Herod's grandsons, but Agrippa died in 44 and the entire kingdom was reabsorbed under a procurator.

We now come to the end of our digression, and indeed of independent Jewish history in antiquity. If the Romans felt only contempt for Jewish traditions, the Jews felt only hatred for the unbearable pollution of a conquering, foreign race. The mad emperor Caligula had even made plans, luckily forestalled by his death, to erect his own statue in the Temple at Jerusalem. The final revolt broke out in 66 AD, when the procurator Gessius Florus seized 17 talents of Temple treasure owed for back taxes. The revolt ended with the siege, capture, and destruction of Jerusalem in 70 by the future emperor Titus. With the simultaneous destruction of the Temple, the Sanhedrin, and the High Priesthood, Jewish political identity came to an end. It must be emphasized that it was during this final period of political and national upheaval that Jesus was born, preached, and died.

The Jews reacted to national slavery in two opposite but nonetheless complementary ways. They tried violence, most successfully against the Seleucids, and then with disastrous results against the Romans. Thus in 6 or 7 BC the fanatical Zealots were founded to fight a revolt against the governor Quirinius (the famous Cyrenius of Luke 2: 2); after the death of Julius Agrippa a prophet named Theudas called for open revolt and had to be beheaded by the procurator Cuspius Fadus (see Acts 5: 34-36); and, most tragically, Simon bar Cochba, "The Son of a Star," liberated Jerusalem in 132-135 AD, only to be put down by the emperor Hadrian with brutal efficiency.

Apart from this violence–though largely inspiring it–was a growing conviction among the Jews that God would not abandon his people, that he would intervene by supernatural means to set the world right again. It was a hope repeated three times a day during the ritual recitation of the *Shemoneh' esse* (the 18 Benedictions):

> Sound the great horn for our freedom;
> lift up the ensign to gather our exiles. . .
> Restore our judges as at the first,
> and our counsellors as at the beginning. . .
> And to Jerusalem, thy city, return in mercy
> and dwell therein as thou has spoken;
> rebuild it soon in our days as an everlasting building,
> and speedily set up therein the throne of David.[21]

Starting from the time of Antiochus Epiphanes, this attitude developed into a form of prophetic literature called *apocalyptic*. The term is from the Greek ἀποκάλυψις or "uncovering," since apocalyptic writings usually take the form of a revelation about the future placed in the mouth of a prophet or king from the past. In general, an apocalyptic vision foresees a period of great evils which foreshadows the coming of the end of the world by the supernatural agency of God, at which time a new kingdom on earth, an earthly paradise without death and suffering, will be established for the faithful. The oldest version we have of this vision is the Book of Daniel, dating from the time of the revolt against Antiochus IV:[22]

> In the first year of Belshazzar King of Babylon Daniel had a dream and visions of his land upon his bed: then he wrote the dream, and told the sum of the matters. Daniel spake and said, "I saw in my vision by night, and, behold, the four winds of the heaven strove upon the great sea. And four great beasts came up from the sea, diverse one from another.
>
> The first was like a lion...a second like a bear...and lo another, like a leopard...and behold a fourth beast, dreadful and terrible, and strong exceedingly; and it had great iron teeth: it devoured and brake in pieces and stamped the residue with the feet of it: and it was diverse from all the beasts that were before it; and it had ten horns...
>
> "I saw in the night visions, and, behold, one like the Son of Man came with the clouds of heaven, and came to the Ancient of Days, and they brought him near before him. And there was given him dominion and glory, and a kingdom, that all people, nations, and languages, should serve him: his dominion is an everlasting dominion, which shall not pass away, and his kingdom that which shall not be destroyed."[23]

After the Book of Daniel, the only apocalyptic writings to survive in Hebrew are the famous Dead Sea Scrolls, which were accidentally discovered by an Arab boy in 1947 in a cave near Qumran. They were written by a community of Essenes, a monastic, apocalyptic cult that was probably wiped out by the great revolt of 70 AD. The *War Scroll* especially speaks in apocalyptic terms, describing an end time when the "Children of Light" will fight against the "Children of Darkness."[24]

After the bar Cochba uprising the Jews understandably turned against such heady stuff and destroyed their original copies. We do, however, have Greek versions of many of these works, each generally inspired by some disaster in Jewish history. Thus the *Psalms of Solomon* follow Pompey's invasion; *4th Ezra, Baruch,* and the *Assumption of Moses* the destruction of the Temple; and the famous Book of Revelations the persecutions of Domitian. It might be helpful to quote from the 10th chapter of the *Assumption of Moses*, for its language is clearer than the highly charged imagery of Daniel:

> And then his kingdom shall appear
> throughout all his creation,
> And then Satan shall be no more...
> For the Heavenly One will arise from his
> royal throne,
> And he will go forth from his holy habitation
> with indignation and wrath on account of his sons.
> And the earth shall tremble: to its confines
> shall it be shaken:
> And the high mountains shall be made low
> And the hills shall be shaken and fall.
> And the horns of the sun shall be broken and he
> shall be turned into darkness;
> And the moon shall not give her light, and be
> turned wholly into blood.
> And the circle of the stars shall be disturbed...
> For the Most High will arise, the Eternal God alone,
> And he will appear to punish the Gentiles,
> And he will destroy all their idols.[25]

All this is clearly written under Persian influence, for it assumes the presence in the world of another force, led by Satan, as a permanent threat to God, just as it promises a life after death to the faithful—both of which concepts are absent from the Old Testament.[26] We are also introduced to the Son of Man, who as "Son of David," "Chosen One," or "Messiah" ("the anointed one") is none other than the Zoroastrian Soshyant, the mediator (just as Mithra was called μεσίτης[27]) whose intercession would establish *Freshegird*, the cleansing of the world.[28] This apocalyptic Messiah had evolved gradually, under the shock of repeated disappointments, from the original, nationalistic messiah prophesied by Isaiah in the 8th century BC as a King of the Jews who, with God's help, would reestablish the Kingdom of David:

> For unto us a child is born, unto us a son is given: and the government shall be upon his shoulder: and his name shall be called Wonderful, Counsellor, the mighty God, the everlasting father, The Prince of Peace. (Isaiah 9: 6)

This new messiah was a supernatural figure who would come from the clouds with the angels to end the world as we know it. First called the Son of Man he was consistently confused, as we'll see, with the earthly messiah promised by Isaiah.[29]

There can really be no doubt that Jesus believed in this apocalyptic vision.[30] Each of the synoptic gospels offers a close parallel version of Jesus' prophecy about the end of the world: we'll start this discussion by quoting from the one in Mark:

> Take heed lest any man deceive you, for many shall come in my name, saying, "I am Christ," and shall deceive many. And when ye shall hear of wars and rumors of wars, be ye not troubled: for such things must needs be; but the end shall not be yet. For nation shall rise against nation, and kingdom against kingdom: and there shall be earthquakes in diverse places, and there shall be famines and troubles: these are the beginnings of sorrows...Now the brother shall betray the brother to death, and the father the son; and children shall rise up against their parents, and shall cause them to be put to death...
>
> But in these days, after that tribulation, the sun shall be darkened, and the moon shall not give her light, and the stars of heaven shall fall, and the powers that are in heaven shall be shaken. And then shall they see the Son of man coming in the clouds with great power and glory. And then shall he send his angels, and shall gather together his elect from the four winds, from the uttermost part of the earth to the uttermost part of heaven...
>
> Verily I say unto you, that this generation shall not pass, till all these things be done. Heaven and earth shall pass away: but my words shall not pass away.
>
> But of that day and that hour knoweth no man, no, not the angels which are in heaven, neither the Son, but the Father. Take ye heed, watch and pray: for ye know not when the time is. For the Son of man is as a man taking a far journey, who left his house, and gave authority to his servants, and to every man his work, and commanded the porter to watch.
>
> Watch ye therefore: for ye know not when the master of the house cometh, at even, or at midnight, or at the cockcrowing, or in the morning: Lest coming suddenly he find you sleeping. And what I say unto you I saw unto all, watch![31]

This is a typical apocalyptic prophecy which can be compared with those cited above or with the 6th chapter of the Book of Revelations, which tells of the "four horsemen of the Apocalypse," of the stars falling out of the sky, and so forth. It should be noted also that Jesus, while denying exact knowledge of when the end will come, nonetheless is convinced that it must happen within the generation of those hearing his words.[32] The difficulties that arose when this prophecy did not come to pass will occupy a considerable chunk of the next chapter.

"The Kingdom of God" whose coming Jesus consistently says is "at hand" and for whose coming Christians pray every day in the Lord's Prayer ("Thy Kingdom come," which means "let your kingdom come"), is not the little world of the apostles, nor the projected rule of the Church, nor a Christianity-inspired paradise on earth; it is, rather , the apocalyptic kingdom of Daniel's vision, ushered in by the Son of man coming from the clouds with the angels, just as Christ predicted to Caiaphas at his trial. It is, briefly, Armageddon and the end of the world. Jesus' whole ministry was devoted to destroying this world so that the Kingdom of God could be established in its place.[33]

Because of this supernatural view of the Messiah's nature, Jesus could not and did not claim during his lifetime that he was the Messiah. Such a claim would have been patently absurd: the Messiah couldn't be a carpenter's son who died a human death. He was supposed to be a glorious, supernatural being who would come in the clouds with the angels. Jesus could only have looked upon himself as the future Son of man, and that future role could only be assured after his death. That's why he told the demons "who knew him" not to reveal his secret (Mark 1: 34 and 3: 12), and it also explains the incredible fact that even his own disciples didn't know he was the Messiah.

For when he asks them at Caesarea Philippi (Mark 8: 27-30, Matt. 16: 13-20, Luke 9: 18-21) who he is, they don't know! It takes a divine revelation to inform Peter of Christ's messiahship, and indeed it's Peter who reveals the secret, not Jesus, who tells the Twelve to keep it to themselves. Finally, although Jesus certainly makes a messianic entry into Jerusalem by riding upon an ass (see Zechariah 9:9), there is absolutely nothing to suggest that the people recognized him as the Son of Man. How indeed could they have guessed, and who would have told them? It's to be noted that even at his trial the Sanhedrin brought forth no witnesses to accuse Jesus of blasphemous claims to the messiahship—a fact which strongly suggests that Jesus' messianic claims were not general knowledge. The crowds on Palm Sunday were hailing Jesus as Elijah come again—the same guess the apostles made a Caesarea Philippi and (according to the prophets) a necessary prelude to the future coming of the real Son of man.[34]

Since, therefore, Jesus saw his death as a necessary initiation into his messiahship, we can only see his entering into Jerusalem, his belligerent cleansing of the Temple, and his passivity before the treason of Judas as suicidal acts meant to trigger Armageddon and the end of the world. It is, indeed, tempting to imagine with Schweitzer that Judas, shocked at Jesus' claim at Caesarea Philippi to be the Son of Man, betrayed his master to the High Priest to cleanse himself of the blasphemy. If this was Judas' treachery, it explains Caiaphas' question to Jesus at the trial and his violent reaction to Christ's unequivocal response.[35]

I deliberately concluded my condensed version of the Gospels in the last chapter with the ending of Mark as it appears in the oldest manuscripts.[36] For in that version the two Mary's found the tomb empty, but as yet no one had seen Jesus. The women are afraid because they know what the subsequent appearance of Jesus will mean. At this early stage of Christianity the followers of Jesus are not expecting a beatific resurrection on Easter Sunday; when Jesus comes it will be as the Son of Man in power and glory to preside over judgement day, This immediate and cataclysmic second coming was expected, as we've seen, within their generation, and it would be the end of the world.[37]

It's only in this apocalyptic context that the Sermon on the Mount makes any sense.[38] For those of us brought up comfortably in middle America it's so tempting to prevaricate and hedge and assume that of course Jesus didn't mean us to take him literally when he told us to turn the other cheek, to love our enemies, and to give away all our money. But whatever we deny to Jesus, we shouldn't deny him the common courtesy of assuming that he meant what he said. If he tells us that "It is easier for a camel to go through the eye of a needle, than for a rich man to enter into the kingdom of God" (Mark 10: 25, Matthew 19: 24, Luke 18: 25), he means, quite frankly, that rich men are damned to hell.[39] It cannot be otherwise, for if the end of the world is at hand, then extreme measures are necessary. At the edge of destruction there is no time for half measures.

38 "What Do I Do With the Christians?"

Since there were so many rival mystery religions knocking about Rome in the first three centuries AD, each competing for souls and promising salvation, a question naturally arises as to why Christianity won out in the end. The historical approach can no more accept answers like "it was the best" or "God willed it" than it can assume that Akhnaton was a prophetic, religious visionary. We have to be more cynical than that. Historical cynicism accordingly lays us open to the temptation of proposing a list of reasons for Christianity's success. I hope to have made it clear by now that lists are conveniences for the historian; no one who's alive and active makes up lists to justify the fundamental motives of his life, and any list composed after the fact can be expanded or shrunk at its author's pleasure. So instead of composing a list, I'm going to concentrate on one important factor in Christianity's success, the administrative superstructure, or as it's called, the hierarchy (holy order) of the Church.

Two factors (excuse the list) made the Church's hierarchy both possible and inevitable: the managerial talents of the apostle Paul and, by an ironic perversity, the Roman government's persecution of the Church. It was Paul who made Christianity palatable for non-Jews (or Gentiles, as they were called[1]) and thus suitable for export—an export which he helped significantly to organize—and it was the Roman government's persecution of the new religion which, by driving it underground, forced organization upon it as a means of self defense, while simultaneously creating an inspirational pantheon of martyrs. Giving in completely to the historical approach, we'll examine each of these factors in turn—the persecutions in this chapter, and the career of St. Paul in the next.

First off, the very existence of the Christian persecutions comes as something of a surprise since polytheism seems by its very nature both open and democratic. In a world filled with gods and divine personifications, shouldn't there always be room for one more? Jesus should have had no more trouble coming to Rome than did Cybele, Isis, Demeter, or Mithra.

To a certain extent this was true, but the Romans had no concept of toleration as a philosophical virtue. Religion, as we have often observed, is a source of power, and the Romans had little respect for anything else. Foreign religions that fit in neatly with the Graeco-Roman tradition seemed safe and were readily embraced, but the more exotic a cult appeared, or the more it seemed to represent a rival power structure to the state, the more threatening it appeared. Thus temples of Isis were shut down repeatedly in the late Republic and early empire; they didn't become permanent parts of the Roman landscape until the 2nd century AD. Cybele, the Great Mother, with her eunuch priests, baptisms in blood, and wild processions alternately repelled and enticed the Romans. The same Senate that imported Cybele as a hedge against Hannibal also forbade its citizens to join the goddess's priesthood.[2]

Christians seemed exotic, dangerous, and insulting all at once. While demanding that the Romans recognize their god as the one and only, they berated the Roman deities as foul demons whom they refused to worship.[3] Moreover, although emperor worship became increasingly important in the 2nd and 3rd centuries, Christians wouldn't sacrifice to the emperor either. Now no educated Roman thought of his emperor as a god. They certainly assassinated enough of them to realize that. Nonetheless, sacrifice to the emperor's image was looked upon as a harmless expression of patriotism, as a form of loyalty oath. By refusing to engage in it, Christians appeared immediately suspect. They were rightly called atheists—those who don't believe in the gods.

Of course the Jews were in the same boat. They also would not worship the pagan gods; they wouldn't even use Roman money because it had "graven images" on it. But the Jews were a nation with a long and recognized culture. Centuries of empire building had taught the Romans the wisdom of respecting such things.[4] Christians, on the other hand, were a sect, and the Roman government was always mistrustful of secret societies. Indeed, the more secretive the Christians became, the more the Romans mistrusted them. Rumor twisted the symbolic eating of Christ's body and blood in Holy Communion into butchering babies and drinking their blood. It was assumed that if the Christians met in secret, they must be holding wild, drunken orgies.[5]

It is, moreover, frequently overlooked that Christianity was a real threat to the Roman order. Believing as they did that the world was about to end, early Christians refused to engage in commerce or care about money; they ridiculed or shrunk in horror from the holy festivals of their state, from the great ceremonies of thanksgiving, from chariot races, gladiatorial contests (of course!) and from the theatre, all of which were dedicated to the pagan gods.[6]

Even more serious, the Church became increasingly hostile to sex. Abstinence in itself was nothing new to the ancient world. By the time of the Roman Empire the development of self-control was seen by both doctors and philosophers as the only pathway to the cultivation of the spirit and the intellect.[7] By the end of the second century, however, Christians saw the renunciation of sex as something far more revolutionary.

Virginity both for men and women came to be seen as the only possible deliverance from that endless cycle of birth and death which provided not only citizens for the secular state, but also continuity for the "Present Age," the age which was supposed to have been forever altered by the sacrifice of Christ. The pagan philosophers, for all their personal austerity, continued to praise marriage and the joyous procreation of children. The Christians saw marriage as an evil necessity forced upon them by the otherwise unmanageable sexual impulses that corrupted their hearts. Sexual abstinence was seen as Christian heroism, as a revolutionary attack on the City of Man.[8] If everybody became a Christian, the Roman government (as indeed Jesus wanted) would have fallen apart.

The best way to demonstrate the government's attitude towards this new sect is to quote a famous exchange of letters between Gaius Plinius Secundus and the emperor Trajan. Pliny the Younger, as he's called in English, is second only to our friend Cicero as a writer of letters in antiquity. Pliny was typical of an upper class gentleman of the late first and early second century BC. He was well educated both in literature and the law, fundamentally humane, and something of a prig. Pliny was appointed consul in 100 AD, and in 111 received the governorship of Bithynia, a province bordering the south-west coast of the Black Sea. It was in his capacity as governor of Bithynia that Pliny first met up with the Christians:

GAIUS PLINIUS TO THE EMPEROR TRAJAN:

I consider it, master, a duty to consult with you on all matters concerning which I have experienced any doubts. For who can better direct my hesitation or instruct my ignorance?

I have never taken part in an investigation of the Christians; thus I do not know how or to what extent they should be punished or examined. Nor have the following points caused me inconsequential uncertainties: should age make some difference, or should there be no distinction between the youngest and the more mature; should clemency be granted to repentance, or should it be of no benefit to one who has wholeheartedly been a Christian to have ceased; should the name of Christian itself, if without offense, or should the offenses necessarily attaching to the name be punished?

Meanwhile against those who have been denounced to me as Christians this is the policy I have followed: I asked them if they were Christians. Those who concurred I asked a second and a third time with threats of capital punishment. Those who persevered I ordered to be handed over. For I had no doubt, whatever they were confessing, that stubbornness and inflexible obstinacy should be punished. There were others exhibiting similar mental instability whom, because they were Roman citizens, I directed to be sent on to Rome. Presently as a result of this very procedure—as often happens—the accusations becoming more prevalent, several varieties have come to light.

An anonymous list was posted containing the names of many people. Those who denied that they were or had been Christians I thought should be dismissed, if they first invoked the gods in my presence and sacrificed with incense and wine to your image (which I had ordered to be brought forward for this purpose together with the statues of the gods) and moreover cursed Christ, which those who are truly Christians can, it is said, in no way be forced to do. Others named in the list admitted that they had been Christians but presently denied it; they had been once, but had given it up, some three years since, others several years ago, one even twenty years ago. All of these also worshipped your image and the statues of the gods and cursed Christ.

However, they insisted that this was the sum of their fault and error, that they were accustomed to convene of a given day before dawn and sing a hymn antiphonally to Christ as if to a god, and to bind themselves by oath not for the purpose of some crime, but so as not to commit theft, or

brigandage, or adultery, or to betray an oath, or to withhold something held
in trust. It was thereupon their custom to disperse and to join together again
to breakfast, but on common and harmless food. They had even ceased doing
this since my edict which, in accordance with your orders, forbade secret
societies. I am all the more inclined to believe this since, in search of the
truth, I tortured two of their serving girls—whom they call "deaconesses"
(*ministrae*). I found nothing other than perverse and immoderate superstition.

I have therefore suspended my investigations and turned to you for advise.
It seems to me that the affair is worthy of your notice, especially because of
the number of those endangered; for many of every age, or every rank, and
of either sex are called and will be called into danger. The contagion of that
superstition has infected not only the cities, but the villages and farms as well,
though I believe it can be halted and corrected. Certainly it is generally
agreed that the all but deserted temples have once again begun to be filled
and that the long interrupted sacred ceremonies are being performed and
that the victims are being fattened, for which hitherto only an occasional
buyer could be found. From which circumstance one may surmise that the
common throng of humanity can be improved if only given an opportunity
for repentance.

TRAJAN TO PLINY

My dear Secundus, you have acted as you should in conducting the trials
of those denounced to you as Christians. Indeed, no form could be devised
which could be considered universally applicable. They should not be sought
out; if they should be denounced and convicted, they must be punished, but
nonetheless one who has denied that he is a Christian and has proven his
denial by his actions—that is, who has sacrificed to our gods—though suspect
in the past must nonetheless obtain mercy through his repentance. Anony-
mously posted lists should have no place in any trial. Such would be a bad
precedent and unworthy of these times.[9]

Most of the early emperors were like Trajan in their approach
to the Christians, the first exception being, as we've seen, Nero.
When ten of the city's fourteen regions were destroyed by a
terrible fire in 64 AD, Nero was unable to stop the rumor that he
himself, disgusted at the ugliness of the old city, had set the fires.
The rumor was false, for the emperor was actually at Antium when
the fire broke out, and even opened up his pleasure gardens to

provide relief for the homeless. When the rumors persisted, he chose the Christians as his scapegoats and saw to it that they were killed for his own entertainment: Some were dressed up in animal skins so that dogs tore them apart, and others were burned on crosses to illuminate his gardens at night. If anything, the emperors following Nero did what they could to be disassociated from such barbarity.[10]

Christian writers of the 5th century liked to say that Nero's was the first of ten great persecutions, that number neatly tallying with the ten plagues of Egypt and the ten horns on the beast in Daniel's vision. Eusebius and Lactantius offer endless tales of heroic death, of lucky martyrs killed by decapitation, and of less lucky ones torn apart by wild beasts, or ingeniously drawn and quartered, or slowly roasted over hot coals. All of these things undoubtedly happened, but provided as we are with the undeniable records of the Nazi holocaust, there's a tendency to project twentieth century barbarity back into the times of the ancient Romans. That tendency should be avoided or at least modified. The Christians were not massacred and persecuted indiscriminately right up to the time of Constantine; there were instead long periods of toleration. The Antonines generally imitated Trajan, Alexander Severus (ruled 222-235) allowed bishops at his court, and Philip the Arab (244-249) was even said to be a closet Christian. Notable exceptions were Decius (249-251) who made persecution of the Christians part of his campaign to bring back old time Roman morality, Valerian (252-260), and finally Diocletian, whose reign began what Eastern Christians used to call the "era of the martyrs." In chapter 40 we'll take a closer look at this most violent of the persecutions.[11]

The spread of Christianity was amazing, but not so amazing as is commonly assumed. At the time of Constantine's conversion only about 1/20 of the Roman empire was Christian, so that during the early persecutions we shouldn't imagine large numbers of executions. For instance, no bishop was killed until Cyprian in the 3rd century, under the reigns of Valerian and Gallienus; Eusebius tells us (*History of the Church* 6. 41) that the persecution of Decius in Alexandria claimed only 10 men and 7 women; and Gibbon is probably correct in estimating about 1,500 victims for the entire 10 year persecution instituted by Diocletian.[12] Naturally I feel uncomfortable measuring tyranny like salinity. Is one regime a thousand times more civilized than another because it butchers only a few thousand people instead of a few million? I guess not, but intent counts for something too. As we saw in Trajan's letter, most of the Roman emperors weren't out to get the Christians. As they saw it, they were confronted with a clearly treasonable sect which had to be kept under control. There were horrible exceptions to such calculating reasonableness, and we'll study the worst later on. We'll also see how it was turned around, first to toleration, and then to acceptance. As I've pointed out, the ultimate result of the persecutions was the victory of Christianity, a victory which gave the early Church fathers the opportunity to persecute and massacre the pagans. [13]

39 The Brother of Christ

Nero's most famous victims were the saints Paul and Peter. Paul was decapitated, and Peter, at his own request, was crucified upside down.[1] Paul had serious disagreements with Peter and the other disciples, but before his death he had completely revolutionized the Church and set it on the road to success.

Paul is what the Greek Christians called him; his real name was Saul, and he was born into a prominent Jewish family in Tarsus, Cilicia, a province in southeast Asia Minor just north of Cyprus. He was thus a product of the Hellenistic Jewish Diaspora, which explains the excellent Greek of his epistles. The synagogues of the Diaspora conducted their services in that language and read the Bible in the Alexandrian translation of the Old Testament called the Septuagint.[2] This did not, however, make Paul a Greek in culture, nor did it diminish the pride he felt in his Jewish heritage:

> Circumcised the eighth day, of the stock of Israel, of the tribe of Benjamin, an Hebrew of the Hebrews; as touching the law, a Pharisee (Epistle to the Philippians 3: 5).

As a member of the ultra conservative Pharisee sect, Paul was so outraged at the Christian heresy that he became one of its earliest persecutors: "He made a havock of the Church, entering into every house and hailing men and women committed them to prison."[3]

Then, quite inexplicably, Paul was himself converted to Christianity. The author of *Acts of the Apostles* tells the story of Paul's conversion three times, the first time most fully at 9: 1-30. In this version Paul was on his way to Damascus, under commission to persecute the Christians there, when a blinding light appeared along with a voice asking, "Saul, Saul, why persecutest thou me?" And so Paul was converted. His own version of these events in his *Epistle to the Galatians* is considerably less dramatic:

> But when it pleased God, who separated me from my mother's

womb, and called me by his grace, to reveal his son in me, that I
might preach him among the heathen; immediately I conferred not
with flesh and blood: neither went I up to Jerusalem to them which
were apostles before me; but I went into Arabia, and returned again
into Damascus. (Gal. 1: 15-17)

Although Paul did claim elsewhere to have been the last to see
Jesus raised from the dead (I Cor. 15: 8), the author of Acts seems,
as he so often does, to have supplied a simple-minded supernatural explanation for an intensely personal, mystical experience. It
would be fascinating to know the steps by which Paul changed
from committed persecutor to dedicated apostle, but we simply
don't have the evidence to reconstruct them. It's impossible for
twentieth century Americans to reproduce the experiences of first
century religious ecstatics. We only see flying saucers.[4]

Once Paul had been converted, his own logic brought him
inexorably into conflict with his own orthodox Judaism. Like the
other apostles,[5] Paul shared in Jesus' apocalyptic vision and
expected the imminent end of the world:

> For this we say unto you by the word of the Lord, that we which are
> alive and remain unto the coming of the Lord shall not prevent them
> which are asleep. For the Lord himself shall descend from heaven
> with a shout, with the voice of the archangel, and with the trump of
> God: and the dead in Christ shall rise first: Then we which are alive
> and remain shall be caught up together with them in the clouds, to
> meet the Lord in the air: and so shall we ever be with the Lord.[6]

However, unlike the other apostles and their Church in Jerusalem, Paul took this vision a step farther. If Jesus' death was indeed
the beginning of the end, then the new order had already begun,
and the old natural world was becoming something supernatural
and wonderful. Those who believed in Jesus shared through their
baptism in his death and resurrection. As companions of the
Messiah, elected by God from the beginning of time, they had
ceased to be natural men at all. What need had they therefore of
the Jewish law, which had been delivered to normal men?

> Wherefore the law was our schoolmaster to bring us unto Christ,
> that we might be justified by faith. But after that faith is come, we are
> no longer under a schoolmaster. . . There is neither Jew nor Greek,
> there is neither bond nor free, there is neither male nor female: For
> ye are all one in Christ Jesus.[7]

Before Paul, Gentiles who wished to join the new church were put under considerable pressure to become Jews as well. Since Jesus, his disciples, and all of the first Christians had been Jewish, this might seem reasonable, but being Jewish meant dealing with the thorny precepts of The Law. There were about 600 individual rules to follow,[8] including not only the strict kosher dietary rules against eating pork and shellfish, or mixing dairy products with meat, and so forth, but including also the necessity of circumcision, a prospect daunting to even the most devout convert.

Even during its first generation the Church was no monolith. Jewish converts from the Hellenistic Diaspora were a good deal more cosmopolitan than their Aramaic-speaking brethren: They were liberal about the Law and resisted the ruling by the Jerusalem Church that all Christians had to go under the knife. But Paul was even more radical than that. For him the Law had become a trap because it held out the illusion of a grace achievable through ritual and recipe. Such salvation was now impossible, for man was too unworthy to accomplish anything himself that could earn God's mercy. Only faith in Jesus could do that:

> For the Jews require a sign, and the Greeks seek after wisdom:
> But we preach Christ crucified, unto the Jews a stumblingblock, and unto the Greeks foolishness...[9]

By claiming that Christ had made the Law unnecessary, Paul had incidentally made the Church much easier for Gentiles to join. He felt moreover that God had directed him to undertake a Mission to the Gentiles (Acts 22: 17-21), and it was to this mission that he dedicated his career.

Unfortunately, once he had, and with considerable difficulty, convinced the original apostles that he was on their side (Acts 9: 26-28), he came into conflict with James, Jesus' brother,[10] who was dedicated heart and soul to the Jewish Law. As is typical in Eastern countries, a virtual "caliphate" had taken over Jesus' movement after his death, and his eldest brother became the first bishop of the Church of Jerusalem. James, who prayed so much that his knees were callused like a camel's, was nicknamed "The Righteous."[11]

Paul's Mission to the Gentiles further split the primitive Church and formed two warring camps. "Thou seest, brother," James and his elders scolded Paul, "how many thousands of Jews there are which believe; and they are informed of thee, that thou teachest all the Jews which are among the Gentiles to forsake Moses, saying that they ought not to circumcise their children, neither to walk after the customs."(Acts 21: 29-21) Poor St. Peter was caught in the middle, for when he generously broke the Law to eat with gentile Christians in Antioch, he found himself besieged by a delegation from James complaining of his uncleanliness and blasphemy. When he stopped seeing his Gentile friends, he was in turn attacked by Paul:

> We who are Jews by nature, and not sinners of the Gentiles. . . even we have believed in Jesus Christ, that we might be justified by the faith of Christ, and not by the works of the law: for by the works of the law shall no flesh be justified (Gal. 2: 15-16).

A council at Jerusalem described in Acts 15 seems to have arrived at a compromise (Galatians 2: 9), but it was short-lived.[12] During Paul's final visit to Jerusalem in 56 or 58 AD, James, having delivered the speech I've quoted above, asked Paul to perform an act of ritual purification in the Temple to prove to "the zealous" that he still respected the Law. Paul's appearance touched off so violent a demonstration that he had to be rescued by Roman troops. Paul had to endure two years of house arrest until the governor Festus decided to hand him over to the Sanhedrin. As a Roman citizen Paul appealed to Caesar. He was accordingly shipped off to Rome just in time for the persecutions.[13]

By the time of his death, however, Paul had changed everything, for his mission to the Gentiles was as resounding a success as James' to the Jews was a failure. It was James' and his followers' misfortune to offer the Jews hope through an apocalyptic myth just as events in Judaea were shattering that apocalyptic hope forever. James was killed about the same time as Paul, in 62 AD, during a period of confusion between the reigns of the procurators Festus and Albinus. The high priest Ananus II, fed up with James' proselytizing, told him to mount the parapet of the Temple and explain to the Jews the true nature of Jesus. "Why do you question me about the Son of Man?" James shouted down to the crowd, deliberately and provocatively employing his brother's apocalyptic title. "He is sitting in heaven on the right hand of the great power, and He will come upon the clouds of heaven." Outraged, the priests cast him down into the street, where he was stoned to death.[14]

James' Jewish-Christian church stayed on in Jerusalem until the destruction of the Temple, when it withdrew to Pella, a small town beyond the Jordan. Both its loss of the prestigious seat of Jerusalem and the success of rival, Gentile congregations in Antioch, Alexandria, Ephesus, Corinth, and Rome crippled its effectiveness. Finally, after the bar Cochba revolt, when Hadrian forbade Jerusalem to the Jews and constructed a rival capital in its place, the remnant of James' church elected a Gentile bishop named Marcus, who abrogated the Mosaic law for his flock. The conservative hold-outs were eventually labeled heretics.[15]

This is not to imply that everything was idyllic back in the Gentile Church, even though Acts certainly does present it as a communist paradise:

> And all that believed were together, and had all things in common; and sold their possessions and goods, and parted them to all men, as every man had need (Acts 2: 44-54).

Rich landowners sold their property and gave their money to the Church (4: 34-37); happy Christians in Ephesus gathered together their pagan books and burned them in a holy bonfire (19: 19); and we've already read in Pliny's letter how the Christians sang morning hymns to their God,[16] ate church breakfasts together, and were even open minded enough to appoint women as deacons.

Such harmony and coöperation is easy for people who believe that the world is about to blow up. When the end didn't come, and persecutions put increasing pressures on the Christian community, there is clear evidence that this voluntary discipline began to break down. Perhaps an even more insidious cause of unrest was Paul's own doctrine that the elect, through their mystical unity with Christ, were inspired by their faith to righteousness. Such heady stuff was easily open to exaggeration, and in his Second Epistle to the Corinthians Paul railed against a crowd of "superapostles" who had twisted his ideas into a premature and self-indulgent enjoyment of the Kingdom. It didn't take long for the Church to be filled up with phony prophets who sponged off the community, or with an embarrassing number of hysterics who would habitually disturb proceedings by going into convulsions and "speaking in tongues"–i.e. screaming a divinely inspired babble that only angels could understand.[17]

Paul himself had taken the first steps to curb this by assuming a position of authority as a God chosen apostle. The New Testament probably began as a collection of Paul's letters (or "epistles") of instruction to churches throughout the Roman world–to Galatia in Asia Minor, To Thessaly, Philippi, and Corinth in Greece, and to Rome. Acting like a pope centuries before such a concept or title even existed, Paul established the precedent of authority from above which the Catholic Church has followed ever since. "For, brethren," as he wrote, "ye have been called unto liberty; only use not liberty for an occasion to the flesh, but by love serve one another." (Gal. 5: 13)

The most famous of these instructional letters is the first epistle Paul sent to the swinging congregation at Corinth. He tells the Corinthians to drive fornicators, drunkards, and extortionists out of their church (I Cor. 5). He's shocked that members of the congregation were standing in the law courts before pagan judges. Better to suffer injustice! In one of the Church's earliest calls for a separate, canon law, he tells them to settle such matters among themselves. "Know ye not that we shall judge angels? How much more things that pertain to this life?" (6: 3) The famous and often recited chapter 13[18] is designed to diminish the respect accorded to hysterical speakers in tongues. Most of them (as in our own Salem witch trials) must have been women, for Paul tells women to keep quiet in Church and if bothered by any questions to ask their husbands at home! (14: 34-35)

Paul is very concerned with keeping women in their place, and with freeing men from their temptation. "It is good for a man not to touch a woman," he says (7: 1):

> I say therefore to the unmarried and widows. It is good for them if they abide even as I. But if they cannot contain, let them marry: for it is better to marry than to burn (7: 8-9).

It's because of Paul's instructions to the Corinthians that women wear hats in church today. As he explains it, the man is the image of God, and so shames God to cover his head, while women belong to men and so should be covered in church.

> Doth not even nature itself teach you, that, if a man have long hair, it is a shame unto him? But if a woman have long hair, it is a glory

to her: for her hair is given her for a covering (I Cor. 11: 14-15).

Again, we should point out that Paul's unrealistic sexual stance only makes sense within the apocalyptic concept of the last days. Cold showers can't work forever. Eventually the Church had to deal with the disappointed apocalyptic hope in a more fundamental fashion. This involved nothing less than abandoning Jesus' and Paul's concept of the Kingdom of God and shifting the whole message of the Church. As early as the Gospel of Matthew,[19] the author of which clearly believes in the *parousia* (παρουσία), or the second coming of Christ, the end of the world has been delayed to allow for the development of the Church as an institution.[20] As we've seen, the very concept of a second coming was foreign, both to Jesus' beliefs and to those of the evangelist Mark. Originally the resurrection and the *parousia* were conceived of as one act.

In Luke the *parousia* is even further postponed until some indefinite future, "until the times of the Gentiles be fulfilled" (Luke 21: 24). There is even textual evidence that in Luke's version of the Lord's Prayer (11: 2-4) the words "Thy kingdom come" were replaced by "Thy Holy Spirit come upon us and cleanse us." Most significant is the very presence of Luke's continuation, *The Acts of the Apostles.* Mark couldn't have written a "Gospel part II" because he didn't believe there would be time for a sequel to take place. For Luke, the creation of the Church becomes important for its own sake, so that his story of Paul clearly parallels his Gospel's account of the life of Jesus. Finally, by the Gospel of John, the concept of an apocalyptic return has been replaced by a vision of salvation upon earth through Jesus and his Church:[21]

> For God so loved the world, that he gave his only begotten son, that whosoever believeth in him should not perish, but have everlasting life. For God sent not his son into the world to condemn the world: but that the world through him might be saved (John 3: 16-17).

Primitive Christianity thus contained two dangerous ideas which had to be suppressed once the Church, as a self-perpetuating institution, began to evolve. First was the doctrine of the imminent end of the world, with its heady promise of rewards for the salt of the earth and dire punishments for the beautiful people. That would certainly attract the lower classes of Roman society, but it would also create dangerous unrest when their expectations for a better life were not fulfilled. *The Book of Revelation*, an almost hysterical exception to this movement away from apocalyptic, barely made it into the Bible and was almost rejected by the Council of Laodicea in 360.[22] Of course there are still apocalyptic cults today—the Jehovah's Witnesses, for example—but most Christian sects have always followed the attitude of the evangelist John. I can even remember a television preacher shouting at his flock, "Don't wait for pie in the sky bye and bye when you die! You can have it right now, with ice cream on top!"

Second, and perhaps even more dangerous, was Paul's belief in "justification by faith." As we've seen, the congregation at Corinth had already perverted this doctrine into the belief that a true follower of Christ was not a normal man hemmed in by the Law, but was rather joined with Christ and incapable of sin. It's not surprising that, with the exception of St. Augustine, Paul's theories have faded into the theological background. Significantly, Martin Luther in the 16th century would use the doctrine of justification by faith to rebel against what he felt to be the oppressive and tyrannical law of Mother Church.

Obviously, if the Church had to exist for an indefinite time upon the earth, if it had to discipline its members after the example of St. Paul, and if it were to survive the intermittent but nonetheless severe pressures of the persecutions, some sort of formal discipline would have to be imposed upon it. Back in the carefree, communistic days of the early Church the leaders of the separate congregations had been elected by the members. We call them bishops; the Greek term was *episkopos* (ἐπίσκοπος), literally overseer. As the power of the bishops increased, local clergy increasingly interfered in their election, until the democratic basis of the Church was destroyed. Bishops administered the sacraments, managed the ever increasing property of the Church, and eventually assumed the sole right to consecrate priests. Priests had originally, like the bishops, been elected by the people, but by the 3rd century bishops were claiming to be the direct heirs of the apostles. The Holy Spirit, it was believed, had descended upon the original 12 apostles at Pentecost. These had handed it on to their successors who, rather in the manner of an unbroken electric current, passed it on through an unbroken chain of bishops. Thus only a duly consecrated bishop, by laying his hands upon a candidate, could create a priest.

During the third and fourth centuries those bishops resident in the principal towns of a secular province assumed authority over the bishops in minor towns. These arch-bishops were called metropolitans (i.e. of the mother city) and were well on their way to becoming princes of the Church. Bishop Cyprian of Carthage, who was martyred in 258, was thus regally outraged at the suggestion of insult to a bishop:

> If such irregularities are suffered with impunity, there is an end of episcopal vigour; an end of the sublime and divine power of governing the Church; an end of Christianity itself.[23]

We'll have to look ahead almost to the 5th century for clear signs of these metropolitan bishops jockeying themselves into a hierarchy. Rome gradually claimed precedence, and not only because she was the traditional seat of empire. Hadn't two of the most famous apostles been martyred there, and hadn't Jesus offered to Peter, the first bishop of Rome, "the keys of the kingdom of heaven" (Matt. 16: 19)? The first Roman bishop to wage a real disciplinary authority over the West and issue what were really the first papal decrees was Bishop Sirice (384-399). He did not go unchallenged. The bishops of Constantinople and Alexandria were fiercely independent; Antioch in Syria had been one of the first Gentile churches; and of course Jerusalem, as the true metropolis, claimed a special allegiance. After the Council of Chalcedon in 451 these five metropolitan bishops were well on their way to becoming the five great patriarchs of early medieval Christianity.[24]

40 What Price Glory?

Literary historians have long since grown accustomed to using Hesiod's ages of metal[1] as a critical metaphor, so that the Golden Age of Augustus is perceived to degenerate into the Silver Age, covering the period between Tiberius and Hadrian (*i.e.* 14-135 AD).

The authors Pliny, Juvenal, Tacitus, and Suetonius, who wrote during this time, have already been woven into our story. They are great writers, but the sophistication and cynicism that characterize their style inevitably imply a certain lack of confidence, a loss of optimism. Later, as the Roman Empire reached its economic and territorial heights in the reign of the Antonines (Antoninus Pius, Marcus Aurelius, Lucius Varus, and Commodus, [138-192 AD]), its writers declined into slavish imitators and bombastic rhetoricians.[2]

No satisfactory diagnosis for the decline of the Roman Empire is possible–unless, of course, an appeal to the Second Law of Thermodynamics[3] can be called satisfactory. The best we can do is to point out some glaring symptoms and then in this and the following chapter to explain how the fall was delayed by a second Augustus named Diocletian. Like the first emperor he was a brilliant though fundamentally unattractive manager. His cure, the next logical step after Augustus's, froze the Roman state in place to stand against the final shock of the barbarian invasions.

As early as our chapter on Tiberius Gracchus we saw evidence for Rome's fundamental weakness: the gradual concentration of land and wealth into the hands of the aristocracy. Just as Marius was forced to recruit in the slums of Rome, by the 2nd century the emperor Hadrian was scouring the provinces for semi-barbaric troops. Hadrian had no choice, for by his day Italy had no free farmers left. It was a land of agribusiness and impoverished tenant farmers. As a logical culmination of this process, when the Antonines gave way to Septimius Severus in 193, he naturally seized the land of his rivals, concentrating virtually all of the arable land of the empire in the imperial household. This move turned farmers into serfs imprisoned on the imperial estates. They couldn't be recruited, for it was their duty to stay on the land and grow crops for the army. When Septimius's son Caracalla extended the Roman citizenship to all members of the empire, it wasn't in a gesture of reconciliation and unification. It simply extended the government's power of exploitation over its entire population of citizen-slaves. Caracalla put it most succinctly: "No one but myself ought to have money, and that in order to give it to the soldiers."[4]

Of course the army remained the force which made exploitation possible. Two violent revolutions framed the century of peace and prosperity that followed on the Julio Claudian emperors. The first, which resulted in the death of the fiddler Nero, also taught the army the fateful lesson that "emperors could be made elsewhere than at Rome."[5] Having already been corrupted by large increases in pay since republican times and by donatives that were now little more than bribes, the army created four emperors that year (69 AD). The soldiers happily followed the winners, Titus Flavius Vespasianus and his son Titus, who are most characteristically remembered by the Colosseum they built and the Jewish Revolt they put down. Their imperialist policy of necessity increased the state's dependency on the army that had put them on the throne.

The army, however, changed radically under Vespasian. He had no faith in the Roman rabble: They had murdered his own brother Sabinus, Prefect of the City of Rome (Suetonius, *Vitellius* 15. 3) and had contributed disastrously to the chaos of the end of the Republic. Vespasian thus banned the Roman citizens of Italy from the regular legions, turning instead for his troops to the landowners and farmers of the provinces. So in the second century the army was still made up of Roman citizens, at least on paper, but they were no longer townspeople, who now did their best to avoid military service, but rather provincial peasants and country folk. At least socially the Roman army returned to its roots.[6]

The palace plot that killed Vespasian's younger son, the monster Domitian, set the stage for "the good emperors," Nerva, Trajan, Hadrian, and the Antonines, who nonetheless continued the imperialist, expansionist policies of their Flavian predecessors. Trajan's interminable wars stretched the boundaries of Rome to their greatest extent, annexing Dacia (i.e. Rumania), Arabia (Jordan and the Sinai), and Mesopotamia—a policy designed more to keep the army busy than to keep it under control.

The wars were expensive too, and despite the outward appearance of prosperity, the empire of the 2nd century established the pattern of taxation which led to its own destruction. Ruinous and unexpected emergency taxes were constantly inflicted upon the prosperous commercial classes, who were gradually driven into bankruptcy. The empire started to cannibalize its own capital.[7]

The murder of Commodus, the deranged son of the philosopher king Marcus Aurelius, marked the second great revolution and the inauguration of the time of troubles. We have already seen what Septimius Severus, the survivor of that revolution, did to the economic basis of the state. He similarly instructed his son Caracalla "to secure the affection of the army, and to esteem the rest of his subjects as of little moment."[8] Taking that advice Caracalla bribed his soldiers shamefully, a necessary precaution since he had murdered their favorite, his own brother Geta. It did him no good, for while relieving himself by the side of the road he was knifed by one of his soldiers.[9] In the 67 years between Caracalla's death and the accession of Diocletian, the empire was treated to no less than 30 "barrack room emperors," only one of whom managed to die a natural death.

Of course the old peasant army fell apart under such pressure and was replaced by gangs of mercenaries recruited among the most uncivilized inhabitants of the wild frontier: northern Greeks and Illyrians, Arabs, Celtic Britains, and even Germans.

With the army so preoccupied with civil war and revolution, the empire's borders began to collapse. Franks, Alamanni, and Goths broke through the Rhine and Danube frontiers, while to the East the Sasanian Persians under Ardashir I (Artaxerxes) overthrew the Parthians, reëstablished Zoroastrianism in their land, and threatened the eastern half of the Roman Empire. In 260 their king Shabuhr I (Sapor) captured the emperor Valerian and used him as a stepping stone to mount on his horse. When the emperor died he was stuffed and kept in the Persians' temple as a momento.[10]

Wildly increasing military expenses required increased revenues. The government could always steal food and supplies from the peasants—which benighted action drove them from their farms

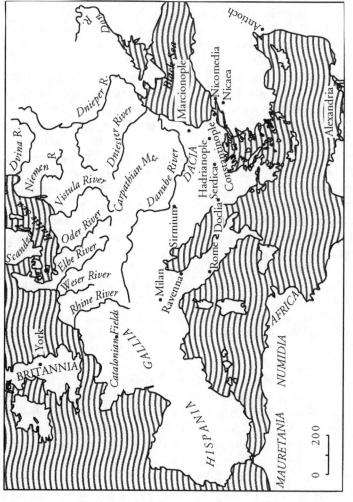

Europe at the Time of the Later Roman Empire

and so further decreased production—but the only source of ready cash was debasement of the currency, the ancient equivalent of printing more money. Here are some figures: under the emperors Augustus and Tiberius the *denarius*, at that time a coin weighing about 4 grams of almost pure silver, was valued at 1,050 to the pound of gold. It was only 67% pure silver under Commodus and reached only 43% under Septimius Severus; by the time of Diocletian's edict of prices (301 AD), the *denarius* (now only a nominal currency used for calculations) had fallen to 50,000 to the pound of gold![11]

Such conditions might well have ended the Roman empire by the end of the 3rd century, but instead the new Persian empire became distracted by its own internal problems while the German tribes, who never had been united, were still waiting like vampires for the foolish Romans to invite them in as destroyers of their own house. Thus the final set of barrack room emperors, even though they still tended to be murdered by their troops, began to turn the tide.

The last and most successful of these was Valerius Diocles, named after Doclia, the village in Illyria (modern "former Yugoslavia") where his mother was born. His father had been a slave who, just like the poet Horace's father in the days of Augustus, had earned his freedom and taken work as a government scribe. Diocletian, as he came to be called, entered the army and worked his way up through the ranks to the command of the imperial body guard. Having achieved a considerable reputation fighting against the Persians, he was hailed as emperor by the troops on Sept 17, 284 after the emperor Numerian, long in poor health, was "nosed out" to be dead in his tent. Diocletian marched west to defeat his former employer's brother Carinus, a self-indulgent and roundly despised weakling, and then went on to remake the Roman state in a pattern that would hold for another 300 years.[12]

Diocletian's major talent, as has already been pointed out, was managerial, so that his first important move was to delegate authority. On March 1, 286 he appointed as junior partner in the empire another Illyrian peasant from Sirmium (Sremska) named Maximian. He was illiterate and cruel, but undeniably efficient and loyal to his master. Diocletian took the title "Jovius" and gave his colleague that of "Herculius," and they fit. In the role of Jupiter Diocletian could act as the father of the state, while the club-wielding, lion skin clad Hercules could act the part of enforcer. Six months later Maximian was officially raised to the rank of Augustus.

There was, however, so much fighting to do that in 293 Diocletian decided on a second level of command to be called "Caesar." The idea was that each Augustus would appoint a second in command who would both help him in his military duties and eventually succeed him as Augustus. Such a system would prevent both civil wars and body counts upon the death of every emperor, and would also divide the too powerful and independent army into four units, each of which could be encouraged to keep an eye out on the other.

As his own colleague Diocletian chose an obscenely fat and violently tempered peasant from Dacia (Rumania) named Galerius whom, to cement the union, he married off to his daughter Valeria. In 297 Galerius proved himself by defeating the Persian king Narses in Armenia, capturing the king's family during the battle, and subsequently at Nisibis negotiating a highly favorable treaty which kept the peace between the two empires until the time of Constantine.

As his Caesar, Maximian chose Flavius, nicknamed Chlorus ("Whitey"). He was another Yugoslavian peasant, this time from Dardania in south Serbia. In order to marry Maximian's step-daughter Theodora, Constantius Chlorus was forced to divorce the bar maid Helena to whom he was already married. That in itself wouldn't be important to us, except that Helena was the mother of a young boy named Constantine, the hero of our next chapter and, eventually, the first Christian emperor of Rome. Though we probably can't go along with bishop Eusebius and say that Constantine's palace "differed in no respect from a Church of God,"[13] it will be apparent that Constantius was the least savage of the four tetrarchs. Thirty years later Constantine's mother would reappear from hiding, transformed into a saint of the Catholic Church. In the meantime young Constantine was shipped off to Diocletian's court to serve as a hostage for his father's loyalty—just like Moses, a comparison Eusebius never tires of making.

Constantius's military chore was to reconquer England, which had risen in rebellion under a leader named Carcusius. Carcusius was killed by a subordinate shortly before Constantius launched his invasion, which quickly reconquered the island. The empire could then settle down into a neat, four-part division: The two Augusti received the more honorable, which is to say the richer, part of the empire—Diocletian the East (Thrace, Egypt, and Asia), and Maximian Italy along with Africa. The Caesars were placed on the more risky Danube and Rhine frontier: Constantius guarded Britain, Gaul, and Spain, while Galerius was placed on the banks of the Danube to watch the Illyrian provinces.[14]

More important than the four-part division or "tetrarchy," however, and certainly longer lasting, were the fundamental changes which Diocletian imposed upon the Roman empire. As can be seen, he had already taken the first steps which would eventually lead to the Roman Empire's being split into two halves, a Latin speaking West and a Greek speaking East. That would happen officially after the death of the emperor Theodosius the Great in 395, who on his deathbed bequeathed the two halves of his realm to his sons Honorius and Arcadius. Diocletian certainly wasn't contemplating such a disfigurement, but it's characteristic of states in their decline that the central government loses its authority and thus its ability to control and organize large areas. Virtually as an admission of this, Diocletian was forced further to subdivide his four part empire into twelve new units called dioceses. He similarly began a long process of chopping up the old provinces–the larger ones into four or five pieces.[15] Later on the Christian Church would appropriate the term "diocese" into its own hierarchy.

Another indication of the slippage of authority was the conscious imposition of Persian court ceremonial upon court life. We described in chapter 35 the easy access and relatively simple lifestyle of Augustus's court; this had been exaggerated during the period of the barrack room emperors when, thanks to the dreary succession of assassinations, it could perhaps be said "that a military government is, in certain regards, more republican than monarchical."[16] Like a fanatic who's lost his sense of humor, however, Diocletian insisted that the emperor be treated like a god. He crowned himself with the diadem,[17] dressed in sumptuous silks, and barricaded himself in his palace behind a wall of eunuchs.

> I heard from my father that the emperor Diocletian, once he became a private citizen, remarked, "Nothing is more difficult than to rule well." Four or five men get together and make up a plan to deceive the emperor. They say what he must approve. The emperor, who is shut up in the palace, does not know the truth. He is forced to know only that which they tell him. He appoints judges when he shouldn't; he removes those from the republic whom he should retain. In short, as Diocletian himself put it, "Even a good, careful, and excellent emperor is up for sale."[18]

Those who were ushered into the emperor's divine presence were made to prostrate themselves in the self-same gesture that had caused one of Alexander's Macedonian officers to snicker.[19]

Completely in accordance with the conception of the divine emperor, the portraits of Diocletian on his coins lose individuality and become not only idealized, but identical with those of the other three tetrarchs. It's no longer the individual who is being honored, but rather the idea of emperor.[20]

We have earlier made mention of the seemingly obvious fact that governments depend ultimately upon the consent of those they pretend to govern. Since Diocletian could no longer depend upon the functioning of this social contract, he consistently set out to force civic responsibility upon his subjects. Because peasants were going bankrupt through inflation, taxation, and the organized brigandage of soldiers and bureaucrats, they now had to be forced by law to stay on the farms and act the part of good serfs. Similarly the sons of soldiers, who were now chopping off toes and fingers to get out of the army, had to be turned into an hereditary caste of state servants. Most surprising was the plight of town counselors or decurions; formerly a sought after position of honor, the decuriate had become an intolerable burden since its holders were now responsible for all the taxes that the impoverished peasants of their towns could no longer afford to pay. Decurions were desperately paying bribes to escape their hereditary honors and so now had to be forced by law to accept them.[21]

Such a character as Diocletian's inevitably succumbed to the enticing allurement of wage and price controls when inflation, fueled in fact by his own practices, threatened to ruin the Roman economy. Diocletian's victories in the East had provided him with a lot of gold and silver, from which he struck coins of fine quality, but their presence in the economy only emphasized the worthlessness of the huge amount of cheap silver-washed copper coins already in circulation. Industry in the empire was, by our standards, ridiculously labor intensive; virtually everything was made by hand. When this primitive industry was unable to produce goods in the abundance demanded by a new, peace time economy, prices shot up and the worthless coinage collapsed—"not fourfold or eightfold, but more than human speech could possibly describe."[22]

To stop this inflation, Diocletian issued in 301 his "Edict of Prices" containing the maximum prices for all goods and services in the empire.[23] In his incredibly turgid preface, he blamed the inflation not, of course, on his own policies, but rather on the greed of speculators who would stoop even to astrology and black magic to ruin the harvests of the empire. "Since," he continued, "fear has always been found to be the most efficient instructor in duty," he determined to punish all violations of the maximum with death.

It didn't work. All the edict managed to do was to drive now unprofitable goods into the black market. Clumsy enforcement led first to bloody riots and then to the complete abandonment of controls. That made matters worse, for with no controls at all inflation drove the good money off the market, condemning the entire empire to an economy of barter.[24]

The final and most dramatic change which Diocletian imposed upon the state was his organized persecution of the Christians. It is, indeed, hardly surprising that as autocratic an emperor as Diocletian would object to a new religion which in accordance with the commands of its founder inspired loyalties superior to those normally reserved for state and family. This wasn't of course the state's first persecution against the Christians, but since the death of Domitian in 96 AD the Church had been treated to an imperial attitude much closer to Trajan's than Nero's. The change instituted by Diocletian was so violent that his reign came to be looked upon by the Church as the "era of the martyrs."[25]

It began during the Persian campaign in 298. During a sacrifice the chief priest Tagis told the emperor that the sacrifices were being spoiled by unbelievers who were making the sign of the cross. Diocletian, who was as dedicated to the old-time religion as his predecessor Augustus, angrily ordered all those in his palace and in his army to sacrifice to the gods or be whipped and driven from service. He was satisfied at that, but not so his Caesar Galerius, whose mother had been a pagan priestess and who apparently fostered a rankling hate against the Christians.

Following the campaign the two tetrarchs wintered in Nicomedia, where Galerius began working on his master. He bribed the oracle of Apollo at Miletus to announce that his oracles were fallacious since "the righteous men on earth were a bar to his speaking the truth." When Diocletian asked a priest who these righteous men were, he was naively told "the Christians." That did it, and the emperor unleashed the persecutions.

February 23, 303, which was the Festival of the Terminalia, was chosen as the opening date. Armed troops and treasury officers marched into the great cathedral at Nicomedia, had the doors torn off, burned the scriptures, and leveled the Church to the ground. Next day in Nicomedia an edict was posted announcing that Christians were stripped of all dignities and were liable to punishment without any recourse to law. Some brave fellow tore down the edict in public and was slowly roasted to death for his trouble.

Subsequently within a two week period two fires broke out in the royal palace. Lactantius, who was living in Nicomedia at the time, repeats a local rumor that both fires were set by Galerius in order to frame the Christians. Whether or not that's true, after Galerius fled the palace—to escape being burned alive, as he put it—Diocletian turned vicious. Faithful and previously all powerful eunuchs were executed, priests and deacons were arrested, and the faithful perished "wholesale and in heaps"—either burned or cast into the sea.[26] Letters were sent both to Maximian and Constantius to go along with the persecutions. Maximian obeyed happily, being a man of slight mercy by nature, but Constantius dragged his feet, confining his actions to church buildings and property while sparing the Christians themselves. Like Diocletian, Constantius apparently had Christians at court, but he seems to have looked upon them with favor.[27]

The persecutions brought Diocletian to the 20th anniversary of his reign, which he decided to celebrate by going to Rome, apparently for the first time in his life. He didn't like the city, however, and left for Ravenna even before ceremoniously assuming his ninth consulship on January 1, 304. It was winter, however, and he fell sick; by the time he got back to Nicomedia the illness had become serious—so much so that by mid December it was assumed that the emperor was dead. When he suddenly made a public appearance on March 1, he appeared so ravaged as to be barely recognizable. Shortly afterwards he announced his intention of resigning.

Diocletian abdicated before his army in a ceremony held three miles from his palace in Nicomedia. At the same time Maximian tendered his resignation in his palace at Milan—not, as subsequent events would prove, at all voluntarily. Although there were two sons among the tetrarchs who might have seemed to be the logical successors—Maxentius, the son of Maximian, and Constantine, the son of Constantius—both of these were passed over. Galerius, who had joined Diocletian at Nicomedia, may have had something to do with this. After all, both he and Diocletian had no legitimate sons of their own, and the two men may have been jealous of their colleagues. There was also the example of the "good emperors" Nerva, Trajan, Hadrian, and Antoninus Pius, each of whom had appointed his successor, as well as the inescapable fact that Maxentius was an idiot, and that Constantine was too young.

Still, the substitutes were not too promising. In the West a peasant soldier named Severus would take over Pannonia, Italy, and Africa, nominally serving as Caesar under the Augustus Constantius, but actually loyal to Galerius. Diocletian is supposed to have called him "that turbulent, drunk dancer, who makes day into night and night into day." As Caesar of the East the new Augustus Galerius chose his nephew, a former shepherd named Daia, whom he renamed after himself Maximin Daia. The soldiers in Nicomedia were thunderstruck when Galerius shoved aside the popular, young Constantine and invested this "semibarbaric young man" with Diocletian's own purple robes.[28]

It did not bode well for the future peace of the Empire. Maximian had obviously been forced into retirement and would certainly not be content to take Diocletian's advice to give up glory for the joy of raising cabbages. Also waiting in the wings was an old tent companion of Galerius named Licinius. Galerius had passed him over as Caesar but promised one day to make him Augustus and guardian of his love child Candidianus, then a boy of nine years. Constantine certainly felt less than safe in the court of his former emperor. Having cajoled Galerius into signing him a safe conduct, he galloped off to the West before the new Augustus changed his mind. Constantine met his father at York, where Constantius had just time enough to commend him to his soldiers before he died. The British army hailed Constantine as Augustus. He was about twenty years old.[29]

41 Onward, Christian Soldiers!

Galerius had a lot to worry about. Young Constantine would have been trouble enough, but Galerius foolishly made an enemy of Rome, a city which he had never even seen. He leaked plans to tax the lazy Roman people for the first time in their history, to disband their spoiled Praetorian Guard, and perhaps even to change the name of the empire from "Roman" to "Dacian." Since he had also insulted Maxentius, the idiot son of Maximian, by passing him over as a candidate for the purple, it was only natural for these two common enemies to gang up against him: Some soldiers in Rome revolted, killed their magistrates, and declared Maxentius as their emperor. Maxentius, temporarily gushing with good will and toleration, wooed the Christians by abandoning the persecutions and the pagans by rebuilding the Temple of Venus.

Galerius retaliated by ordering his protégé Severus to march on Rome. This proved to be a mistake. It gave Maximian the very excuse he needed to come out of his forced retirement and rescue a son whom he seems genuinely to have despised. Severus's men deserted him under the walls of Rome. He fled to Ravenna where the old soldier Maximian besieged him, accepted his surrender, and graciously permitted him to slit his wrists.[1]

Fearing that his actions would force Galerius to link up with Maximin Daia and invade Italy, which indeed proved to be the case, Maximian crossed the Alps for a meeting with Constantine. He could offer Constantine both the authority of the old tetrarchy and marriage to his little daughter Fausta. Constantine accepted and so (just like his father) had to divorce his wife Minervina, who had just given him a son named Crispus. Galerius meanwhile fell on Maxentius in Rome, but was defeated both by the unexpected size of the city and by the disloyalty of his own troops, many of whom deserted to Maxentius in disgust. Galerius scurried back east, looting as he went; when he arrived in Nicomedia he replaced Severus with his old friend Licinius, whom he now promoted to the rank of Augustus. Constantine had the good sense to stay out of the fighting. He was primarily interested in the balance of power, which could only be tilted in his favor if his friends and enemies killed each other off.[2]

There were now, by the way, six emperors: Maximian, Maxentius, and Constantine in the West; Galerius, Licinius, and Maximin Daia in the East. Under such conditions peace was impossible. The best that could be hoped for was truce. Such truce as there was, however, was destroyed between the years 308-310 by the death of the two senior emperors.

Maximian went first, driven on by what Lactantius calls his "puerile jealousy" of his son. In what seems to have been an attempted coup, Maximian tore the purple robes of imperial office from his son's shoulders during a general convocation of their troops. The plan backfired, however, and as the soldiers hooted their disapproval, the old man was driven from Rome "like another Tarquin the Proud."[3] He fled to Galerius in Illyricum where he met briefly with his old boss Diocletian, who had left his cabbages to attend the coronation of Licinius. Diocletian and Galerius forced the old tetrarch to retire once again; frustrated and disappointed, Maximian fled to his son-in-law Constantine in Gaul.

It was in Gaul that Maximian made his final play for power. As soon as Constantine marched off to the Rhine frontier to chastise some Gauls, Maximian seized the royal treasury at Arles and declared himself emperor again. Constantine hurried back by forced marches to bottle up a surprised Maximian in Marseilles. While he attempted to negotiate a treaty from the walls, the city was betrayed to Constantine by the disgruntled soldiers. After some friendly encouragement the emperor Maximian seems to have hanged himself in his cell.[4]

Constantine now broke with the tradition of the tetrarchy, tearing down the statues of Maximian and, by necessity, the images of Diocletian attached to them. The original Diocletian collapsed at about the same time and died of the long, lingering illness that always seems to attack persecutors of the Christians in our surviving sources. Instead of the old image of the tetrarchy, the likeness of Sol, the son god, now appears on Constantine's coins.[5]

The last surviving member of the tetrarchy soon followed his master, for in 310 the inevitable malady attacked Galerius's fat, flabby body: Starting in his genitals it spread inward to his bowels, which swelled and filled with worms until his whole carcass stank and rotted.[6] Before his death however, he had a change of heart, the motives for which may tell us much about the subsequent conversion of Constantine. Very possibly under the influence of his friend Licinius, Galerius decided on his deathbed that his vicious persecution of the Christians might have been the cause of his terrible disease. From the wording of his edict it doesn't sound like a conversion; rather Galerius simply seems to have recognized the power of the Christian demons and to have decided to pay them their due. In this "Edict of Serdica" Galerius says that he originally persecuted the Christians in an attempt to get them to return to the religious practices of their ancestors. Given the fact, however, that their persistent obstinacy had not only cost many of them their lives, but had also prevented them from praying to any gods at all, he decided to allow them to rebuild their churches and recommence the worship of their god:

> As a result of this our indulgence they should prey to their own god for our salvation and for that of the Republic and of themselves, so that the state may be safe all around, and so that they may live secure in their own homes.[7]

The original preamble contained the names of all four emperors: Galerius, Constantine, Licinius, and Maximin Daia. As future events would prove, Maximin was an unwilling participant, whose forced signature may have only increased the jealousy he felt of both Licinius and Constantine. At any rate, both the edict and the prayers it inspired seem to have done no good, for the worms won out, and Galerius died the following month, May 311.

Licinius and Maximin Dia split his empire at the Bosporus, where they met like Napoleon and Czar Alexander to shake hands. Given the location of Licinius's territory, which reached westward to the Alps, it's not surprising that he would gravitate towards Constantine, the ruler of Gaul and England. So when Constantine contracted yet another marriage bed alliance by giving his half-sister Constantia to Licinius, Maximin Daia sent word to Maxentius in Rome to formulate their own *entente*. Constantine might have had no direct reason to fear Maxentius or to attack Italy, but the Roman senatorial class had become fed up with Maxentius's exorbitant taxes and heavy-handed government. In Eusebius this dissatisfaction has been transformed into stories of the rape of Christian virgins and the vivisection of babies. Undoubtedly senatorial embassies visited Constantine and without much difficulty reinforced his own dissatisfaction with the presence of a disgruntled in-law on his southern flank. Constantine was forced to leave over half his troops behind to guard the Rhine frontier, but he nonetheless marched into Italy with 40,000 infantry and 8,000 cavalry. Maxentius could boast 170,000 foot soldiers and 18,000 cavalrymen, numerous but soft from long residence in the capital.[8]

Constantine fought two difficult battles at Turin and Verona, but the fight everyone remembers was at the Milvian Bridge about nine miles outside of Rome. There Constantine faced Maxentius and his army stationed with the Tiber at their backs, and there occurred one of the most famous miracles of early Christianity. The story comes from Eusebius's *Life of Constantine:*

> And while he was thus praying with fervent entreaty, a most marvelous sign appeared to him from heaven, the account of which it might have been hard to believe had it been related by any other person. But since the victorious emperor himself long afterwards declared it to the writer of this history, when he was honored with his acquaintance and society, and confirmed his statement by an oath, who could hesitate to accredit the relation, especially since the testimony of after-time has established its truth? He said that about noon, when the day was already beginning to decline, he saw with his own eyes the trophy of a cross of light in the heavens, above the sun, and bearing the inscription, CONQUER BY THIS. At this sight he himself was struck with amazement, and his whole army also, which followed him on the expedition, and witnessed the miracle.[9]

Everyone knows this story, and the miraculous Latin inscription *in hoc signo vinces* even appears on packages of Pall Mall cigarettes. Rationalists have even suggested natural phenomena to account for the miracle and thus have attributed Constantine's conversion to a freak of nature.[10] Nonetheless, the miracle never happened. Eusebius himself makes no mention of it in his earlier account of the same battle (*History of the Church* 9. 9), nor does it appear on the Arch of Constantine (where the victory is attributed to the pagan sun god!), in contemporary coins and panegyrics (*i.e.* set speeches of praise delivered in the emperor's presence) or in the account of Lactantius. This silence contrasts suspiciously with the wide publicity on coins and statues granted by Marcus

Aurelius to the "miraculous storm of rain" which saved a Roman army in Moravia.[11]

The origin of the legend seems to be Lactantius's report of a dream that visited Constantine at some unspecified location. The sign in that dream was our old friend the Egyptian *ankh* ♀ which the emperor was told to inscribe on the shields of his soldiers as the sign of Christ.[12] At any rate, back at the battle the now Christian soldiers of Constantine drove Maxentius and his followers back to the Milvian bridge, which they had foolishly cut behind them. As they crowded onto a pontoon bridge hastily assembled next to the original stone structure, Maxentius was pushed off into the Tiber; he and his armor sank like a stone, and the battle was quickly decided.[13]

It makes no sense either to claim that Constantine lied to the gullible Bishop Eusebius or to look for rationalistic, quasi-scientific explanations. The conversation we quoted above most certainly occurred, but it took place many years after the event, by which time Constantine's Christianity had become a good deal more sophisticated (relatively speaking) and exclusive than it had been in the early days. We should warn ourselves not to think of Constantine and Eusebius in twentieth century terms, nor to expect historical accuracy from historians and emperors who were concerned with loftier matters. For someone like Constantine one miracle was as good as another. Indeed, is a flaming cross any more a miracle than the conversion of a sinner?[14] What the emperor told the bishop was a dramatization of his internal conversion, and there's no reason to doubt that he came to believe it himself.

Once in Rome Constantine executed Maxentius's two sons along with a flock of trouble-makers, but he didn't set up the general executions which were normal in those days. He remodeled a basilica recently completed by Maxentius and placed in its western end a colossal statue of himself, seven times life size. Eusebius tells us that the statue held a cross in its right hand and bore the inscription, "By virtue of this salutary sign, which is the true test of valor, I have preserved and liberated your city from the yoke of tyranny. I have also set at liberty the Roman Senate and people, and restored them to their ancient distinction and splendor."[15]

What Constantine didn't restore was that ancient freedom from taxation on account of which the Romans had supported Maxentius in the first place. The richest were especially hard hit, and from now on owed the emperor eight pounds of gold annually. Constantine only stayed in Rome for two or three months and only visited the city twice more during his lifetime. Rome would never have especially pleasant associations for him.[16]

In January 313 Constantine proceeded to Milan to meet with his brother-in-law Licinius. Their main problem was Maximin Daia, who was disobeying Galerius's edict of toleration and slaughtering Christians in the East. Maximin had even paid the Church the ultimate compliment of imitating its organization: He set up pagan bishops whom he called "great priests" in each city and "pontifices" (i.e. archbishops) in each province, while he himself would only eat meat sacrificed by his pagan priests.[17] In response to this outrage and of course to undermine the authority of Maxentius's ally, the two western emperors issued the famous Edict of Milan in March of 313. It does not establish Christianity as the state religion, which establishment would not occur until the year 395; it is instead an edict of general toleration, and that in surprisingly general terms:

> ...we give both to the Christians and to all people the freedom to follow whatsoever religion each wishes, so that whatever divine power is seated in heaven may be well and kindly disposed to us and to all who have been constituted under our power.[18]

The same generalized terms were heard again in April when Licinius and Maximin fought a great battle. Maximin Daia had invaded Licinius' s territory and besieged Byzantium, so that Licinius was forced to march from Milan, raising troops on the way, to meet the enemy at Hadrianople. He had about 30,000 troops to the 70,000 of Maximin Daia. As Lactantius tells it, the night before the battle an angel appeared to Licinius and told him to have his men pray to God in the following prayer:

> Highest god, we beseech you, highest god, we beseech you: we entrust to you all justice, we entrust to you our safety, we entrust to you our dominion. Through you we live, through you are we victorious and blessed. Highest, holy god, hear our prayers: we stretch out our arms to you: Hear us, holy, highest god.[19]

The prayer is remarkably non-sectarian, assuming that the an-

gel who delivered it was a Christian. Of course its very vagueness
made it suitable both to the Dacian pagans in Licinius's army and
to the closet Christians in Maximin's, many of whom would be
seriously disgruntled by the persecutions in the East. Licinius won
a great victory. Maximin Daia fled to Tarsus, executed his pagan
priests for having deceived him, took poison, and died in agony
four days later. Licinius quickly arrived to execute a revenge
roundly praised by our Christian sources: he killed the surviving
children of Maximin, Galerius, and Severus along with the daughter and widow of his old benefactor Diocletian.[20]

It should be obvious by now that originally there was nothing
exclusive about Constantine's Christianity. There is no need to
imagine some compromise between the Christianity of
Constantine and the paganism of Licinius in order to explain the
vague wording of the Edict of Milan; the wording reflects the typical, almost militant syncretism of the educated classes in late antiquity, who looked upon all eastern mystery cults as separate
manifestations of the same, universal god. This can be seen as early
as the second century in Apuleius's novel *The Golden Ass*, especially where the goddess Isis addresses the assified hero Lucius:

> Behold me, the primordial parent, the mistress of all elements, the
> initial progeny of the world, highest of the gods, queen of shades,
> first of the heavenly powers, the uniform manifestation of gods and
> goddesses...whose single power the whole world worships in
> multifarious forms, in various rites and under diverse names.[21]

As late as 390 Maximus of Madaura could use language strikingly similar to that of the Edict of Milan or of Licinius's prayer:

> There is only one God, sole and supreme, without beginning or
> parentage, whose energies, diffused through the world, we invoke
> under various names, because we are ignorant of his real name. By
> successively addressing our supplications to his different members
> we intend to honor him in his entirety. Through the mediation of
> the subordinate gods the common father both of themselves and of
> all men is honored in a thousand different ways by mortals who are
> thus in accord in spite of their discord.[22]

In his coinage, Constantine himself successively addressed
Christ Jesus, Hercules the Victorious, Mars and Jupiter the Pre-
servers, and of course Aurelian's cult favorite, the Invincible Sun

(Sol Invictus).[23] Even as late as 321 Constantine could publish
simultaneously two edicts, one setting up the observance of Sunday and the other demanding regular consultation of the Aus-
pices.[24] Constantine did not convert to Christianity all at once,
nor did he take the first steps in a flash of religious enthusiasm.
We've already seen how Maximin Daia tried to ape the organiza-
tional strength of the Church by imposing its order upon the
Roman state cult. Constantine did him one better and embraced
not only Christianity's bishop-managers, but the salutary magic
of the new cult as well.[25]

As we saw in the story of Akhnaton, a country with only one
God requires a government with only one emperor. Constantine
and his surviving partner first fell out in 314 when Licinius encouraged Constantine's brother-in-law to revolt. After the battle
of Cibalae from which, Eusebius tells us, Constantine graciously
allowed his enemy to escape, the two Augusti kept a formal truce
for eight years. During that time Constantine grew stronger thanks
to victories won by both himself and his son Crispus over the
Germans and the Goths; Licinius meanwhile became excessive
in his persecution of the Christians, eventually giving Constantine
the excuse he needed to invade the East.

Licinius was defeated three times, first at Hadiranople, then at
Byzantium, where Crispus sank his fleet, and finally across the
straits at Chrysopolis, on Sept. 18, 324. Thanks to his wife
Constantia he was given a safe conduct to Thessalonika where,
however, Constantine had him hanged on a trumped-up charge
of conspiring with the barbarians.

> Thus, as he was the first to proclaim to all the sole sovereignty of
> God, so he himself, as sole sovereign of the Roman world, extended
> his authority over the whole human race.[26]

42 One Substance

Symbols are important, both to people and to nations, so it's hardly surprising that the new Augustus would set out to found a new Rome. It was consecrated on May 11, 330, and was naturally constructed in the East, where there was still a draftable pool of soldiers, a healthy urban life, and what we nowadays call a viable economy. Instead of starting from scratch, Constantine rebuilt the ancient city of Byzantium, which is located on the European side of the Bosphorus at the end of one of the best natural harbors in the world. His title of "New Rome" was quickly changed by popular usage into Constantinople, "the City of Constantine."

Constantine raided the plantations of Italy and the temples of Asia to populate and embellish his new city, whose walls by the time of Theodosius the Great enclosed 2,000 densely populated acres. At the eastern end of the city Constantine constructed a stately forum, in the center of which, on a 120 foot high porphyry and marble pillar, was a colossal bronze statue of himself. To the southeast, closer to the Propontis, was the city's (or *hippodrome* in Greek), the racetrack, which measured 320 by 79 yards;[1] it will play a large part in our penultimate chapter. In the same district was the extensive palace, within whose walls the modern meaning of "Byzantine" took shape.

As has earlier been pointed out, the eastern Roman empire only begins officially with the death of Theodosius in 395, and we'll examine it most closely under the reign of the 6th century emperor Justinian. Since it would be cumbersome to refer to the "Constantinopolitan Empire," the eastern Roman empire and its culture are always called "Byzantine." For now we can simply describe it as a logical continuation of Diocletian's divine emperorship. There were numerous titles and endless court ceremonials. The Senatorial or "Illustrious" Class was divided into the *spectabiles* and the *clarissimi*. Palace officials below senators were called *perfectissimi* and *egregii*. In most unrepublican fashion, officials were mechanically called "your Sincerity, your Gravity, your Excellency, your Eminence, your Sublime and Wonderful Magnitude, your Illustrious and Magnificent Highness."[2]

Constantine saw himself and his city as towering symbols of imperial unification. He had latched onto Christianity for the same reason, but even before the foundation of Constantinople there were disturbing indications that he might have made the wrong choice.[3] He had no sooner defeated Maxentius when Africa became embroiled in a most un-Christian tiff over the appointment of Caecilian as bishop of Carthage. It seems that one of the attending bishops, ironically named Felix ("Happy"), was accused of handing over his sacred books during Diocletian's persecutions. Caecilian was replaced by Donatus, an uncompromising survivor of the persecutions. The Church split between those who chose to forgive the "Surrenderors," and those like Donatus who refused to do so.

The heresy promised serious consequences, for the Donatists insisted that marriages, baptisms, and ordinations performed by surrendering priests were necessarily invalid. Moreover, since the Donatist heresy tended to appeal to the lower classes in Africa, it took on political overtones of resentment against Roman imperial rule and against the harsh economic conditions of the times. For instance, when a crowd of Donatist vagabonds came upon a sedan chair before which a slave was running interference, they set the slave in the chair and forced the rich owner to run ahead in his place.[4]

Constantine was furious that his chosen, unifying force was itself becoming disunited. In a fatherly-sounding decree he expressed his imperial displeasure:

> For all these reasons it has come to pass that the very men who should demonstrate brotherly love and single-minded accord instead stand apart from each other in most loathsome fashion and thus give pretext for mockery to men whose hearts are estranged from the most holy faith.[5]

No less than five tribunals were held in a vain attempt to settle this matter, that at Milan of November 10, 316 being presided over by Constantine himself. In was eventually decided, as indeed it had to be for the unity of the Church, that a holy sacrament was valid of its own accord, regardless of the personal sins of the officiating priest. Of course the Donatists refused to be satisfied, and they were still causing trouble when the Germanic Vandals mooted the problem by taking Africa out of the Roman Empire in 429.

The Donatist heresy was, however, small potatoes compared with another theological dispute named after its originator, the Alexandrian priest Arius. From Constantine's point of view, Arius's problem was that he thought too much. What he thought about was a very old Greek philosophical concept called the Logos. The Greek word λόγος means something like *word, reason,* and *thought,* all at once, but it was given special, philosophical overtones by the late 6th century BC philosopher Heraclitus, the fellow who's still famous for having said that you can't step into the same river twice. Heraclitus saw fire as the primary element of the cosmos; he identified with fire a universal governing force over all things, and he called it Logos.[6] Plato inherited the concept, as can be seen in the following passage about the nature of his philosopher king:

> Nor, Adeimantos, do I suppose that one who truly understands the way things are would have leisure to look down upon the affairs of men and, struggling with them, drink deeply of envy and disharmony. Rather he would look upon harmony and eternity, contemplating those things which harm neither themselves nor others but exist in order and according to reason (κατὰ λόγον ἔχοντα), and he would imitate and copy them as much as he could.[7]

Especially important for the Logos' development is the 3rd century BC philosopher Zeno, founder of the Stoic philosophy, so called from the *Stoa* or porch in Athens where he delivered his lectures. Zeno developed Heraclitus' Logos into the divine mind of the universe, a philosophical concept which is actually quite difficult to distinguish from the Judaeo-Christian concept of God.

As we've already seen in the story of the noble assassin Brutus, Stoicism became the upper class's philosophy of choice in the late republic and early empire, culminating in the famous *Meditations* of the emperor Marcus Aurelius. All these threads were ultimately united in the mystical-philosophical doctrine of Neoplatanism, founded in the early 3rd century AD by Plotinus, who saw the universe created by an indivisible monad, itself existing over and above the realm of pure thought to which the Platonic *ideas* were relegated.[8]

It would thus have been quite easy for the Gospel of John, which was probably written about AD 100, to identify the Logos with Jesus Christ:

> In the beginning was the Word (Logos), and the Word was with God, and the Word was God (John 1: 1). And the Word was made flesh, and dwelt among us, (and we beheld his glory, the glory as of the only begotten of the Father,) full of grace and truth (1: 14).

Now, Arius made the very serious mistake of pondering the relationship between Jesus Christ the Son and Jehovah, or God the Father. Of course this rather overstates the problem, for despite what his enemies might have said, Arius's thinking wasn't crude enough for him to ask bluntly, "which came first, the Father or the Son?" The identification of Son with Logos was only a popularization anyway and had more in common with deep-rooted pagan attitudes than with the Stoic and Neoplatonic idea of the Mind of the Universe. But nonetheless Arius seems to have been so concerned with maintaining the philosophical and theological supremacy of God that of necessity he downplayed the importance of the popular Logos concept. He probably never went so far as to say (though his enemies have put it into his mouth) that there was a time when God existed and the Logos had not yet been created, but the Arians' favorite Bible verse, Proverbs 8: 22, certainly implied such an interpretation.[9] What he did insist was that the Logos "is not himself eternal, co-eternal with the Father, like him un-created, for it is from the Father that he has received both life and being."[10]

Arius was facing head-on a problem which has plagued Christianity from its inception. In accordance with its Jewish antecedents, Christianity is supposed to be a monotheistic religion, but in reality it worships two Gods, the Father and the Son. Again under Platonic influence,[11] this was expanded into a tripartite god, the Trinity: the Father, the Son (Logos), and the Holy Spirit, which descended upon Christ at the time of his baptism by John, and again upon the Apostles at the Pentecost. To the pagans, this made Christianity as polytheistic as everyone else.

By attempting to apply logic to the problem of the Trinity, Arius deeply offended his boss, Bishop Alexander of Alexandria, who attempted to halt his underling's investigations. When Arius refused, Alexander convened a council of nearly 500 bishops from Egypt and Libya, who forthwith excommunicated Arius from the

Church. But Arius, like Donatus before him, had powerful friends. They included Bishop Eusebius of Caesarea, whose name has frequently appeared below in the footnotes, the other Eusebius (of Nicomedia), a host of Asian bishops, two renegade bishops from Egypt itself, seven presbyters, twelve deacons, and no less than three hundred pious virgins. Once questions about the precedence of the Logos were being parodied in the pagan theatres of Alexandria, Constantine realized with disgust that the unity of his Church was again destroyed. Only a general council could repair the damage.[12]

The council, which met on May 20, 325 at Nicaea (modern Izmik), near Nicomedia, was meant to be world-wide, or "ecumenical." Almost 250 bishops assembled from as far away as Spain and Persia, but because of the distances involved most came from Asia and Syria; Pope Sylvester, for instance, who was too old to travel, sent only two presbyters. The chairmanship seems to have been entrusted to Bishop Ossius of Cordoba, but Constantine himself, present as a "non-voting member," directed the proceedings from a low gold throne set at the upper end of the seats. Eusebius reports in his affable manner that the emperor set about reconciling the disputants "by the affability of his address to all, and his use of the Greek language, with which he was not altogether unacquainted." He admits elsewhere, however, that Constantine generally composed his orations in Latin and then had them put into Greek by his staff of translators.[13]

But Constantine labored under handicaps far beyond those of language. It's first of all very clear that he never really understood what everyone was getting so excited about. As he wrote to Alexander and Arius before the council opened,

> And yet, having made a careful enquiry into the origin and foundation of these differences, I found the cause to be of a truly insignificant character, and quite unworthy of such fierce contention.[14]

Constantine furthermore faced a room of hopelessly divided disputants. On what could be called the extreme left were Arius and his faithful. Our friend Eusebius of Caesarea led a sort of left-center, made up of those who were willing to grant the Logos some sort of moderate subordination, but who were, like Constantine himself, more interested in Church unity than in theological quibbles. On the right were those that felt the real danger of

Arianism to the monotheistic integrity of the Trinity; they were led by Bishop Alexander along with his deacon and eventual successor, the Arian-hater Athanasius. The far right was represented by followers of the 3rd century Libyan bishop Sabellius, the mirror image of Arius, who maintained that there was only one God under three names, and who thus relegated the Logos to the position of divine attribute. The best Constantine could hope for was a compromise.[15]

That compromise was the traditional creed of Caesarea, introduced into the debate by its bishop Eusebius. The creed itself was innocuous, for many such existed for local catechism classes; they were generally written in biblical language and were based on Jesus' own baptismal formula cited at Matthew 28: 19:

> Go ye therefore and teach all nations, baptizing them in the name of the Father, and of the Son, and of the Holy Ghost.

Arius and his followers were perfectly willing to accept the Caesarean creed as proposed, but Constantine wasn't. By the end of the conference it was apparent that the Arians represented a small minority; an earlier, pro-Arian creed had attracted only twenty votes and was subsequently torn to pieces by the bishops. Constantine saw the chance to stamp out division once and for all, so he took it. He suggested that the term *homoousion* (ὁμοούσιον) be added to the Caesarean creed to explain the relationship of the Logos to the Father.

The Arians were outraged. They complained that the term was disgustingly materialistic. Indeed, Aristotle had used it to describe the stars, remarking that they are *homoousion* to each other—i.e. of one substance in kind. They complained that the term was against tradition, for it had been specifically rejected by the Council of Antioch in 269 when Paul of Samosata was thrown out of the Church. That didn't matter, Athanasius retorted. "Paul of Samosata used the word in one sense; Arius denied it in another."

For the first time in Church history a word from outside scripture was adopted officially to explain the nature of God.[16] To the horror of Eusebius of Caesarea, his old, familiar creed was transformed into the now famous Nicene creed. Many Christians still memorize it in childhood:

I believe in one God the Father Almighty, maker of heaven and earth. And of all things visible and invisible: And in one Lord Jesus Christ, the only-begotten Son of God; Begotten of his Father before all worlds, God of God, Light of Light, very God of very God; Begotten, not made; Being of one substance [*homoousion*] with the Father; By whom all things were made; Who for us men and for our salvation came down from heaven, And was incarnate by the Holy Ghost of the Virgin Mary, And was made man. And was crucified also for us under Pontius Pilate; He suffered and was buried: And the third day he rose again a cording to the Scriptures: And ascended into heaven, And sitteth on the right hand of the Father: And he shall come again, with glory, to judge both the quick and the dead; Whose kingdom shall have no end.[17]

Arius and his faithful of course refused to sign the imperial communiqué which concluded the council; they were banished to Illyricum. In exile the Arian sect itself became divided, the most numerous of the Arians reaching the mighty conclusion that the Father was of a *similar* substance with the Son—in Greek *homoiousion*. Although Constantine's vacillating son Constantius would accept this doctrine at the Council of Jerusalem in 360, for the present it was looked upon as the most insidious heresy of all—insidious because it was only one *iota* from the truth. For Constantine at least the Council of Nicaea had shown the path to Christian and imperial unity, so that the subject could be considered closed.

It should be remembered, however, that Constantine, far from being fascinated with the intricacies of Christian doctrine, was deeply bothered by their very existence. Christianity for him was a means to the unification of his empire. He was therefore more interested in bringing Arius and his followers back into the fold than in maintaining some incomprehensible theological purity. Moreover, his sister Constantia, the widow of Licinius, was an Arian and put considerable pressure on him to reconcile her favorite priest to Mother Church.

When Arius responded with a suitably Christian display of humility and reconciliation, Constantine in 327 reconvened the Council of Nicaea, which obligingly readmitted Arius into the Church. Within five months, however, consensus vanished with the death of Bishop Alexander and his subsequent replacement by deacon Athanasius, a fanatic as devoted to the *homoousion* as was Arius to the unassailable glory of the Father. The forces of patriotism and theological purity (often the same forces in history) rose up against the new bishop; at the Council of Tyre, chaired by Eusebius of the footnotes, Athanasius was accused of violent abuse of his episcopal power, extending even to the charge of murder. Although Athanasius dramatically produced the very man he was accused of having murdered, he sensed that the Council was stacked against him and fled to Constantinople in advance of the inevitable verdict.

There he actually waylaid the emperor in the street and, in a scene typical of the melodrama that was his entire life, he persuaded Constantine to change his mind and to embrace once again his own Nicene creed. What is now considered Orthodoxy might have triumphed then and there, but the two Eusebii arrived with the trumped-up charge that Athanasius was plotting to intercept the vital grain shipments from Alexandria to Constantinople. Constantine abandoned the Nicene creed once again, and Athanasius was exiled to Trèves in Gaul, where ha was to spend twenty-eight months. As Gibbon remarks, "His various adventures might have furnished the subject of a very entertaining romance."[18]

Much to Constantine's chagrin, the exile of Athanasius had no effect upon the bishops of Egypt, who still refused to accept Arius into their brotherhood. As a gesture of his new support, the emperor therefore invited Arius to the capital, where the resident bishop was ordered to admit him into communion in the cathedral. Arius came, but on the day set aside for his triumphal entry into the emperor's church, he felt obliged to enter an outhouse first, where he died from a sudden and violent attack of diarrhea. Arius's enemies called it the fitting vengeance of God; his friends called it poison.[19]

Still, Constantine dared not fire Athanasius, who served as bishop of Alexandria for forty-six years—twenty spent in exile under four successive emperors. Thanks partly to his long residence in the West, the *homoousion* came to be accepted there as the word of God. Constantine and his successors kept Arianism (or its *homoiousion* variety) alive in the East even though Constantine's pagan nephew Julian ("the Apostate") cleverly decreed religious toleration in the hope that the pesky Christians would self-destruct in civil war. In 379, as we'll see in the next chapter, the Spanish general Theodosius became Augustus of the East and brought back Nicene Christianity with him. It has been considered "orthodox" ever since.[20]

The year after the Council of Nicaea, while on his way to Rome to celebrate his twentieth anniversary in office, Constantine suddenly executed his first son Crispus, the same prince who, following his victory over Licinius, had been called "an emperor most dear to God and in every way resembling his father."[21] Shortly thereafter he also executed his second wife Fausta, apparently by suffocating her in a steam bath. As in the case of Athanasius, a whole romance could be built around these incidents, but the emperor's motives are simply unknown.[22] Constantine seems to have enjoyed good health for the remaining ten years of his life, finally succumbing in 337 to a brief illness. On his deathbed he finally consented to baptism in the Christian faith, feeling that

> the time was come at which he should seek purification from sins of his past career, firmly believing that whatever errors he had committed as a mortal man, his soul would be purified from them through the efficacy of the mystical words and the salutary waters of baptism.[23]

Constantine's three sons by Fausta divided the empire among themselves, executed seven of their cousins and two of their uncles, and then began the civil wars which led to the eventual extinction of their house.

43 The Earthly City

The extinction of Constantine's family allowed two opportunistic generals, the Illyrian Valentinian (364-375) and the Spaniard Theodosius (378-395), to spawn families which, upon interbreeding, produced the West's last dynasty of "legitimate" emperors. Of course it was not simply the incompetence of their degenerate offspring that produced the famous decline and fall of the Roman Empire. We've already looked at some of the underlying causes—economic, political, and moral—which accomplished that. What we've been ignoring is the primary cause: the barbarian invasions.

It would take a book as long as the one we're finally drawing to a close to do justice to all of these Germans, Slavs, and Ural-Altaians who swarmed over the Rhine-Danube frontier. What we'll do is to take a general look at the Germanic peoples first and then go on to examine more closely the Goths, who had, if not the most permanent, certainly the most dramatic effect upon the history of the West.

The very word "barbarian" immediately raises hackles, and not surprisingly, since the Greeks invented it as an insult meaning "non-Greek." Its modern use, however, only implies a people without writing and settled urban life. Furthermore, although the Romans wrote about the Germans with their "cruel, blue eyes, blonde hair, and great bodies,"[1] as though they had descended upon them from another planet, it should be remembered that the Germans are also Indo-Europeans, and thus members of the same linguistic group as the Persians, Greeks, and Latins. Thus their social organization closely resembles that of the early Spartans, Athenians, and Romans themselves.

In theory at least their assembly of adult males, called the *thing*, possessed supreme authority. Normally it chose leaders called *grafs*, but in times of emergency it could elect a supreme ruler or *king* (itself one of our Germanic words; it's *cyning* in Anglo-Saxon, and *König* in modern German). Anybody could be a *graf*, but kings were always chosen from ancient royal families, resident in all the

Germanic tribes. Their presence acted as a leveling influence upon their communities. Even a king couldn't simply command. He had to convince the folk to follow his lead and was always in danger of being shouted down in open assembly. Being king was a risky business. Each great man in the community had his own gang. The gangs struggled incessantly for supremacy, and it was considered shameful to survive your leader in battle. Like the ancient Myceneans, these Germans lived by predatory warfare and defined manhood in terms of military prowess. "Indeed, it is thought cowardly and slothful to earn with sweat what you could take with blood."[2]

Ancient German gods were as bloody as ancient German politics. We're still worshipping the gods too, for after the 3rd century several of them became identified with traditional Graeco-Roman deities and have taken over their week-names.[3] For example, the Romans quickly identified Wodan with their own Mercury, both originally gods of trade. *Dies Mercurii,* the French *mercredi* and Italian *mercoledi,* became *Vodanstag* or Wednesday. Similarly Tiu, the god of war, took on Mars' Day (*Dies Martis, mardi, martedi*) and made it *Tuesday* while Thor and Frija lurk behind *Thursday* and *Friday.* Wodan especially, but also the mother-earth goddess Nerthus, were worshipped with human sacrifice, a fact confirmed in most grisly fashion by the hundreds of bog mummies—many of them strangled or decapitated—that have turned up in northwest Europe.[4]

Originally a pastoral people, the Germans only took up farming when hemmed in by rival peoples like the Celts or the Romans, and even then their settlements were scattered and all their land held in common by the tribe.[5] They were inveterate gamblers and hard drinkers—mostly of beer, which the Romans thought a most amusing beverage—and lived on a high cholesterol diet of meat and dairy products. Their private morals, at least, were universally praised. Except for their *Gräfen* and *Könige,* whose duty it was to increase the size of their noble families, the Germans were strictly monogamous. Pre-marital sex was so discouraged that it was considered shameful to reach puberty before one's twentieth year.[6]

In his short ethnological study of the German peoples, Tacitus lists upwards of sixty different tribes, many of whom disappeared or later turned up under different names. The only way to make any sense of them all is to divide the German people roughly into two groups, the East and West Germans, separated eventually by the river Elbe.

For the last time, therefore, we have to return to the period of the Indo-European invasions, about 2,000 BC, when the Germans first appeared in Denmark, southern Scandinavia, and the western coast of the Baltic Sea. They began to move out in two groups about one thousand years later. The westernmost group, settled originally between the Oder and the Elbe, pushed westwards against the Celts of Gaul and, eventually, the Romans under Julius Caesar. These West Germans included some of the tribes most important for medieval history: The Franks, after whom modern France is named (the kings Clovis, Charlemagne, and Pippin were all Franks), the Alamanni (the polite French word for *German* is still *Allemand*), and the Angles (England is of course Angle-land). These people, however, did not overthrow the Roman Empire. Though piratical by nature, they were far more settled than their cousins to the east and had even begun some simple farming. The East Germans, on the other hand, moved out towards the Carpathian Mountains of modern Poland between 600 and 300 BC. Their most important representatives are the Goths.[7]

The Goths themselves remembered their ancient Scandinavian homeland, "the womb of nations," as the island of Scandza. Their eastern migrations brought them to the shore of the Black Sea during the reign of Caracalla, at which time they broke into two groups: the Ostragoths, or east Goths, who eventually built a kingdom stretching north and west from the river Dniester; and the Visigoths, or West Goths, who settled south of the Dniester to the Danube. They caused the Romans a lot of trouble and in 251 even killed the emperor Decius, who had foolishly pursued them into a swamp on the lower Danube, where he fell off his horse and was never seen again. The Visigoths were eventually allowed to settle in Dacia (i.e. Rumania), which for all intents and purposes thus slipped away from the Roman Empire. The emperor Constantine accepted the Goths as federated allies, a convenient fiction which allowed him to claim that he had reconquered Dacia, and which cost him a fortune in bribe money paid yearly to the Goths as foreign aid.[8]

The Goths were gradually converted to Christianity thanks largely to the work of a missionary named Wulfilas. Originally a

Cappadocian, he had been captured by the Goths and then sent to Constantinople as a hostage, where he adopted Christianity. Unfortunately for the later history of the West, that Christianity was of the Arian variety, and indeed Wulfilas was consecrated as bishop by our old friend Eusebius of Nicomedia. He invented a Gothic alphabet based upon the Goths' own runic inscriptions and the Greek letters, and he translated the Bible into Gothic. The fragments of this which survive are the very beginning of German literature.[9]

This uneasy truce between Goths and Romans was broken by a sort of transcontinental billiard game when the nomadic Huns were forced westward, looking literally for greener pastures. Although the allied press during World War I typically referred to the Germans as "Huns," they were not Germanic at all, but rather a Mongolian people, speaking a language distantly related to modern Turkish and even more distantly to Hungarian and Finnish. They were a pastoral people who lived in wagons among their herds, got drunk on fermented cow's milk, sucked blood from their cattle in time of drought, and slashed the cheeks of their infants to make them tough. To the terrified Goths they seemed unbelievably ugly:

> ...a stunted, foul, and puny tribe, scarcely human and having no language save one which bore but slight resemblance to human speech...their swarthy aspect was fearful, and they had, if I may call it so, a sort of shapeless lump, not a head, with pin-holes rather than eyes.[10]

Fleeing before these invaders but also (just like the Huns) looking for greener pastures themselves, the Goths crowded to the bank of the Danube. In the year 376 their chiefs Fritigern and Alavivus sent envoys to the emperor, who was at Antioch, begging to be allowed to cross the Danube and settle in Thrace. Unfortunately for Rome, the emperor of the East was Valens, the idiot brother of Valentinian I. He had no fear of the Goths, for he had gone along on a successful war against them in 367-369, nor had he any concept of the tremendous logistical problems involved in settling some 80,000 refugees in his territory. To Valens the Goths represented only a potential labor force. His advisors told him that the Goths would serve his empire as soldiers, and that the provinces, freed from the necessity of sending recruits, could fill the imperial coffers with gold instead. So Valens gave his consent and had his officials ferry over the Goths by boat, raft, and hollowed-out tree trunk.[11]

Valens didn't invent short-sighted exploitation of the barbarians. As we've seen already in the stories of Diocletian and Constantine, the urban populations of the empire had long since become unsuitable for military service. In Diocletian's day only his hill-billy compatriots from Dalmatia and the tough, yeomen farmers of the Anatolian plateau provided suitable soldiers from within the empire's borders. By the 3rd century the army was mostly Illyrian, just like the emperors, and a dangerous pattern was established. To save costs, army units were reduced in size and settled closer to their civilian sources of supply. We can think of them either as corrupted by easy living or, perhaps more accurately, as diverted from soldiering into exploiting protection money from their civilian neighbors.

As provincial recruits thus became increasingly—shall we say—civilized, Germans were recruited to fill their places. By the end of the fourth century, most high ranking officers in the Roman army were of German origin, and the practice of hiring one band of barbarians to pillage and slaughter another had become commonplace. It's interesting to note that the Germanic dragon came to replace the imperial eagle as the typical legionary standard. Valens was, in effect, following standard operating procedure, while Fritigern and his Goths, far from attacking the Roman empire, were just anxious to join the party.[12]

Valens made two demands upon the Goths: They were forced to hand over as hostages their young noblemen, who were subsequently scattered throughout Asia under the guardianship of Count Julius, the Master General of the Troops, and they were to surrender all their arms. The hostages were indeed marched off, but everything else fell apart. Lupicinus, the military governor of Thrace, was both incompetent and crooked. More interested in collecting bribes than weapons, he made no provision for the refugees beyond a market where rotten dog meat was sold at the rate of ten pounds for a slave.

Starving and in despair, the Goths marched off towards Marcianople. In what seemed to be an attempt at conciliation, Lupicinus invited Fritigern and Alavivus to a banquet; meanwhile, as the Goths rioted outside the walls of Marcianople, Lupicinus

ordered his troops to slaughter the honor-guard of his two guests.
Fritigern drew his sword, hacked his way to freedom, and reorga-
nized his troops. An attack by Lupicinus was easily swatted aside.
Moving northwards into the Mount Haemus range of Thrace, the
barbarians fought a more serious battle at a place called Salices
("The Willows"). It was a bloody draw, but the Goths were able
to break out of the mountains and plunder the rich villas in the
countryside, advancing eventually right up to the Hellespont.

Valens' co-emperor in the West was his 19-year-old nephew
Gratian, the son of Valentinian. Gratian was handsome, courageous, and already well launched upon a career of military glory
and personal dissipation. He was preparing to come to his uncle's
aid when the West German Alamanni, taking advantage of his
preoccupation, crossed the Rhine and invaded his territory.
Gratian was thus delayed for some time while he cleaned house.
When he finally set out eastwards in 378, he sent Valens word of
his great victories over the Alamanni along with an urgent request
to make no move until he arrived with reinforcements.

Valens received the message at Constantinople and turned green
with envy. His flatterers kept telling him he was invincible. The
racing fans in the Hippodrome were screaming at their emperor
to take some action against the Gothic menace. Most encouraging, intelligence reports were reaching him that Fritigern, with a
piddling force of 10,000 men, was in his vicinity. Prodded to un-
characteristic decisiveness, Valens announced that he would save
the Roman world all by himself. At the head of a great imperial
army (great on paper, that is, though it probably amounted to no
more than 20,000 troops) he left Constantinople and proceeded
on a forced march northwestwards to the suburbs of Hadrianople,
where he finally located Fritigern's wagons. The wily Goth sent
priests to negotiate terms while the exhausted imperial troops
wilted in the August heat.

The battle began by mistake when a Roman patrol skirmished
with the Goths. The barbarians' heavy cavalry completely over-
ran Valens' men, who were so compacted that the Gothic arrows
couldn't miss. Even Valens was hit, after which some loyal troops
hauled him off to a near-by farmhouse. Not realizing who was
inside, a Gothic raiding party burned it to the ground.

The Battle of Hadrianople was easily the worst disaster since
Cannae. Hardly a third of the army escaped; along with the em-

peror two generals were lost and thirty-five tribunes. In petty revenge for the disaster, Count Julian summoned all of his hostages
to the fora of their respective cities, supposedly to receive a
present. The young Goths were met by squads of archers on the
surrounding roof-tops and were all massacred on the same day.[13]

With Valens dead, Gratian needed a new colleague for the East.
He chose an experienced soldier named Theodosius, the son of a
Spanish general his court had executed only three years earlier.
Theodosius made no rash moves. He waited until the death of
Fritigern broke up the Goths into disorganized raiding parties and
then invited Fritigern's successor Athanaric to Constantinople.
Like all barbarians before and after him (including the European
knights of the First Crusade), Athanaric was flabbergasted at the
size of Constantinople. "Now I see," he explained,

> what I have often heard with unbelieving ears...Truly the emperor
> is a god on earth, and whoso raises a hand against him is guilty of
> his own blood.[14]

Athanaric ate and drank himself to death in the big city, and
only four years after the disaster of Hadrianople, Theodosius
managed to bribe the Goths back to the federated status they had
enjoyed under Constantine.

As long as Theodosius was alive the Goths stayed quiet. When
he died, however, the short-sighted, greedy ministers of his sons
cut off their foreign aid, which act reëmbarked the Goths on their
old career of predatory warfare. In preparation for this new national emergency, the Visigothic assembly elected its first king, a
nobleman from their royal Balthi (i.e. "Bold") family named
Alaric. Alaric and his Goths had no reason to hurl themselves
against the walls of Constantinople. They headed west.

Theodosius had left behind no appropriate provisions for such
a crisis. Hopelessly deceived by his fatherly affections, he had
determined to divide the Roman world between his two worthless sons. When Theodosius died in 395, his 17-year-old boy
Arcadius had already been playing co-emperor at Constantinople
for three years. In the West little Honorius, aged eleven, was entrusted to Theodosius's Master of Both Services, an East German
of the Vandal tribe named Stilicho. The bureaucrats who ruled
Arcadius were broken reeds at best; the only Roman hero available to stand up to King Alaric was this fellow German Stilicho.[15]

The two combatants had a lot in common. It should be understood at the outset that Alaric had no intention of destroying the Roman Empire. Like Stilicho, he looked upon it as a source of security and wealth. Theodosius had promised to make Alaric a general in the Roman army, and he led his people in revolt partly because Theodosius' death had cheated him of his rank. It's typical of a barbaric people, existing on the fringes of a decaying empire, to hunger after the good life their very enemies have to offer. Alaric was no different, but his aspirations for respectability, if we can call it that, were contradicted by his role of king. He ruled over a nation of pirates whose very concept of manhood was based on theft and violence. Alaric didn't want to destroy Rome; he wanted to earn its respect and obedience.[16]

Stilicho had even more grandiose ambitions. He dreamed of uniting the entire Roman empire, just as his master Theodosius had done. Of course as a German, Stilicho couldn't rule by himself, so he would recover the East in the name of his malleable patron Honorius. Dynastic marriages greatly increased his chances. After he had become Theodosius's right-hand man, the emperor had married him to his niece and adopted daughter Serena. That produced a semi-royal daughter named Maria, whom Stilicho and Serena eventually married off to Honorius. But like Alaric, Stilicho was forced to live a contradiction. Although the Goths were his enemies, Stilicho needed their man power in his schemes of conquest. He had to defeat Alaric, but it was against his interests to wipe him out.

The first battles were fought in Greece. Alaric was kind enough to inform Antiochus, the proconsul of Greece, that he was invading his province, and the proconsul abandoned Thermopylae in a panic. The Visigoths looted Greece from north to south. Athens, a city now more famous for its honey than its philosophers,[17] bought its safety with a huge bribe, but the nearby Eleusinian mysteries were sacked out of existence. Sparta, "defended by neither arms nor brave men,"[18] fell with all the rest. Stilicho landed an army in Greece, but he quickly made a deal with Alaric, who moved north to Epirus in 397. Eutropius, the emperor Arcadius's favorite eunuch, obligingly bribed Alaric with the title "Master of Soldiers in Illyricum," allowing him to use Epirus as his base of operations for years.[19]

The Visigoths grew restless in Epirus, so Alaric led them out whenever the West seemed sufficiently distracted. The first chance came in 402, when an Ostrogoth named Radagaisus formed a coalition of Germanic tribes to invade the West. Alaric moved over the Alps into northern Italy, where Stilicho defeated him twice, first at Pollentia and then at Verona. Of course Stilicho didn't press his advantage, and to the Romans' chagrin the Visigoths were allowed to run back to Epirus.

The second chance came in 408. Stilicho had begun the history of Florence by killing Radagaisus there in 405, but on Christmas eve of the year 407 the survivors of his coalition danced over the frozen Rhine and effectively removed Gaul from the Roman Empire. Britain then revolted, Spain broke away, and of course the Visigoths appeared at the foot of the Julian Alps.[20] Alaric then proceeded to send Honorius a bill for his protracted stay in Epirus and his expensive invasion of Italy! Stilicho hurried to Rome, where he convinced the Senate to give into Alaric's extortion. One Senator, named Lampadius, mumbled, "That isn't peace, it's piece-meal surrender!" but four thousand pounds of gold was shipped north to the happy barbarians.[21]

This treaty sealed Stilicho's fate. It now seemed painfully obvious that he had been dealing with Alaric all along. The spoiled soldiers of Italy resented Stilicho's fondness for barbarians. They also blamed him for the great territorial losses in the West—perhaps rightly, for Stilicho had withdrawn thousands of troops from the Rhine frontier to defend Italy. Honorius was less attached to him now too, for the emperor's child bride Maria had died that year. Maria had never reached adulthood, a fact which dampened even Honorius's passion. When his cousin Serena, Stilicho's wife, forced their second daughter upon him, he was similarly unmoved. Little Thermantia also remained untouched.[22]

The Eastern Emperor Arcadius finally brought about Stilicho's downfall when he died on May 1, 408. Honorius immediately made plans to sail east and—as he put it—safeguard the interests of his nephew, little Theodosius. Citing the length of the voyage and the revolt in Britain, Stilicho persuaded the emperor that the trip would be a bad idea and instead made plans to set out himself. His actions, being patently opportunistic, gave Stilicho's political enemies all they needed to move against him. Chief among these enemies was the Master of the Offices, a Christian bureaucrat from the Black Sea named Olympius. Olympius convinced the emperor

Honorius that Stilicho was out to murder little Theodosius and put his own son Eucharius on the throne in his place. Since the hapless Eucharius was both Honorius's brother-in-law and the grandnephew of Theodosius the Great, the story gained some credibility. Olympius was most successful in haranguing Roman troops, who already hated Stilicho as Alaric's creature and a traitor to the Empire.

The soldiers' riots began in Ticinum, where they ran wild through the town and killed several important officials, one of whom was even clinging to the knees of the (as ever) terrified Honorius. Stilicho was afraid to act, for to do so would have meant leading barbarians against Roman troops. Disgusted with his cowardly inactivity, a hot-headed Goth named Sarus (whom we'll meet again later) massacred Stilicho's personal body-guard of Huns. Stilicho fled to Ravenna and sought sanctuary in a church. Imperial troops surrounded the building; their leader Heraclianus offered a safe conduct, only to produce a contravening order for execution as soon as Stilicho stepped outside. As Cicero had done almost five hundred years earlier, Stilicho forbade his followers to fight for a losing cause and offered his neck to Heraclianus's sword. As an afterthought, young Eucharius was similarly tracked down and killed.

When the Roman soldiers heard of Stilicho's death, they seized the families of their barbarian compatriots and slaughtered all the women and children. As a result 30,000 outraged barbarian troops fled northwards to Alaric, screaming for revenge.[23]

Acting on Olympius's advice, Honorius refused Alaric the bribe money negotiated by Stilicho and scoffed at an offer to exchange hostages. Courage is indeed a noble emotion, but it came at little cost to Honorius. Terrified by Stilicho's great battle of Pollentia, Honorius had long since moved his court to the swamp-bound, impregnable city of Ravenna. Snug and safe amidst the city's mosquitoes, Honorius took no precautions to back his courage up. Alaric marched down the Flaminian Way towards Rome. Meeting with no opposition he quickly surrounded the capital and proceeded to starve it into submission.

Cities have been going up in smoke at an alarming rate for the past several chapters, so it's important to realize the symbolic importance of this particular siege. Even Hannibal had been unable to touch Rome. It had suffered frequently in civil war, but no foreign enemy had touched Rome since the Gauls sacked it way back in 390 BC. Stilicho had instinctively denuded the Rhine frontier in order to save Italy from attack. Rome was the traditional seat of the empire, even though Honorius had visited it only once in his life. It was also by far the greatest city in the West. We still possess an urban survey compiled in the 4th century AD. It states that Rome consisted of 1,797 private homes (i.e. *domus*, a term including everything from town houses to palaces) and 46,602 tenement buildings. That would mean about 50,000 citizens and slaves housed in *domus* and about 1,677,000 more in the tenements. The fall of this great, historic metropolis would indeed signal *der Untergang des Abendlandes*.[24]

In the face of Alaric's siege, the land-owning senatorial class, "living in ostentatious, futile luxury amidst their thousands of slaves,"[25] could come up with no more original solution to their dilemma than to execute Serena, Stilicho's widow. It didn't help. Finally, after famine had littered the streets with rotting corpses, the Senate sent a delegation out to Alaric. As they had been ordered, the delegation warned Alaric that the people of Rome were prepared to march out against him. Laughing at the threat, Alaric told them, "The thicker the grass, the easier it is to mow." His own terms were brutal: he wanted all the city's gold and silver, all its moveable property, and all of its barbarian slaves. When the ambassadors asked him what they would have left, he laughed again. "Your lives," he said.[26]

Having exhausted the advantages of strangling women, the Senate now turned to black magic. Pompeianus, the City Prefect, reported that the town of Narnia had been miraculously delivered from the Visigoths through the intervention of the pagan gods. Elated at such glad tidings the Senate's pagan caucus turned on their Christian brethren and demanded the reinstitution of the old time religion. Even Innocent, Bishop of Rome, had no objections. All that was needed was a pagan senator to perform the salutary rites in public and thus risk offending his most Christian majesty, the emperor Honorius. None could be found.

Instead, another deputation crept out to Alaric, who this time agreed to moderate his terms. He would set Rome free for 5,000 pounds of gold, 30,000 pounds of silver, 4,000 silk tunics, 3,000 scarlet skins, and 2,000 pounds of pepper. The deal was struck, and Alaric graciously opened a market for the starving citizens of the capital. The Visigoths then withdrew to Tuscany to winter quarters. Virtually all of the barbarian slaves of the city followed in his wake, raising the strength of his army to some 40,000 troops.[27]

But Honorius, listening as always to his eunuch Olympius, wouldn't pay the ransom. The desperate Romans sent two deputations to Ravenna, the second led by Bishop Innocent himself, but still Honorius wouldn't pay. Even the removal of Olympius failed to make any difference. The ambitious eunuch bungled a military assignment against Alaric's brother-in-law Ataulphus; he was eventually whipped to death for his trouble. His successor Jovius, the Praetorian Prefect, was a former colleague of Alaric, but even he couldn't convince the emperor to settle with a barbarian. Alaric was willing to compromise; he was demanding land for his troops and the magic title Master of Both Services for himself.

When he got neither he marched on Rome a second time. At his urging the Senate appointed Attalus, one of its members, as an anti-emperor. Alaric marched into Rome behind his puppet, who began to spout grandiose schemes for uniting the empire under his make-believe authority. An attack on Ravenna made no progress, especially after reinforcements from the East made it more impregnable than ever. Attalus proved a disappointment. As Alaric saw it, he "went about things like a rash fool, without reason or chance of success." Alaric finally deposed him personally, even sending his purple robes to Honorius as a conciliatory gesture. He then set off to Ravenna in an attempt to reopen negotiations. Beneath the walls of the city he fell in with the troops of the hothead Sarus, the Hun killer, now acting as a freelance. Apparently as a result of a quarrel with Ataulphus, Sarus attacked. Outraged at the insult and fed up with Honorius's lack of faith, Alaric marched on Rome for a third time.[28]

This time Rome was betrayed: disaffected slaves opened the Salerian gate, through which the Visigoths entered the city on the night of August 23, 410. Conveniently ignoring the fact that they were Arians, St. Augustine boasted later that the Visigoths, inspired by their Christian faith, set aside the larger churches as sanctuaries for their Christian brethren. He goes on, however, to admit that

Whatever devastation, murder, plunder, arson, or misery was committed in the most recent destruction of Rome, it all happened according to the custom of war.[29]

Christians and pagans alike were tortured into revealing the whereabouts of their wealth; wives, maidens, and even nuns were raped; thousands died of famine and disease; and countless more were carried off into slavery.[30] The Visigoths stayed in Rome for six days, after which they moved south, hoping eventually to pass into Sicily and then into the rich Roman province of North Africa.

Of course Rome recovered. It's still, after all, the capital of Italy. But to a great extent the reputation of Rome as a great imperial city was shattered. All empires depend upon their reputations, which is to say upon the terror they inspire. No other event in Roman history so clearly foretold change than this loss of Roman invincibility. St. Jerome, one of the founders of Catholic monasticism and the translator of the Bible into Latin, was in the Holy Land when he heard the news:

A terrible rumor was brought from the West that Rome was besieged, that its citizens' safety had been redeemed for gold, and that once plundered they were once again surrounded, losing both their livelihood and their lives. My voice sticks in my throat and sobs interrupt my words. The city is captured which captured the whole world. Indeed it has fallen to hunger before the sword could take it, and few were found to be captured.[31]

Alaric didn't outlive his revenge by much. That same year, after his plans to cross into Sicily were sunk in the Straits of Messina, he suddenly took sick and died. The Goths buried him in the river Busentus, which flows near the city of Consentia. They had captives divert the river's channel so that a secret tomb could be excavated for Alaric's corpse and the great treasures buried with it. The river was then returned to its bed and the captives slaughtered so as to keep their secret.[32]

The Visigoths built a kingdom for themselves in Aquitaine. Later, in the 470's, their king Euric took advantage of the political collapse in the West to conquer Spain, where the Goths ruled until the Moslem invasion of the 8th century. Meanwhile the West absorbed one shock after another. Taking over Alaric's plan, the East German Vandals crossed to Africa and so seized the West's principle bread basket. The Huns followed next under King Attila, whose name has become almost a common noun for savagery. He was defeated in 451 by the Roman general Aëtius. Aëtius was the exception to the rule in those days: he was a Roman who could fight. His boss, Valentinian III, ran him through during a typical royal temper tantrum. That same year, 455, the Vandals sacked the poor city of Rome again and actually succeeded in making their name a common noun.

Valentinian III was the last legitimate emperor, which is to say the last direct relative of the first Valentinian and of Theodosius the Great. After his inevitable assassination anybody could be emperor. The West was actually ruled by a series of Stilicho imitators who, being German, could not be emperors themselves but only emperor-makers. They were constantly torn between appointing either idiots who inspired no loyalty at all or else talented generals who became threats to their authority. The last of these emperor-makers was the German mercenary Odovacer, who deposed the emperor Romulus Augustulus in 476. Augustulus was young and good looking, so Odovacer was merciful: he granted the boy a pension of 6,000 *solidi* and exiled him to the beautiful Campanian villa built centuries before by Lucius Lucullus.[33]

You'll frequently find the date 476 on time lines as the fall of the Roman Empire in the West. Legally there is some truth to that, but it's important to realize that at the time no one really noticed. As far as he was concerned, Odovacer was the loyal servant of the Eastern emperor Zeno, and indeed even sent that emperor a delegation requesting that he not send the Romans another emperor as a replacement. "The majesty of a sole monarch," cried the deputation, toady-like, "is sufficient to pervade and protect, at the same time, both the East and the West."[34] The common peasant certainly noticed no change. He had been living as a serf since the days of Diocletian, a condition which would see no material change until after the French Revolution.

As it turned out, however, the West never did get another Roman Emperor. Zeno certainly didn't approve of the upstart barbarian Odovacer taking over, for he had on hand his own barbarian, an Ostrogothic prince named Theodoric, whom Zeno found it politically expedient to ship out of the East. Theodoric the Ostrogoth had spent ten years of his boyhood in Constantinople as a hostage. Like Philip, Alexander's father, he passed his captivity well, learning much about the Byzantines and making powerful friends.

He became a real threat to Zeno, a crafty Balkan hillbilly (his real name was Tarasicodissa!) who had married into the royal family. For ten years Theodoric alternated the roles of enemy and supporter of the royal house. He was appointed Master of Soldiers in 483, became consul in 484, and then attacked Constantinople in 487. Zeno ultimately bribed Theodoric with the job of taking care of Odovacer, whom he dutifully killed following a three year siege of Ravenna.[35] Theodoric then ruled Italy nominally as the agent of his Byzantine master Zeno, but in actuality as an independent, Germanic king. Britain had fallen to the Angles and the Saxons, Africa to the Vandals, Gaul to the Franks, and Spain to the Visigoths. If anyone cared to notice, there wasn't a Roman Empire in the West.

44 The Prince and the Showgirl

Despite the forced retirement of Romulus Augustulus, the Roman Empire lasted all the way till 1453. By that time, of course, the Empire had shrunk to little more than the walled city of Constantinople, and it would take a considerable stretch of the imagination to trace the line of Constantine XI back to the first Augustus. Still, if Constantine Palaeologus could die on the walls of Constantinople bravely defending his city against the Turkish conquerors, we can at least take a closer look at the Byzantine culture he was trying to preserve.

The Byzantines are to a great extent still with us. All of the emperors who followed Constantine I imitated his mania for caesaropapism, so that in the Eastern Roman Empire, as in old Republican Rome, the Church was always looked upon as a department of state. This attitude changed only in the increasingly barbarized West, where throughout the Middle Ages the upstart German kings (styled, to the amusement of the Byzantines, "Holy Roman Emperors,") carried on a bloody conflict with the Bishops of Rome (called, to the amusement of the Patriarchs of Constantinople, "Popes"). It was this conflict which separated Church and State in the West and ultimately fostered that thoroughly secular delight in the individual so necessary for all Western style democracies. Such a split never occurred in the East, neither among the Byzantines nor among the many peoples, such as the Russians for instance, whom they converted to Christianity and brought within their sphere of culture. The Russian Czars, ruling from the city they called The Third Rome, treated their patriarchs and their subjects as part of a divine plan entrusted to their care. Their successors, who traded Orthodoxy for communism, treated their people the same.

Starting with Theodosius' son Arcadius, there were over 1,000 years of Byzantine emperors. For medievalists, I suppose, the most famous of the sequence would be Alexius Comnenus, who called for the First Crusade in the 11th century. But for the period we're

discussing, the leading light has to be Petrus Sabbatius, who, after adoption by his uncle the Emperor Justin, took the name
Flavius Petrus Sabbatius Iustianianus. We'll call him Justinian I.
He was the last man to attempt to be emperor of both the East
and the West, and even though his plans of conquest proved ultimately futile, if not fatal to the empire, his overheated sense of
vision helped to create Romanesque architecture and to preserve
the body of Roman law.

If Justinian has come down to us as something of a split personality, that is due partly to the nature of our information. The
principal source for Justinian's story is the contemporary Byzantine historian Procopius, who composed a long, detailed, rather
fulsome history of Justinian's wars of conquest. However,
Procopius also wrote in secret a short collection of outrageously
scurrilous attacks on his boss, called the *Anecdota*. The two
Justinians are difficult to reconcile, but much of the confusion was
probably inherent in the man himself. Justinian rather reminds
me of King James I of England: autocratic, pedantic, and devoted
to his own anachronistic ideals, but still able to inspire a literary
masterpiece through committee.

Justinian's family which, like Diocletian's, came from Illyria (i.e.
the area we now call "The Former Yugoslavia") had no claim to
the throne, but that was hardly unusual in an age when the title
Porphyrogenitos—born in the royal purple maternity ward—was a title
that few emperors could claim.[1] Royalty was first achieved by
Justinian's uncle Justin, a peasant boy from Skopje who, because
of his "very fine figure," was enrolled in the palace guard of the
Emperor Leo I. Justin rose to be Commander of the Palace Guard
under the Emperor Anastasius, a position the old man used to seize
the throne when Anastasius died.

Justin was the first illiterate emperor. His staff had to provide
him with a wooden stencil through which he could trace the word
legi ("I've read it") onto documents that required imperial initial-
ing. Procopius is pretty hard on Justin, at least in the *Anecdota*,
calling him "extraordinarily simple-minded and exceedingly like
a stupid donkey, inclined to follow the man who pulls the rein,
his ears waving steadily the while." Not surprisingly, the elderly
emperor depended upon his bright, big-city educated nephew
Justinian to manage the administration of the empire.[2]

That's not to say, however, that Justinian managed alone, for his name is forever linked with the beauteous Theodora, his wife and empress. Theodora's strong-willed and passionate personality neatly complemented the cold blooded reserve of her husband, just as her devotion to the Monophysite heresy helped tone down her husband's fanatical orthodoxy.[3] Their romance is the original version of "The Prince and the Showgirl."

Theodora was the daughter of a bear trainer in Constantinople's Circus or Hippodrome. Upon his death and the impoverishment of his family, the young and beautiful Theodora went on the stage with a strip-tease act performed with the aid of a gaggle of geese. She became even better known, however, as a highly paid prostitute, in which capacity she toured the East as part of the entourage of a governor named Hecebolus. Dumped by him in Alexandria, she worked her way back to Constantinople, where she made the acquaintance of Justinian. Apparently the dour politician was swept off his feet by the accomplishments of a woman so perverse, Procopius tells us, that she was dissatisfied with having only three bodily orifices.

Marriage, however, was out of the question, not only because of the objections of Justinian's adoptive mother, the virtuous Yugoslav peasant woman Lupicina, but also because of the prohibitions of the law, which forbade marriage between a man of Senatorial rank and a prostitute. Lupicina's death solved the first difficulty, after which it was easy for Justinian to talk his senile co-emperor into changing the law so as to offer a "glorious repentance" to retired prostitutes. Not many days after the marriage, and just three days before Easter of 527, the Emperor Justin died an apparently natural death, leaving his throne to the joint occupation of Theodora and the 45-year-old Justinian.[4]

Their style of rule is most conveniently illustrated by the famous Nika Revolt of 532. Νίκα, meaning "Vanquish!" became the rallying cry of the Hippodrome's Blue and Green factions, so named after the colors of the competing jockeys' silks. Constantinople, like Rome, was a sports-crazed city; for the Romans the sport of choice was always the chariot races. Everybody followed one of the two teams, which even controlled the 4 self-governing demes into which Constantinople was divided. The heretic emperor Anastasius had been a Green; thus Uncle Justin and Justinian were Blues. Under Justinian's patronage the Blues became arrogant and unmanageable, wearing their hair cropped on the sides and long in back after the fashion of the Huns, and mugging rich Greens with impunity in the streets. As if that weren't enough, Justinian himself was mugging the entire city with unbearably high taxes.[5]

The riot started, naturally enough, in the Hippodrome, where the Greens screamed complaints about their treatment through-out 22 of the usual 25 heats into which the racing day was divided. Finally exasperated at their whining, Justinian had a public crier howl down at them from the royal box, "Be patient and attentive, ye insolent raiders! Be mute, ye Jews, Samaritans, and Manichaeans!"

"We are poor, we are innocent, we are injured, we dare not pass through the streets!" the Greens yelled back. When that didn't work, their cries degenerated into insults: "Homicide! Ass! Per-jured tyrant!"

"Do you despise your lives?" cried Justinian, and the Blues rose in their seats. The Greens then rioted, and Justinian fled to the palace.[6] The mob burned public baths and porticoes, the ancient church of St. Sophia, and even outlying buildings of the palace itself. Inflamed by the destruction they were causing and drunk with a new sense of power, the Blues and Greens called a truce and broke into the prison of the city prefect, where some of their followers had been confined. They butchered the imperial offi-cials and set the prisoners free. Justinian tried placating the mob by firing his corrupt and hated praetorian prefect, John the Cappadocian, and his quaestor Tribonian, but the rioting went on unabated for five days.

Hiding away in his palace, Justinian became suspicious of Hypatius and Anastasius, the nephews of the late emperor Anastasius, and so dismissed them to their homes. The mob, be-ing in need of a leader, obligingly stormed into Hypatius's house and, over the screams of his wife, carried him off to the forum of Constantinople, where they placed a make-shift crown fashioned from a gold necklace on his head. Spurred on by some traitorous senators of the old guard who roundly hated Justinian and his whole upstart dynasty, Hypatius marched his crowd of support-ers to the Hippodrome and seated himself in the imperial box.

Back at the palace Justinian was preparing to flee in the royal yacht. It was Theodora who rose up in Council and shamed him into staying. "May I not live that day on which those who meet me shall not address me as mistress!" she cried. "Royalty is a good burial-shroud!"[7] Hiding in the palace, however, would eventually prove fatal, for the loyalty of the troops was suspect. They were waiting to see which emperor would come out on top. Fortunately for Justinian, the general Belisarius had just returned victorious from the Persian Wars. Belisarius, a Thracian peasant who, like Uncle Justin, had risen through the ranks, owed his career to Justinian. He was loyal, and his troops were fanatically loyal to him. Justinian dispatched Belisarius to the Hippodrome along with Mundus, general of the Illyrians, who happened to be in town with a band of his barbarians.

Belisarius first tried to get into the royal box, but the soldiers on guard refused to obey him. He then charged into the Hippodrome itself, causing the huge blue-green mob to panic. Hearing the noise, Mundus rushed in with his barbarians through a gate called the "Gate of Death." The soldiers cut down some 30,000 unarmed civilians, which effectively squashed the rebellion. Hypatius was dragged from his throne and delivered to Justinian, who executed him along with his brother Pompeius. John the Cappadocian and Tribonian were re-hired.[8]

After such devoted service, both in the Persian Wars and in the riot, Belisarius became the chosen instrument for Justinian's imperial dream:

> We have good hopes that God will grant us to restore our authority over the remaining countries which the ancient Romans possessed to the limits of both oceans and lost by subsequent neglect.[9]

Of course every aggressor needs a specious excuse, and Justinian's came through a revolution in North Africa.

For four generations Gaiseric's successors had ruled peacefully over the Vandals. King Gaiseric had originally led the Vandals to Africa and, as we saw in the last chapter, vandalized the city of Rome in 455, but his successors learned the advantages of peaceful coexistence. When, however, the current king Hilderick, a grandson of Valentinian III and an old friend of Justinian, was overthrown by the Arian rebel Gelimer in 530, Justinian unleashed the wrath of Belisarius upon him.[10]

The most effective part of the wrath was the Cataphracts, or heavy armed cavalry, some 6,000 of whom constituted Belisarius' main force. The battle of Hadrianople had proven the uselessness of undisciplined foot soldiers against well trained, heavily mounted troops, and the Romans learned their lesson well from the Goths. The Cataphracts were recruited from Asia Minor; Procopius describes them as follows:

> But our archers are mounted on horses, which they manage with admirable skill; their head and shoulders are protected by a casque or buckler; they wear greaves of iron on their legs, and their bodies are guarded by a coat of mail. On their right side hangs a quiver, a sword on their left, and their hand is accustomed to wield a lance or javelin in close combat. Their bows are strong and weighty; they shoot in every possible direction...and as they are taught to draw the bowstring not to their breast, but to the right ear, firm indeed must be the armor that can resist the rapid violence of their shaft.[11]

In September and December of 533 Belisarius won two crushing victories near Carthage. Gelimer fled into the desert to hide among the Bedouin, but at last he surrendered in disgust. The Vandal kingdom of North Africa collapsed. Tripoli, Sardinia, and Corsica also surrendered, as did the islands of Majorca, Minorca, and Ivitza. Taking advantage of another civil war among the Visigoths, the Romans were able to cross over to the Spanish mainland and seize some coastal cities as well.

Naturally after such a triumph the courtiers in Constantinople became jealous of Belisarius and manufactured rumors of his treason. To squelch them Belisarius hastened back home with Gelimer in tow. After acting as the principle float in Belisarius' victory parade, the ex-Vandal king lived out his life on an estate in the suburbs of Constantinople.

All suspicions were tranquilized as Belisarius was hailed "the third Africanus" and granted one of the empire's last consulships. Justinian abolished the office in 542 as archaic and unbearably expensive for its holders, who were responsible both for private charities and for the public games. Henceforth the year was dated from the beginning of Justinian's reign or else from the year 5508 BC, the date calculated from Genesis as the beginning of the world.[12]

The Vandals were certainly not what they had been under Gaiseric. A century of soft living had left them easy prey for the Cataphracts, whom they outnumbered at the start of the war 10 to 1. Like so many would-be conquerors before them, they were simply swallowed up into the teeming native populations of the

East. Justinian, however, failed to consolidate his rule. He replaced Belisarius with a succession of greedy exarchs who plagued the land with taxes and sucked it dry. The Arian heresy was forbidden after a rigged synod of bishops, which infuriated the natives, and Justinian generally failed to pay his troops, which infuriated them.[13]

Next on the list was Italy, with Rome as the grand prize. Once again civil war among the barbarians offered an excuse. Our old friend Theodoric the Ostrogoth had married a Frankish lady named Audefleda, sister to Clovis, the first king of France. Their daughter, the princess Amalasuntha, was regent of Italy since old man Theodoric had named her 10-year-old son, his grandson Athalric, as his heir. After Theodoric's death, unfortunately, the boy turned into a spoiled brat and rebelled against his mother's stern discipline. With the aid of self-seeking yes-men at court he broke away from his mother's tutelage and managed to drink himself to death by the age of sixteen.

Left without a man in the house, Princess Amalasuntha married her cousin Theodahad. Being both ungrateful and ambitious, Amalasuntha's new husband carried her off from Ravenna and exiled her upon an island in Lake Bolsena in his native Etruria, where he had her strangled in her bath tub. Whether or not Theodahad was encouraged in his murderous treachery by Peter, the Byzantine ambassador to Italy, and whether or not Peter was acting on instructions from Theodora, jealous of Amalasuntha's legendary beauty, Justinian expressed outrage over the foul murder of a useful barbarian ally. Of course that meant war.[14]

In 535 Belisarius took Sicily, as always the breadbasket of Rome, and crossed almost unopposed into the toe of Italy. The Gothic army turned on the incompetent Theodahad and hailed his armor-bearer Witigis as their king. King-elect Witigis sent a hit man to murder his boss and, as insurance, married Amalasuntha's daughter Mathesuantha. By this time Belisarius had taken Naples and marched into Rome amid the cheers of a population long since sick of barbarians. Witigis and the Gothic army moved in and besieged Belisarius in Rome for one year and nine days. The city was relieved by the timely arrival of imperial reinforcements under the general John "the Sanguinary," and Witigis scurried north to the safety of Ravenna.

7,000 more reinforcements arrived under the eunuch Narses,

Justinian's imperial treasurer, but the war against Witigis dragged on for two more years. The three generals Belisarius, John, and Narses disagreed to such an extent that the great city of Milan was allowed to fall to the Goths, who brutally executed the entire male population. Only after the recall of Narses was Belisarius able to besiege the Gothic capital of Ravenna.

Desperate, the Goths offered Belisarius the crown of Italy. He pretended to accept, marched into the city in triumph, and then secured it for his emperor Justinian. As had happened in the Vandal War, however, a mere hint of treason was enough to make Justinian nervous; he recalled Belisarius at once with promises of a command in the interminable Persian Wars. Belisarius obediently sailed again to Constantinople with Witigis as his trophy. The valuable Gothic hostage was promoted to the rank of Patrician and retired to the suburbs. If he entertained with Gelimer he had to do it without his wife Mathesuantha, who was married off to Justinian's cousin Germanus. Jordanes ended his *History of the Goths* with the naive hope that their offspring would unite the Byzantine and Gothic people forever.[15]

The recall of Belisarius was a costly mistake. The Italian population, who had greeted Belisarius as their liberator, gradually turned against the Byzantines as their hero was replaced by a hoard of ravenous *logothetes*, or financial agents. Alexander, who was put in charge of Rome, was nicknamed "the scissors" by the population. He so defrauded his own soldiers that they stole from the people. The Goths, meanwhile, taking advantage of the lull in operations, elected Totila to be their next[16] king. He not only proved to be the hero the Goths had been waiting for, he also took care to keep his troops under optimum discipline, thus presenting a most favorable contrast to the Byzantines.

Justinian and Theodora dispatched Belisarius once again to Italy to save the day, but this time the general's effectiveness was seriously curtailed. While Belisarius had been off fighting Persia's King Chosroes, Justinian had nearly died of the bubonic plague, which reached Constantinople in 542; it decimated Europe and the Near East for the rest of the century. The inevitable rumors filtered back to the convalescing emperor that Belisarius, along with other traitors, was exulting in the possibility of Justinian's death. "If the Romans should set up a second Justinian over us," the traitors were supposed to have said, "we shall never tolerate it!" The ever suffering and, one begins to think, overly obliging Belisarius was thus recalled once again. "And he went about, a sorry and incredible sight, Belisarius a private citizen in Byzantium, practically alone, always pensive and gloomy, and dreading death by violence."[17] Of course instead of a death sentence yet another commission came to save Italy, but Belisarius was in no condition to demand the best of terms. He promised the emperor that he would never ask him for money, but would support the war with his own funds.[18]

The rescue mission was a failure. Dispatched in 544, Belisarius spent five years sailing from one armed fortress to another while Totila campaigned virtually unopposed in Italy. By the winter of 545, when he wasn't even able to relieve towns under siege by the enemy, Belisarius broke his promise and sent the following letter to Justinian:

> We have arrived in Italy, most mighty emperor, without men, horses, armor, or money, and no man, I think, without plentiful supply of these things, would ever be able to carry on a war...Consequently, since we have fallen behind in regard to the payment of the soldiers, we find ourselves quite unable to impose our orders upon them; for the debt has taken away our right to command. And this also thou must know well, my master, that the majority of those serving in the armies have deserted to the enemy. If, therefore, it was only necessary that Belisarius be sent to Italy, then thou hast made the best preparation possible for the war; for I am already in the very midst of Italy. If, however, it is thy will to overcome thy foes in the war, provision must also be made for the other necessary things...[19]

Totila could now move in on Rome itself. When Belisarius botched an attempt to send provisions up the Tiber, conditions in the city became desperate. A detachment of Isaurian guards, sharing Belisarius' disgust with lack of pay, agreed to betray the city and open the Asinarian Gate to the Goths. On the evening of Dec. 17, 546, Totila sent a platoon of commandos shimmying up a rope let down by the traitors. With axes they cut through the great beam that secured the gate. It was opened wide, and the Gothic army marched in. Procopius says that only 500 defenders were left within the city. Totila allowed most of them to escape and even stopped the massacre of refugees in the Church of the Apostle Peter.[20]

This loss of Rome was certainly less traumatic than Alaric's sack 136 years earlier, but Rome was able to bounce back after Alaric. It didn't recover this time. Like her sister city Alexandria after the Arab conquest, Rome became not a city, but a settlement nestled amidst ruins, ruled by petty noble families and the popes they created, inhabited by a mob of illiterate peasants who habitually smashed the marbles of their ancestors to make cement.

Belisarius was able to reoccupy the deserted capital, but without proper supplies he had no chance of consolidating his position. Finally, following the death of Theodora in 548, the general's wife Antonina convinced Justinian to heed her husband's wish to be recalled. When Belisarius got back to Constantinople he washed his hands of the Gothic war and settled into comfortable retirement, much admired, at least for the present, for his past successes.[21]

The recapture of Italy was entrusted to Justinian's cousin Germanus, the great hope of the historian Jordanes. He, unfortunately, sickened and died in Italy, to be replaced by Narses, Belisarius's insubordinate auxiliary from 14 years earlier. The Goths laughed at the choice, for Narses was an imperial eunuch. It might seem incredible that Byzantine emperors habitually surrounded themselves with these unfortunate creatures, but in the back-stabbing court of Constantinople they were the only servants who could be trusted. Eunuchs could not be emperors, nor could they produce children to form a rival imperial dynasty.[22]

Narses was given all the support that Belisarius had lacked; he landed in Italy with 35,000 troops, the bottom of the Byzantine barrel, forcing Totila to march out from Rome to stop him. Their final battle was fought in Umbria in the Apanine mountains, near the village of Tadinum. Totila, who had not read my chapter on the battle of Cannae, sent a massed cavalry formation against the Romans' crescent-shaped battle line. His horsemen, mowed down by the powerful bows of the Cataphracts, fell back in disorder upon the Gothic infantry. Six thousand Goths were slaughtered while King Totila, who ran off with a retinue of only five men, was cut down in flight and hastily buried by his terrified companions. The Romans dug up the grave to confirm his death, took away his crown and bloody cloak as trophies, and reburied the corpse.[23]

Rome was retaken by Narses' lieutenant Dagisthaeus. This was the fifth time the poor city had been captured in Justinian's reign:

by Belisarius in 536, by Totila in 546, by Belisarius again in 547, by Totila again in 549, and now by Dagisthaeus in 552.[24] Rome's barbarian allies looted the town, 300 noble Roman youths held hostage by the Goths were slain in revenge, and most of the Senators were cut down in their Campanian villas before they could return to the city. Justinian had already abolished the consulship; now he indirectly shut down the Senate of Rome as well. Narses had some difficult mop-up operations to perform, especially since the Franks sent military aid to their Gothic cousins, but disease and strategy eventually wiped out all resistance. Narses spent 15 years as Exarch of Ravenna ruling over the exhausted Italians.

Back at Constantinople neither Belisarius nor Justinian was allowed a peaceful end. In 558, when an earthquake damaged the long walls of Constantinople, a Hunnic tribe called the Kotrigurs ran through the breach and looted the suburbs. Since the bulk of the army was in Italy and Africa, old Belisarius was called out of retirement to save the day. The people of Constantinople welcomed him back home with a triumph; Justinian gave him a cold hug. Two years later, after a palace coup was uncovered, Belisarius was inevitably suspected. Justinian imprisoned him for six months, only to let him go with a begrudging acknowledgement of innocence. The general survived his imprisonment only 8 months. After another 8 months Justinian died too, at the age of 83.[25]

Justinian was a tireless ruler. The fact that the scandal-mongering *Anecdota* contains no attack on his morals is perhaps the best evidence for the kind of private life he led. He ate little and slept less, frequently startling his courtiers as he paced aimlessly through the palace at night. Still, his boundless energy must be judged as woefully misdirected and ultimately fatal to the Roman Empire. While he frittered away his time attempting to reconquer the western heritage of Augustus, the real threat from the North and the East grew apace. Huns and Slavs ravished the Balkans, swarming over the extensive frontier fortifications bragged about by Procopius in his book the *Buildings*. Neither Procopius nor Justinian seems to have realized that great walls and defensive works are inevitably a sign of internal weakness and decay. The Persians too, safe behind the natural frontiers of the Taurus mountains, the Caspian and Black Seas, and the Persian Gulf to the South, ravaged the eastern borders in spite of the military pomp of Belisarius. King Chosroes I agreed to the first "everlasting peace" in 532 because he was anxious about securing his own throne. In 540, while Belisarius was busy with the sieges of Ravenna, Chosroes attacked again, even destroying the great city of Antioch. He only agreed to a 50-year peace in 562 when his army was hit by the Bubonic Plague, and even then his high-sounding offer cost the Empire a bribe of 30,000 gold pieces a year! So Justinian's reconquest of the West was a failure, and by misjudging where the true danger lay, he exposed the Empire to future, fatal attacks by the Arabs and Turks.[26]

Such a gloomy summing up might make you wonder why I haven't written chapters on other imperial disasters like Caligula, Nero, Domitian, Commodus, and Elagabalus. Well, despite all the negative aspects of his reign, Justinian doesn't really belong among the losers. I remarked at the outset of this chapter that the emperor Justinian has come down to us as a split personality. He can, after all, be looked upon as a heroic last hurrah, while his positive contributions to Roman culture, ignored by us so far, are among the most important in the history of the Empire. These contributions were both plastic and literary.

Justinian was as inveterate a builder as he was a conqueror. Of all his public and ecclesiastical projects, he's most remembered for the great Church of St. Sophia that he built to replace the church destroyed in the Nika rebellion. Despite its desecration by the Turks, it still stands today as one of the few, and certainly as the most physically impressive, remains of classical antiquity. It is the crowning achievement of Byzantine architecture: 250 feet across by 350 feet deep, with a dome, symbolizing the heavens and, if we want to push it, Justinian's reunification of the Roman world, rising 180 feet from the pavement.

The Romans had, of course, built domed structures before—most notably Hadrian's Pantheon in Rome—but in those the dome rests easily upon a round stone drum. Justinian's architects, Anthemius of Tralles and Isidorus of Miletus, set their dome upon a square. The square is composed of 4 massive pillars connected each by a high arch. From the corners rise broadly sweeping triangles called pendentives upon which the great dome rests.

Two side isles or "colonnaded stoa" run the length of the church, one aisle for men, the other for women. Their vaulted ceilings and the dome itself were covered in gold and colored stones. Light from 24 windows pierced in the lower course of the dome flooded the interior with light, giving the effect, as Procopius put it, of a meadow in full bloom.[27] From the Basilica of St. Peter's in Rome to the Capital Building in Washington D.C., the Cathedral of St. Sophia has been one of the world's most imitated structures.

Buildings, however, tend to fall down. St. Sophia, for instance, is Justinian's second edition; the first was wrecked by an earthquake. The direct effect of a building is also limited by the horizon, so that we historians are much more impressed with ideas. It is clearly the most contradictory part of Justinian's story that this morose, hen-pecked insomniac was in the right place and time to preserve Roman Law for the West.

By Justinian's day Roman Law was over 1,000 years old and in a shambles. Not even a life-time of study could establish mastery over the mass of material available, and even if that were possible, *leges, plebescita, senatus consulta,* praetorian edicts, and endless imperial pronouncements and decrees hopelessly contradicted one another. At a time when all books were copied by hand and when Latin studies in the East were slowly dying out, it would just have been a mater of time until the legal writings of the Republic and Empire disappeared from neglect. To prevent this, Justinian ordered the compilation, not of a law code, which would have been of only temporary interest, but rather of an abridged law library. It's known today as the *Corpus Iuris Civilis.*

That means *The Body of Civil Law,* but that's *civil* in the sense of "belonging to Roman citizens," so that the work might be called *The Roman Law Collection.* In bulk it is about the size of three Bibles. The man put in charge of its production was the same Tribonian we saw fired during the Nika riots. It eventually came to be issued in four parts: The *Codex, Novels, Digest* (or *Pandects*), and the *Institutes.*[28]

The first edition of the *Codex* came out right at the start of Justinian's reign in 528; a second edition (which is what we have) in 534. It doesn't mean "code," for the Latin word *codex* only means a book that's bound in pages, rather than strung out in a long continuous roll like paper towels (that's a *liber*). The *Codex* therefore is a bound collection of imperial pronouncements (*constitutiones*).

There's a strange circularity in all of this. Originally, all law in Rome depended upon the authority of the king. After the Tarquins were kicked out, the king's law-making powers were divided

among the various parts of the Roman republican government—
as indeed we saw in earlier chapters. With the establishment of
Augustus' principate, the reverse process began, as the emperors
absorbed law-making powers back into themselves. Augustus, it
will be recalled, only allowed the Senate and Assemblies to continue meeting as window dressing. In the 2nd century the emperor
Hadrian first dropped all pretense and literally claimed the power
to make laws.

The *Codex* replaced earlier collections made during the reigns
of Diocletian and Theodosius II. Of courses the tide of imperial
babble didn't stop, so eventually a collection of Justinian's own
pronouncements, the *Novels*, was issued in Greek.[29]

The letter from the emperor Trajan to Pliny in chapter 38 is
actually an example of an imperial "pronouncement." Like many
of them, it's a response to a specific question. It was also rendered
obsolete, despite having been written by the *optimus princeps* himself, by virtue of its anti-Christian bias. It was the sum total of all
these contradictions that made the *Codex* necessary.

The *Digest* comprises the bulk of the *Corpus Iuris*. It is therefore
rather surprising to learn that it isn't a collection of Roman laws,
but rather of the opinions of Roman legal scholars. Strictly speaking, Roman laws, which could only be passed by our old friends
the *comitia centuriata,* the *comitia tributa,* and the *concilium plebis,*
had only a minimal impact on the lives of most Roman citizens.
Only about 40 of them were really important, most notably the
Law of the 12 Tables, passed by the *comitia centuriata* way back in
450 BC (Remember?). The noble Senate had never officially had
anything but an advisory capacity, despite its great influence, and
by Justinian's day it "sat as in a picture, having no control over its
vote and no influence for good, but only assembled as a matter of
form and in obedience to an ancient law."[30]

From the middle of the 2nd century BC, however, jurists had
been sought out for their learned opinions, and aspiring young
orators like Cicero studied under their guidance. Augustus first
gave selected jurists the right to issue sealed opinions on his authority, and such jurists in the imperial employ eventually formed
the emperor's council and probably drafted most of his pronouncements. The law in Rome would have remained static without the interpretations of these influential scholars.

Thirty-nine jurists are quoted in the *Digest,* the earliest being

Quintus Mucius Scaevola, who was consul in 95 BC and murdered during Marius' proscriptions, and the last Domitius Ulpianus, a praetorian prefect murdered by his own troops in 228 AD. Ulpian's death ended the productive period of Roman jurisprudence—not surprisingly, given the unsettled conditions of the 3rd century and the obvious risks of being a jurist. Learning sank to such a low ebb that during the reign of Theodosius II the Law of Citations had to be invented. Theodosius' judges, when confronted with conflicting legal authorities, were as helpless as a jack-ass between two bales of hay. Theodosius decreed that his bewildered judges should therefore only have to consult a canon of five jurists, and in case of confusion always side with the majority. With one of the bales of hay artificially removed, the judges could feel less like jack-asses.[31]

Justinian decided to end this nonsense. In 530 he put Tribonian in charge of a learned commission of 15 men, who were given the job of condensing 300 years of legal scholarship to moderate length. The commission claimed to have reduced 3,000,000 lines of commentary about $\frac{1}{20}$ in bulk, but it's certain that the original monographs and commentaries of the classical legal scholars were no longer preserved by the 6th century. The commission probably based its work on excerpts long since prepared for law students at the schools of Berytus (Beirut) and Constantinople. The work was published in Dec. 16, 533.[32]

Great work though the *Digest* is, it is not organized and thus presents a singularly formidable front to any beginning law student. Always willing to oblige, Justinian ordered the faithful Tribonian to compile what he subsequently called "an elementary framework, a cradle of the law."[33] This short treatise, called the *Institutes,* was based on a work of the same title by the 2nd century jurist Gaius, who was also one of the stars of the Law of Citations. It divides the whole of Roman Law into the sub-groups Persons, Things, and Actions.[34] "Study our law," Justinian encouraged his students. "Do your best and apply yourselves keenly to it. Show that you have mastered it. You can then cherish a noble ambition; when your course in law is finished you will be able to perform whatever duty is entrusted to you in the government of our state."[35]

Near the beginning of this book we examined Hammurabi's Code as a way of getting closer to the peoples of the ancient Near

East. It seems fitting to end up with a similar look at Roman Law in accordance with Justinian's institutional scheme. A facile comparison of the two, however, would be pointless. Hammurabi's Code is a rather simple compilation of precedents. The *Corpus Iuris Civilis* is a sophisticated, theoretical work whose style sounds amazingly modern. As we'll see, that's because Roman Law is modern law, and as such is one of antiquity's greatest contributions to us. It will form the subject of our final chapter.

45 Live Honorably, Harm Nobody, Give Everyone His Due

The Romans always felt embarrassed before Greek culture. Even today it is considered an intellectual sin to prefer Tacitus to Thucydides, or Virgil to Homer. Virgil himself, devoted to Greek culture as he was, felt the same uneasiness. As a Roman, however, he could make one unqualified boast.

> Others, no doubt, will better mould the bronze
> To the semblance of soft breathing, draw, from marble,
> The living countenance; and others plead
> With greater eloquence, or learn to measure,
> Better than we, the pathways of the heaven,
> The risings of the stars: remember, Roman,
> To rule the people under law, to establish
> The way of peace, to battle down the haughty,
> To spare the meek. Our fine arts, these, forever.[1]

For all their intellectual precocity, the Greeks could never forge themselves into a nation under law. That accomplishment was to be Rome's greatest achievement; for all his faults we have Justinian to thank for passing it down to us.

The Romans saw all law as pertaining to either persons, things, or actions.[2] Persons makes a particularly good start for us, for it allows a closer look at how the Romans actually lived as a people. This Roman people was divided into dependent and independent persons. Only a male head of household was independent; everyone else was subordinate in one sense or another to him.[3]

This was especially true of children. In the early days of the Republic, they could even be executed by their fathers, as in the famous story of Titus Manlius, the consul who killed his son for disobeying orders.[4] That had softened by historical times, but not much.[5] Not only were children in their father's power, but their children and grandchildren were as well. Father was the *paterfamilias*; his son was the *filiusfamilias* and remained so until his father's death. Sons had no property of their own; it belonged to their *paterfamilias*–though Justinian softened this so that the father could only use and take profit from his children's property, not own it outright.[6] Sons were so completely absorbed into their father's *potestas* (i.e. power) that they had virtually no legal identities of their own:

> That a head of household cannot proceed against his son for theft is not a ruling of the civil law as such; the very nature of the case makes it impossible; for we can no more sue those in our power than we can sue ourselves...[7]

Although women, the next element of the household, were originally subject to either their father or their husband, they gradually gained more rights under the empire. In the old Republican style of marriage, called *manus*, the wife passed under the authority of her husband or his *paterfamilias*, thus becoming technically the sister of her own children. Even by the time of the Punic wars this unfortunate arrangement had been replaced by something called *liberum matrimonium* (free marriage), by which again only the use of the wife's property passed into the power of her husband. Furthermore, that property couldn't be sold off by the husband without the wife's consent, in order "to stop men exploiting the weakness of the female sex and ruining them financially."[8]

Divorce from *liberum matrimonium* was easy. Augustus in the *Lex Papia-Poppaea* provided that only the presence of seven witnesses was needed. As in old Babylon, a divorced woman got back her dowry; if the husband was at fault, he would have to cough it up in only 6 months, rather than in the usually allotted grace period of 2 years. If the wife was at fault she lost $\frac{1}{6}$ or $\frac{1}{8}$ of the marriage portion. Adultery on the wife's part, of course, was a much more serious affair. In the sterner days of the Republic it was punished with death. Augustus was content simply to exile both parties to separate islands. Justinian, unfortunately, like Constantine and the other Christian emperors, followed the lead of the Christian Church which, in accordance with the attitude of the New Testament,[9] increasingly restricted the circumstances under which divorce by mutual consent could take place.[10]

Women who became legally independent, either through divorce or through the death of their male authority figure, were originally placed under the care of a *tutor*, without whose authority they couldn't even sign contracts or sell property. By the time of Gaius, however, this practice had become obsolete:

> Virtually no valuable argument seems to have established that women of legal age be in guardianship. For what is commonly believed—that because of their frivolous intellects they are frequently deceived and that it is equitable that they be regulated by the authority of a tutor—seems more specious than true. Women who are of legal age generally handle their business for themselves, and in certain cases the tutor interposes his authority only for the sake of appearances. Indeed, unwilling guarantors must frequently be compelled to serve by the praetor.[11]

It is, however, under the laws of inheritance that women's rights—or lack of them—are most clearly documented, so I'm going to discuss them here, even though wills properly belong to the Law of Things. The Romans, as is obvious from the passages above, didn't like the idea of women controlling property. This loosened up a bit by Justinian's time, but generally speaking, this bias remained intact. Thus succession was always passed down, if possible, in the male line of descent—through the agnatic line, as the Romans put it.

Under the 12 Tables all agnates were treated alike, so that brothers and sisters shared equally in their father's estate, but the Voconian Law of 170 BC virtually abolished all rights of female inheritance. Justinian bragged about returning to the equal treatment of the 12 Tables. He allowed mothers to inherit their children's estates (provided the kids had no heirs), and he even allowed children to inherit directly from their mothers. Formerly, the mother's property passed back instead to her father's family.[12] Still, after immediate heirs (i.e. "the sons and daughters, also grandchildren through a son and so on down the line, who were within the authority of the deceased on his deathbed"[13]), agnates always had priority over cognates, or descendants in the female line. Agnatic relations counted all the way down to the 10th degree, which is pretty far from a kissing cousin; cognates only counted to the 6th.[14]

Even if women's rights gradually improved under the Empire and Justinian had some justification for his claims of even-handedness, the following seems to be the final word on rights of inheritance:

General statements such as that the nearer cognate has the stronger claim, or that all cognates are entitled on an equal footing, are only good on the assumption that there is nobody with priority as an immediate heir or equivalent, or as an agnate, under the rules we have given.[15]

After women and children, the family of a *paterfamilias* was completed by his slaves. All slaves were, by definition, dependent persons, and all slaves were treated the same by the law, regardless of individual living conditions. Slaves were generally battle captives or their descendants. The Romans, however, attached no racial prejudice to slavery and were quite willing to enslave anybody. Even a full Roman citizen, if captured in battle by the enemy, was thought of as having lapsed into slavery; the rights of his children were thus held in suspension until either his death or his automatic rehabilitation upon return. Similarly, any will he wrote while still a foreign captive was considered invalid.[16] A Roman citizen over 20 could even sell himself into slavery for a share of his own price![17]

As a result of this mercenary attitude, Blacks in Rome were not saddled with the stigma of having been an enslaved race. Blacks, called Ethiopians by the Romans, were common enough in the cosmopolitan population of the capital, where they were just as easily regarded as merchants, mercenaries, or ambassadors as slaves.[18] Surviving Roman comedy, which was composed at the time of the Macedonian Wars described in chapters 26-27, habitually depicted slaves with red hair[19] since at that time fair-skinned northern Greeks were flooding the slave market. The modern circus clown, with his pasty face, red hair, bulbous nose, and huge feet is quite possibly the direct descendant of this Roman slave stereotype.

Slaves were absolutely thought of as the property of their masters, to the extent that a run-away slave-girl could be accused of theft of herself, and that the kidnapping of her child was handled as theft of her master's property.[20] Killing a slave brought the same penalty as killing a valuable piece of four-footed livestock, although there was some debate over whether pigs should be included in the same category. As the jurist Paul put it, "If you kill my slave, I think that personal feelings should not be taken into account...but only what he would be worth to the world at large."[21]

Senseless cruelty, however, was not allowed, for "it is in the public interest that nobody should treat his property badly." Masters who killed their slaves without good reason would be punished just as if they'd killed the slave of another—which is to say with a fine equal to the slave's highest value in the preceding year. Similarly, masters who were notoriously cruel to their slaves would have them sold by the state to someone else.

Though these rules against cruelty included prohibitions against sadistic torture, it was standard operating procedure to torture any slave called as witness in a trial—just to make sure he was telling the truth. As the Digest puts it, "By torture we mean the infliction of anguish and agony on the body to elicit the truth. Mere interrogation or mild initmidation does not come within this edict."[22]

Slaves could be set free by a process called *manumission* (literally "setting free from the hand"). A manumitted slave became a freedman, and as such the client of his former master, who now became his patron. Patrons could claim ½ (under Justinian lessened to ⅓) of their freedmen's estate unless expressly excluded by the freedman's children, so the relationship was not looked upon as a casual one. Freedmen didn't usually even have the right of suing their patrons for injury, "for the praetor does not have to tolerate the slave, now a freedman, complaining against his master that the latter abused him verbally or moderately chastised or corrected him."[23]

Slaves had their own "pocket money" (*peculium*) over which they had some legal right, and could use this to buy their freedom (though some used it to buy their own slaves!). Many slaves were set free in their masters' wills. This practice had become so prevalent that in 2 BC Augustus passed the *Lex Fufia Caninia* to restrict it. It was also forbidden to free all of one's slaves in order to defraud a creditor, who would thus find the estate of his debtor impoverished. Slaves could be made heirs too, as long as they had not been the adulterous lovers of their mistresses. Slaves were compulsory heirs, which is to say that they were forced to accept their legacies. They did automatically gain their freedom thereby, but there could be a catch, for they were also liable for all the debts owed by their dead and beneficent masters.[24]

The next major branch of the Roman law is the Law of Things. This sounds like simply the law of property and contracts, but it's actually much broader than that, for the Roman jurisconsults divided things into the corporeal and the incorporeal, the latter of which embraced the legal concepts of rights and obligations. That would include inheritance, by which whole estates as well as individual things were transferred; obligations entered into voluntarily, like contracts; and obligations caused through injury, which we call torts and the Romans called delicts. Even theft was looked upon as an obligation caused by delict and was originally handled as a civil suit. So the Law of Things is a major chunk of the law.[25]

Naturally the Romans were very concerned about how ownership of things—i.e. property—is transferred. In the early days of the Republic this had to be accomplished through a cumbersome process called *mancipatio*, literally "grasping by the hand." It was a ceremony requiring five witnesses and a pair of scales. The buyer had to grasp the object for sale with one hand and the copper he could give in exchange with the other. He then said, "I declare this slave [cow, or whatever] to be mine by the law of the Quirites and purchased by me with this piece of bronze upon these bronze scales." He then struck the scales with the copper or bronze he was holding.

That would make a colorful performance, but it would greatly hold up action on the stock exchange. Thus the Romans gradually substituted simple delivery of goods, backed up by the concept of *usucapio*, or "grasping by use." Under this concept if any moveable property were held in someone's possession for 3 years, then ownership passed to him. For immovable property the period was 10 years, unless of course the object had been fenced. Stolen property could never be usucapted.

As far as the seller was concerned, his liability ended once the price had been agreed upon. The law said that "goods are at the purchaser's risk," so that if any honest accident occurred before delivery, the buyer was obliged to absorb the loss.[26]

We've already touched upon wills under the Law of Persons, but as a legal concept inheritance belongs here in the Law of Things. Roman lawyers, like modern ones, must have spent a good deal of their time writing wills, for the sections on wills, legacies, and trusts take up fully one third of Justinian's *Institutes*. In brief, though: A Roman will didn't even have to be written; it just needed seven witnesses, each of whom was a full citizen and himself capable of making a will. No one under another's authority could write a valid will, and of course no one mentioned in the will could serve as a witness. These rules were considerably relaxed for soldiers on active duty, for "soldiers know little of such matters."

Anyone could be named as an heir, but thanks to a law passed by Sulla's extraordinary courts of *Centumviri*, a son could not be disinherited by simple omission. Such an insulted son could have the will declared null and void and automatically have himself named principal heir. If you were angry enough to disinherit, you actually had to write "Let Titius [the Institute's customary generic name] my son be disinherited." You could also appoint a substitute heir in case of the death of your child, but Justinian warns that such a clause could be dangerous to the child's health, and recommends that such instructions be kept sealed at the lawyer's office.[27]

Originally, Roman law didn't look upon promises as legally enforceable obligations unless they were performed under certain formulas, just as sales had to be performed under the strict formula of *mancipatio*. There was only a gradual evolution towards "the modern view that promises are binding unless the law excludes them, as opposed to the old view that they are not binding unless the law makes them so."[28] For instance, verbal contracts or stipulations—which to the Romans were as valid as written ones—used to be made in accordance with strict, formulaic exchanges.[29] These were abandoned by the emperor Leo, who said that any words would do, either in Latin or Greek, if the parties understood each other. Furthermore, such stipulations became invalid if one of the parties were deaf, dumb, insane, or underage, or if an impossible stipulation were set, such as "Do you promise to give if I touch the sky?"[30] We'll have more to say about legal formulas later.

Other obligations from contract included debt (both in kind and in money), sale (which we've touched upon), hire, mandate (i.e. engagement without charge) and partnership. A characteristic wrinkle in the law of partnership is the limit placed upon liability of a partner for loss through laziness or carelessness. The standards set are not the highest, but rather such as could be expected from the partner's personality: "Someone who chooses a careless partner has only himself to blame."[31]

Moving out of the guiltless society, we come to obligations from delict, or wrong-doing. They were divided into theft, robbery, loss wrongfully caused, and contempt. Historically, these would be cases in which the king had been forced to intervene after a defendant had been dragged, kicking and screaming, into court.[32]

The king would naturally attempt to bring about a compromise; failing that he could hand over a thief to be his own victim's slave. Later, the 12 Tables called for "tit for tat" justice, just as we saw in Hammurabi's day. The Empire added exile and penal servitude as punishments, and of course execution was always available for certain heinous crimes not considered among delictual obligations. We'll discuss them later. But for delicts the usual penalty was a fine. Fines were thus imposed as punishment to the wrongdoer, not as compensation for the victim, who had other actions available to recover his property—assuming, of course, that a victim was lucky enough to have been mugged by a solvent thief. The Romans did not consider prison an option, "for prison should be used to hold men, not to punish them."[33]

Even if a thief paid his fine and managed to avoid slavery or penal servitude in the mines or gruesome slaughter by the beasts in the arena, the praetor could still brand him with *infamia*. He would be in grim company:

> The following incur infamia: one who has been discharged from the army in disgrace...one who has appeared on the stage to act or recite; one who has kept a brothel; one who in criminal proceedings has been judged guilty of vexatious litigation or collusion in anything; one who has been condemned in his own name for theft, robbery with violence, insult, fraud, trickery or compromised in such a case...[34]

Someone condemned as infamous could neither vote, hold office, serve as a witness, represent a client, nor make a will. As we shall see later, by Justinian's time actions for delict, which sound to us moderns like civil suits, were replaced by summonses before governmental courts. As the digest puts it:

> It must be remembered that now criminal proceedings for theft are common and the complainant lays an allegation. It is not a kind of public prosecution in the normal sense, but it seemed proper that the temerity of those who do such wrongs should be punishable on extraordinary scrutiny.[35]

Theft was divided into manifest and non-manifest. Manifest theft meant basically "red-handed" theft, and it was costly. If you caught your thief before he got to stash his loot, you could collect fourfold damages. Non-manifest theft only paid double. It didn't matter how many thieves were caught in the act, for as the jurist Paul rightly argued, all the thieves who helped carry off a heavy beam were equally guilty.

Robbery, which meant theft with violence (*rapina*) also brought four-fold damages, but since those damages included the return of the stolen object the penalty was actually only three-fold. Willful injury, as we saw in the cases of slaves, required the highest price the object would have brought in the last 30 days.

Contempt meant insult inflicted through violence, verbal abuse, or published libel. It also included sexual harassment. It was possible to sue for contempt if someone under your authority had been insulted, so that you could even sue for insult to a slave. Technically a slave could not be insulted, but the insult could be seen as reflecting upon his master. It was also necessary to react at once, for an insult once swallowed ceases to exist.[36]

The final division of the law is that of Actions (i.e. legal processes), an understanding of which will bring us a long way towards grasping the fundamental nature of Roman jurisprudence. Going all the way back to the 12 Tables, Roman Law was not a collection of rights, but rather of specific remedies. In order to plead your case, it was necessary to know the specific formula available. You then filled in the blanks and argued accordingly before a magistrate. This is similar to the importance we saw formulas take in contracts. Precision here was no light matter, for Gaius tells of a case where a plaintiff lost his suit simply because he made a claim for "damaged vines" when the statute he was using demanded the formula "damaged trees."[37] It was thirst for knowledge of this sort that led to the publication of the 12 Tables themselves and to the first important legal monographs of the 2nd century.

Although the formulas were set by law, "criminal trials are not ordered by forms of action."[38] Originally, they involved crimes so terrible that the king stepped in on his own, without waiting for a defendant to be dragged into his court. They were called "Public Trials" because any Roman citizen was free to prosecute such a wrong-doer. Some of these crimes invoked only fines or disgrace (i.e. loss of legal status), but many were capital offenses that automatically called for death, banishment, or condemnation to the mines.

Ten capital offenses were listed in the 12 Tables: 1) Treason, 2) nocturnal assembly in the city, 3) murder, 4) arson, 5) perjury, 6) corruption of a judge, 7) composition of libels or satires (which could get their author clubbed to death), 8) destruction of a neighbor's crops, 9) witchcraft, and 10) debt (If several creditors remained unsatisfied after 60 days, they could, Shylock-like, carve up the debtor.).

For once the list in the *Institutes* doesn't present much of an improvement. It includes murder, adultery (despite the more humane decree of Augustus), homosexuality (despite emperors like Trajan and Hadrian), rape, poisoning, and the casting of magic spells.

Actions for criminal cases were held before standing courts, the first of which was set up in 149 BC to deal with extortion by provincial governors. Sulla, in a reform which lasted through the time of Augustus, set up seven permanent courts to try the crimes of murder, forgery, extortion, treason, electoral bribery, embezzlement, and assault.

From the time of the kings it had always been the right of a citizen to appeal to the people–i.e. to the Assemblies–but there was no appeal from these standing courts. With the growth of Rome, trials before the Assembly had become increasingly impractical, and with the advent of the Revolution even undesirable.

Some punishments depended upon the status of the criminal. Thus if a man were "highly placed" his punishment for seducing "an unmarried girl or a respectable widow" would be confiscation of half his property; if the seducer were lowly, he'd be whipped and banished. While the rich could always buy a favorable verdict, the poor were invariably tortured into a confession. The crime of parricide, which meant killing either a son or a father, brought a famous and symbolic penalty:

> He is not put to the sword nor to the fire, nor to any other custom-hallowed death, but is sewn into a sack with a dog, a cock, a snake, and a monkey; and, sealed in with these bestial intimates, he is thrown, as the nature of the place allows, into a nearby sea or river.

In reality, however, given the paucity of monkeys in Italy, parricides were usually fed to the lions or burned at the stake.[39]

Civil actions took the form of arbitration before a private judge (*iudex privatus*) empowered for each case by the urban praetor, who approved the legal formula under which the case would be tried.

As both commerce and life in the big city grew increasingly complex, the rigid formulae of the old law proved inadequate for the growing number of civil cases, so about 150 BC the *Lex Aebutia* gave the urban praetor the right to create new *formulae in factum,* or to fit the requirements of each case. Each year the incoming *praetor urbanus* would publish an edict explaining his formulaic procedures; the collection of these edicts formed the *ius honorarium,* a major component of the Law of Actions.[40]

What we would call a civil suit thus was divided into two parts. In part one the plaintiff and defendant would appear before the urban praetor to explain their complaint. The praetor would then draw up the formula appropriate to the circumstances. This formula would in effect represent instructions to the private judge who would hear the case. By creating new formulas the praetor would actually create new law.

As a simple example, let's imagine an argument between two Romans over whether one owed the other 10,000 sesterces. In part one the two men would appear before the praetor who would hear their arguments and issue the following traditional formula:

> Let X be *iudex.* If it appears that the defendant ought to pay 10,000 sesterces to the plaintiff, let the *iudex* condemn the defendant to pay 10,000 sesterces to the plaintiff. If it does not so appear, let the *iudex* absolve him.

X would then be selected from a list of rich Romans who sat in judgement from a sense of civic duty. He would hear the actual arguments of plaintiff and defendant and decide the case.[41]

Dry cleaning presents a good theoretical example of actions in action. Suppose that you've sent off your cloak to Titius' One-Hour-Cleaners, and a thief breaks into Titius' and steals it. If the thief is caught, you do not have an action for theft of the cloak; that belongs to Titius, in whose interest the safety of the cloak now rests. Your proper action against Titius is for hire. Furthermore, if Titius wore your cloak on a date without your permission and had it stolen off his back by the thief, Titius still had his action for theft against the mugger, but now you also would have an action for theft against Titius since, technically, he stole your cloak. As the jurisconsult Ulpian proudly announced, "it can thus happen that even the thief himself has an action for theft"[42]

Examples for defense against an action can be taken from the

Lex Aquilia, originally passed as a plebiscite in 287 BC, which established actions for wrongful loss. The trick was to prove that you were not at fault. Thus, just as in America, you could be charged under the act for killing a robber, but not if you could prove that there had been no other way for you to escape injury. This was also the act under which an owner could sue you for killing his slave. If you ran the poor creature through with one of your practice javelins, for instance, it was judged to be the slave's fault if he had wandered onto a known athletic field; it was your fault if you were tossing your javelin in a public place. If you had crushed the slave with the branch of a tree you were pruning, the judge would want to know if the tree were by a roadside or in the middle of a field (where you could argue the slave was trespassing), or if you had shouted "Look out!" before letting loose with the branch.

Damages under the *Lex Aquilia* were simple if the defendant confessed, but double if he denied liability. That could be a hefty sum, for the *Lex* called for fourfold damages, which was the maximum allowed under the law. Actions under the *Lex Aquilia* were considered punitive. Others, designed solely for regaining property, were called restorative. A third type, like the action for robbery mentioned above, was hybrid.[43]

By Justinian's day, however, the concept of actions was largely obsolete. Its preservation in the *Institutes* is due mainly to the influence of Gaius' original scheme. Even Augustus found the old system difficult to control, so he gradually replaced the old judges with imperial officials directly responsible to him. Hadrian put an end to yearly praetorian edicts by making that of his praefect Salvius Julianus the Perpetual Edict. The permanent courts for criminal trials had disappeared by about 200; the last *iudex privatus* we hear of sat in the year 261 AD; and by Justinian's day all cases were heard before "extraordinary courts." They were composed of imperial delegates and can be thought of historically as extensions of the old provincial courts run by governors. Once Augustus had received the *imperium maius* in 27 BC it was entirely logical for him to extend his proconsular power over the legal system of the entire empire.

These extraordinary courts acted much more like courts of today. Instead of searching for the appropriate formula, litigants had only to appear before the imperial judge and tell their story. Thus by Justinian's time the concept of a living Roman tradition had been replaced by the arbitrary will of a single judge, himself the mouthpiece of an authoritarian emperor.[44]

Persons, things, and actions: I would hate to conclude this brief survey of the *Corpus Iuris Civilis* with nothing more than a collection of examples. What about the work as a whole? What about its destiny?

The strongest overall impression made by the *Corpus* is one of fairness. As implied in the title of this chapter, which comes from the very start of the *Institutes*, this fairness is not the child's concept of "treat everyone the same." Roman law only promises "everyone his due." The class structure was a permanent part of Roman society, but still the emperors Severus and Antoninus could boast, "Although we stand above the law, we live by it."[45] The weak were to be protected: neither children, idiots, nor dumb animals could be held responsible for their actions,[46] and even an honest mistake in the courtroom—what we would call a technicality—could be forgiven.[47] Conversely, the careless are constantly admonished to stop whining and accept the responsibility of their actions.[48]

It might be assumed that the Romans possessed no concept of what we like to call "basic human rights." That isn't true. In passages that could easily have been composed in the Enlightenment, the *Institutes* develops a whole theory of natural law:

> The law of nature is the law instilled by nature in all creatures. It is not merely for mankind but for all creatures of the sky, earth, and sea. From it comes intercourse between male and female, which we call marriage; also the bearing and bringing up of children (1.2 pr).

It is even admitted, most surprisingly, that slavery is fundamentally unjust:

> Wars broke out. People were captured and made slaves, contrary to the law of nature. By the law of nature all men were initially born free (1.2.2).

To the practically minded Roman, however, natural law reflected the myth of the Golden Age and had nothing to do with everyday life. The Romans lived in the world as they found it; it never occurred to them to strive for a realization of the Golden Age.

Roman Law does not concern itself with individuals. It looks at society, the high and the low, and tells the individual where he fits in. In practical terms, Roman justice had more to do with one's status than with abstract concepts of right and wrong. A Roman's duty was never to himself. It was divided between his family and his ever present extended family, the state.[49]

In the West, knowledge of the *Corpus* didn't die out during the Middle Ages. It just got epitomized and condensed to death, gradually to be buried under the more barbaric law codes of the Germans, such as the Salian Code of the Franks issued around 510 by Clovis. By the late 11th century, however, complete manuscripts of the *Corpus Iuris* surfaced; they were studied, glossed, and circulated, especially by students of the great University of Bologna. The Romance-speaking countries of Europe have always taken the *Corpus Iuris* as their national heritage; the ever evolving national states of Europe in the 12th and 13th centuries abused Justinian's authoritarian principles in their struggle against the traditional forces of feudalism. Oddly enough it was in Germany that ancient Roman law had its greatest influence. Because Germany was not united into a nation until the 19th century, the *ius civile*, at least as it had been misinterpreted by medieval scholars, actually had practical legal force until the promulgation of the German Civil Code in 1900. Even the concept of "natural law" so pervasive in our own Declaration of Independence owes its existence to a non-historical respect for the concepts imbedded in Roman law.

England and America (except for Louisiana!) have not directly followed the *Corpus Iuris*. Their laws are based upon the precedents, parliamentary acts, and royal decrees that make up English Common Law. Still, we know that by 1150 the Italian scholar Vacarius was teaching Roman Law in England, and of course interest in the classics during the English Renaissance made Roman influence inevitable in the development of English Law. This has been most obvious is successive attempts to codify the confused mass of Common Law. Blackstone, who first tried in the 18th century, based his *Commentaries* upon Justinian, and modern law schools, consciously or not, organize their courses the same way.[50]

So, just as I said at the start of the last chapter, the Byzantines are still with us. I hope that I have confused you by pointing out that the Roman Empire lasted almost till the time of Columbus, and that the Middle Ages can easily be said to have begun during the reign of the Roman Emperor Diocletian. Books like this one which artificially divide history into chunks called ancient, medieval, and modern only perpetuate a false illusion. It is sickening to think of history as a melodrama in three acts whose finale is us.

Notes to Chapter 23

1. The 5th century Greek historian Hellanicus, whose work is now lost, was apparently the first author to record the relationship of Aeneas to the Romans. See *CAH* VII. 2 pp. 57-61. As both Gruen and Heurgon point out, the legend may have been introduced into Rome from Etruria rather than from Greece, and probably no earlier than the 4th century. See Erich S. Gruen, *The Hellenistic World and the Coming of Rome* (Berkeley: University of California Press, 1980) pp. 250-251 and Jacques Heurgon, *Rome et la Méditerranée occidentale jusqu'aux guerres puniques,* 3rd ed. (Paris: Presses Universitaires de France, 1993) pp. 224-226.

2. Livy, 1. 4. See above pp. 31 and 60-61. As Livy himself confesses (1. 3.2) *Quis enim rem tam veterem pro certo adfirmet?*

3. Michael Rostovtzeff, *A History of the Ancient World, vol. II Rome* (Oxford, 1927) pp. 7-8. Howard H. Scullard, *A History of the Roman World 753 to 146 BC,* 4th Edition (London: Methuen and Co., 1980) pp. 18-25; Heurgon pp. 53-61. Alexander Grandazzi, *The Foundation of Rome: Myth and History* (Ihaca: Cornell University Press, 1997) emphasizes the complexity of Rome's Indo-European origins and stresses that ethnic and linguistic interaction throughout all periods was fluid. "Whoever they were, the people who lived on the plains of Latium at the dawn of the second millennium B.C.E. were not Latins, but rather became Latins (p. 116)."

4. Heurgon pp. 118-119.

5. Herodotus, I. 94. A rival theory, first offered by Dionyssius of Halicarnassus 1. 30.2, makes the Etruscans an aboriginal people. Massimo Pallottino sees the evolution of the Etruscans in Italy as a result of complex interactions *in situ,* but which nonetheless show an unbroken line from the Villanovans of the iron age to the historical Etruscans. See *A History of Earliest Italy* (London: Routledge, 1991) pp. 51-53.

6. Most interestingly an inscription scratched onto a 7th century vase from Caere reads *mi laucies mezenties,* i.e. "I belong to Laurus Mezentius." The "mythical" Mezentius was King of Caere, and Virgil tells us that his son's name was Laurus! See Vergil, *Aeneid* 7. 647-654 and Heurgon p. 434.

7. The traditional date was set by Varro. It was arrived at by adding 7 generations of 35 years each to the traditional date of the founding of the Republic, 509 BC. It is quite possible, however, that the number of seven kings is the manipulated figure, if indeed a founding date in the middle of what we call the 8th century had been handed down in tradition. See Heurgon pp. 226-228.

8. The story of Aeneas in Italy is told by Virgil in the second half of

his great epic the *Aeneid.* For the story of Romulus and Remus, see Livy, 1. 3-7 and (with endless rhetorical embellishments) Dionysius of Halicarnassus, 1. 76-87. See also Rostovtzeff, *Rome* pp. 15-16, Scullard pp. 46-47, and Theodor Mommsen, *The History of Rome,* vol. 2 (New York: Scribner, Armstrong, and Co., 1873) pp. 547-548.

9. I didn't make that up! It's from a fragment of Ennius's *Annals* preserved for us by Cicero and listed at I.48 in Ernout's collection: *certabant urbem Romam Remoramne vocarent.*

10. For the story of the Horatii and the Curiatii, who dueled dramatically over the fate of Alba Longa, see Livy, 1. 24-29; Scullard pp. 61-62 and 33-4; Rostovtzeff, *Rome* pp. 14-16. See also Mommsen vol. 1 pp. 75-79, 143-144, and 147-148; Heurgon pp. 74-79, 87; Grandazzi pp. 129-139.

11. Grandazzi pp. 149-161; Heurgon pp. 430-431.

12. Livy 1. 34-35 and 39-41; Scullard pp. 53-56; *CAH* VII.2 pp. 93-96.

13. Livy 1. 8 and 35, who says that it was Romulus himself who adopted these symbols from the Etruscans; Dionysius of Halicarnassus 3.61; Rostovtzeff pp. 9-10 and 20-21; Scullard pp. 28-33 and 60; Heurgon pp. 208, 237-240.

14. Scullard pp. 63 and 67-68; Rostovtzeff, *Rome* pp. 17-21; Mommsen I. 110-113; Heurgon pp. 216-219.

15. Livy 1. 35; Cicero, *De Re Publica* 2. 20.

16. Rostovtzeff, *SEHRE* pp. 11-13; Scullard pp. 39-41, 45; Mommsen I. 128-132 (who thinks that the plebs were descended from non-Roman Latins); *CAH* VII.2 pp. 98-104, 167-168 and 178-182, 260, 325, and 443-444 (where even within one volume different articles disagree); Heurgon pp. 196-200; Grandazzi p. 119; Michael Crawford, *The Roman Republic,* 2nd ed., (Cambridge: Harvard University Press, 1993) pp. 24-25, 28.

17. Lest you wonder forever, the names of the 7 kings of Rome are Titus Tatius, Numa Pompilius, Tullus Hostilius, Ancus Marcius, Tarquinius Priscus, Servius Tullius, and Tarquinius Superbus. The magic number 7 tells something against their authenticity, for a list of 7 seems too pat to be true. It's to be noted that Rome has seven hills too, though you have to cheat a bit in the counting to make them come out that way. Lest you wonder about the fabled 7 hills of Rome, they are the Janiculum on the west bank of the Tiber, and on the east bank, proceeding clockwise from north to south, the Capitoline, Quirinal, Viminal, Esquiline, Aventine, and Palatine. Some critics believe, however, that the ancient "Seven Hills Festival" (*Septimontium*) celebrated on December 11 was originally the festival of the "fortified hills" (*Saeptimontium*), and that the list is thus a relatively modern conceit. See Heurgon p. 89 and Mommsen I.156 note. Grandazzi pp. 139-141 sees the *Septimontium* as preceding the founding of Rome and thus representing the scattered condition of the city's early history.

18. Scullard pp. 50-51 and 69-71; Rostovtzeff pp.16-17; Heurgon pp. 201-211.

19. Cicero, *De Re Publica* 2. 52

20. Livy 1. 46-48, 56-60; 2. 1; Dionysius of Halicarnassus, 4. 64.1-76.2. The consular Fasti list six consuls for the year 509/508, of whom Heurgon accepts only M. Horatius as historical. If so, he would have ruled over the surviving regal band of *praetors* as *praetor maximus*. See Heurgon p. 268. For the Fasti themselves see *CAH* VII.2 pp. 627 ff. and E.J. Bickerman, *Chronology of the Ancient World* (Ithaca: Cornell University Press, 1980) pp. 140 ff., both with bibliography.

21. Livy, 2. 10.

22. *Ibid.* 2. 14.1-7 and Dionyssius of Halicarnassus, 7. 5-6.

23. Livy, *Praef.* 9 (my translation).

24. See Sandra R. Joshel, "The Body Female and the Body Politic: Livy's Lucretia and Verginia," in Amy Richlin, ed., *Pornography and Representation in Greece and Rome* (New York: Oxford University Press, 1992) pp. 112-130.

25. Tellingly, in the Greek version of Dionysius she drives in a carriage from Collatia to appeal to her father in Rome. See Joshel p. 122.

26. Livy 2. 14.8-9.

27. Tacitus, *Histories* 3. 72 is comparing the riots in Rome in 69 AD, "The Year of the 3 Emperors" to other disasters of the past, such as when the city was surrendered to Porsenna. Pliny the Elder (*Natural History* 34. 139) in a typical note, comments: "It has been variously attempted to demonstrate that iron can be innocent. In the treaty, which Porsina gave to the Roman people when the kings had been expelled, we find it specifically stipulated that iron be used only in agriculture."

28. Heurgon pp. 261-267; *CAH* VII.2 pp. 93-96, 256-259; Scullard pp. 74-76. For the nickname Ἀριστόδημος ὁ Μαλακὸς see Dionysius of Halicarnassus, 7. 4.3.

29. Samuel Johnson, "The Vanity of Human Wishes" vv. 221-222.

Notes to Chapter 24

1. Livy 2. 1; Howard H. Scullard, *A History of the Roman World 753 to 146 BC,* 4th ed. (London: Methuen, 1980) p. 79.

2. M. Rostovtzeff, *A History of the Ancient World, vol. II Rome* (Oxford, 1927) pp. 7-8.

3. Like the Greek word τύραννος, the Latin word *dictator* has come to take on evil connotations in its modern usage that it didn't have in the old days.

4. Livy 3. 26; Scullard pp. 80, 95-96; Mommsen I. 330; *CAH* VII. 2 p. 288.

5. Plutarch, *Cato* 17 [p. 424]. "[Cato] said that, as for himself, his wife never came into his arms except when there was a great thunder; so that

it was for a jest with him, that it was a pleasure for him, when Jupiter thundered." See also 16 [pp. 422-423] and Scullard pp. 90-91.

6. Livy, 2. 1.

7. Polybius, 6. 13; Crawford pp. 26-27.

8. Plutarch, *Pyrrhus* 19 [p. 481].

9. Scullard pp. 80 and 126-127; *CAH* VII. 2 pp. 393-394.

10. In the days of the kings, when Rome was divided into 3 tribes of 10 centuries each, the Roman army consisted of 3,000 infantrymen. Each tribe was also responsible for a century of cavalry, making a total of 300 knights. Even by the time of the Republic this form of reckoning was out of date. See Heurgon p. 216.

11. The story of "Good King Servius Tullius" has proven to be very complex. In the traditional narratives of Livy and Dionysius of Halicarnassus he is portrayed as a slave who became the son-in-law and successor of his master Tarquinius Priscus. However, another tradition preserved fortuitously in a speech of the emperor Claudius (*CIL* 13. 1668) shows that he also went by the name Mastarna (*nam Tusce Mastarna ei nomen erat*) and was the "most faithful companion" of Caelius Vivenna. In Vulci's François tomb, which we looked at in the last chapter for its depiction of Gnaeus Tarquinius's murder, Mastarna is indeed depicted freeing one Caelius Vibenna. It looks as though the real Servius Tullius (whom Dionysius of Halicarnassus at 3.65.6 calls ξένον δὲ καὶ ἄπολιν – "a stranger and a man without a country") was an Etruscan *condottiere* whose conquest of Rome represents a rival Etruscan threat to the Tarquins. His title *Mastarna*, which is written *Macstrna* on the François Tomb, seems to be an Etruscan version of the Latin *magister*. If so, it's uncomfortably close to *il Duce*. Heurgon pp. 244-247. *CAH* VII. 2 p. 96 is less comfortable with Claudius's identification.

12. These are not the social class of Knights from which, for example, Cicero arose, but rather the *equites equo publico*, whom Mommsen calls "the patrician-plebeian nobility." They eventually came to be made up of senators' sons who were looking forward to a political career.

13. Cicero, *De Re Publica* 39-40; Lily Ross Taylor, *Party Politics in the Age of Caesar* (Berkeley: University of California Press, 1971) pp. 56-57, 203 note 35; Mommsen II. 417-422.

14. Livy 1. 42-44; Dionysius of Halicarnassus, 4. 16-21; Scullard pp. 72-74, Taylor p. 203 note 34; Mommsen I. 132-138; Heurgon pp. 247-251. The census qualifications, provided in coined money by Livy and Dionysius, are obviously anachronistic. At the time of Servius Tullius, as at the time of Solon, they would have been expressed in kind.

15. Taylor pp. 51-55, 60, and 207 note 63; Scullard p. 46; 56-7; *CAH.* VII. 2 p. 402.

16. Mommsen III. 289-290.

17. Heurgon pp. 273-275.

18. Livy, 2. 32.

19. Livy, 2. 33; Polybius, 6. 16; Taylor 72-73 and p. 211 note 121. For convenience's sake I'm anticipating a bit. The first tribunes were created by the plebs assembled in *curiae*; for the Concilium Plebis only dates from 471 BC. See Mommsen I. 350-362. Scullard p. 468 note 15 doubts Livy's statement that the election of tribunes was transferred in 471 to the Comitia Tributa; it was probably recognized in the Concilium Plebis.

20. Livy, 3. 34.6. As Livy tells the story, the decemvirs only fell when their leader Appius Claudius attempted to debauch the fair maiden Verginia whose father, unable to rescue her from the tyrant's clutches, stabbed her dead in the Forum. This is obviously a doublet of Lucretia's story.

21. See Alfred Ernout, *Recueil de Textes Latins Archaïques* (Paris: Klincksieck, 1957) pp. 114-121 and Barry Nicholas, *An Introduction to Roman Law* (Oxford, at the Clarendon Press, 1962) pp. 15-16.

22. Livy 4. 2 (my translation). See Heurgon p. 283.

23. Cicero, *De Legibus* 3. 3.7 (C.W. Keyes, tr.).

24. Scullard pp. 89-91; 115-117; Mommsen I. 382-385; *CAH.* VII. 2 pp. 225-226; 335, 438; Justinian, *The Digest of Roman Law: Theft, Rapine, Damage, and Insult*, ed. and trans. C.F. Kolbert (Harmondsworth, England: Penguin Books, 1975) pp. 14-16.

25. *CAH.* VII. 2 pp. 400-401; Heurgon pp. 312-315; Crawford p. 195.

26. See Ronald Syme, *The Roman Revolution* (Oxford University Press, 1960) p. 18: "In any age of the history of Republican Rome about twenty or thirty men, drawn from a dozen dominant families, hold a monopoly of office and power." See also Scullard pp. 332-333; *CAH* VII. 2 pp. 345-347; Heurgon pp. 306-308.

27. Taylor pp. 29-32 and Scullard p. 332.

28. For instance, we find: "P. Paquium Proculum II vir. virum b. d. r. p. o. v. f. A. Vettium Caprasium Felicem II vir. v. b. d. r. p. o. v. f., digni sunt...scripsit...sius dealbatore Onesimo" Which is short-hand for "Publium Paquium Proculum duumvirum, virum bonum dignum re publica, oro vos faciatis etc." and means, "I ask you to elect Publius Paquius Proculus to the Board of Two—a good man, and worthy of the Republic. Likewise Vettius Caprasius Felix—they are worthy. Written for ...sius by the whitewasher Onesimus." Similarly is found: "I ask you to elect Gaius Iulius Polybius as aedile; he'll bring good bread." There are even take-offs, such as: "The after-hours drinkers (*seribibi*) all ask you to elect Marcus Cerrinius Vatia as aedile" or "The muggers recommend Vatia as aedile" ! See W.B. Sedgwick, *The Cena Trimalchionis of Petronius* (Oxford: at the Clarendon Press, 1964) p. 136.

29. For a description of the election process, see Taylor pp. 59-71

30. Polybius, 6. 11-18.

Notes to Chapter 25

1. Sicilian coins issued by Carthage in 410 bear the inscription QRTHDST. *CAH* VII. 2 pp. 506-7.

2. Serge Lancel, *Carthage: A History* (London: Blackwell, 1995) pp. 1-34. Lancel points out that archaeology has so far dated burials to about a century later than the traditional date of Carthage's founding. For a good discussion of the transformation of the Phoenician into the Greek alphabet, see pp. 351-356.

3. Al. N. Oikonomides, ed., *Hanno the Carthaginian: Periplus* (Chicago: Ares, 1977). Mr. Oikonomides believes (p. 39) that the work is genuine, but Lancel pp. 102-109 takes a closer look at the strange story of gorillas which concludes the work. We're told by Hanno that on an island (which appears to be in Sierra Leone) his men caught and skinned 3 wild and hairy women whom his interpreters called *gorillas*. This gruesome tidbit has long been recognized as a probable reference to Perseus's battle with the three Gorgon sisters. Indeed, the Greek word *Gorgadas* could easily have turned into *Gorillas*. Curiously, as Mr. Oikonomides also points out at p. 37, modern gorillas were first named in a direct reference to this passage by the American missionary and naturalist Thomas Savage (*Boston Journal of Natural History*, 1847).

4. Pliny the Elder, *Natural History* 18. 22-23. At the same time the Senate also directed the 28 books of Mago's treatise on agriculture to be translated from the Punic into Latin. The work was completed and influenced later writers on farming like Varro, Columella, and Pliny himself, but it has also been lost. The story of the library's rescue reminds me of the tale (Plutarch, *Antony* 58 [p. 1137]) that Antony, some years after Caesar accidentally burned down the great library of Alexandria, gave Cleopatra the 200,000 volumes of the library of Pergamum. I rather doubt that too; however, the story at least brightens Caesar's reputation among book lovers.

5. Aristotle, *Politics* 2. 11; Polybius, 6. 50-51; Howard H. Scullard, *A History of the Roman World 753 to 146 BC.* (London: Methuen and Co.,1980) pp. 157-161; Lancel, *Carthage* pp. 110-120.

6. Plutarch, *Moralia* 799D (Harold North Fowler, tr.); Jeremiah 7:30-31; See *CAH* VII .2 pp. 512, 514-517; Lancel, *Carthage* pp. 227-256. See also the highly colored account of infant sacrifice in the 4th century by Diodorus Siculus 20. 14.4-7, and the railings of the church father Tertullian (*Apologeticum* 9. 2-4) against secret continuation of the practice even under the early Empire.

7. Even in the Linear B tablets *po-ni-ki-ja* means red. *DMG* p. 91.

8. The story of the First Punic War is told brilliantly by Polybius in the first book of his history. If you like historical novels, one of the best is Gustave Flaubert's *Salammbô*, an imaginative reconstruction of the

mercenary revolt.

9. Polybius, 3. 11 (Shuckburgh, tr.); Livy, 21. 1.

10. *CAH* VIII pp. 24-25.

11. Polybius, 3. 15-3.17.; Scullard pp. 34 and 159; Mommsen II.116-118; Serge Lancel, *Hannibal* (London: Blackwell, 1998) pp. 46-51.

12. Polybius, 3. 20-30 (Shuckburgh, tr.) and 33; Livy, 21. 18.

13. Polybius, 3. 34-49.

14. *Ibid.* 3. 56 and 35. Scholars and tourists have for centuries tried to retrace Hannibal's route across the Alps, but as Lancel remarks (*Hannibal* p. 72), "Crossing the Alps with Livy and Polybius in one's hand is an even more fanciful enterprise than trying to find the true site of the battle of Alesia by matching Caesar's text with an Ordnance Survey map." The famous but ridiculous story of using heated vinegar to crack rocks is at Livy, 21. 37.

15. Polybius, 10. 3. See also Livy, 21. 46 where Livy added, however, that the historian Coelius Antipater gives credit for the rescue to a Ligurian slave.

16. Polybius, 3. 65-74

17. Polybius, 3. 80-82 (Shuckburgh, tr.). Cf. Livy, 22. 3. We should, however be careful about accepting this very negative picture of the unfortunate Flaminius. As a military expansionist he was a consistent enemy of Carthage. When he decided to establish Roman colonists south of Ariminum as a bulwark against the pesky Gauls, he angered the Senate twice over. First he went over their heads by passing a *plebiscitum* through the Concilium Plebis; then he had the audacity to propose full Roman citizenship for his colonists. These imperialist policies brought him into conflict with Quintus Fabius "the Delayer" (whom we'll meet in a moment), who was related to the early Roman historian Fabius Pictor (who wrote in Greek). Writers are always biased, so I'm afraid that historiography is filled with conspiracy theories like this. See *CAH.* VII pp. 432-436, 451-453; *CAH* VIII P. 69; Lancel, *Hannibal* pp. 51-52, 88-89; and Michael Crawford, *The Roman Republic* pp. 53-55.

18. Polybius, 3. 82-86; Livy, 22. 4-7.

19. Of course no one called him "Delayer" to his face! At 30.26 Livy refers to the famous lines from book 12 of Ennius's Annals: "One man by delaying restored our republic./ For he didn't place public opinion before safety./ Therefore has his glory shone increasingly with the passing of time (My translation of lines 200-202 in Ernout's collection). See also Lancel, *Hannibal* p. 101.

20. Polybius, 3. 87-94. Livy at 22. 31 points out that only Servilius had the power to appoint Fabius dictator, but since he was away in Cisalpine Gaul the people took it upon themselves, unconstitutionally, to name Fabius acting dictator.

21. Livy, 22. 34-35 and 39. Once again a word of caution: Polybius,

who is the ultimate source for Livy's account, would certainly have been biased towards "the good consul" Aemilus Paulus, who (as you can see from the chart following chapter 28) was the grandfather of his friend and patron Scipio Aemilianus. See *CAH* VIII pp. 51-52 and 80; Crawford p. 55.

22. Polybius, 3. 107-114; Livy, 22. 40-45.

23. Polybius, 3. 115-116; Livy, 22. 47-48.

24. Polybius, 3.1 16 and Livy, 22. 49.

25. Preserved in a fragment of Polybius, 7. 9.

26. Livy, 22. 51.

27. Polybius, 6. 58 and Plutarch, *Marcellus* 13 [p. 375]; Livy, 22. 58-61.

28. Livy, 26. 24 and 28; Scullard pp. 215-216; Mommsen II.179-184; *CAH* VIII pp. 102-106; Lancel, *Hannibal* pp. 132, 153-154; Erich S. Gruen, *The Hellenistic World and the Coming of Rome* (Berkeley: University of California Press, 1984) pp. 373-381.

29. Polybius, 8. 6-8 and 37; Plutarch, *Marcellus* 19 [p. 380]; Livy, 25. 31. There's a famous story that Archimedes used huge magnifying glasses to burn the rigging of the Roman ships, but that seems to be just another myth traceable to the satirist Lucian (cf. the story of the first Marathon race in chapter 16). Lucian says in his *Hippias* chapter 2: "The former [i.e. Archimedes] burned the ships of the enemy by means of his science," but none of our earlier sources mention the trick. See Edward Gibbon, *History of the Decline and Fall of the Roman Empire* (Modern Library Edition) vol. 2 p. 505 note 99.

30. Polybius, 3. 95-96; Scullard pp. 211-214; Mommsen II. 184-189; Lancel, *Hannibal* pp. 133-136.

31. Livy, 26. 18 and Scullard p. 225-226; Mommsen II. 189-191; *CAH* VIII pp. 175, 179-180; Lancel pp. 136-138.

32. Livy, 27. 40-51 and Polybius, 11. 1-3; Scullard pp. 226-232; Mommsen II. 191-196 and 209-212; Lancel pp. 144-149.

33. Livy, 28. 40-44; Scullard pp. 232-233. Fabius and his supporters controlled the consulship from the defeat of Cannae until 207. Thus Scipio's Spanish command of 210 had to be granted by the Tribal Assembly, where his family's popular support had more punch than in the aristocratically controlled Centuriata. After 205 the Scipionic alliance and their imperialistic policy took over. See *CAH* VIII pp. 68-74.

34. Polybius, 14. 1-8.

35. Scullard pp. 232-236; Mommsen II. 218-219; Lancel pp. 172-173; Polybius, 15. 1-2.

36. Polybius, 15. 9-14; Livy, 30. 32-35.

37. Scullard pp. 236-238; Mommsen II. 222-223.

38. Students always ask, "How much is that worth?" Please look ahead to my remarks about the Edict of Prices in Chapter 40 to see why it is impossible to answer that question. That having been said, and just for

fun, it is possible to come up with a modern figure. Lancel in *Hannibal* p. 177 puts the tribute at 10,000 Euboic talents, adding helpfully that a Euboic Talent equals 26 kilograms of silver. We know that the indemnity was to be paid in silver thanks to the note by Pliny the Elder at *N.H.* 33.51. Currently, in March of 1999, one troy ounce of silver is valued at $5.549. Since one troy ounce=.0311 kilograms, we come out with the "current market value" of $46,390,351 for the full indemnity.

39. Polybius, 15. 18-19; Livy, 30. 37.

40. Livy, 38. 50-54.

41. Livy, 39. 51-52 and Plutarch, *Flamininus* 20-21 [pp. 463-465.]

42. Juvenal, 10. 147-167 (Rolfe Humphries, tr.).

Notes to Chapter 26

1. This certainly seems to have been the attitude of Rome in the first two wars she waged in 229 and 219 against Illyria, which occupied the then (as now) ethnically and politically fragmented area of "Yugoslavia." Rome acted to contain the Illyrians when they tried to graduate from piracy to imperialism. It was in Rome's interest to keep the Adriatic shipping lanes open that were important both to her new southern possessions and to herself. Neither Illyrian War brought Rome any territorial advances. See Erich Gruen, *The Hellenistic World and the Coming of Rome* (Berkeley: University of California Press, 1984) pp. 359-373.

2. Livy, 31. 1-2 and Polybius, 15. 20. For working out the confusing chronology of the opening years of the 2nd Macedonian War, I'm especially indebted to Scullard pp. 245-248 with notes pp. 504-506. For a different interpretation, which puts both the Senatorial Commission and the embassy from Athens before the Comitia's initial refusal to declare war, see Mommsen II. 274-276 and *CAH* VIII pp. 255-258, and Gruen pp. 392-393.

3. Livy, 31. 5-7.

4. Polybius, 16. 24-27.

5. *Ibid.* 18. 5. (Shuckburgh, tr.)

6. *Ibid.* 16. 28-35.

7. Livy, 31. 5-7.

8. Livy, 31. 8 and 1. 32 (my translation). Livy's script is certainly anachronistic, and the story may be too. As early as the 3rd century BC the ever practical Romans, irritated at the expense of sending priests overseas, set aside a convenient plot of land in Rome as foreign soil onto which bloody spears could be tossed. See Mary Beard, John North, and Simon Price, *Religions of Rome* (Cambridge: Cambridge University Press, 1998) volume 1 pp. 132-133 and volume 2 pp. 7-8 and 131-132.

9. Plutarch, *Flamininus* 1-2 [pp. 449-450].

10. *Ibid.* 3-5 [pp. 450-453]. We should of course expect Plutarch to overemphasize the philhellenism of his hero. Unfortunately for

Flamininus's reputation, an inscription has preserved a letter, supposedly by him, addressed to the Chyretians. It isn't in very good Greek. *CAH* VIII pp. 439-440.

11. Plutarch, *Flamininus* 6 and 2 [pp. 453 and 450]; *CAH* VIII pp. 265-267.

12. Polybius, 18. 8-11 and Plutarch, *Flamininus* 7.[p. 453].

13. Plutarch, 7 [p. 453]; Polybius, 18. 18-19.

14. Polybius, 18. 29-32 and Plutarch, 8 [p. 454].

15. Polybius, 18. 20-27; Plutarch, 8 [p. 454].

16. Polybius, 18. 27 and 34; Plutarch, 8-9 [pp. 454-455].

17. Polybius, 18. 46; Livy, 33. 32; Plutarch, 9 [pp. 455-456.]

18. Polybius, 18. 42 and 45; Plutarch, 10 [p. 456].

19. Polybius, 18. 46; Livy, 33. 32; Plutarch, 10-11 [pp. 456-457].

20. See Rostovtzeff, *Rome* pp. 70-71; *CAH* VIII pp. 269, 272-273, 443, and especially Gruen pp. 132-157.

21. Plutarch, 15 [p. 460]. For the war with Antiochus, see Polybius book 21. The final treaty is quoted at 21. 45. See also *CAH* VIII pp. 286-289.

22. 33. 33 (my translation). An inscription (*SEG* XI.923.7-40) found near Sparta shows that a festival in Flamininus's honor was still being held in 15 AD! See Beard, *Religions of Rome*, vol. 2 p. 254.

Notes to Chapter 27

1. Even by Roman times there had been virtually no cultural mixture between the Greek rulers and the native Egyptian population. See Rostovtzeff *SEHRE* pp. 278-286.

2. Juvenal, 3. 6o-65, 73-78, 109-112. This is again from the wonderful translation by Rolfe Humphries.

3. Plutarch, *Aemelius Paulus* 8 [p. 324].

4. *Ibid.* 8 [p. 325]; Polybius, 22. 8-17; 23. 1-3, 7; Livy, 40. 5-24, 54-57; Erich Gruen, "The Last Years of Philip V," *Greek Roman and Byzantine Studies* 15 (1974) pp. 221-246.

5. Polybius, 25. 3.

6. Livy, 42. 11-14.1.

7. Polybius, 27. 1-6. Scullard pp. 278-279; Mommsen II. 342-348; Gruen, *The Coming of Rome* pp. 403-419; William Reiter, *Aemilius Paulus Conqueror of Greece* (London: Croom Helm, 1988) pp. 50-51, 124-132.

8. Scullard pp. 279-281; Mommsen II.349-354; *CAH* VIII pp. 310-312; and Polybius, 27. 7-8. See also Plutarch, *Aemilius Paulus* 9 [p. 325].

9. Plutarch, 10 [p. 326].

10. *Ibid.* 13-16 [pp. 328-330].

11. Scullard note 6 pp. 513-514; Mommsen II.355; Plutarch, 17 [p. 331]; Livy, 44. 37.5-9.

12. Plutarch, 19-37 [pp. 332-344]; Livy, 44. 40-43; 45. 4.2-8.8.

13. *Scriptores Historiae Augustae*, "Hadrian" 5.3, cited by Gruen *The*

Coming of Rome p. 429.

14. Scullard p. 282; Mommsen II.365-367; *CAH* VIII 316-317; Plutarch, 29 [p. 339]; Polybius, 30. 16.

15. Rostovtzeff, *Rome* pp. 72-3; Scullard pp. 282-283; Mommsen II.357-358; *CAH* VIII 317-318; Plutarch, 28 [p. 338]; Livy, 45. 18, 29, and 32; Gruen, *The Coming of Rome* pp. 424-429.

16. Rostovtzeff, *Rome* pp. 73-75; Scullard p. 289-290; Mommsen III.57-60; *CAH* VIII. 321; Gruen, *The Coming of Rome* pp. 431-436. Note Gruen's cautionary remarks that evidence for actual Roman provincial machinery is virtually nonexistent. Nonetheless even he admits that the "Macedonian era" of Roman domination begins with the victory of Metellus in 148.

17. Scullard pp. 290; Mommsen III.60-63.

18. Polybius, 38. 7-11. See also Arthur Pickard-Cambridge, *The Dramatic Festivals of Athens* (Oxford: Clarendon Press, 1968) pp. 289 and 365; Scullard pp. 291; Mommsen II. 63-70; *CAH* VIII 321-323.

Notes to Chapter 28

1. Plutarch, *Cato* 26-27 [pp. 430-431]; Appian, *Book 8, The Punic Wars* 10.67-68 (who does not, unfortunately, confirm this famous story about Cato). See also Sallust, *Bellum Iugurthinum* 41-42.

2. *CAH* VIII pp. 486-487; 496-498; Gruen p. 293; Lancel, *Carthage* pp. 404-409; W. Beare, *The Roman Stage* (London: Metheun, 1964) p. 66. The opening 2 lines of Hanno's speech (930-931) read:
Ythalonimualonuthsicorathisymacomsyth
chymlachchunythmumysthyalmycthybaruimysehi

3. Gruen pp. 300, 307, 313-315. See also Tenny Frank, *An Economic History of Rome to the End of the Republic* (Baltimore: The Johns Hopkins Press, 1920) pp. 108-110. Frank points out that Rome made little effort to compete economically in the 2nd century, either with Carthage or even with Delos, the free market she had set up and handed over to Athens. "Indeed, the ancient world has no record of any state of importance so unconcerned about its commerce as the Roman Republic." See also *CAH* VIII pp. 152-157 and Michael Crawford, *The Roman Republic* p. 47. For the opposite and more traditional view, see Rostovtzeff *SEHRE* p. 21 and note 15, and again p. 314.

4. Cicero, *De Oratore* 2.25: "Increasing your patrimony? But that is not the mark of the nobility!" cited by Gruen p. 306.

5. Cato, *De Agri Cultura* 2.7 (my translation).

6. Appian *Pun.* 10. 69-11. 81 and 13. 92-13. 93; Polybius, 36. 3-6.

7. Polybius, 38. 1 (Shuckburgh, tr.).

8. Appian, *Pun.* 13. 93-97; Lancel, *Carthage* pp. 415-417.

9. Appian 14. 98.

10. Livy, 44. 44.1-3; Plutarch, *Aemilius Paulus* 22 [p. 334]. As it turned

out, Scipio had been having such a fine time slaughtering the fleeing enemy that he lost tract of the time! For the story of Scipio's family, see Plutarch 2, 5 [pp. 321-323].

11. According to the old law of the Twelve Tables, an adopted son would be "emancipated" by his natural father and would thus lose all rights to his original inheritance. This embarrassment was however avoided in typical Roman fashion by a technicality in the praetor's court which would grant *bonorum possessio* to emancipated children. See Nicholas p. 249.

12. Appian, *Pun.* 15. 101-16. 105.

13. Polybius, 36. 8 (Shuckburgh, tr.); Plutarch, *Cato* 27 [p. 431].

14 Appian, *Pun.* 16. 105-108.

15. *Ibid.* 17. 112.

16. The communal graves prepared for the victims in the assault have been uncovered. See Lancel, *Carthage* p. 426.

17. Appian, *Pun.* 17. 114-19. 131.

18. *Iliad* 6. 447-449 (Richmond Lattimore, tr.). See Polybius 39. 5 and Appian, 19. 132.

Notes to Chapter 29

1. H.H. Scullard, *From the Gracchi to Nero* (London: University Paperbacks, 1966) pp. 19-20; Mommsen II.441-448 and 462-467; Frank pp. 51-57. In Sicily land attached to the cities paid one tenth of their produce to Rome. See Rostovtzeff *SEHRE* p. 207; David Stockton, *The Gracchi* (Oxford: Clarendon Press, 1979) pp. 13-14.

2. *CAH* VII 122-124; 328-329. Though it isn't clear that the Licinian Sextian laws themselves imposed the 500 iugera cap, it certainly was in force by the mid second century. See Alvin H. Bernstein, *Tiberius Sempronius Gracchus: Tradition and Apostasy* (Ithaca: Cornell University Press, 1978) pp. 124-125.

3. See for example Scullard *From the Gracchi to Nero* p. 20.

4. Cicero, *De Officiis* 2.73, quoted by Stockton p. 7.

5. Appian, *Bella Civilia* 1. 7-8. Plutarch, *Tiberius Gracchus* 8 [pp. 997-8]; Frank pp. 51-57; 89-93; *CAH* VIII 186-188; 197-204; 232-233; Luciano Perelli, *I Grachi* (Rome: Salerno Editrice, 1993) pp. 76-80; Bernstein pp. 77-96; Stockton pp. 11-19.

6. Plutarch, *Tiberius Gracchus* 8 [p. 998].

7. *Ibid.* 1 [pp. 993-994].

8. *Ibid.* 5-7 [pp. 996-997]. The Spanish "barbarians" had a good deal more class than their conquerors, for they refused to accept the Romans' gift of the scapegoat Mancinus. The hapless commander was sent back home, where he was unceremoniously kicked out of the Senate. He seems to have been allowed back in later, however, and may even have risen to the praetorship. See Mommsen III. 27-28, Scullard, *History* pp 110-

111 and 296, and *Der Kleine Pauly* under "Hostilius 10."

9. Perelli pp. 80-82; Stockton pp. 40-41; Bernstein pp. 131-164. It is quite probably that in its original form Tiberius's bill did not limit the number of children who could earn their parents additional 250 iugera exemptions. Tiberius seems to have removed some of the concessions once senatorial opposition solidified and he was forced to make his bill more palatable to the mob.

10. Appian, *BC* 1.9; Plutarch 8-9 [pp. 998-999]; Rostovtzeff p. 97; Scullard, *From the Gracchi to Nero* pp. 26-7; Mommsen III.123-126.

11. Plutarch, 9 [p. 999].

12. Appian, *BC* 1. 10-12; Plutarch 10-12 [pp. 999-1001].

13. Appian, *BC* 1. 13; Plutarch 13 [p. 1001].

14. Appian *Ibid.*; Plutarch 13-14 [pp. 1001-1002]; Gruen, *The Coming of Rome* pp. 592-608. Gruen calls the move "politics, not foreign policy" (pp. 599-600). Bernstein (pp. 208-209) labels it "premeditated demagoguery."

15. Perelli p. 98.

16. Scullard pp. 29-30; Mommsen III.115-117.

17. Plutarch (19 [p. 1005]) presents an elaborate explanation of this signal, saying that Gracchus was pointing to his head so that those out of ear-shot should understand, "My head is on the block.!" It is, however, important for the moral that Plutarch is trying to point in his story to keep Gracchus as altruistic as possible. Still, even he admits (10 [p. 1006]) that Tiberius's mob of 3000 supporters was largely responsible for the violence that occurred. Appian says flat out (2. 15) that the signal had been agreed upon the night before between Gracchus and his friends. Bernstein (p. 221) follows Appian; Perelli (p. 135) believes Plutarch.

18. Appian, *BC* 3. 14-16; Plutarch 19 [pp. 1005-1006].

19. Plutarch 20 [p. 1006] and Appian, *B.C.* 1. 2.

20. Plutarch, *Gaius Gracchus* 5 [p. 1010].

21. Cited by Mommsen III 128, Scullard p. 32, and Perelli pp. 94-96.

22. *CIL* I 551, cited by Frank p. 123.

23. Tiberius may have included Italians allies among the original beneficiaries of the bill only to abandon them to the self centered prejudices of the Roman mob. See Bernstein pp. 137-159.

24. Appian, *BC* 1. 27; 2. 18-20; and 4. 27.

Notes to Chapter 30

1. Sallust, *Bellum Iugurthinum* 35. 10.

2. *Ibid.* 86. 2-3.

3. In reality the bottom had fallen out of the minimum property requirement during the 2nd century. It had originally been 11,000 bronze asses. By the end of the century it was 1,500. Rome's growing empire needed soldiers more than it needed scrupulous recruiting officers. See

Perelli p. 83 and Bernstein pp. 74-75.

4. S.A. Cook *et al.* ed., *The Cambridge Ancient History* vol. IX (Cambridge: at the university Press, 1932) pp. 133-137; Rostovtzeff, *Rome* pp. 106-107; Mommsen III. 201 and 242-247.

5. Plutarch, *Sulla* 30 [p. 569.]

6. Suetonius, *Caesar* 1. 1-3; Plutarch, *Caesar* 1 [p. 855].

7. Plutarch, *Pompey* 21 [p. 753].

8. Plutarch, *Crassus* 6 (pp. 653-654). Crassus's father and elder brother were both executed by Cinna, leaving him with a fortune, probably in land, of 300 talents (7,200,000 sesterces), which was actually moderate for a nobleman. Like Pompey, he raised a private army of clients to aid Sulla; indeed, Plutarch tells us that it was Crassus's support at the Coline Gate which earned Sulla his victory. Crassus also earned a lot of money buying up burned out property in Rome, which he converted into expensive town houses for ambitious new senators. See Arthur Mason Ward, *Marcus Crassus and the Late Roman Republic* (Columbia: University of Missouri Press, 1977) pp. 48-49, 62-77.

9. Plutarch, *Crassus.* 45 [p. 771] (Dryden, tr.). For this brief survey of Pompey's early career, see Plutarch's life 6-46 [pp. 743-770]. As Mommsen points out in IV 174 note, the inclusion of Media in the list is an exaggeration of diplomatic pressures placed by Pompey upon his new neighbor, the great Parthian Empire.

10. Suetonius, *Caesar* 55. 1-2.

11. Suetonius, *Caesar* 4.2 and 74.1; Plutarch, *Caesar* 1-2 [pp. 855-6]. I've always been a little suspicious of this story, since it balances so neatly Pompey's exploits with the pirates—so neatly, in fact, that it might be a product of anti-Pompean propaganda from the time of the Civil War. It could be true, too. See Matthias Gelzer, *Caesar, Politician and Statesman* (Cambridge: Harvard University Press, 1968) p. 23-24.

12. Suetonius 9-12 and Plutarch 6 [pp. 851-852].

13. Suetonius 13; Plutarch 7 [p. 858].

14. The cognomen is a happy coincidence, but it wasn't a nickname. The Pulchri were a branch of the Clodius family, just as the Caesares were of the Julii. See Syme, *The Roman Revolution* p. 19.

15. Plutarch, *Caesar* 10 [p. 860] (Dryden, tr.).

16. Suetonius, *Caesar* 74.2 (my translation). Gelzer p. 60 note 3 questions whether it is chronologically possible to place this famous quote at the trial itself.

17. For the trial see Suetonius 6.2, Plutarch 9-10 [pp. 859-860], and Warn, *Marcus Crassus* pp. 205-209 and 229-320. For details, however, see Marcus Cicero, *Epistulae ad Atticum* 1. 13.3 and especially 1. 16.2-5. This first appearance of Cicero's letters requires an explanation. Marcus Cicero, as I've already mentioned, was Rome's greatest lawyer and orator. He had served as consul in 63, and that was unusual, for Cicero wasn't

a Roman; he was a hick from the town of Arpinum. That year, however, a rogue nobleman named Catiline was also running for the consulship, and the aristocrats figured that the hick was preferable to the rebel. With all the fervor of a convert and the enthusiasm of a self-made man who has finally been allowed to play with the big boys, Cicero embraced the senatorial aristocracy. When Catiline attempted a revolution (in which, by the way, there were hints about Caesar's involvement), Cicero crushed him. Cicero's four great orations against Catiline and his co-conspirators are today the bane of every third year high school Latin student. Besides his oratory, however, Cicero was also an important poet, who unfortunately spent too much of his time writing endlessly about the great deeds of his consulship. He also wrote voluminously about philosophy. No philosopher himself, he translated and adapted Greek works. Since it was Cicero's philosophical tracts that were most frequently studied during the Middle Ages and Renaissance, when Europe had forgotten Greek, Cicero should be credited with virtually inventing the modern philosophical vocabulary. Most important for our purposes, however, are his letters. These were collected in great numbers after his death and have largely survived. Since he didn't mean them for publication, they are the most intimate and certainly one of the most important historical sources preserved from antiquity. During the years when he was writing regularly to his friend Atticus in Athens, we can recreate almost day to day the goings on in the Capitol. For the whole period covered by this book, Cicero's letters and the war memoirs of Caesar offer just about the only first rate, first hand accounts written by major participants in the events we're attempting to describe.

18. Plutarch, *Caesar* 11 [p. 861]; Suetonius 18.

19. Plutarch, *Pompey* 43 [p. 770].

20. Cicero, *ad Att.* 2. 1.8 (my translation).

21. See Hortensius's objection to the Lex Manilia: "If everything must be entrusted to one man, Pompey is most worthy, but nonetheless everything should not be deferred to one man." Cicero, *Oratio pro Lege Manilia* 17.

22. Cicero, *ad Att.* I. 14.1 (my translation).

23. Frank, *Economic History of Rome*, pp. 126-127, 138-140, 223-226; Gelzer p. 75; Ward pp. 211-212; Peter Greenhalgh, *Pompey: The Roman Alexander* (Columbia: University of Missouri Press, 1981) pp. 197-203; David Shotter, *The Fall of the Roman Republic* (London: Routledge, 1994) p. 62.

24. *i.e.* Celts. The Celtic peoples, who at the time of the Minoans occupied much of northwestern Europe, including Germany, France, Spain, and the British Isles, were gradually exterminated by the Roman empire until they only survived beyond its northern fringes in Wales, Scotland, and Ireland. Can ye say it's a braw bricht moon-lit nicht?

25. Suetonius, *Caesar* 18-19.2. For the motives behind the First Trium-virate, see H.H. Scullard, *From the Gracchi to Nero* pp. 116-118; Lily Ross Taylor, *Party Politics in the Age of Caesar* (Berkeley: University of Califor-nia Press, 1971) pp.130-137; *CAH* IX. 509-513; Mommsen IV. 235-244; Syme, *The Roman Revolution* pp. 33-35, and note 23 above.

26. Suetonius 20. 1-2; Plutarch, *Caesar* 14 [p. 862-3]; *Pompey* 47-48 [p. 773]; *CAH* IX. 516.

27. Suetonius, *Caesar* 20.3. cf. Polybius 6.17.

28. Suetonius, *Caesar* 20.4; 22. 1-2; Plutarch, *Caesar* 14 [p. 863], *Pompey* 48 [pp. 773-774]; *CAH* IX. 518-519; Gelzer pp. 86-87.

29. By Caesar's time this was such a formality that the 30 curiae were usually represented by the 30 lictors in attendance upon the consul. See Barry Nicholas, *An Introduction to Roman Law* (London: at the Clarendon Press, 1962) p. 62.

30. *CAH* IX. 523-527; Mommsen IV. 251-254; Suetonius, *Caesar* 20. 4; Plutarch, *Caesar* 14 [p. 863].

31. Suetonius, *Caesar* 21 and 50-51; Plutarch, *Caesar* 14 [p. 862]; Plutarch, *Pompey* 47 [p. 773].

32. For a description of the trial see Cicero, a*d Q. Fratr.* 2. 3.2. For Clodius, see Plutarch, *Pompey* 49 [pp. 774-775]; *CAH* IX. 528; and W.W. How and A.C. Clark, *Cicero Select Letters with Historical Introductions Notes and Appendices* (Oxford, 1926), vol. II. p. 149; A.J. Langguth, *A Noise of War* (New York: Simon and Schuster, 1994) pp. 134-137.

33. Plutarch, *Pompey* 51-52 [pp. 776-7]; Plutarch, *Crassus* 14-15 [p. 659-660]; Plutarch, *Caesar* 21 [pp. 867-8]; Suetonius, *Caesar* 24.1; Cicero *ad Fam.* 1. 9.8-9; How and Clark pp. 150-151; *CAH* IX. 535; Taylor p. 69; Gelzer pp. 120-122, 127; Langguth pp. 187-196; Shotter pp. 72-74.

34. Plutarch, *Crassus* 33 [p. 674].

35. Plutarch, *Pompey* 53 [pp. 777-778]; Plutarch, *Caesar* 23 [p.869]. Cae-sar offered to marry Pompey's daughter in place of his wife Calpurnia and to have Pompey marry Octavia, his grand-niece. Pompey refused. This Octavia was the sister of Octavian, the future emperor Augustus, and she subsequently became the wife of Mark Antony. See Gelzer p. 151.

36. Plutarch, *Pompey* 54 [p. 779]; Plutarch, *Caesar* 28 [p. 872]; How and Clark pp. 160-161; *CAH* IX. 620-621, 624-625; Taylor pp. 68-69; Mommsen IV. 387-391.

37. See, for instance, Suetonius, *Caesar* 49 and 53.

38. My version of Catullus 29.

Notes to Chapter 31

1. For this date's being assigned to the *Lex Pompeia Licinia* see F.E. Adcock's arguments in *CAH* IX. 616-617. Now in a series of chapters devoted to Caesar, the term Ides—thanks to the "Ides of March"—requires

some explanation. The Romans, practical though they were, never thought of the simple idea of assigning a number to each day of the month. Instead, they had 3 linchpin dates, the Kalends (New Moon), Nones (First Quarter), and Ides (Full Moon), from which they counted backwards. The Kalends were always the first of the month, which is the origin of our word "calendar." The Ides normally fell on the 13th, except in the months of March, May, July, and October, when they fell on the 15th. I can remember a New York D.J. once making a joke about Income Tax Day's being the "Ides of April," only to be inundated with calls and letters from angry Latin teachers. *Nones* means "ninth day before the Ides," but Romans always counted both ends of a sequence, so that whereas we would say that the ninth day before the 13th is the 4th, a Roman would say that it is the 5th. So the Nones usually fall on the 5th, except of course in March, May, July, and October, when they fall on the 7th. Therefore April 15th isn't the Ides of April, but rather (counting, remember, both ends of the sequence) 17 days before the Kalends of May—*ante diem septimum decimum Kalendas Maias*, or for short *a.d. xvii. Kal. Mai.* If you think that's complicated, try long division with Roman numerals.

2. Suetonius, *Caesar* 28. 2-3; Plutarch, *Pompey* 56 [pp. 780-781]; *CAH* IX. p. 627; Mommsen IV. 419-420.

3. Cicero, *ad Fam.* 8. 14. 2 (my translation).

4. Gelzer pp. 175-177.

5. Caesar, *Bellum Civile* 1. 1-3, 5, 8; Suetonius, *Caesar* 29-30.1; Plutarch, *Caesar* 30 [p. 873]; Gelzer p. 192.

6. Plutarch, *Pompey* 57 [p. 781] (Dryden, tr.).

7. Cicero, *ad Att.* 10. 8.2 (my translation). For the stolen 2 legions, see Hirtius, *De Bello Gallico* 8. 54-55; Plutarch, *Pompey* 56 [p. 781]; and Caesar, *BC* 1. 4. See also Plutarch, *Pompey* 64 [p. 785].

8. In his life of Pompey (60 [p. 783]), Plutarch insists that Caesar said it in Greek: ἀνερρίφθω κύβος, which is certainly correct, since the line would have been recognized in Caesar's day as a quote from the Greek playwright Menander (Men. 65). Suetonius gives the better known version of this in Latin, *iacta alea est* (32), which is usually translated "The die is cast." Indeed, Suetonius gets rather carried away with the drama of the scene, so that Caesar ends up snatching a bugle, blowing "charge!" and galloping across the river. In his own account, Caesar characteristically passes over the whole scene: "Once he had learned the will of his soldiers, he proceeded to Ariminum with that legion (1.8.1)." See also Plutarch, *Caesar* 32 [p. 874].

9. Caesar *BC* 2. 8.3. The Cicero quote, from *De Officiis* 82, is cited by Suetonius in *Caesar* 30.5. For Plutarch's remarks see *Pompey* 51 [p. 776] and *Caesar* 28 [pp. 871-2]. See also Hirtius *BG* VIII. 50.

10. Plutarch, *Pompey* 64 [p. 785] and 16 [p.750]; Plutarch, *Marcus Brutus*

4 [p. 1188].

11. Cicero, *ad Att.* 8. 12D.

12. Caesar, *BC* 1. 15-23.

13. Caesar, *BC* 1. 24-27; Cicero, *ad Att.* 9. 13A; Plutarch, *Pompey* 62 [pp. 784-5]; Robin Seager, *Pompey: A Political Biography* (Oxford: Basil Blackwell, 1979) pp. 164-176.

14. Cicero, *ad Att.* 8. 16.1: *quem ego hominem* ἀπολιτικώτατον *omnium iam ante cognoram, nunc vero etiam* ἀστρατηγητότατον. See also 9. 9.2; Caesar, *BC* 1. 29-31; Plutarch, *Pompey* 63 [p. 785].For Curio's disaster in Africa, see Caesar, *BC* 2. 23-44.

15. Plutarch, *Caesar* 35 [p. 876] and *Pompey* 62 [p. 784];Caesar, *BC* 1. 32-33; Gelzer pp. 209-210.

16. Suetonius, *Caesar* 34.2 (my translation).

17. Caesar, *BC* 1. 34-2. 22.

18. *Ibid.* 2. 21.5 and 3. 1-6.3.

19. *Ibid.* 3. 10 and 18; Seager pp. 179-180.

20. *Ibid.* 3. 8, 13, 15-18.2.

21. Plutarch, *Caesar* 38 [pp. 877-8]; Suetonius, *Caesar* 58.2, who associates the incident with Caesar's first crossing. Of course Caesar doesn't mention it at all in his own book. Suetonius, however, frequently gets his chronology mixed up. cf. *CAH* IX. 658; Mommsen IV. 486; Gelzer pp. 228-229; Christian Meier, *Caesar* (New York: Harper Collins, 1995) p. 390.

22. Caesar, *BC* 3. 25-6, 29-30, 41-42.

23. Suetonius, *Caesar* 68.2; Caesar, *BC* 3. 48.

24. Plutarch, *Pompey* 65 [p. 786] (Dryden, tr.); Suetonius, *Caesar* 36. For the Dyrrhachium campaign, see Caesar, *BC* 3. 43-72.

25. Caesar, *BC* 3. 73.1-2; Plutarch, *Caesar* 41 [p. 879]; Plutarch, *Pompey* 67 [pp. 787-788] See also *Pompey* 76 [p 794]: "And, in truth, neither did Pompey during all the war commit a greater oversight, nor Caesar use a more subtle stratagem, than in drawing the fight so far off from the naval forces." (Dryden, tr.) See Seager pp. 181-182; Meier pp. 394-397.

26. Caesar, *BC* 3. 75-80.

27. Cicero, *ad Fam.* 7. 3.2 (my translation). Plutarch, *Pompey* 67 [p.788];Caesar, *BC* 3. 82-83.

28. Caesar, *BC* 3. 84-88. Plutarch, *Pompey* 69 [p. 790].

29. Plutarch, *Pompey* 69 [p. 789] (Dryden, tr.); Caesar, *BC* 3. 88-89.

30. Caesar, *BC* 3. 92 (my translation).

31. This quote sounds a bit melodramatic, but both Suetonius (30.4) and Plutarch (*Caesar* 46 [p. 882]) attribute it to Asinius Pollio, an eyewitness. Anyway, if a battle doesn't make you histrionic, what will? For the battle itself, see Caesar, *BC* 3. 93-99, Plutarch, *Caesar* 42-45 [pp., 879-882], and Plutarch, *Pompey* 70-72 [pp. 790-792].

32. Caesar, *BC* 3. 102-104; Plutarch, *Pompey* 76-80 [pp. 794-797].

Notes to Chapter 32

1. Plutarch, *Caesar* 48 [p. 883]. That's 17 ½ million *denarii*. In order to get back his throne, Ptolemy "the Fluteplayer" had borrowed this back in 59 from the financier Gaius Rabirius Postumus, who had gone bankrupt due to the king's extravagance. Caesar helpfully bought up the financier's bad paper, and it was this debt that the young Ptolemy owed him. See Gelzer p. 247.

2. This famous story is in Plutarch, *Caesar* 49 [p. 883].

3. Caesar, *BC* 3. 106-112; Plutarch, *Pompey* 80 [p. 797]; Plutarch, *Caesar* 48-49 [pp. 882-884]; Suetonius, *Caesar* 35. 1.

4. Suetonius, *Caesar* 35. 2 and 37. 2. cf. Plutarch, *Caesar* 50 [p. 884].

5. Gelzer pp. 252-254; 261-262; Meier pp. 416-417.

6. Plutarch, *Caesar* 51-56 [pp. 884-886]; Suetonius, *Caesar* 35.2-36.70.

7. For Caesar's reforms see Suetonius, *Caesar* 37-44 and Plutarch, *Caesar* 59 [p. 888]. For the calendar in particular, see Suetonius 40, Plutarch 59, Mommsen IV. 661-662, How and Clark Vol. II pp. 448-449, and Bickerman, *Chronology of the Ancient World* pp. 43-51. Caesar's calendar still needed some fiddling, by the way, for Sosigenes' year of 365 days 6 hours was 11 minutes longer than the true solar year. This was fixed in the year 1582 by Pope Gregory XIII, at which time our modern calendar was introduced. As might be guessed, only the 16th century Russians refused to go along with Gregory's reforms. This causes some confusion in later European history, for by the year 1917 the Julian calendar had fallen 13 days behind the Gregorian. Thus the February Revolution actually occurred in March, and the October Revolution in November. As Trotsky remarked, "before overthrowing the Byzantine calendar, the revolution had to overthrow the institutions that clung to it."

8. Suetonius, *Caesar* 52. 1-2; Gelzer p. 287.

9. Suetonius, *Caesar* 77.

10. *Ibid.* 41.2, where Suetonius even gives the form recommendation Caesar used.

11. Cicero, *ad Fam.* 7. 30.1.

12. Suetonius, *Caesar* 76. 1,3.

13. See the arguments of F.E. Adcock (*CAH* IX. 722-723 and 736-738), of Elizabeth Rawson (*CAH* IX² pp. 463-465), of Ronald Syme, *The Roman Revolution* pp. 54-57, of Christian Meier, *Caesar* pp. 470-479, and of David Shotter p. 85. Mommsen IV. 566 argues that Caesar avoided the hated name of king only to establish an actual monarchy under the title of Imperator, and Gelzer more or less agrees pp. 277-278 and 313-320. Meier feels that Caesar, unlike Sulla, was insensitive to institutions such as the Senate and was too concerned with his personal dignity to care about abstractions like "monarchy" and "republic." See pp. 438, 449-450. For the king stories, See Suetonius, *Caesar* 79-80.1 and Plutarch

Caesar 60-61 [pp. 888-891]. See especially Plutarch, *Marcus Brutus* 9 [p. 1191]: "Now the flatterers of Caesar were the occasion of all this, who, among other invidious honours which they strove to fasten upon Caesar, crowned his statues by night with diadems, wishing to incite the people to salute him king instead of dictator." (Dryden, tr.)

14. Caesar, *BC* 3. 106 (my translation).

15. Plutarch, *Caesar* 62 [p. 890]; Plutarch, *Marcus Brutus* 4-12 [pp. 1188-1192]; Suetonius, *Caesar* 80.4; Cicero, *ad Fam.* 6. 6.10; and Clark and How vol. II p. 414. The Shakespeare quote is from Act I scene 2.

16. Suetonius, *Caesar* 80.4; Plutarch, *Marcus Brutus* 14 [p. 1194]; Plutarch, *Caesar* 66 [p. 892].

17. Plutarch, *Antony* 13 [p. 1112]; Plutarch, *Caesar* 66 [p. 892].

18. Suetonius, *Caesar* 82.1-3; Plutarch, *Caesar* 66 [pp. 892-3], *Marcus Brutus* 17 [p. 1196]. Caesar's famous last words "Et tu, Brute!" appear only in Suetonius, who has them in Greek: καὶ σὺ τέκνον; ("You too, son?") and similarly in the 3rd century Greek historian Dio Cassius (44. 19.5). The Latin version was made famous by Shakespeare's play *Julius Caesar* (act 3 scene 1), but doesn't occur in any ancient source. It was probably coined by an unknown Elizabethan dramatist and had become something of a dramatic cliché by Shakespeare's time. See Arthur Humphreys (ed.), *The Oxford Shakespeare: Julius Caesar* (Oxford: Clarendon Press, 1984) pp. 24-25. Suetonius expresses considerable doubt about the outcry, but I'll leave the final word on the subject to Bernard Shaw, who in the notes to his play *Caesar and Cleopatra* remarks: "As to Caesar's sense of humor, there is no more reason to assume that he lacked it than to assume that he was deaf or blind. It is said that on the occasion of his assassination by a conspiracy of moralists (it is always your moralist who makes assassination a duty, on the scaffold or off it) he defended himself until the good Brutus struck him, when he exclaimed "What! you too, Brutus!" and disdained further fight. If this be true, he must have been an incorrigible comedian."

19. Suetonius, *Caesar* 83-85; Plutarch, *Caesar* 67-68 [pp. 893-394]; *Antony* 14-15 [pp. 1112-1113]; and *Marcus Brutus* 18-20 [pp. 1196-1198]. For Cleopatra, see *CAH* X. p. 4 note 2.

20. Suetonius, *Caesar* 83 and *Augustus* 8.2-3.

21. Oswald Spengler, *The Decline of the West* vol. I (London: George Allen, 1926) p. 38. If Spengler is correct in seeing Cecil Rhodes (!) as the prototype of our Caesar-of-the-future, then we're in worse shape than I thought.

Notes to Chapter 33

1. Plutarch, *Antony* 16 [p. 1113]; Appian, *Civil War* 2. 130-132.

2. Cicero, *ad Att.* 15. 11.1-2; Plutarch, *Brutus* 21-24 [pp. 1198-1202].

3. Cicero was acutely aware of the propaganda power of being Caesar's

son, and for that reason wrote to his friend Atticus that he was not calling the boy "Caesar." *ad Att.* 14. 12.2.

4. Cicero, *ad Att.* 16. 8.1-2; Plutarch, *Antony* 16 [pp. 1113-1114];Plutarch, *Brutus* 22 [p. 1199]; Suetonius, *Augustus* 10. 1-3. For the chronology of this period I am indebted to *CAH* X. 4-12; H.H. Scullard, *From the Gracchi to Nero* (London: Methuen, 1963) pp. 161-162; Ronald Syme, *The Roman Revolution* pp. 125-127; Jochen Bleicken, *Augustus: Eine Biographie* (Berlin: Alexander Fest Verlag, 1998) pp. 94-101.

5. Thus in a letter to Cassius dated from early Feb. 43 BC :"I wish you had invited me to dinner on the Ides of March. There wouldn't have been any left-overs." (*ad Fam.* 12. 4.1) (my translation).Cf. *ad Att.* 14. 12.1 and 14. 21.3.

6. *Ibid.* 16. 18.1.

7. Hirtius and Pansa were old political cronies of Caesar. Cicero's brother Quintus wrote of them in a letter of 44 BC (*ad Fam.* 16.27): "I know very well that they are filled with lust, sloth, and a most effeminate spirit." Cited by Gelzer p. 171 note 5.

8. Augustus, *Res Gestae* 1. 1-3

9. Servius Sulpicius Galba (an eyewitness) to Cicero, *ad Fam.* 10. 30.1-5. See also Decimus Brutus' letter to Cicero, *ad Fam.* 12. 5.2.

10. Plutarch, *Antony* 17 [p. 1114] (Dryden tr.).

11. See Tacitus, *Annals* 1. 10.1-2 and Suetonius, *Augustus* 10. 4-11 for the expected accusations that Octavian poisoned the one and stabbed the other in the back. We can readily agree with the remark in *CAH* X p. 5 n. 1 that this is only a "canard." Similarly Bleicken p. 116, who characterizes the remark as typical of the slanders hurled by both sides.

12. Cicero, *ad Fam.* 11. 10.4.

13. Suetonius, *Augustus* 12; Scullard p. 182; Syme pp. 176-178, 181-182; Bleicken pp. 116-119, 123-124.

14. Cicero, *ad Fam.* 10. 24.6 (my translation).

15. Suetonius, *Augustus* 26. 1. Syme calls this "a picturesque and superfluous anecdote" p. 185 note 7. Bleicken accepts it without comment p. 131, as does Karl Galilnsky, *Augustan Culture: An Interpretive Introduction* (Princeton: Princeton University Press, 1996) p. 47.

16. Syme pp. 185-186; *CAH* X 16-17; Bleicken p. 133.

17. Plutarch, *Antony* 18 [pp. 1114-1115]; *CAH* pp. 15-17; Syme pp. 178-179.

18. Cicero, *ad Fam.* 10. 35 (my translation).

19. Bleicken pp. 135-137.

20. Plutarch, *Cicero* 49 [p. 1069] (Dryden tr.). See also *Antony* 19-20 [p. 1115]; Suetonius, *Augustus* 62.1 and 27.1-2; and Scullard pp. 163-164. Lord Byron was a good deal less sympathetic to our friend Marcus Tullius Cicero than Plutarch had been: "—but why do they abuse him for cutting off that poltroon Cicero's head? Did not Tully tell Brutus it was a

pity to have spared Antony? and did he not speak the Philippics? and are not "words things"? and such "words" very pestilent "things" too? If he had had a hundred heads, they deserved (from Antony) a rostrum (his was stuck up there) apiece–though, after all, he might as well have pardoned him, for the credit of the thing." Leslie A. Marchand (ed.), *Lord Byron Selected Letters and Journals* (Cambridge: Harvard University Press, 1982), p. 85.

21. Plutarch, *Brutus* 28-52 [pp. 1203-1218]; *Antony* 21-22 [p. 1116]; Suetonius, *Augustus* 13.

Notes to Chapter 34

1. Suetonius, *Augustus* 16. 2 (my translation).

2. *CAH* X p. 26; Scullard p. 166; Syme pp. 206-207; Bleicken pp. 173-176.

3. Appian, *BC* 5. 62-67, cited by Bleicken p. 186.

4. Suetonius, *Augustus* 13. 3, 14-15; Plutarch, *Antony* 30 [p. 1121]; Scullard p. 167; *CAH* X pp. 28-29; Bleicken pp. 189-194. The lead slingshot bullets found at the site are notorious, covered as they are with typical soldiers' graffiti aimed at their targets. These always remind me of the messages chalked onto bombs and torpedoes in WW II by American soldiers–"Eat this, Adolph!" "Open wide, Tojo!" etc. See my comments in *The Priapus Poems* pp. 135-136, or another example cited by Bleicken p. 711: *L. Antoni calve, Fulvia, culum pandite!* Which could be charitably rendered, "Hey, baldy Luke Antony, hey, Fulvia, spread 'em!"–the same old joke we saw on the Eurymedon pot back in chapter 18.

5. Appian 5. 122-131. Octavian absorbed the title of pontifex maximus when Lepidus died in 12 BC. Augustus, *Res Gestae* 10. 1-2. See also Suetonius, *Augustus* 16. 1-2,4; 31. 1; *CAH* X. 29-30; Scullard p. 169; Syme p. 232; and Bleicken pp. 228-230.

6. Plutarch, *Antony* 26 [p. 1118] (Dryden, tr.).

7. Asinius Pollio would later write an important history of the Civil Wars–now lost (alas!) but nonetheless a major source for many of the ancient authors I've cited. Maecenas continued to be an important general for Octavian, and later became the emperor's official patron of the arts. It's thanks to his support that we have the works of Horace and Virgil.

8. Plutarch, *Antony* 31 [p. 1121]. For the Brundisium conference, see Bleicken pp. 194-200.

9. Plutarch, *Antony* 33-35 [pp. 1123-1124]; Scullard p. 167 and 171-172; Syme pp. 214-226; Bleicken pp. 214-221.

10. *CAH* X. p. 66. Bleicken pp. 256-257 doubts that a formal "marriage" was set up at this time, but rather suspects that Cleopatra, as part of Antony's grand re-ordering of the East, was raised to the status of a

full client in Antony's provincial service. Bleicken sees the final break as coming in 35 when Octavia dutifully returned from Rome to Athens with a care package of 2,000 soldiers and supplies for her husband. Antony unceremoniously told her to send on the supplies and to head back to Rome herself. Colin Wells, *The Roman Empire,* 2nd edition (Cambridge: Harvard University Press, 1997) pp. 23-24 accepts the marriage and compares it to the foreign brides of Alexander the Great. Wells finishes up by saying, "Perhaps the scholars cannot imagine themselves being carried away and sacrificing all for love, like Antony." Well, despite my cautionary remark in the next paragraph, I can imagine that quite easily.

11. Plutarch, *Antony* 37-51 [pp. 1125-1134].

12. *Ibid.* 54 [p. 1135].

13. Livia Drusilla, the woman Octavian married after divorcing his own wife Scribonia. She was already pregnant by her then husband, Tiberius Claudius Nero. Octavian stayed married to her for 50 years. Her son Tiberius, by her former husband, became Octavian's successor.

14. Suetonius, *Augustus* 69. 2 (my translation).

15. *Ibid.* 17.1. See also Syme pp. 281-283, Scullard pp. 173-175, *CAH* X. pp. 90-95; and Bleicken pp. 269-274.

16. Horace *Ep.* 9. 17-18: "But here Galatians shouting 'Caesar!' turned their 2,000 horses..."

17. *Ibid.* 19-20.

18. Plutarch, *Antony* 56-68 [pp. 1136-1143]. See especially Tarn's amazing reconstruction of the battle in *CAH* X. pp. 100-106, where of course he gives Cleopatra's influence first place. For his use of Horace's 9th epode, compare Eduard Fraenkel, *Horace* (London: Oxford University Press, 1966) pp. 71-75, who demonstrates that Horace wasn't actually at the battle. Bleicken's equally careful reconstruction is on pp. 275-286. He believes that Antony's plan all along was not to defeat Agrippa's fleet, but rather to break out of Actium and regroup; similarly Wells p. 28.

19. Virgil, *Aeneid* 8. 678-713 (John Dryden, tr.—and yes! Dryden wrote a lot more than his translation of Plutarch!).

20. Suetonius, *Augustus* 17. 3-4; Plutarch, *Antony* 69-77 [pp. 1143-1148].

21. Plutarch 78-86 [pp. 1148-1152].

22. Suetonius, *Augustus* 17. 5; Plutarch, *Antony* 81 [pp. 1149-1150]; Scullard p. 176. Syme p. 273 n. 1 doubts that Caesarion was Caesar's son; Gelzer p. 257 n. 1 is certain that he was. See also Suetonius, *Caesar* 52. 2. This is one of the last references I'll be making to the author Plutarch, who has been with us since the early chapters of this book. Plutarch was a Boeotian, born sometime around the year 50. He lived to a ripe old age and thus wrote at the time of the Flavians. His *Parallel Lives* was Harry Truman's favorite book and has inspired a lot of literature, from Shakespeare's *Julius Caesar* to Mary Renault's *Fire from Heaven.*

Plutarch didn't think of himself as an historian; he wrote biographies "to point a moral, or adorn a tale," but his forte was historical color and dramatic narrative. As the author of an introductory text (which is, after all, meant to entice you to further reading), I have therefore plundered the good Plutarch with (I hope!) more discretion than mercy.

Notes to Chapter 35

1. Livy 1. 19.3. cf. Augustus, *Res Gestae* 13 and Suetonius, *Augustus* 22, who both say that the gates had been shut twice before.

2. Scullard p. 216; Colin Wells p. 83. Plutarch (*Moralia* 207D8) has preserved for us Augustus's surprise "that Alexander did not regard it as a greater task to set in order the empire which he had won than to win it." Cited by Green, *Alexander* p. 473.

3. Suetonius, *Augustus* 35. 1,3-4; Dio Cassius 52. 42.1-3, 6-7; 53. 21.4-5.

4. Dio Cassius 53. 21.6-7; Suetonius, *Augustus* 56. 1 and 49. 2.

5. Bleicken pp. 310-315.

6. Dio Cassius 53. 4; 5.4; 8.1 (Earnest Cary, tr.). On the rich rhetorical irony of Dio's set speech and on the disingenuousness of Octavian's motives, see the commentary of J.W. Rich, *Cassius Dio: The Augustan Settlement (Roman History 53-55.9)* (Warminister: Aris and Phillips, 1990) pp. 15-16, 134-137. cf. Augustus, *Res Gestae* 34, in Octavian's own words: "In my 6th and 7th consulships, after I had extinguished the civil wars, even though by universal consent I was in complete charge, I transferred the republic from my power into the control of the Senate and the Roman people." For the very complex relationship between Augustus and the symbols of the Republic (or republic), see Galinsky pp. 58-71 and 76-77.

7. Dio Cassius 53. 11-13, 15.4-5; Suetonius, *Augustus* 47. For "Augustus" see Suetonius 2 and Dio 16. 7-8. See also Bleicken pp. 323-327. Syme pp. 313-314 and 326-330 corrects Dio's anachronistic list of senatorial and Augustan provinces. He also points out that governors and legates tended not to come from the surviving senatorial families, whom Augustus still feared. The provinces were now ruled by new men who owed their advancement to Augustus alone.

8. Suetonius, *Augustus* 66. 2; 18.2. Dio Cassius 53. 13.1-2, 23.

9. Suetonius, *Augustus* 47; Dio Cassius 14. 3-4 and 16. 1-3.

10. Tacitus, *Annals* 1. 12; 15. 1

11. Augustus, *Res Gestae* 34. 3 (my translation).

12. Tacitus, *Annals* 1. 3.7 (my translation).

13. Colin Wells pp. 52-53 dates the conspiracy to the year 22.

14. Dio Cassius 53. 25-26; 28.2; 30; 32.3-6, 9-10; Suetonius, *Augustus* 26. 2-3; 27. 4; *CAH* X pp. 136-140; Scullard p. 226; Bleicken pp. 348-354; Wells pp. 51-52. See especially Syme pp. 333-348, where the delicate balance of power between Augustus, Maecenas, Agrippa, and Livia

is explored. Indeed the whole theme of Syme's book, which we haven't the space to go into here, is the structure and development of party politics in the age of Augustus. As he points out (p. 346): "A democracy cannot rule an empire. Neither can one man, though empire may appear to presuppose monarchy. There is always an oligarchy somewhere, open or concealed."

15. Dio Cassius 53. 17.1-7.

16. Suetonius, *Augustus* 53. 2 *quasi elephanto stipem*, 72-73.

17. Suetonius, *Augustus* 23; Tacitus, *Annals* 1. 11.4. This was of course making the best of a bad deal. The Rhine-Danube frontier was neither inevitable nor especially suitable. Augustus was a committed imperialist who would have conquered Germany had he been able to pull it off. See Colin Wells pp. 73-78.

18. Suetonius 28. 3, 30. 1, 32. 1, 45. 1-3; Augustus, *Res Gestae* 22. 1.

19. *CAH* X pp. 441-456 and XI p. 834; Galinsky pp. 128-138. See also Suetonius, *Augustus* 34.

20. Suetonius 65. 2-4; 101. 3; Tacitus 1. 6.1-3.

Notes to Chapter 36

1. See especially Matthew 2-4, 46; Mark 1, 11, 14-16; Luke 2; and John 18-19.

2. Albert Schweitzer, *The Quest of the Historical Jesus* (New York: Macmillan 1968) pp. 123-124. Norman Perrin supplies some very useful examples of the kinds of stylistic comparisons that have led to this conclusion, as well as a brief summary of the sources of the Gospels in *The New Testament: An Introduction* (New York: Harcourt Brace, 1974) pp. 8-10. The argument, first developed by Christian Weisse in 1838, is that if the 3 most similar Gospels, Matthew, Mark, and Luke (the synoptic gospels, as they're called), are placed side by side, a pattern of interrelationships in language and in the ordering of incidents can be observed. Basically, many places can be found where Matthew and Mark agree, but Luke doesn't, or where Luke and Mark agree, while Matthew doesn't, but you won't find passages where Matthew and Luke agree against Mark. The only explanation for such a relationship would be that Mark came first and has been copied by the other two evangelists. See also Bart D. Ehrman, *The New Testament: A Historical Introduction to the Early Christian Writings* (New York: Oxford University Press, 1997) pp. 73-75. The Gospel of John with its developed concept of "The Logos," is clearly a later Christian invention. Schweitzer quotes Weisse on p. 125: "It is not so much a picture of Christ that John sets forth, as a conception of Christ; his Christ does not speak in His own Person, but of His own Person." Cf. also Günther Bornkamm, *Jesus of Nazareth* (New York: Harper and Row, 1960) p. 14: "The Gospel according to John has so different a character in comparison to the other three and is to such a

degree the product of a developed theological reflection, that we can only treat it as a secondary source." In the same book see also Appendix I, "Introduction to the History and Sources of the Synoptic Gospels" pp. 215-220; in Ehrman see pp. 152 and 224. Investigations of inconsistencies in the Biblical stories of Jesus' life are nothing new. See the article "Mages" (probably by Voltaire) in the *Encyclopédie* of Diderot and D'Alembert.

3. It's modern at least to the extent that I wrote it in the spring of 2000! The Greek text used was the one assembled for *The New English Bible* (Oxford and Cambridge University Presses, 1964). See "Ancient Sources" under "Bible."

Notes to Chapter 37

1. Ananda Coomaraswamy, *Buddha and the Gospel of Buddhism* (New Hyde Park, New York: University Books, 1964) p. 13; Paul Radin, *The Trickster* (New York: Schocken Books, 1972) p. 63; Ovid, *Metamorphoses* 3. 253-315.

2. Coomaraswamy pp. 13-14; Plutarch, *Alexander* 2 [pp. 801-2].

3. Suetonius, *Caesar* 88. Of course, to give the pathetic fallacy its due, I should point out that a comet did appear the year of Caesar's death—it was Halley's. See the deliberately disingenuous remarks of Edward Gibbon, *The Decline and Fall of the Roman Empire* vol. 1 (New York: The Modern Library) pp. 443-444. (end of Chapter XV). The star announcing Jesus' birth was also meant to fulfill Balaam's prophecy in Numbers 24: 12. See also Tacitus, *Histories* 5. 13 on the portents attending the fall of the Temple.

4. Ramsay MacMullen, *Paganism in the Roman Empire* (New Haven: Yale University Press, 1981) pp. 23-24; Walter Burkert, *Ancient Mystery Cults* (Cambridge: Harvard University Press, 1987) pp. 3-11.

5. See the frequency of inscriptions chart in MacMullen, *Paganism* p. 6, and his remarks pp. 118-119, which provide a good cautionary warning against usual claims that Mithra was primarily a religion for soldiers.

6. Mary Boyce, *Textual Sources for the Study of Zoroastrianism* (Totowa, New Jersey: Barnes and Noble, 1984) pp. 9 and 29. See also Franz Cumont, *Oriental Religions in Roman Paganism* (1911; reprint, New York: Dover, 1956) pp. 139-143 and 155-156. Also Franz Cumont, *The Mysteries of Mithra* (1903; reprint, New York: Dover, 1956) pp. 2-3.

7. Boyce p. 52, translating the Greater Bundahishn ch. 34. 23: "The Soshyant with his helpers will perform the yasna for restoring the dead. For that yasna they will slay the Hadayans bull; from the fat of that bull and the white haoma [the pressing of the primordial plant] they will prepare ambrosia and give it to all mankind; all men will become immortal, for ever and ever."

8. Manfred Clauss, *Mithras: Kult und Mysterien* (München: C.H. Beck,

1990) p. 89.

9. *Ibid.* pp. 117-122; Burkert pp. 73-74 and figure 11; Mary Beard, John North, and Simon Price, *Religions of Rome: Volume 1: A History* (Cambridge: Cambridge University Press, 1998) pp. 285-286. What have survived, besides the elaborate Mithraic temples (or caves), which seem to have represented the vault of the heavens, are pagan guesswork (especially Porphyry's commentary *On the Cave of the Nymphs in the Odyssey*), Christian attacks, and a few fragmentary graffiti from the caves themselves. See Beard, North, and Price, *Religions of Rome: Volume 2: A Sourcebook* pp. 305-319.

10. See R.L. Gordon, "Franz Cumont and the doctrines of Mithraism," *Mithraic Studies: Proceedings of the First International Congress of Mithraic Studies* (John R. Hinnells, ed.) (Manchester University Press, 1975) note 119 pp. 245-246; also in the same collection, John R. Hinnells "Reflections on the bull-slaying scene" pp. 29-293; and Clauss p. 18. David Ulansey, in a book which reads like a J.F.K. conspiracy case [*The Origins of the Mithraic Mysteries* (New York: Oxford University Press, 1989)], interprets Mithraism as an allegory for the precession of the equinoxes. See also Beard, North, and Price vol. 1 pp. 279-280; vol. 2 p. 308.

11. Sir James George Frazer, *The Golden Bough, 1 Volume Abridged Edition* (New York: Macmillan, 1963) pp. 416-417; Cumont, *Mysteries of Mithra* pp. 167 and 196; Clauss pp. 74-76.

12. The naming and ordering of the weekdays was based upon astronomers' calculations of the distances of the seven planets from the earth, which was supposed to be the center of the universe. Thus the farthest planet, which takes nearly 30 years to complete its orbit (actually, of course, around the sun) was named by the Romans Saturn, after the old, slow father of Jupiter. Before the popularity of the sun cult of later antiquity, Saturn's Day was the beginning of the week. The planet closest to the earth was the moon, which took only one month to make its orbit—hence Moon's Day. The order of the planets was Saturn, Jupiter, Mars, Sun (in the glorious center), Venus, Mercury, and Moon. To get our order for the days of the week, descend along the list in groups of four (remembering, as in counting dates, to count both ends of the sequence). Thus SATURN jupiter mars SUN venus mercury MOON saturn jupiter MARS (hence the French Mardi) etc. This odd arrangement probably resulted from astrologers' naming each day after the planet sacred to its first hour; since there are 7 planets and 24 hours in a day, 7 into 24 goes 3 times with 3 left over; 3 plus one for the 1st hour of the next day explains the groupings into 4. If you're still with me and curious about this, see George Sarton, *A History of Science* vol. 2 (Harvard University Press, 1959) pp. 326-333 and E.J. Bickerman, *Chronology of the Ancient World* pp. 58-61.

13. Burkert p. 43.

14. *Phaedrus* 247a (my translation).

15. Exodus 20: 2-5.

16. As has often been done. See Cumont, *Oriental Religions in Roman Paganism* pp. 42-43, and Frazer *The Golden Bough* pp. 413-420. For a similar reconstruction of the mithraic iconography, see Clauss on the cult meal (pp. 117-122) and on the sacrifice of the bull (p. 91). All such arguments, however, are based on analogy and assumption. Actual evidence for the European mysteries themselves is surprisingly absent. We should also remember the Saducees who mocked Jesus' preaching about the resurrection (Matthew 22: 23-33; Mark 12: 18-27; Luke 20: 27-40). The Old Testament does not teach the resurrection of the soul. See Rudolf Bultman, *Primitive Christianity in its Contemporary Setting* (London: Thames and Hudson, 1956) p. 46.

17. MacMullen, *Paganism in the Roman Empire* pp. 53-57 and *Christianizing the Roman Empire* (New Haven: Yale University Press, 1984) pp. 11-12, 18-19, and 70; Burkert pp. 23-29, 48-53, 75-76, 86-87; Beard, North, and Price vol. 1 pp. 286-291.

18. Jaroslav Pelikan, *Jesus Through the Centuries* (New York: Harper and Row, 1987) p. 11.

19. 2 Macabees 4: 13-15.

20CAH VIII pp. 346-350.

21. Quoted in Rudolf Bultman, *Primitive Christianity in its Contemporary Setting* (London: Thames and Hudson, 1956) p. 80. See also pp. 65-67.

22. Daniel 8-12 is a lament for the destruction of the Temple by Antiochus in 168 BC, but there is no mention of its rededication in 165, so that it's sensible to date the book to somewhere between these two incidents. See Perrin pp. 69-70.

23. Daniel 7: 1-7 (condensed) and 13-14. cf. above p. 252.

24. Ehrman pp. 208-210.

25. Quoted in Perrin pp. 67-68.

26. *CAH* IX. 417-421; Franz Cumont *ORRP* p. 138; Bultman pp. 82-3.; Ehrman pp. 215-217. Note that at Mark 12: 18-27 the Saducees, who were the conservatives of the Temple aristocracy, mocked Christ for his belief in the afterlife.

27. Cumont *MM.* p. 127, which is based on the testimony of Plutarch, *De Iside et Osiride* 46 (369E). For the concept of the messiah as mediator, see Claude Lévi-Strauss, *Myth and Meaning* (New York: Schocken Books, 1978) pp. 32-33. For a warning, however, that this does not constitute evidence for a link between Zoroastrianism and western Mithraism, see Gordon pp. 228-229 ("This mediation of Mithras is not Avestan.").

28. cf. above chapter 11.

29. Bultman p. 86; Ehrman pp. 217-219; Johannes Weiss, *Jesus' Proclamation of the Kingdom of God* (Chico, California: Scholars Press, 1985) pp.

114-117. In Weiss see note 85 p. 117 by the editors Hiers and Holland.

30. Naturally there are plenty of people to disagree with this central point. Even Bultman remarks: "Though Jesus' teaching about the will of God is hardly influenced by his expectation of an imminent end of the world and the threat of judgement, yet, when he is confronted by the indifference and hostility of the authorities and the people, his preaching does assume the form of denunciation and a summons to repentance." (p. 76). See also Perrin p. 300: "I am convinced that all sayings or teachings ascribed to Jesus in the gospels that give a definite form to a future expectation—for example, a future coming of the Son of man—fail the test of the criteria for authenticity." For the point of view I'll be taking in this chapter, see Johannes Weiss (who wrote his book in 1892) p. 93: "Naturally, we should avoid at the outset any kind of reformulation of this idea, however strange it may seem to us. As it now stands, it expresses what the early Christians meant: This old world cannot assimilate the Kingdom of God." See also Gibbon vol. I pp. 402-403 and Bornkamm pp. 203-204 note 40.

31. Mark 13: 5-37. cf. Matt. 24 and Luke 21: 5-36.

32. Mark 13: 30 ἀμὴν λέγω ὑμῖν ὅτι οὐ μὴ παρέλθῃ ἡ γενεὰ αὕτη μέχρις οὗ ταῦτα πάντα γένηται. Very similarly Matt. 24: 34 and Luke 21: 32. See especially Mark 9:1: "And he said unto them, Verily I say unto you, that there be some of them that stand here, which shall not taste of death till they have seen the Kingdom of God come with power."

33. See Weiss pp. 65, 73-4, 92-96. For a good, extended definition of the Kingdom of God, see Albert Schweitzer, *The Psychiatric Study of Jesus* (Boston: The Beacon Press, 1948) p. 48.

34. See Voltaire, *Dictionnaire philosophique* (Paris: Garnier, 1964) pp. 307-308 (under the entry "Messie"). See also Weiss pp. 81-83 and 118-121; Schweitzer, *The Quest of the Historical Jesus* pp. 148-151, 337, 347-8, 371-373, 386, and 393-395; and Ehrman p. 64. Going further than I would, Bultman believes that Jesus did not even think of himself as the Messiah, but only as the prophet of the Kingdom. It was, Bultman believes, the early Church which foisted the Messiahship upon Jesus. "Jesus proclaimed the message. The Church proclaims him." (pp. 90-93). Günther Bornkamm reaches the (I believe) contradictory conclusion that although the "messianic secret" is only a "literary device" of the evangelist Mark (p. 171), nonetheless Jesus scrupulously avoided applying the messianic titles Messiah, Son of God, Son of David, or Son of man to himself (p. 173 and 226-231).

35. Schweitzer, *Quest* pp. 389-391 and (on Judas) 396-7; Weiss pp. 86-9; Ehrman p. 230.

36. At 16: 8 in the King James Version. See R.V.G. Tasker (ed.), *The Greek New Testament* (Oxford and Cambridge, 1964) pp. 416-417.

37. See Perrin p. 148 and Ehrman pp. 67-68.

38. Frazer pp. 419-420; Weiss pp. 105-114; Schweitzer pp. 354 and 402; Ehrman pp. 227-228. For an opposing view, see Bornkamm pp. 109 and 223-225; for a more historically based compromise (which sees Jesus' death as the start of the promised kingdom), see Pelikan pp. 22-33.

39. As Pelikan points out, the more familiar form of the Beatitude "Blessed are the poor in spirit: for theirs is the kingdom of heaven" should be compared with its alternate in Luke 6: 20, 24: "Blessed be ye poor: for yours is the kingdom of God. . . But woe unto you that are rich! for ye have received your consolation." *Jesus Through the Centuries* p. 218.

Notes to Chapter 38

1. *i.e.* those of the *gentes* (nations) other than Israel. The usage is from St. Jerome's Latin translation of the Bible (the Vulgate) where, for instance, Jerome translates St. Paul's ῞Ηλλην (Greek) as *Gentilis* (Gal. 2: 3).

2. Beard, North, and Price, vol. 1 pp. 161, 211-214, 250, 313, 343-344; vol. 2 pp. 209-210.

3. Tertullian, *Apology* 23.

4. A good example of the official Roman attitude to the Jews occurs in Acts 18: 12-17. In this section the Jews of Corinth, fed up with Paul's Christian proselytizing, haul him before Gallio, the governor of Achaea. Gallio refused to listen to their complaints, saying: "If it were a matter of wrong or wicked lewdness, O ye Jews, reason would that I should bear with you: But if it be a question of words and names, and of your law, look ye to it; for I will be no judge of such matters." See also Ramsay MacMullen, *Paganism in the Roman Empire* (New Haven: Yale University Press, 1981) pp. 2-3 and Beard, North, and Price vol. 1 pp. 221-223, who point out that this relative tolerance was characteristic of the late Republic and all but disappeared by the 2nd century AD.

5. Gibbon I. 395-8, 410-417, 444-452; Perrin pp. 80-81; Beard, North, and Price vol. 1 pp. 225-226; vol. 2 pp. 280-281; 331. Tertullian, 7. 1.

6. Tertullian, 38. 4; 42-43. For the intimate relationship between the official Roman religion and daily life, see *CAH* VII pp. 598-609.

7. Michel Foucault, *Le Souci de Soi* (Paris: Gallimard, 1984) pp. 53-59 and 90-93.

8. Peter Brown, "Bodies and Minds: Sexuality and Renunciation in Early Christianity," in David M. Halperin et al., *Before Sexuality* (Princeton University Press, 1990) pp. 479-493. Beard, North, and Price vol. 1 pp. 375-376. See St. Paul's famous remarks at I Corinthians 7: 8-9, which we'll discuss in the next chapter.

9. Pliny, *Epist.* 10. 96 and 97 (my translation). Pliny, unlike Cicero, edited his own litters for publication, so he meant them to show him at his best. They don't always do that, as here where he matter-of-factly reports torturing women for evidence. Pliny's letters tell us a lot about upper class life in his day, filled as they are with menus of his luncheons

and floor plans of his new villas. He was also an eye-witness to the eruption of Mount Vesuvius, which he described to the historian Tacitus in 6. 16 and 20.

10. Tacitus, *Ann.* 15. 38-44; Suetonius, *Nero* 38.

11. Gibbon I. 455-465 and 473-485. See also Eusebius, *History* 8. 1.

12. Gibbon I. 434-440; 468-72; 501-503. See also A.H.M. Jones, *The Decline of the Ancient World* (New York: Holt, Rinehart and Winston, 1966) pp. 7-8. Of course Gibbon's numbers are only guesses, but pagans were probably in the majority throughout the fourth and, in some places, even into the fifth century. For evidence see MacMullen, *Paganism* pp. 132-134 with notes, and *Christianizing* p. 134 note 13.

13. MacMullen, *Christianizing* pp. 107-108 and 118-119. As J.B. Bury points out (*History of the Later Roman Empire*, vol. 1 [1923, reprint New York: Dover Publications, 1958] pp. 365-366), Early Christians believed that persecution of the heathen was not only a moral obligation, but the necessary price for God's protection of the state.

Notes to Chapter 39

1. Eusebius, *History of the Church* 2. 23 and 3. 1.

2. By the time the early Church was under way, however, this Greek tradition was abandoned so that Hebrew became once again the classical language of the synagogue. See H.-I. Marrou, *Histoire de l'Éducation dans l'Antiquité* (Paris: Éditions du Seuil, 1965) p. 616 note 6: "The Jews of Alexandria, in the time of Philo, celebrated a festival to commemorate the translation of the Septuagint...later...that day became a day of fasting and grief 'in expiation for the sin committed when the Torah was exposed in the language of the Goyim.' "

3. Acts 8: 3. Paul confesses this himself at Gal. 1: 13-14, 23-24, and in I Cor. 8-9. See Günther Bornkamm, *Paul* (New York: Harper and Row, 1971) pp. 8-10, and Jerome Murphy-O'Connor, *Paul: A Critical Life* (Oxford: Clarendon Press, 1996) pp. 65-70.

4. For this section on Paul see Perrin pp. 89-94. Perrin is convinced that Paul had a vision of Christ. So was Carl Jung, apparently: "I want to make clear that by the term 'religion' I do not mean a creed. It is, however, true that on the one hand every confession is originally based upon the experience of the numinosum and on the other hand upon πίστις, the loyalty, trust, and confidence toward a definitely experienced numinous effect and the subsequent alteration of consciousness: the conversion of Paul is a striking example of this." C.G. Jung, *Psychology and Religion* (New Haven: Yale University Press, 1938) p. 6.

5. See Bo Reicke, *The Epistles of James, Peter, and Jude* (The Anchor Bible) (Garden City: Doubleday, 1964) p. xxxviii and also Peter's clearly apocalyptic speech in Acts 2: 16-21.

6. I Thess. 4: 15-17. cf. Rom. 13: 11-12; I Cor. 7:29, 10: 11.

7. Gal. 3: 24-28. cf. Rom. 6: 3-5. See Albert Schweitzer, *Aus meinem Leben und Denken* (München: Siebenstern Taschenbuch, 1965) pp. 102-105 and 177-179; *CAH* XI 270-271, 277-280; Bornkamm, *Paul* 115, 120-129.

8. Bultman, *Primitive Christianity* p. 66.

9. Bornkamm, *Paul* pp. 13-14, 120-123; Ehrman pp. 241-242; Robert Eisenman, *James the Brother of Jesus* (New York: Viking, 1996) pp. 126-129, 160. The quote is I Cor. 1: 22-23.

10..Many people are upset by the suggestion that the Virgin Mary had any children other than Jesus. In fact, the Bible lists four others: James, Joses, Judas, and Simon (Mark 6: 3 and Matt. 13: 55). See also 1 Cor. 9: 5 and especially Gal. 1: 19. Indeed, the incident recounted at Mark 3: 31-35 and Matt. 12: 46-50 (and only slightly altered at Luke 8: 19-21) makes no sense if we deny Jesus his actual brothers. Nonetheless, the cult of the Mother of God, which, though absent from the Gospels, has much in common with the pagan worship of Diana of Ephesus, has brought the Greek Orthodox Church to assume that Joseph had a previous wife, and the Roman Church to insist that James is merely Jesus' cousin. See Gibbon I. 461 note 49; Bornkamm, *Jesus of Nazareth* pp. 199-200 note 4; Eisenman pp. xxvii-xxviii, 8-9, 139, 185-186, and 198-199.

11. Eusebius, *History* 2. 1.1 and especially 7. 19; *CAH* XI.272; Reicke pp. xviii-xix. Eisenman pp. 136-137 quotes from the *Gospel of Judas Thomas*, the so-called twin-brother of Jesus, that was discovered with the Nag Hammadi cache in Egypt in 1945: "The Disciples said to Jesus, 'We know that you will depart from us. Who is it that shall be great over us?' Jesus replied to them: 'In the place where you are to go, go to James the Just, for whose sake Heaven and Earth came into existence." (12). See also pp. 154-208, where Eisenman develops his theory that the election of Matthias to replace the traitor Judas in Acts 1: 15-26 is actually a doublet for the immediate election of James to the episcopate of Jerusalem.

12. Murphy-O'Connor pp. 90-95, 132-144. See also Eisenman pp. 127-128.

13. Acts 21: 15-22: 30. See Perrin pp. 90-96; *CAH* XI 268-272; Reicke p. xviii; and Bornkamm, *Paul* 97-106; Murphy-O'Connor pp. 341-351.

14. Eusebius, *History* 2. 23.13 (my translation).

15. Gibbon I. 388-390.

16. cf. Eusebius 2. 17.22: "And our customary hymns, and how while one sings in a regular rhythm the others, listening in silence, join in at the end of the line." (my trans.)

17. Gibbon I. 418; *CAH* XI. 286-290; Schweitzer, *Leben und Denken* p. 178; Ehrman pp. 272-285.

18. 13: 1: "Though I speak with the tongues of men and of angels, and have not love, I am become as sounding brass, or a tinkling cymbal."

19. Perrin (p. 7) dates the composition of the gospels to the years 70-

100.

20. *Ibid.* p. 172.

21. *Ibid.* pp. 216-217; *CAH* XI. 276-7 and 281; *The Greek New Testament* p. 420 under "11: 2."

22. Reicke pp. xxiv-xxv; Gibbon I. 404 and note 68; Eusebius, *History* 3. 25; *CAH* XI. 272-5.

23. Quoted in Gibbon I. 430. Ignatius, bishop of Antioch about 115, took a similar view: "It is good to recognize God and the bishop. He that honoureth the bishop is honoured of God; he that doth aught without the knowledge of the bishop rendereth service to the devil." See *CAH* XI. 291.

24. Henri-Irénée Marrou, *L'Église de l'Antiquité tardive* (Paris: Éditions de Seuil, 1985) pp. 26-28 and 95-97; Gibbon I. 418-424; Bury *HLRE* I.64-65; Jones, *Decline of the Ancient World* pp. 88-89, 261.

Notes to Chapter 40

1. Hesiod, *Works and Days* 109-201.

2. "Perhaps there is some connection between the wealth acquired, the enjoyment of that wealth, the resultant indolence, the acquiescence in slavery and in a government which by its benevolent despotism saved the citizens from the need of keeping awake except to gather in the profits. If we know the real meaning of the Antonine period, perhaps we should find a formula of some value for our own future." Tenney Frank, *An Economic Survey of Ancient Rome, vol. 5 Rome and Italy of the Empire* (Baltimore: The Johns Hopkins Press, 1940) p. 298. See also the 2nd chapter of Gibbon's *The Decline and Fall of the Roman Empire* (vol. 1 pp. 25-52).

This is a good time to recommend Patrick Brantlinger's fascinating book, *Bread and Circuses: Theories of Mass Culture as Social Decay* (Ithaca: Cornell University Press, 1983), which presents a history of what he calls "negative classicism." By that he means the use of the decline and fall of the Roman Empire as a metaphor for the decline and fall of whatever happens to be modern society at the moment. This is a particularly attractive pose for traditionalists like me who hate television and love Tibullus. See also Ramsay MacMullen, *Corruption and the Decline of Rome* (New Haven: Yale University Press, 1988) pp. 1-5, who has a lot of fun with the image of literary decline developed above in the text. Both authors sagely point out the subjectivity (and indeed class consciousness) of any such judgement, and consequently the danger of generalization. Thus Brantlinger: "The bread and circuses analogy seems to be largely accurate insofar as it detects widespread social, cultural, and environmental decay behind the façade of technological progress; it seems to be most inaccurate when it finds in mass culture or the mass media a primary cause—in some versions, the primary cause—of that decay." (p.

282) MacMullen: "In these and other expressions of its nature, the 'Rome' that 'declines' is thus not one single thing but many things, and the search for any one cause across the board is futile. So, too, is the search for any one period in which all aspects of Roman civilization were much changed. No such crucial period exists." (p. 5) The reader is also reminded of the brief discussion of cultural determinism in note 23 of chapter 18, which dealt with the decline and fall of the Athenian Empire.

3. The second law defines the limits of heat systems by pointing out that the amount of their unavailable energy (called entropy) necessarily increases. Thus heat always flows from hot objects into cold ones, and organized systems necessarily degenerate into chaos. Of course the second law refers to closed physical systems like stars so it's very bad physics to employ it metaphorically for cultural analysis or for hare-brained arguments against the theory of evolution. Still, for a well reasoned application of this basic law of physics to cultures, see Leslie A. White, *The Evolution of Culture* (New York: McGraw-Hill, 1959) pp. 33-40.

4. Cassius Dio 77. 10.4, cited by Rostovtzeff, *SEHRE* pp. 417-420; see also pp. 203-206 and his *Rome* pp. 271-277; Frank, *Economic Survey* pp. 297-301; *CAH* XI.828-9; Montesquieu pp. 137-138.

Serf is a loaded word and of course anachronistic here in its medieval sense. I wanted to use it early in the discussion, however, so that Diocletian's later reforms would not seem so revolutionary.

5. Tacitus, *History* 1. 4.

6. Rostovtzeff, *SEHRE* pp. 89-111, 126-129.

7. *Ibid.* pp. 378-392. MacMullen, *Corruption and the Decline of Rome* pp. 41-43 points out that it is not simply the rate of taxation that proves ruinous, but rather its unequal distribution and collection.

8. Cited in Gibbon I. 119.

9. *Ibid.* p. 120.

10. Lactantius, *De Mortibus Persecutorum* 5. See also A.H.M. Jones, *Constantine and the Conversion of Europe* (London: The English Universities Press, 1961). pp. 2-4

11. Jones pp. 4-5; Frank pp. 90-93.

12. Gibbon I. 300-304; Jones, *Constantine* 12-13; Rostovtzeff, *Rome* pp. 270-271; Averil Cameron, *The Later Roman Empire* (Cambridge: Harvard University Press, 1993) pp. 30-31.

13. Eusebius, *Life of Constantine* 1. 17 (Richardson, tr.).

14. Gibbon I. 304-312, 319-326, 332-333; Montesquieu p. 138; Jones, *Constantine* pp. 1-2, 13-18; Cameron pp. 31-32; Lactantius 8 and 9.

15. Lactantius 7. 1-4; Jones, *Constantine* p. 23; Cameron pp. 39-40.

16. Montesquieu p. 132.

17. The diadem, which was clearly Persian in origin, seems later to have been formally introduced by Constantine. Its wearing became regular in the 5th century, by which time it was conferred upon the emperor by

the patriarch of Constantinople. J.B. Bury, *HLRE* I. 10-11 and 15.

18. *Scriptores Historiae Augustae: Aurelian* 42 (my translation). See MacMullen, *Corruption* pp. 147-148, where the above passage is cited in somewhat different form.

19. Gibbon 328-332; Montesquieu pp. 135-137; Franz Cumont, *Oriental Religions in Roman Paganism* p. 141. For a description of the kind of Byzantine nonsense to which these practices led, see Procopius, *Anecdota* 15. 13-16. It should be pointed out that not only the details of court ceremonial, but also what we think of today as the civilized treatment of international ambassadors, can be traced back to Sassanid Persian influence. See Bury, *HLRE* I .92-93. Cameron p. 42 is careful to point out, as she is throughout her presentation of Diocletian's reforms, that the changes in his reign represent intensifications more than innovations.

20. Martin Henig (ed.), *A Handbook of Roman Art* (Ithaca: Cornell University Press, 1983) pp. 173-175. See also (pp. 91-92) the famous porphyry statue group of the tetrarchs now in the Piazzo San Marco, Venice.

21. Jones, *Constantine* pp. 6-12, 22-28 and *Decline of the Ancient World* pp. 20-21, 240-250; Frank, *Economic Survey* p. 303; Bury, *HLRE* I. 55-63; Rostovtzeff, *SEHRE* pp. 148, 521-522; MacMullen Corruption pp. 43-52, 162-164, 194-195. Cameron pp. 45-46 stresses again the gradual and evolutionary nature of the changes, a point which MacMullen had already carefully developed. See also the somewhat later laws from the Theodosian Code cited in Donald Kagan, *Problems in Ancient History volume two: The Roman World* (London: Macmillan, 1972) pp. 420-422, especially 12.1. 13 and 7. 21.1. The constant repetition and even hysterics of imperial pronouncements against decurions show that the laws could not be enforced.

22. A Grenier, *La Gaule Romaine*, vol. 3 in *An Economic Survey of Ancient Rome* (Tenney Frank, ed.) (Baltimore: The Johns Hopkins Press, 1937) pp. 606-607. See also Jones, *Constantine* p. 27 and Cameron pp. 27-28, 36-39. The quote is from lines 18-19 of the introduction to Diocletian's Edict of Prices.

23. This document is one of the most fascinating to survive from antiquity since it provides something of a shopping list of goods available in the empire along with their relative prices. The edict's monetary unit is the *denarius*, the first question about which would be naturally "What's it worth today?" Equivalencies are of course impossible—especially since the prices set by the edict couldn't be enforced—but just for fun it is possible to set a "pork denarius" or a "beef denarius" by dividing the ancient price per-pound into the current dollar-per-pound figure at the butcher's. Confusion starts at once, however, for in Diocletian's Rome, pork (the most commonly consumed meat) was more expensive than beef! Simon Corcoran, *The Empire of the Tetrarchs: Imperial Pronouncements and Government AD 284-324* (Oxford: Clarendon Press, 1996) p. 227 notes

the same ratio of 2:3 in a papyrus from Oxyrhynchus dating to 290. Neither should we expect consistency across cultures. Figuring the value of the denarius based on the current (summer of 1998) price of gold (Diocletian set the value of the denarius at 50,000 to the pound of gold, and I'm using Troy ounces), the "gold denarius" comes out to 7¢. Based, however, on the current value of pork roast at my local supermarket, the "pork denarius" is 12¢. At any rate, here are some representative prices (in denarii) gleaned from Graser'edition of the edict, printed in volume 5 of Tenney Frank's *An Economic Survey of Ancient Rome* pp. 307-421.

pork and lamb:	(pound) 12
beef and mutton:	(pound) 8
ham:	(pound) 20
1 pair of chickens:	60
2 jumbo melons:	4
garden asparagus, 25 to the bunch:	6
gym teacher:	(boy/month) 50
arithmetic teacher:	(boy/month) 75
Greek or Latin literature teacher:	(boy/month) 200
running sandals:	60
1st quality traveling bag:	1,500
carriage with tires minus hardware	7,000

24. Lactantius 7. 6-7; Diocletian, *Edict of Prices proem.* 46; Grenier pp. 608-612; Rostovtzeff, *SEHRE* p. 516; Jones, *Decline* pp. 167-168; Corcoran pp. 229-233.

25. Lactantius 3-6; cf. Gibbon pp. 485-6 and Beard, North, and Price vol. 1 pp. 242-244.

26. Lactantius 10-15.5; Eusebius, *Life of Constantine* 2. 50-51; Eusebius, *History of the Church* 8. 2-6. Cf. Jones pp. 46-49 and Gibbon 485-496.

27. Lactantius 15. 6-7; Eusebius, *Constantine* 1.16. Eusebius's story that Constantius banished from his palace those who obeyed the imperial edict and were consequently "faithless to God" is, to put it mildly, an exaggeration.

28. Lactantius 17-19; Eusebius, *Constantine* 1. 18; Zosimus 2. 8.1; Jones, *Constantine* pp. 56-57; Gibbon I. 342-343.

29. Lactantius 20.24; Eusebius, *Constantine* 1. 20-21; Eusebius, *History of the Church* 8. 2-6. Cf. Jones, *Constantine* pp. 46-49 and Gibbon 485-496.

Notes to Chapter 41

1. Lactantius, *The Death of the Persecutors* 26 and 27. 8; Eusebius, *History of the Church* 8.14; Zosimus 2. 9.2-10.2; Gibbon I. 347-350, 496-7; Ramsay MacMullen, *Constantine* (London: Weidenfeld and Nicolson, 1969) pp. 59 and 62-3.

2. Lactantius 27. 107; Zosimus 2.10.3-11; Gibbon I. 350-352;

MacMullen 59-60.

3. Lactantius 28; Zosimus 2. 11.

4. Lactantius 29. 2-30; Eusebius, *History* 8 App.; Gibbon I. 353-355; MacMullen, *Constantine* pp. 60-61.

5. MacMullen, *Constantine* p. 61; Lactantius 42; Eusebius, *History* 8 App.

6. Eusebius, *History* 8.16; cf. Lactantius 33. This is the same malady that felled Herod the Great (see above, chapter 37), not to mention Herod Antiphas and Antiochus I. One marvels at their stubborn perversity, given the apparently inevitable consequences.

7. Lactantius 34 (my translation). There's a Greek version (including the preamble) in Eusebius 8. 17. Michael Grant, *The Emperor Constantine* (London: Weidenfeld & Nicolson, 1993) pp. 136-138 rejects the story of the illness and invokes "cold political considerations" to explain the edict.

8. Eusebius, *Life of Constantine* 1. 26 and 33-35; Lactantius 43-44; Zosimus 2. 15.1-2; Gibbon I. 356-360; MacMullen, *Constantine* pp. 64-65 and 70-72.

9. Eusebius, *Constantine* 1. 28 (Richardson, tr.).

10. A.H. Jones in *Constantine and the Conversion of Europe* pp. 96-102 calls upon the "halo phenomenon" which results from ice crystals obscuring the face of the sun.

11. Cited by MacMullen, *Constantine* pp. 73-74. See *CAH* XI.358-359.

12. Lactantius 44.5: *facit ut iussus est et tranaversa X littera summo capite circumflexo Christum in scutis notat*–"He did as he was told and marked Christ upon his shields with the letter X turned on its side and its top bent over." In order to turn this into the better known chi-rho, ☧, it's necessary to emend the text, as indeed Moreau suggests (11. 434-436). Eusebius does precisely that and expands Constantine's dream into instructions to create the *labarum*, a golden standard surmounted by the magical device and bearing the pictures of Constantine and his children. Both Gibbon (I. 645) and MacMullen (73-74) point out that it's too early for Constantine's children and, indeed, for the *labarum* itself, which wasn't used for another ten years. Camron p. 56 remarks, "Some degree of mythologizing has evidently taken place." Michael Grant pp. 138-146 also discusses conflation between the dream and the vision, but he is more credulous: "But there is no reason why both events, vision and dream, should not have occurred, or have been believed to occur." (p. 145)

13. As a further elaboration, Eusebius in the *Life of Constantine* presents the wooden bridge as a trap constructed for Constantine's army, by means of which Maxentius's death can therefore be viewed as an act of poetic justice. More details are added by the 6th century pagan historian Zosimus (2. 15.3-4). However, this contradicts both the illustration on the Arch of Constantine and the earlier account in Eusebius's own *History of the Church* (9. 9). The elaboration seems to be the result of

Eusebius's desire to compare Constantine to Moses drowning Pharaoh in the Red Sea, and of his wish to quote dramatically Psalm 7:15, "He made a pit, and digged it, and is fallen into the ditch which he made." Zosimus' elaborations should also be no surprise, for despite his own pagan bias, he portrays Maxentius as exercising a "savage tyranny" (16.3) over the Romans.

14. Mark 2: 9, "Whether is it easier to say to the sick of the palsy, Thy sins be forgiven thee; or to say, Arise, and take up thy bed, and walk?" For this whole discussion of the miracle at the Milvian Bridge, see Gibbon I. 644-650 and MacMullen, *Constantine* pp. 70-78. For Eusebius as an historian, see Cameron pp. 15-18. In judging the historicity of Constantine's vision, it might be helpful to compare the vision of Jesus that appeared to Elvis Presley in the sky above Flagstaff Arizona in March, 1965. See Peter Guralnick, *Careless Love: The Unmaking of Elvis Presley* (Boston: Little Brown, 1999) pp. 193-196.

15. Eusebius, *Constantine* 1. 40, also quoted in his *History of the Church* 9. 9. The head, hands, and feet of the colossal statue survive and are now in the Palazzo dei Conservatori at Rome. Eusebius never went there to see the statue himself, so we really don't know whether its religious iconography was any less generalized than that on the famous arch. See Beard, North, and Price vol. 1 p. 366.

16. Gibbon I. 366-7 and MacMullen, *Constantine* p. 84.

17. Lactantius 36. 3-5 and 37. 1-2; Eusebius, *History* 8. 14.

18. Lactantius 48. 2 (my translation). See Corcoran, *The Empire of the Tetrarchs* pp. 158-160.

19. Lactantius 46. 6.

20. *Ibid.* 49-51; Eusebius, *History* 9. 10-11; Eusebius, *Constantine* 1. 58-59.

21. Apuleius, *Metamorphoses* 11. 4 (my translation).

22. Quoted by Franz Cumont, *ORRP* p. 207. Cf. Michael Grant, *The Emperor Constantine* pp. 125-126 and Tertullian, *Apology* 24. 3: "Now even granting that these [pagan divinities] are gods, would you not concede, in accordance with the common opinion, that there exists someone more sublime and more powerful, as it were the prince of the world in perfect majesty?"

23. Jones, *Constantine* pp. 93-94. In MacMullen's biography see plate IIIb for illustrations of Constantine's famous coins bearing the chi-rho and, issued the same year, the image of the emperor standing with Sol Invictus himself. Cameron p. 49 cites an anonymous Panegyric from 310 (Pan. Lat. VII (6).21) crediting Constantine with a vision of Apollo! Michael Grant, *The Emperor Constantine* pp. 131-134 conveniently denies the authenticity of the vision, suggesting that it was a crude shake down from a greedy priest.

24. Gibbon I. 636.

25. "The passive and unresisting obedience which bows under the yoke of authority, or even of oppression, must have appeared in the eyes of an absolute monarch the most conspicuous and useful of the evangelic virtues." *Ibid.* p. 640.

26. Eusebius, *Constantine* 2. 19. For the story of the wars with Licinius see Gibbon I. 371-381; Eusebius, *Constantine* 1. 49-2.56; Eusebius, *History* 10. 8-9; and especially Zosimus 2. 18-28.

Notes to Chapter 42

1. Gibbon I. 506-518; Montesquieu pp. 137-138.

2. Gibbon pp. 521-523. Cf. MacMullen, *Corruption* pp. 62-63 and Corcoran pp. 103-104.

3. Michael Grant, *The Emperor Constantine* pp. 161-164.

4. Henri-Irénée Marrou, *L'Église de l'Antiquité tardive* (Paris: Éditions de Seuil, 1985) pp. 31-35; Gibbon I. 671-675.

5. Eusebius, *History of the Church* 10. 5.22.

6. G.S. Kirk and J.E. Raven, *The Presocratic Philosophers* (Cambridge, 1966) pp. 187-188 and 214-215. cf. Albin Lesky, *A History of Greek Literature* (New York: Thomas Y. Crowell, 1966) pp. 211-212.

7. Plato, *Republic* 500c (my translation).

8. Lesky pp. 674-675 and 878-886. Cf. Tertullian, *Apology* 21. 10-14.

9. The Arian sense of the verse is clearest in the Vulgate: *Dominus possedit me in initio viarum suarum / Anteguam quidquam faceret a principio.* This has been understandably fudged in the King James translation: "The Lord possessed me in the beginning of his way, before his works of old." The translation in the Anchor Bible is, "The Lord possessed me, the first principle of his sovereignty, / Before any of his acts..." See R.B.Y. Scott, *The Anchor Bible: Proverbs, Ecclesiastes* (Garden City: Doubleday, 1965) p. 68, along with Scott's note p. 73.

10. Cited by Marrou p. 37. For this discussion of Arianism, see also Gibbon I. 675-683 and Jones, *Decline of the Ancient World* p. 328.

11. See the tripartite division of the soul in *Republic* 434D-441C. Of course there are numerous pagan triads too. See Cumont, *Oriental Religions in Roman Paganism* p. 250 note 55.

12. Marrou pp. 37-38; Gibbon I. 683-684; Henry Melvill Gwatkin, *Studies of Arianism* (Cambridge: Deighton, Bell, and Co., 1882) p. 30.

13. Eusebius, *Constantine* 3. 13-14 and 4. 32. For the convocation see 3. 7-9 and Timothy Barnes, "Constantine, Athanasius and the Christian Church," in Samuel N.C. Lieu and Dominic Montserrat, ed., *Constantine: History, Historiography and Legend* (London: Routledge, 1998) pp. 10-11; Marrou pp. 38-9; MacMullen, *Constantine* pp. 171-172; Michael Grant, *The Emperor Constantine* pp. 172-173.

14. Eusebius, *Constantine* 2. 68. Still, we shouldn't be too hard on Constantine, for even St. Thomas More, in his letter to Martin Dorp,

could say, "Finally, so you may know briefly my views on this whole subject—I am not criticizing all theologians, and I do not condemn all the problems advanced by the moderns; but those which are not at all relevant, which contribute nothing to learning and are a great hindrance to piety—those problems, in my opinion, should be censored, and furthermore, completely rejected." Elizabeth Frances Rogers (ed.), *St. Thomas More: Selected Letters* (New Haven: Yale University Press, 1961) p. 40.

15. Marrou p. 39. Gibbon I. 684-685.

16. Eusebius's letter to his diocese, quoted in Theodoret, *The Ecclesiastical History* 1. 11; Gwatkin pp. 37-49; Gibbon I. 685-687; MacMullen, *Constantine* p. 174; Jones, *Constantine* p. 161; Marrou pp. 39-40; Michael Grant pp. 173-174. For Paul of Samosata, see Eusebius, *History of the Church* 7. 29-30, where the pastors' letter against him is preserved. Paul, who lived during the reign of Aurelian, said that Jesus is "from below"—i.e. that he was a man who became a God, not the other way around. He was thus a precursor of Arius, a strange fact, given the fate of his term *homoousion*.

17. I am simplifying a bit here. This famous version of the Creed—it's from the now (alas!) defunct *Book of Common Prayer*—is not precisely the Nicene Creed, but seems to be a revision of the local creed of Jerusalem written by bishop Cyril when he returned from exile in 362. See H.M. Gwatkin, *The Arian Controversy* (London: Longmans, 1898) pp. 159-161, a somewhat expanded version of his *Studies of Arianism* pp. 260-262. The original versions of the creed can be found in Eusebius' letter in Theodoret 1. 11; they are quoted conveniently by Jones (Caesarean version) in *Constantine* p. 159-160 and MacMullen (Nicean version) in his *Constantine* pp. 174-175.

18. Gibbon I. 713.

19. Athanasius *Letter to Serapion* (also quoted in Theodoret 13); Jones, *Constantine* pp. 172-203; Gibbon I. 693-4, 697-702.

20. As A. Harnack has remarked of the homoousion, "One of its most serious consequences was that from this time forward Dogmatics were forever separated from clear thinking and defensible conceptions, and got accustomed to what was anti-rational...The thought that Christianity is the revelation of something incomprehensible became more and more a familiar one to men's minds." Quoted by Bury *HLRE* I. 349. Cameron points out p. 69 that this formal attempt to define correct thought set a disastrous precedent for the freedom of ideas.

21. Eusebius, *History* 10. 9.7.

22. Zosimus 2. 29.1-2; Gibbon I. 565-570; MacMullen, *Constantine* p. 187, and Jones, *Constantine* pp. 243-246.

23. Eusebius, *Constantine* 4.61.

Notes to Chapter 43

1. Tacitus, *Germania* 4. 2.

2. *Ibid.* 14. 4. For this whole discussion see 7. 1-3 and 11-14 as well as Caesar *BG* 6. 23.4-6. cf. J.B. Bury, *The Invasion of Europe by the Barbarians* (New York: Norton, 1967) pp. 11-15 and C.W. Previté-Orton, *The Shorter Cambridge Medieval History* (Cambridge, 1953) vol. 1 pp. 37-38; Fergus Millar, ed., *The Roman Empire and its Neighbours* (New York: Delacorte Press, 1967) pp. 311-312.

3. Cf. Above note 12 in chapter 37.

4. For human sacrifice see Tacitus, *Germania* 9. 1, 12. 1-2, 39. 1-2, 40. 2-5 and Jordanes, *History of the Goths* 5.45. A good, ghoulish survey of the bog mummies is P.V. Glob, *The Bog People: Iron-Age Man Preserved* (New York: Ballantine Books, 1970). For the Tacitus passages, see the commentary of J.G.C. Anderson (Oxford, 1938).

5. Bury pp. 6-10; Tacitus 16. 26.1-3; Caesar, *BG* 4. 1.7 and 6. 22. Millar pp. 309-311 traces the development, under Roman influence, of independent hamlets into farmsteads dominated by the "big house" of an established family.

6. Tacitus 18-24 and Caesar 4. 1-2 and 6. 21-23.

7. Bury, *Invasion* pp. 4-6 and *SCMH* pp. 38-39.

8. Jordanes 1-5, 14, 18, 21, and 23; Ammianus Marcellinus 31. 13.13; *SCMH* p. 39; Bury, *Invasion* pp. 15-17, 22-26.

9. *SCMH* pp. 56-7; Bury, *Invasion* pp. 45-47; cf. Jordanes 51.

10. Jordanes 24. 122 and 127 (Mierow, tr.). cf. Ammianus Marcellinus 31. 2.2.; Bury, *Invasion* pp. 48-51; Gibbon I. 914-922; Cameron pp. 136-137; and Millar pp. 299-301, 317-319.

11. Ammianus Marcellinus 31. 4.1-5; Jordanes 25; Gibbon I. 922-3; *SCMH* pp. 57-58; Bury, *Invasion* pp. 55-58; Cameron pp. 137, 140. MacMullen, *Corruption* pp. 183-184 uses this story as an example of imperial corruption and incompetence.

12. Bury, *Invasion* pp. 38-44; Bury, *HLRE* I. 38-39, 99; Montesquieu pp. 144, 155; Gibbon I. 538-540; Zosimus 2. 34. See also MacMullen, *Corruption* pp. 175-177, which is really a summary of his third chapter (pp. 122-170).

13. Ammianus Marcellinus 31. 4-16; Zosimus 4. 20-24.2, 26; Jordanes 25-26; MacMullen, *Corruption* pp. 184-185.

14. Jordanes 28. 142-144 (Mierow, tr.).

15. Gibbon I. 943-956 and II. 91-92; *SCMH* pp. 59, 77-80; Bury, *HLRE* I.106-107; *Invasion* pp. 60-69; Zosimus 4. 56-5.1; Jordanes 27-29.

16. Alaric's successor and brother-in-law Athaulf inherited that same conflict and described it to the historian Orosius: "In the full confidence of valour and victory, I once aspired to change the face of the universe; to obliterate the name of Rome...By repeated experiments I was gradu-

ally convinced...that the fierce untractable humour of the Goths was incapable of baring the salutary yoke of laws and civil government. From that moment I proposed to myself a different object of glory and ambition; and it is now my sincere wish...not to subvert, but to restore and maintain, the prosperity of the Roman empire." Cited by Gibbon II. 173. cf. Zosimus 5. 26.1-2.

17. Cynesius, cited by Gibbon II. 93 note 8. I couldn't resist quoting this famous gibe though as Bury points out (*HLRE* I. 375) it was at least partly inspired by the Alexandrian philosophers' jealousy of the Neoplatonic revival at the Academy under Priscus and his successors.

18. Zosimus 5. 6 (Ridley, tr.).

19. *Ibid.* 5. 5-5.12. See also Gibbon II. 92-98; Bury, *Invasion* pp. 69-71; Bury, *HLRE* I. 119-121; and *SCMH* p. 80.

20. Gibbon II. 99-122; Bury, *Invasion* pp. 76-83; Bury, *HLRE* I.160-170; *SCMH* pp. 81-83; Zosimus 5. 26-27.

21. Zosimus 5. 29.1-5. That pun is the best translation I can come up with of Lampadius's bon-mot, which Zosimus quotes in Latin: *non est ista pax sed pactio servitutis.*

22. *Ibid.* 5. 28-29. See Ronald T. Ridley's remarks on p. 217 note 105 in his translation of Zosimus (Sidney: Australian Association for Byzantine Studies, 1982) and cf. Bury, *Invasion* pp. 84-86 and *HLRE* I.170. Jones in *Decline of the Ancient World* p. 76 is kinder to Stilicho than I am in the remarks that follow.

23. Zosimus 5. 30-35; 37. 6.

24. Jérôme Carcopino, *Daily Life in Ancient Rome* (New Havens: Yale University Press, 1975) pp. 18-21. cf. Gibbon II. 137 and 149-150.

25. Thus Previté-Orton, *SCMH* p. 84.

26. Zosimus 5. 36-40.

27. *Ibid.* 5. 41-42. The pepper is no joke. It was imported all the way from India and was very expensive. That section of Diocletian's edict of prices covering spices is unfortunately fragmentary, but we can reconstruct the relative price of pepper. The edict does preserve the price of dried ginger at 250 *denarii* a pound, and in the first century Pliny the Elder priced both ginger and black pepper at about the same rate (6 and 4 denarii respectively. Talk about inflation!). See Tenney Frank, *An Economic Survey of Ancient Rome* vol. 5 pp. 285 and 421, and cf. above chapter 40 note 22. Of course by the 5th century commodities like pepper and silk tunics were far more valuable than the hopelessly devalued currency of the West.

28. Zosimus 5. 43-6.13

29. Augustine, *City of God* 1. 7. St. Augustine wrote *The City of God* to answer accusations by pagans that Rome fell because the Christians had abandoned the pagan religion of their ancestors. St. Augustine's answer was that, first of all, the pagan gods had been unable to save Rome from

disasters in the past. Even more important, and indeed downright apocalyptic in its implications, is his explanation that God doesn't care about
the materialistic, earthly city of Rome. He cares only for the heavenly
City of God: "And so two loves have created two cities: the earthly city,
created by love of the self extending even to the contempt of God, and
the heavenly city, created by love of God extending even to the contempt
of self."(14. 28)

30. *Ibid.* 1. 10, 11, 12, 14, 16, 17, 22. Like Augustine, Jordanes also boasts
that the Goths spared the holy places: "They merely sacked it and did
not set the city on fire, as wild people usually do." (30. 156). Later, however, Jordanes adds that Alaric's successor Ataulphus sacked the city
again, "and whatever had escaped the first sack his Goths stripped bare
like locusts, not merely despoiling Italy of its private wealth, but even of
its public resources." As often, Jordanes is confused, for Ataulphus never
sacked Rome. Could not this second description record another, non-
Christian tradition of what the Goths did to Rome?

31. St. Jerome, *Ep.* 127. 12 (my translation).

32. Jordanes 30. 157-158.

33. *Ibid.* 45-46 and Gibbon II. 343-4 and note 127. For Lucullus, cf.
above chapter 30.

34. Gibbon II. 342. The situation was actually rather complex.
Romulus Augustulus, for all his fame in the time lines, was never legitimate emperor. Augustulus's doting father Orestes, who had once been
secretary to Attila the Hun, had served as Master of Soldiers to Rome's
last legitimate emperor, Julius Nepos, who was married to the niece of
the Eastern emperor Zeno's mother-in-law Verina. Orestes overthrew his
master, who fled to the Dalmatian coast. He survived five more years
(until he was assassinated), recognized by both Gaul and the imperial
court at Constantinople. The death of Julius Nepos in 480 should be
thought of as the legitimate end of the Western Empire, if indeed legiti-
macy still counts for anything at this point. See Bury, *HLRE* I. 404-411
and Jones, *Decline of the Ancient World* p. 92.

35. Jordanes 52 and 57. See Bury, *HLRE* I. 316-318, 411-428.

Notes to Chapter 44

1. Montesquieu p. 165.

2. Procopius, *Anecdota* 6. 1-19; 8. 2-3 (H. B. Dewing, tr.). The same story
about the stencil is also associated with King Theodoric the Ostrogoth.
See Bury, *HLRE* I. 467 note 2. For Justin see *HLRE* II. 16-19.

3. Having dragged you over the coals with the Arian Heresy, I'll spare
you the details of the Monophysite. In brief, though, the sect, which was
centered in Syria and Egypt, insisted upon the indissoluble nature of the
divine and human elements in Jesus. The Monophysites arose in opposition to the orthodox (i.e. politically successful) theologians of Antioch

and Constantinople, who not only tended to separate the two natures of Christ but even objected to the title "Mother of God" for the Virgin Mary. That final blasphemy drove the devout mobs of Alexandria crazy. Justinian couldn't abide any opposition, be it theological or otherwise. He shut down the philosophical schools of Athens as pagan abominations, even though their leaders were the direct successors of Plato and Aristotle. He would have attacked the Monophysites too, but Theodora realized, as we've often pointed out in the text, that religious wars are almost always camouflage for political disagreements. Egyptians and Syrians used Monophysitism as a rallying cry against the foreign domination of Byzantine culture just as Arabs today use Moslem fundamentalism as a focal point for opposition to the cultural threat of the West. For as long as she lived, Theodora helped keep her husband from tearing the Empire apart, but eventually Justinian's mindless persecution of both Arians and Monophysites made the Byzantine regime so hateful to its non-Hellenic subjects that they welcomed the Moslem invaders of the 7th century as liberators. For a good survey of this religious dilemma, see *SCMH* pp. 118-122, 187-188, and 194-196 and Jones, *Decline* pp. 85-86, 355. Fuller treatments can be found in Gibbon II. 805-865 (Chapter 47); (more sympathetically) in Henri-Irénée Marrou, *L'Église de l'Antiquité tardive* (Paris: Éditions du Seuil, 1985) pp. 126-167; and J.A.S. Evans, *The Age of Justinian: The Circumstances of Imperial Power* (London: Routledge, 1996) pp. 71-75. See especially Bury, *HLRE* I .349-359; II. 360-394. Today the Coptic and Armenian Churches are still Monophysite, while the Catholic and Orthodox faiths remain Dyophysite.

4. Procopius, *Anecdota* 9. 1-34, 47-54.

5. *Ibid.* 7. 1-38; Procopius, *History of the Wars* 1. 24.1-7; Steven Runciman, *Byzantine Civilization* (Cleveland: The World Publishing Company, 1967) pp. 58-59; *SCMH* p. 188; Gibbon II. 486-489; Bury, *HLRE* I. 84-86 and II. 39-48.

6. Gibbon II. 489, citing Theophanes. This was too good to leave out, but I should confess that Gibbon seems to have collated an actual incident from the riots cited by the *Chronicon Paschale* with a fascinating but apparently unrelated dialogue quoted by the *Chronicle of Theophanes.* The latter is printed in full and analyzed by Bury in an appendix to *HLRE* II. 71-74. For a more detailed reconstruction of the early days of the riots, see Evans pp. 119-122 and Robert Browning, *Justinian and Theodora* (London: Thames and Hudson, 1987) pp. 67-71. Rome had a long tradition of such theatrical public acclamation used to confirm or (more dangerously) challenge status. For earlier examples see MacMullen, *Corruption* pp. 67-69 and cf. Cameron pp. 176-177.

7. Procopius, *History of the Wars* 1. 24.33-37.

8. *Ibid.* 1. 24.7-58. Tribonian lived on for many years and died of natural causes in Justinian's service. We'll meet him again later in the chapter.

John, however, got greedy of Belisarius' power and made an enemy of Theodora. Antonina, Belisarius' wife, framed the praefect as a favor to her mistress. He was eventually deported to Egypt, where Procopius has him begging for "bread and obols" (*History* 1. 25.1-44).

9. *Novels* 30 § 11, cited by Bury at *HLRE* II. 26.

10. Jordanes 33. 170-172; Evans p. 126.

11. Procopius, *History of the Wars* 1. 1.12-15, cited by Gibbon II. 533-534. I've used his translation. See also Runciman pp. 110-111.

12. Runciman p. 71; Gibbon II. 528-553; *SCMH* p. 189.

13. *Anecdota* 18. 1-12; Evans pp. 133-136.

14. Jordanes 59. 304-306; *Anecdota* 16. 1-5; Gibbon II. 554-557; *SCMH* 190; Bury *HLRE* II. 159-167; Evans pp. 136-138.

15. Jordanes 60. 307-314; Gibbon II. 557-581; Montesquieu p. 159; *SCMH* 190-191; Bury *HLRE* II. 180-216; Evans pp. 139-151.

16. After the capture of Witigis the Germans elected the Visigothic general Ildibad as their king. He was assassinated in a private quarrel; Totila was his nephew.

17. *Anecdota* 4.1-6, 16 (Dewing, tr.)

18. *Ibid.* 4. 39.

19. Procopius, *History* 7. 12.3-10 (Dewing, tr.) Cf. also *Anecdota* 5. 1-7.

20. Procopius, *History* 7. 20.1-31. Cf. Gibbon II. 639 note 19; Bury, *HLRE* II. 233-244; Evans pp. 173-174.

21. Procopius, *History* 7. 30.25 and 8. 35.1-3.

22. See Montesquieu p. 159 and Runciman pp. 162-163. This explains why, according to Justinian's own *Institutes*, castrati were not allowed to adopt (1. 11.9). See also *Digest* 9. 2.27. It's also important to note that Narses was an Armenian whose promotion to high rank illustrates Justinian's determination to bring those most eastern subjects of his empire socially and politically into the Roman sphere. See Bury, *HLRE* II. 345-346.

23. Procopius, *History* 8. 29.1-4 and 32.1-36; Gibbon II. 643-648; *SCMH* p. 191; Evans pp. 177-178.

24. Procopius, *History* 8. 33.27.

25. Gibbon II. 649-660; *SCMH* pp. 192-193.

26. Procopius, in describing the situation in 548, just before Belisarius's second recall from Italy, prophetically draws a picture of Justinian's whole reign: "Thus...the final result for them was that not only had they consumed money and lives in prodigal fashion to no advantage, but they had also lost Italy besides, and had to look on while practically all the Illyrians and Thracians were being ravaged and destroyed in a pitiable manner by the barbarians, seeing they had now become their neighbors (*History* 7. 33.1)." cf. *Anecdota* 18. 16-30 and see Montesquieu pp. 160-164; Gibbon II. 512-514; *SCMH* 192-194; Bury, *HLRE* II. 75-123.

27. Procopius *Buildings* 1. 1.20-65; Runciman pp. 206-207; Gibbon II.

507-509.

28. Peter Birks and Grant McLeod (trans. and ed.), *Justinian's Institutes* (Ithaca: Cornell University Press, 1987) pp. 8-11; C.F. Kolbert (trans.), *Justinian: The Digest of Roman Law: Theft, Rapine, Damage, and Insult* (Harmondsworth: Penguin Books, 1985) pp. 35-37; Gibbon II. 687-8; *SCMH* pp. 197-8.

29. I'm especially indebted to Birks and McLeod (pp. 9-10) for their clear translation of Latin technical terms. See also Alan Watson (ed.), *The Digest of Justinian* (Philadelphia: University of Pennsylvania Press) pp. xxvii-xxxix; W.W. Buckland, "Classical Roman Law" in *CAH* XI. 809 and 815-816; Kolbert pp. 16-18, 45-46; Gibbon II. 677-689; *SCMH* p. 198; Mommsen I. 202-203; Olga Tellegen-Couperus, *A Short History of Roman Law* (London: Routledge, 1993) pp. 140-147.

30. *Anecdota* 14. 8.

31..The canon was Papinian, Paul, Ulpian, Gaius, and Modestinus. In case of a tie, the judges were to follow Papinian.

32. For the discussion of the *Digest*, see Birks and McLeod pp. 10-16; *CAH* XI. 811-826; Kolbert pp. 10-19, 27-42; Mommsen III. 567-68; Gibbon II. 681-691; *SCMH* 198.; Hans Julius Wolff, *Roman Law: An Historical Introduction* (Norman: University of Oklahoma Press, 1951) pp. 162-170.

33. Justinian, *Institutes* "imperial majesty" 3.

34. *CAH* XI. 824; Birks and McLeod pp. 12-17; Kolbert pp. 42-43, 49.

35. Justinian, *Institutes* "imperial majesty" 7.

Notes to Chapter 45

1. Virgil, *Aeneid* 6. 847-853 (Rolfe Humphries, tr.).

2. Justinian, *Institutes* 1. 2.12. All translations of the *Institutes* in this chapter are from the edition of Birks and McLeod. Translations of the *Digest* are from Watson's edition.

3. *Institutes* 1. 8; Kolbert p. 49.

4. About 340 BC in the Latin Wars. See Livy 8. 7-8.

5. The right to kill one's child became increasingly abridged under the early empire and was finally abolished by Christian emperors. Constantine did however revive the right to sell one's children into slavery "as an aid to impoverished parents." See Andrew Borkowski, *Textbook on Roman Law* (London: Blackstone Press, 1994) pp. 103-104.

6. Kolbert pp. 52-53; *Institutes* 1. 12; 2. 9.1.

7 *Digest* 47. 2.16.

8. *Institutes* 2. 8 pr. See also Borkowski pp. 114-116.

9. We saw this earlier in the Sermon on the Mount (5: 32). See also Mark 10: 2-12 and Luke 16: 18.

10. Bury, *HLRE* II. 406-409.

11. Gaius, *Institutes* 1. 190 (my translation). See *CAH* XI. 829-830;

Kolbert pp. 52-56; Gibbon II. 700-703, 722, and J.K.B.M. Nicholas, *An Introduction to Roman Law* (Oxford: at the Clarendon Press, 1962) pp. 95-96.

12. *Institutes* 3. 2-3.5. cf. Gibbon II. 710 and 713 and Mommsen I. 210; Ernest Metzger (ed.), *A Companion to Justinian's Institutes* (Ithaca: Cornell University Press, 1998) pp. 117-118.

13. *Institutes* 2. 19.2.

14. *Institutes* 3. 5.5.

15. *Institutes* 3. 6.12. For an excellent discussion of how the legal concept of a father's authority was more important than even blood ties—especially in the case of inheritance—see Yan Thomas, "The Division of the Sexes in Roman Law" pp. 90-102 in Pauline Schmidt Pantel, ed., *A History of Women in the West: I, from Ancient Goddesses to Christian Saints* (Cambridge: The Belknap Press, 1992).

16. *Institutes* 1. 12.5 and 2. 12.5. cf. Kolbert p. 188 note 10.

17. *Institutes* 1. 3.4.

18. See Frank M. Snowden, Jr., *Blacks in Antiquity* (Cambridge: Harvard University Press, 1971) p. 186: "Although evidence with respect to the Ethiopian in the ancient world is not available for the application of all the criteria used by scholars today, we are able to see how the Ethiopian fared in certain crucial areas: occupations, religion, social acceptance, and race mixture. An examination of these areas demonstrates that Greco-Roman practice conformed with Greek and Roman beliefs as to the origins of racial diversity and their utterances as to the insignificance of racial differences in judging men."

19. W. Beare, *The Roman Stage* (London: Methuen and Co., 1968) pp. 186 and 190.

20. *Digest* 47. 2.48.

21. *Digest* 9. 2.33. cf. 9. 2.2 and *Institutes* 4. 3 pr.

22. *Digest* 47. 10.15.41; *Institutes* 1. 8.2.

23. *Digest* 47. 10.7.2; *Institutes* 1. 5.6; 3.7.

24. *Institutes* 1. 5.6; 2. 14 pr-3; 2. 19.1; 2. 20.20; 2. 24.2. *CAH* X. 432-433.

25. Birks and McLeod pp. 13-15; *Institutes* 2. 2.

26. Kolbert pp. 56-60; Mommsen I. 207-208 and IV. 655; Nicholas p. 179; *Institutes* 2. 1.40-41, 47-48; 2. 6; 2. 10 pr; 3. 22; *Digest* 46. 2.14. The famous warning *caveat emptor* does not actually appear in Roman law. Deliberate fraud was however forbidden by the overriding concept that the seller act "in good faith."

27. *Institutes* 2. 10-13, 16.3; Mommsen III. 567 and 448; *CAH* XI. 837-8.

28 W.W. Buckland in *CAH* XI. 385-6.

29. e.g. *"Quinque aureos dare spondes?" "Spondeo!"* The necessary vocabulary is listed in *Institutes* 3. 15.1.

30. *Institutes* 3. 19.

31. *Institutes* 3. 25.

32. It was the responsibility of the plaintiff to do the dragging. In Roman law, if you were not strong enough to take care of yourself—or if you didn't have powerful friends—you were really out of luck. See Alvin H. Bernstein, *Tiberius Sempronius Gracchus* p. 85; Borkowski p. 59.

33. *Digest* 48. 19.8.9, cited by Buckland, *CAH* XI. 843. See also Kolbert pp. 64-67; Mommsen I. 205-6; *Institutes* 4. 1 pr.; Hans Julius Wolff, *Roman Law: An Historical Introduction* (Norman: University of Oklahoma Press, 1951) pp. 52-54; Nicholas pp. 211-212; Metzger p. 233; and Tellegen-Couperus p. 131.

34. *Digest* 3. 2.1.

35. *Digest* 47. 2.93. See Borkowski, *Textbook on Roman Law* pp. 320-321.

36. *Institutes* 4. 1.3; 4. 2; 4. 3.13-16; 4. 4.2-6, 12; *Digest* 46. 2.21; 47. 10.5; and 9. 2.51.

37. Gaius, *Institutes* 4. 11, cited by Wolff pp. 63-64.

38. *Institutes* 4. 18 pr.

39. *Institutes* 4. 18; Gibbon II. 718-719; Mommsen I. 204. For another example of this parricide law, see Apuleius, *The Golden Ass* 10. 8, where a young man is to be sewn into a sack for supposedly having killed his brother. Jones, *Decline of the Ancient World* pp. 194-195; Rostovtzeff, *SEHRE* pp. 197-198; Jacques Heurgon, *Rome et la méditerranée occidentale,* 3rd ed. (Paris: Presses Universitaires de France, 1993) pp. 210-211.

40. *CAH* IX. 852-858; H.H. Scullard, *From the Gracchi to Nero* (London: Methuen, 1966) pp. 15-16, 86, 210-211; Mommsen III. 144-146; Borkowski pp. 60-66.

41. Nicholas pp. 23-25; Tellegen-Couperus pp. 53-57. See also Wolff pp. 77-78, where a formula establishing a fictitious *usucapio* ("grasping by use") is explained, as well as Borkowski pp. 67-69 for further examples.

42. *Digest* 47. 2.48.4; *Institutes* 4. 1.13-15.

43. *Institutes* 4. 3 pr-10; 4. 6.16-19, 21; *Digest* 9. 2.23.

44. *CAH* IX. 862-866; *CAH* XI. 808-813, 839-843; Birks and McLeod pp. 16-18.; Wolff pp. 84-90; Nicholas pp. 27-28; Tellegen-Couperus pp. 88-93, 128-133; Borkowski pp. 73-75. Judges had surprisingly little leeway. A witness's credibility was tied directly to his social rank; written evidence was always preferred to oral witnesses; and heathens and non-Christians couldn't testify under any circumstances.

45. *Institutes* 2. 17.8.

46. *Institutes* 4. 9; *Digest* 9. 2.5; 46. 2.23; 47. 8.2; 47. 10.3.

47. *Institutes* 2 .20.29-31: "False descriptions are not fatal." cf. 4. 6.35.

48. *Digest* 9. 2.28: "...and many cases of this sort can be seen in which the plaintiff fails, because he could have avoided the danger." cf. *Digest* 9. 2.11 and *Institutes* 3. 14.3: "A person who gives something to a negli-

gent friend to look after should blame his loss on his own complacency."

49. MacMullen, *Corruption* pp. 87-96. Of the Great Men, the powerful land owners and the well connected who could defy the courts as easily as they could the tax collectors, MacMullen remarks: "There is no sign of them within the empire of Trajan's day, hardly any for a century after that. To explain their triumphant challenge, only broad changes in the empire's types and structure of power will suffice."

50. Charles Homer Haskins, *The Rise of Universities* (Ithaca: Cornell University Press, 1957) pp. 6-8, 35-44; Birks and McLeod pp. 18-26; Gibbon II. 669 note 2; Wolff pp. 177-225. Curiously, as recently as 1988, the Roman concept of *confusio* (see *Institutes* 2. 2.27) was used in Great Britain when two types of crude oil were wrongfully mixed during transport. Borkowski pp. 346-347 cites the case as "Indian Oil Corporation Ltd v Greenstone Shipping SA (Panama) QB345."

Abbreviations Used in Notes

ANET	Pritchard, *Ancient Near Eastern Texts Relating to the Old Testament*
BC	Caesar, *de Bello Civili*
BG	Caesar, *de Bello Gallico*
CAH	*Cambridge Ancient History*
CIL	*Corpus Inscriptionum Latinarum*
DMG	Ventris and Chadwick, *Documents in Mycenean Greek*
DS	Diodorus Siculus
HLRE	Bury, *History of the Later Roman Empire*
J	Justinian, *Institutes*
MM·	Cumont, *Mysteries of Mithra*
OPW	Kagan, *Outbreak of the Peloponnesian War*
ORRP	Cumont, *Oriental Religions in Roman Paganism*
QC	Quintus Curtius
SCMH	Previté-Orton, *Shorter Cambridge Medieval History*
SEHRE	Rostovtzeff, *Social and Economic History of the Roman Empire*

Introduction to Bibliography and Further Reading

The bibliography has been divided into two sections: ancient and modern.

Ancient Sources lists all of the primary material mentioned in the text or the notes. Anthologies and selections are listed under the editor. The editions and translations cited are not necessarily the most recent, but rather those which I happen to have used in writing the book. They represent the eccentric population of my own library, where I have been obliged to do most of my work over the past twenty years. It seemed pointless to list the translations of the works available yesterday in paperback. Readers can do that more accurately themselves simply by consulting *Books in Print,* which can be found in any bookstore or library. Students, in my experience, always settle for whatever translation happens to be on the shelves of their library or in stock at the local book store, while teachers on short budgets are frequently forced to order the cheapest editions available. Furthermore, my notes frequently refer to the commentaries and introductions listed in *Ancient Sources*.

We translators are competent hacks at best anyway, and using a translation always feels like a concession to sloth and expediency. Still, we can't live forever, so some general suggestions about translations are in order.

The best and most convenient introductory anthology to the literature of ancient Egypt and Mesopotamia is still James Pritchard's *Ancient Near Eastern Texts Relating to the Old Testament* (1969). Although this is now consistently referred to as "out of date" by scholars, there is nothing else of comparable scope and competence. Mistakes at this level are mostly the concern of specialists, and many of the translations—such as E.A. Speiser's of *Gilgamesh*—have virtually become English classics. If you want to look more closely at the literature of ancient Egypt, try the clearly written and well chosen selections of William Kelly Simpson, *The Literature of Ancient Egypt* (1972), or (more generously) the three volumes of Miriam Lichtheim's *Ancient Egyptian Literature* (1973).

Once you get to the Greek and Latin classics, virtually all of the selections are available in neat, bilingual editions in the Loeb Classical Library, published today by Harvard University Press. If you know French, there's a comparable though smaller collection in the Budé series published by Les Belles Lettres, Collection des Universités de France. Budé editions tend to have more ample introductions and commentaries than their Loeb counterparts. Many of the historians can also be found in paperback in the Penguin Classics. These tend to be more modern translations, but the Loeb editors are gradually updating their catalogue.

The one general recommendation I would make, however, is that you avoid prose renditions of works the ancients wrote in verse. All the above series translate most everything into prose, and prose versions of Homer can be especially deadly. Richmond Lattimore's translation of the *Iliad* (1951) is still the best, but for some reason his *Odyssey* has always struck me as less successful. The translation by Robert Fitzgerald (1961) has been a favorite for years, and I will make an exception for T.E. Lawrence's prose version (Oxford, 1932), which turns the *Odyssey* into a novel by Robert Graves.

Greek tragedy is a real conundrum. I still feel that the University of Chicago series, edited by David Grene and Richmond Lattimore, is the most consistently readable. The translators seem to aim at turning Aeschylus, Sophocles, and Eurypides into modernized Shakespeare. For that very reason many readers find the series hopelessly out-of-date.

No two people will ever agree on the suitability of a translation. Your best bet, if you have the time and your library has the resources, is to look over a few pages of the available competition and pick the version that irritates you the least.

Modern Sources available for the study of ancient history are extensive and indeed stretch all the way back to the Renaissance. Here, however, are some suggestions on where to begin and where to find more extensive lists of recent books and articles.

If you're interested in human evolution, Roger Lewin's *Bones of Contention* (1987) is a good start, even if it did come out just before the Out of Africa controversy. For that and a readable summary—popular science in the best sense—try David Johanson *et al.*, *Ancestors: In Search of Human Origins* (1994), based on the PBS series. Paul Mellar's *The Neanderthal Legacy* (1996) will get you off on a new career.

An excellent short introduction to the origins of agriculture is Bruce D. Smith, *The Emergence of Agriculture* (1995). David R. Harris, *the Origin and Spread of Agriculture and Pastoralism in Eurasia* (1996) is a rigorous and stimulating anthology.

For the ancient Middle East, Amélie Kuhrt's *The Ancient Near East c. 3000-330 BC* (1995) is both an excellent narrative and a first-rate bibliographical source. I could say the same thing about a newly updated favorite, *The Ancient Near East: A History* (1998) by William W. Hallo and William Kelly Simpson.

C.W. Ceram's widely available *Gods, Graves, and Scholars* (1967) is still the best general introduction to the science of archaeology itself. For a couple of practical but still non-technical examples of the nitty gritty, you might want to try John Chadwick's *The Decipherment of Linear B* (1970) or Donald B. Redford's *Akhenaten the Heretic King* (1984).

For the Minoans and the Myceneans, volume 2 of the 3rd edition of the *Cambridge Ancient History* (1973) is still a good starting point, even though it's nearly 30 years old. There is an excellent and provocative collection of articles (in French) edited by René Treuil, *Les civilisations égénnes du Néolithique et de l'Age du Bronze* (1989), and of course you don't need French to consult the extensive bibliographies. See also William A. McDonald and Carol G. Thomas, *Progress into the Past: The Rediscovery of Mycenean Civilization* (1990). For the Minoans Rodney Castledon's *Atlantis Destroyed* (1998), despite its fixation with Plato's myth, is a useful aid.

The best book on early Sparta, I think, is still Pavel Oliva's *Sparta and her Social Problems* (1971), but Lukas Thommen's *Lakedaimonion Politeia* (in German, 1996) will help you catch up with bibliography.

A good narrative on early Athens is the relative chapters in Christian Meier, *Athens: A Portrait of the City in its Golden Age* (1998), but Meier is little help with bibliography. For that, try volume 3 part 3 of the 2nd edition of the *Cambridge Ancient History* (1982), as well as the helpful short monograph by Charles W. Fornara and Loren J. Samons, *Athens from Cleisthenes to Pericles* (1991).

The best book on the Graeco-Persian Wars is Peter Green, *The Greco-Persian Wars* (1996). J.F. Lazenby's *The Defense of Greece 490-479* (1993) is more pedantic but for that reason more helpful with bibliography. A special surprise (in French) is Pierre Briant's *Histoire de L'Empire Perse* (1996), which approaches the Persian Wars, up to Alexander the Great, from the Persian perspective. This is a generous, large scaled treatment with excellent bibliography.

After Thucydides, the next step in studying the Peloponnesian War is to read Donald Kagan's masterful four volume study: *The Outbreak of the Peloponnesian War* (1969), *The Archidamian War* (1974), *The Peace of Nicias and the Sicilian Expedition* (1981), and *The Fall of the Athenian Empire* (1987). Fornara and Samons will help with more recent bibliography, as will volume 5 of the *Cambridge Ancient History* (1992) and David Cartwright's *A Historical Commentary on Thucydides* (1997).

The two best books on Alexander are W.W. Tarn, *Alexander the Great* (1948) and Peter Green, *Alexander of Macedon* (1991). They are mirror images. More recent bibliography, especially that dealing with Philip's tomb, can be found in N.G.L. Hammond, *The Genius of Alexander* (1997).

The best modern introduction to ancient Rome is to take a deep breath and read Theodor Mommsen's *Römische Geschichte* (*The History of Rome* [1873]), and then to take an even deeper breath and read Edward Gibbon's *The History of the Decline and Fall of the Roman Empire* (1776-1788). Mommsen is the only ancient historian ever to have been awarded the Nobel Prize for Literature, and the *Decline and Fall* is the greatest history book in the English language. Of course there has been a good deal of scribbling since Gibbon:

The new second edition of the *Cambridge Ancient History* again provides a lot of helpful bibliography. Volume 7 part 2 and Volume 8 (both published in 1989) will bring you down to the year 133 BC.

For early Rome, Alexander Grandazzi, *The Foundation of Rome: Myth and History* (1997) is both well written and provocative. See also Massimo Pallattino, *A History of Earliest Italy* (1991); (in French) Jacques Heurgon, *Rome et la Méditerranée occidentale jusqu'aux guerres puniques* (1993 ed.); and T.J. Cornell, *The Beginnings of Rome: Italy and Rome from the Bronze Age to the Punic Wars c. 1000-264 BC* (1995)

For the expansion of Rome over the Mediterranean, the classic work remains Erich S. Gruen, *the Hellenistic World and the Coming of Rome* (1980), an object lesson in careful scholarship. For recent work on the Punic Wars specifically, see Serge Lancel's two books, *Carthage: A History* (1995) and *Hannibal* (1998), now available in English.

I should also recommend two widely consulted studies by H.H. Scullard: *A History of the Roman World 753 to 146 BC* (1980) and *From the Gracchi to Nero* (1982). Besides their clear narrative, both are extremely useful for their surveys of the ancient sources.

The best biography of Tiberius Gracchus is Alvin H. Bernstein, *Tiberius Sempronius Gracchus: Tradition or Apostasy* (1978). Luciano Perelli, *I Gracchi* (1993), in Italian, is a bit of a socialist whitewash, but contains good references.

For the late Republic and the Civil War, once again the new editions of *Cambridge Ancient History* provide a god jumping-off point for bibliography. Volume IX (1994) and volume X (1996) cover the period from 146 BC to 69 AD. Two good recent surveys with bibliography are David Shotter, *The Fall of the Roman Republic* (1994) and Colin Wells, *The Roman Empire* (1997), the latter of which brings its survey and bibliography down to "Max Thrax."

The best biography of Caesar is still Matthias Gelzer, *Caesar:*

Politician and Statesman (1968), while for the foundation of the principate you shouldn't miss the classic by Ronald Syme, *The Roman Revolution* (1939). An excellent and up-to-the-minute biography of Augustus is (in German) Jochen Bleicken, *Augustus: Eine Biographie* (1998).

Any study of Jesus should begin with Albert Schweitzer, *The Quest of the Historical Jesus* (1906), itself a bibliography with commentary of work from the Enlightenment up to Schweitzer's own day. It glows with Schweitzer's humanity, common sense, and scholarship. The best recent survey is Bart D. Ehrman, *The New Testament* (1997). A good contemporary biography of Paul is Jerome Murphy-O'Connor, *Paul: A Critical Life* (1996). Robert Eisenman, *James, the Brother of Jesus* (1996) is very useful if you don't cut yourself on any of the axes it has to grind. Mary Beard, John North, and Simon Price have written an excellent two volume set, *Religions of Rome* (1998), volume one a history and volume two a generous anthology of primary sources, many not easily available elsewhere. These are stimulating surveys which carefully put Christianity and the mystery cults into a clear historical perspective.

Two specialized surveys of the later Roman Empire should be mentioned at the outset: Michael Rostovtzeff, *The Social and Economic History of the Roman Empire* (1957) and A.H.M. Jones, *The Later Roman Empire 284-602* (1964). Jones' *The Decline of the Ancient World* (1966) is an abridgement, prepared by Jones himself, of his longer work. It is now out of print, though Johns Hopkins University Press has reissued *The Later Roman Empire* (1986).

For the whole period of the later empire, Averil Cameron has prepared two excellent, brief surveys with bibliography: *The Later Roman Empire AD 284-430* (1993) and *The Mediterranean World in Late Antiquity AD 395-600* (1993). Just out is *Cambridge Ancient History* volume 13, *The Late Empire, A.D. 337-425* (1998). The best biography of Constantine is Ramsay MacMullen, *Constantine* (1969).

The study of Roman Law, like the study of ancient music, will drive you crazy. A good and seductively clear start is Olga Tellegen-Couperus, *A Short History of Roman Law* (1993). More detailed and technical, but still readable, is Andrew Borkowski, *Textbook on Roman Law* (1994).

Ancient Sources

Aeschylus. *The Persians.* Translated by Seth G. Benardete. In *The Complete Greek Tragedies.* Edited by David Grene and Richmond Lattimore. Chicago: University of Chicago Press, 1956.

Ammianus Marcellinus. *Ammianus Marcellinus.* With an English Translation by John C. Rolfe. 3 vols. Cambridge: Harvard University Press, 1939.

Andocides. *On the Mysteries.* In *Selections from the Attic Orators.* Edited by E.E. Genner. Oxford: At the Clarendon Press, 1955.

Appian. *Appian's Roman History.* With an English Translation by Horace White in 4 volumes. London: William Heinemann, 1958.

Apuleius. *The Transformations of Lucius Otherwise Known as The Golden Ass.* A New Translation by Robert Graves from Apuleius. New York: Farrar, Straus & Giroux, 1951.

Aristotle. *The Athenian Constitution.* Translated with Introduction and Notes by P. J. Rhodes. Harmondsworth: Penguin Books, 1984.

–. *The Politics.* Translated by T.A. Sinclair. Baltimore: Penguin Books, 1962.

Arrian. *Arrian.* 2 vols. With an English Translation by P.A. Brunt. Cambridge: Harvard University Press, 1976.

Augustine. *Concerning the City of God Against the Pagans.* A New Translation by Henry Bettenson. London: Penguin Books, 1972.

Augustus. *Res Gestae Divi Augusti: The Achievements of the Divine Augustus.* With an Introduction and Commentary by P.A. Brunt and J.M. Moore. Oxford: Oxford University Press, 1967.

Berossus. *The Babyloniaca of Berossus.* Edited by Stanley Mayer Burstein. Malibu: Undena Publication, 1978.

Bible. *The Anchor Bible: The Epistles of James, Peter, and Jude .* Translated by Bo Reicke. Garden City: Doubleday, 1964.

–. *The Anchor Bible: Genesis.* Translated by E.A. Speiser. New York: Doubleday, 1962.

–. *The Anchor Bible: Proverbs, Ecclesiastes.* Translated by R.B.Y. Scott. New York: Doubleday, 1965.

–. *Biblia Sacra Iuxta Vulgatam Clementinam.* 5th ed. Madrid: La Editorial Catolica, S.A. 1977.

–. *The Greek New Testament.* Edited with Introduction, Textual Notes, and Appendix by R.V.G. Tasker. Oxford: Oxford University Press and Cambridge University Press, 1964.

–. *Holy Bible*...Translated out of the Original Tongues...TheText Conformable to That of the Edition of 1611, Commonly Known as the Authorized or King James Version. Philadelphia: A.J. Holman.

Boyce, Mary, ed. *Textual Sources for the Study of Zoroastrianism.* Totowa, New Jersey: Barnes and Noble, 1984.

Caesar. *C. Iuli Caesaris Commentariorum Pars Prior...Pars Posterior.* 2 vols. Renatus du Pontet (ed.). Oxford: Clarendon Press, 1908.

Catullus. *Catulli Carmina.* Robinson Ellis, ed. Oxford: Clarendon Press, 1904.

Cicero. *De Re Publica, De Lebigus.* With an English Translation by Clinton Walker Keyes. Cambridge: Harvard University Press, 1966.

–. *Select Letters with Historical Introductions Notes and Appendices.* 2 vols. W.W. How and A.C. Clark, ed. Oxford: Oxford University Press, 1926.

Demosthenes. "De Corona." In *Demosthenes II.* With an English Translation by C.A. Vince. Cambridge: Harvard University Press, 1971.

Dio Cassius. *Cassius Dio: The Augustan Settlement (Roman History 53-55.9).* Edited with Translation and Commentary by J.W. Rich. Warminster: Aris and Phillips Ltd, 1990.

–. *Dio's Roman History.* With an English Translastion by Easrnest Cary in 9 Volumes. Cambridge: Harvard University Press, 1961.

Diodorus Siculus. *Diodorus of Sicily in Twelve Volumes: IV Books IX-XII.40.* Translated by C.H. Oldfather. London: Heineman, 1970.

–.*Diodorus of Sicily in Twelve Volumes: VIII Books XVI. 66-95 and XVII.* Translated by C. Bradford Welles. Cambridge: Harvard University Press, 1983.

Dionysius of Halicarnassus. *The Roman Antiquities of Dionysius of Halicarnassus.* With an English Translation by Earnest Cary in

Seven Volumes. Cambridge: Harvard University Press, 1937.

Ernout, Alfred. *Recueil de Textes Latins Archaiques.* Paris: Librairie C. Klincksieck, 1966.

Eusebius. *The History of the Church from Christ to Constantine.* Translated with an Introduction by G.A. Williamson. Dorset Press, 1984.

—. *The Life of Constantine.* A Revised Translation with Prolegomena and Notes by Ernest Cushing Richardson. In Philip Schaff and Henry Wace, ed., *A Select Library of Nicene and Post-Nicene Fathers of the Christian Church.* Second Series. *vol. 1: Eusebius.* New York: Charles Scribners Sons, 1904.

Hanno the Carthaginian. *Periplus.* Translated and Edited by Al. N. Oikonomides. Chicago: Ares, 1977.

Herodotus. *The Histories.* Translated by George Rawlinson. New York: Everyman's Library, 1997.

Hesiod. *Hesiod.* Translated by Richmond Lattimore. Ann Arbor: The University of Michigan Press, 1977.

Homer. *The Iliad of Homer.* Tanslated and with an Introduction by Richmond Lattimore. Chicago: University of Illinois Press, 1951.

—. *The Odyssey of Homer.* A Modern Translation by Richmond Lattimore. New York: Harper & Row, 1965.

Horace. *Q. Horati Flacci Opera.* 3rd ed. Fridericus Klingner (ed.). Leipsig: Teubner, 1959.

Jordanes. *The Gothic History of Jordanes.* An English Version with an Introduction and a Commentary by Charles Christopher Mierow. 1915. Reprint, Cambridge: Speculum Historiae, 1960.

Justin. *Justin, Cornelius Nepos, and Eutropius.* Literally Translated with Notes and a General Index by John Selby Watson. London: Henry G. Bohn, 1853.

Justinian. *The Digest of Justinian.* Translation Edited by Alan Watson. 2 vols. Philadelphia: University of Pennsylvania Press, 1998.

—. *The Digest of Roman Law: Theft, Rapine, Damage, and Insult.* Edited and Translated by C.F. Kolbert. Hammondsworth: Penguin Books, 1975.

—. *Justinian's Institutes.* Translated with an Introduction by Peter Birks and Grant McLeod. Ithaca: Cornell University Press, 1987.

Juvenal. *The Satires of Juvenal.* Translated by Rolfe Humphries.

Bloomington: Indiana University Press, 1958.

Lactantius. *Lactance De la mort des persécuteurs.* Introduction, texte critique et traduction de J. Moreau. Paris: Les éditions du cerf, 1954.

Lattimore, Richmond, tr. *Greek Lyrics,* 2nd ed. Chicago: University of Chicago Press, 1960.

Lichtheim, Miriam, ed. *Ancient Egyptian Literature: A Book of Readings.* 3 Volumes. Berkeley: University of California Press, 1973.

Livy. *A History of Rome: Selections.* Translated, with an Introduction by Moses Hadas and Joe P. Poe. New York: Modern Library, 1962.

—. *Livy in 14 Volumes.* With an English Translation by B.O. Foster et al. Cambridge: Harvard University Press, 1976.

—. *The War With Hannibal: Books XXI-XXX of The History of Rome from its Foundation.* Translated by Aubrey de Sélincourt. Harmondsworth: Penguin Books, 1968.

Lucretius. *The Way Things Are: The De Rerum Natura of Titus Lucretius Carus.* Translated by Rolfe Humphries. London: Indiana University Press, 1973.

Lysias. *Lysias,* with an English Translation by W.R.M. Lamb. London: William Heinemann, 1967.

Manetho. *Manetho.* Translated by W. G. Waddell. London: William Heinemann, 1971.

Moore, J.A. *Selections from the Greek Elegiac, Iambic, and Lyric Poets.* Cambridge: Harvard University Press, 1965.

Ovid. *P. Ovidii Nasonis Metamorphoseon Libri XV.* Leiden: E.J. Brill, 1982.

Petronius. *The Cena Trimalchionis of Petronius.* Edited by W.B. Sedgwick. Oxford: At the Clarendon Press, 1964.

Plato. *Apology of Socrates and Crito.* Edited by Louis Dyer. Boston: Ginn & Company, 1895.

—. *Laws.* Translated by A.E. Taylor. In *The Collected Dialogues of Plato.* Edited by Edith Hamilton and Huntington Cairns. Princeton: Princeton University Press, 1961.

—. *Plato in Twelve Volumes. III: Lysis, Symposium, Gorgias.* With an English Translation by W.R.M. Lamb. London: William Heinemann, 1967.B

—. *Plato With an English Translation: Euthyphro, Apology, Crito, Phaedo, Phaedrus.* Translated by Harold North Fowler. London:

William Heinemann, 1966.

—. *The Republic of Plato.* Translated with Introduction and Notes by Francis MacDonald Cornford. New York: Oxford University Press, 1945.

—. *Why So, Socrates?* A Dramatic Version of Plato's Dialogues Euthyphro Apology Crito Phaedo by I.A. Richards. Cambridge: At the University Press, 1964.

Pliny the Younger. *Plinius, Epistulae.* A Critical Edition by Selatie Edgar Stout. Bloomington: Indiana University Press, 1962.

Plutarch. Plutarch: *The Lives of the Noble Grecians and Romans.* Translated by John Dryden and Revised by Arthur Hugh Clough. New York: The Modern Library.

Polybius. *Polybius on Roman Imperialism*: The Histories of Polybius Translated from the Text of F. Hultsch by Evelyn S. Shuckburgh. Abridged, with an Introduction by Alvin H. Bernstein. South Bend: Regnery/Gateway, 1980.

Pritchard, James B., ed. *Ancient Near Eastern Texts Relating to the Old Testament.* Princeton: Princeton University Press 1969.

Procopius. *Procopius.* With an English Translation by H.B. Dewing. 7 vols. Cambridge: Harvard University Press, 1969.

Quintus Curtius. *Quinte-Curce: Histoires.* 2 vols. Texte établi et traduit par H. Bardon. Paris: Société d'édition «Les Belles Lettres» 1961.

Quirke, Stephen and Carol Andrews, tr. *The Rosetta Stone: Facsimile Drawing.* New York: Harry N. Abrams, 1989.

Sallust. *C. Sallusti Crispi: Catilina, Iugurtha, Fragmenta Ampliora.* Alphonsus Kurfess, ed. Leipzig: Teubner, 1957.

Scriptores Historiae Augustae. 3 vols. With an English Translation by David Magie. Cambridge: Harvard University Press, 1960-1961.

Simpson, William Kelly, ed. *The Literature of Ancient Egypt.* New Haven: Yale University Press, 1972.

Suetonius. *C. Suetoni Tranquilli Opera Vol. I De Vita Caesarum Libri VIII.* Maximilianus Ihm, ed. Stutgardt: Teubner, 1978.

Tacitus. *Cornelii Taciti Libri Qui Supersunt.* 2 vols. 2nd ed. Erich Koestermann, ed. Leipzig: Teubner, 1965.

—. *Germania.* Edited with Commentary by J.G.C. Anderson. Oxford: Clarendon Press, 1938.

Tertullian. *Tertullien Apologétique.* Texte établi et traduit par Jean-Pierre Waltzing et Albert Severyns. Paris: Société d'édition

«Les Belles Lettres» 1929.

Theodoret. *The Ecclesiastical History.* In Henry Wace and Philip Schaff, ed., *A Select Library of Nicene and Post-Nicene Fathers of the Christian Church.* Second Series, vol. 3. New York: The Christian Literature Company, 1906.

Thucydides. *The Complete Writings of Thucydides: The Peloponnesian War.* Translated by Crawley. New York: The Modern Library, 1951.

Ventris, Michael and John Chadwick. *Documents in Mycenean Greek.* Cambridge: Cambridge University Press, 1959.

Vergil. *The Aeneid of Virgil:* A Verse Translation by Rolfe Humphries. New York: Charles Scribner's Sons, 1951.

—. *Virgil's Aeneid.* Translation by John Dryden. New York: Airmont, 1968.

Xenophon. "Constitution of the Lacedaemonians" in *Xenophon: Scripta Minora* . With an English Translation by E. C. Marchant. Cambridge: Harvard University Press, 1956.

—. *Cyropaedia.* With an English Translation by Walter Miller. 2 vols. London: William Heinemann, 1968.

—. *Xenophon in Seven Volumes: I and II Hellenica.* With an English Translation by Carleton L. Brownson. Cambridge: Harvard University Press, 1968.

Zosimus. *New History.* A Translation with Commentary by Ronald T. Ridley. Canberra: Australian Association for Byzantine Studies, 1982.

Modern Sources

Aitken, MJ.; C.B. Stringer; and P.A. Mellars. *The Origin of Modern Humans and the Impact of Chronometric Dating.* Princeton: Princeton University Press, 1993.

Andrews, Carol. *Egyptian Mummies.* Cambridge: Harvard University Press, 1984.

Ardrey, Robert. *African Genesis.* New York: Dell, 1961.

Baines, John. "The Dawn of the Amarna Age." In *Amenhotep III: Perspectives on His Reign.* Edited by David O'Connor and Eric H. Cline.

Barnes, Timothy. "Constantine, Athanasius and the Christian Church." In Lieu, Samuel N.C. and Dominic Montserrat, ed., *Constantine: History, Historiography and Legend.* London: Routledge, 1998.

Beard, Mary, John North, and Simon Price. *Religions of Rome.* 2 Vols. Cambridge: Cambridge University Press, 1998.

Beare, W. *The Roman Stage.* London: Methuen and Co., 1968.

Beaulieu, Paul-Alain. *The Reign of Nabonidus King of Babylon 556-539 B.C.* New Haven: Yale University Press, 1989.

Bernstein, Alvin H. *Tiberius Sempronius Gracchus: Tradition and Apostasy.* Ithaca: Cornell University Press, 1978.

Bickerman, E. J. *Chronology of the Ancient World.* Ithaca: Cornell University Press, 1980.

Bleicken, Jochen. *Augustus: Eine Biographie.* Berlin: Alexander Fest Verlag, 1998.

Blumler, Mark, "Ecology, evolutionary theory and agricultural origins." In *Origins and Spread of Agriculture,* ed. David R. Harris, 25-50.

Borkowski, Andrew. *Textbook on Roman Law.* London: Blackstone Press, 1994.

Bornkamm, Günther. *Jesus of Nazareth.* New York: Harper and Row, 1960.

—. *Paul.* New York: Hárper and Row, 1971.

Brace, C.L., and M.F. Ashley Montagu. *Man's Evolution, an Intro-*

duction to Physical Anthropology. New York: Macmillan, 1965.

Brace, C. Loring. *The Stages of Human Evolution.* Englewood Cliffs, New Jersey: Prentice Hall, 1967.

Braidwood, Robert J. "Near Eastern Prehistory," in Fried, 1968.

Brain, C.K. *The Hunter or the Hunted?* Chicago: University of Chicago Press, 1981.

Brantlinger, Patrick. *Bread and Circuses: Theories of Mass Culture and Social Decay.* Ithaca: Cornell University Press, 1983.

Breasted, James. *Development of Religion and Thought in Ancient Egypt.* 1912. Reprint, Philadelphia: University of Pennsylvania Press, 1986.

—. *A History of Egypt.* New York: Scribners, 1909.

—. "Ikhnaton." In *Encyclopaedia Britannica,* 1960 edition.

Briant, Pierre. *Histoire de L'Empire Perse: De Cyrus à Alexandre.* Paris: Fayard, 1996.

Brown, Peter. "Bodies and Minds: Sexuality and Renunciation in Early Christianity." In *Before Sexuality.* ed. David M. Halperin, John J. Winkler, and Froma I. Zeitlin. Princeton: Princeton University Press, 1990.

Browning, Robert. *Justinian and Theodora.* London: Thames and Hudson, 1987.

Budge, E.A. Wallis. *Ancient Egyptian Language: Easy Lessons in Egyptian Hieroglyphics.* 1910. Reprint, Chicago: Ares, 1975.

—. *An Egyptian Hieroglyphic Dictionary.* 2 Volumes. 1920. Reprint. New York: Dover Publications, 1978.

—. *Egyptian Religion.* 1900. Reprint, New York: Bell Publishing Company, 1959.

Buffière, Félix. *Eros adolescent, la péderastie dans la Grèce antique.* Paris: Les Belles Lettres, 1980.

Bultman, Rudolf. *Primitive Christianity in its Contemporary Setting.* London: Thames and Hudson, 1956.

Burkert, Walter. *Ancient Mystery Cults.* Cambridge: Harvard University Press, 1987.

Bury, J.B. *History of the Later Roman Empire from the Death of Theodosius I to the Death of Justinian.* 2 vols. 1923. Reprint, New York: Dover Publications, 1958.

—. *The Invasion of Europe by the Barbarians.* New York: Norton, 1967.

Cambridge Ancient History: Volume II Parts 1 and 2: History of the Middle East and the Aegean Region c. 1800-1380 B.C. 3 Volumes. Third Edition. Edited by I.E.S. Edwards; C.J. Gadd; N.G.L.

Hammond; and E. Sollberger. Cambridge: Cambridge University Press, 1973.

—. *Volume V: Athens: 478-401 B.C.* Seventh Impression. Edited by J.B. Bury; S.A. Cook; and F.E. Adcock. Cambridge: Cambridge University Press, 1969.

—. *Volume V: The Fifth Century B.C.* Second Edition. Edited by D.M. Lewis; John Boardman; J.K. Davies; M. Ostwald. Cambridge: Cambridge University Press, 1992.

—. *Volume VI: Macedon: 401-301 B.C.* Second Impression. Edited by J.B. Bury; S.A. Cook; and F.E. Adcock. Cambridge: Cambridge University Press, 1933.

—. *Volume VII Part 2: The Rise of Rome to 220 B.C.* Second Edition. Edited by F.W. Walbank; A.E. Astin; M.W. Frederiksen; and R.M. Ogilvie. Cambridge: Cambridge University Press, 1989.

—. *Volume VIII: Rome and the Mediterranean.* Second Edition. Edited by A.E. Astin;F.W. Walbank; M.W. Frederiksen; and R.M. Ogilvie. Cambridge: Cambridge University Press, 1989.

—. *Volume IX: The Roman Republic: 133-44 B.C.* Edited by S.A. Cook; F.E. Adcock, M.P. Charlesworth. Cambridge: Cambridge University Press, 1932.

—. *Volume IX: The Last Age of the Roman Republic, 146-43 B.C.* Second Edition. Edited by J.A. Crook; Andrew Lintott; Elizabeth Rawson. Cambridge: Cambridge University Press, 1994.

—. *Volume X: The Augustan Empire: 44B.C.-A.D. 70.* Second Impression. Edited by S.A. Cook; F.E. Adcock; and M.P. Charlesworth. Cambridge: Cambridge University Press, 1952.

—. *Volume X: The Augustan Empire, 43 B.C.-A.D. 69.* Second Edition. Edited by Alan K. Bowman; Edward Champlin; Andrew Lintott. Cambridge: Cambridge University Press, 1996.

—. *Volume XI: The Imperial Peace: A.D. 70-192.* Second Impression. Edited by S.A. Cook; F.E. Adcock, and M.P. Charlesworth. Cambridge: Cambridge University Press, 1954.

—. *Volume XIII: The Late Empire, A.D. 337-425.* Edited by Averil Cameron and Peter Garnsey. Cambridge: Cambridge University Press, 1998.

Cameron, Averil. *The Later Roman Empire AD 284-430.* Cambridge: Harvard University Press, 1993.

—. *The Mediterranean World in Late Antiquity, AD 395-600.* London: Routledge, 1993.

Campbell, Joseph. *The Hero With a Thousand Faces.* New York:

Pantheon Books, 1949.

Carcopino, Jérôme. *Daily Life in Ancient Rome.* New Haven: Yale University Press, 1975.

Carter, Howard and A.C. Mace. *The Discovery of the Tomb of Tutankhamon.* 1923. Reprint, New York: Dover Publications, 1977.

Cartwright, David. *A Historical Commentary on Thucydides: A Companion to Rex Warner's Penguin Translation.* Ann Arbor: The University of Michigan Press, 1997.

Castleden, Rodney. *Atlantis Destroyed.* London: Routledge, 1998.

–. *Minoans: Life in Bronze Age Crete.* London: Routledge, 1990.

Ceram, C.W. *Gods, Graves, and Scholars.* New York: Knopf, 1973.

–. *Hands on the Past.* New York: Knopf, 1966.

Chadwick, John. *The Decipherment of Linear B.* Cambridge: Cambridge University Press, 1970.

Childe, V. Gordon. "The Birth of Civilization." in Fried, 1968.

Clauss, Manfred. *Mithras: Kult und Mysterien.* München: C.H. Beck, 1990.

Coomaraswamy, Ananda. *Buddha and the Gospel of Buddhism.* New Hyde Park, New York: University Books, 1964.

Corcoran, Simon. *The Empire of the Tetrarchs: Imperial Pronouncements and Government AD 284-324.* Oxford: Clarendon Press, 1996.

Cornell, T.J. *The Beginnings of Rome: Italy and Rome from the Bronze Age to the Punic Wars c. 1000-264 BC.* London: Routledge, 1995.

Crawford, Harriet. *Sumer and the Sumerians.* Cambridge: Cambridge University Press, 1991.

Crawford, Michael. *The Roman Republic.* Second Edition. Cambridge: Harvard Univrsity Press, 1993.

Cumont, Franz. *The Mysteries of Mithra.* 1903. Reprint, New York: Dover Publications, 1956.

–. *Oriental Relgions in Roman Paganism.* 1911. Reprint, New York: Dover Publications, 1956.

Dart, Raymond A. "The Cultural Status of the South African Man-Apes" in Fried, 1959.

Dilke, O.A.W. *Reading the Past: Mathematics and Measurement.* Berkeley: University of California Press, 1987.

Dover, K.J. *Greek Homosexuality.* New York: Vintage Books, 1980.

Duff, J. Wight. *A Literary History of Rome: from the Origins to the Close of the Golden Age.* New York: Barnes and Noble, 1960.

–. *A Literary History of Rome in the Silver Age: From Tiberius to Hadrian*. London: T. Fisher Unwin, 1927.

Ehrman, Bart D. *The New Testament: A Historical Introduction to the Early Christian Writings*. New York: Oxford University Press, 1997.

Eisenman, Robert. *James the Brother of Jesus*. New York: Viking, 1996.

Eldredge, Niles, and Ian Tattersall. *The Myths of Human Evolution*. New York: Columbia University Press, 1982.

Evans, J.A.S. *The Age of Justinian; The Circumstances of Imperial Power*. London: Routledge, 1996.

Everyman's Atlas of Ancient and Classical Geography. London: J.M. Dent, 1952.

The First Men. New York: Time-Life Books, 1973.

Flannery, Kent V. "The Ecology of Early Food Production in Mesopotamia," in Fried, 1968.

Fornara, Charles W. and Loren J. Samons II. *Athens from Cleisthenes to Pericles*. Berkeley: University of California Press, 1991.

Forster, E.M. *Alexandria: A History and a Guide*. Garden City: Anchor Books, 1961.

Foucault, Michel. *Le Souci de Soi*. Paris: Gallimard, 1984.

Fraenkel, Eduard. *Horace*. London: Oxford University Press, 1966.

Frank, Tenney. *An Economic History of Rome to the End of the Republic*. Baltimore: The Johns Hopkins Press, 1920.

–. *An Economic Survey of Ancient Rome: Volume V. Rome and Italy of the Empire*. Baltimore: The Johns Hopkins Press, 1940.

Frazer, Sir James George. *The Golden Bough: One Volume Abridged Edition*. New York: Macmillan, 1963.

Frerichs, Ernest S. and Leonard H. Lesko, ed. *Exodus: The Egyptian Evidence*. Winona Lake, Indiana: Eisenbrauns, 1997.

Fried, Morton H. *Readings in Anthropology*. New York: Thomas Crowell, 1959.

–. *Readings in Anthropology Second Edition*. New York: Thomas Crowewll, 1968.

Galinsky, Karl. *Augustan Culture: An Interpretive Introduction*. Princeton: Princeton University Press, 1996.

Gardiner, Alan. *Egypt of the Pharaohs*. London: Oxford University Press, 1964.

Gelzer, Matthias. *Caesar: Politician and Statesman*. Cambridge: Harvard University Press, 1968.

Gibbon, Edward. *The Decline and Fall of the Roman Empire.* 3 Volumes. Edited by Oliphant Smeaton. New York: The Modern Library.

Gilbert, Katharine Stoddert; Joan K. Hold; and Sara Hudson, ed. *Treasures of Tutankhamun.* New York: Ballantine Books, 1976.

Glob, P.V. *The Bog People: Iron-Age Man Preserved.* New York: Ballantine Books, 1970.

Gomme, A.W. *The Population of Athens in the Fifth and Fourth Centuries.* 1933. Reprint, Chicago: Argonaut, 1967.

Gordon, R.L. "Franz Cumont and the Doctrines of Mithraism." In *Mithraic Studies: Proceedings of the First International Congress of Mithraic Studies.* Edited by John R. Hinnells. Manchester: Manchester University Press, 1975.

Gould, Stephen Jay. *The Panda's Thumb.* New York: W.W. Norton, 1980.

Grandazzi, Alexander. *The Foundation of Rome: Myth and History.* Translated by Jane Marie Todd. Ithaca: Cornell University Press, 1997.

Grant, Michael. *The Emperor Constantine.* London: Weidenfeld & Nicolson, 1993.

Green, Peter. *Alexander of Macedon 356-323 B.C.: A Historical Biography.* Berkeley: University of California Press, 1991.

—. *The Greco-Persian Wars.* Berkeley: University of California Press, 1996.

Greenhalgh, Peter. *Pompey: The Roman Alexander.* Columbia: University of Missouri Press, 1981.

Grenier, A. "La Gaule Romaine." In Tenney Frank, ed., *An Economic Survey of Ancient Rome.* Volume 3. Baltimore: The Johns Hopkins Press, 1937.

Grimal, Nicholas. *A History of Ancient Egypt.* Oxford: Blackwell, 1992.

Gruen, Erich S. *The Hellenistic World and the Coming of Rome.* 2 vols. Berkeley: University of California Press, 1984.

—. "The Last Years of Philip V." *Greek Roman and Byzantine Studies* 15 (1974): 221-246.

Gwatkin, Henry Melvill. *Studies of Arianism.* Cambridge: Deighton, Bell, and Co., 1882.

Hadas, Moses. *Ancilla to Classical Reading.* New York: Columbia University Press, 1961.

Hallo, William W. and William Kelly Simpson. *The Ancient Near*

East: A History. Second Edition. Fort Worth: Harcourt Brace College Publishers, 1998.

Halperin, David M. *One Hundred Years of Homosexuality*. New York: Routledge, 1990.

Hamilton, Edith. *Mythology*. New York: Mentor Books, 1953.

Hammond, N.G.L. *The Genius of Alexander*. London: Duckworth, 1997.

—. *A History of Greece to 322 B.C.* Oxford: at the Clarendon Press, 1967.

Harlan, Jack R. *The Living Fields: Our Agricultural Heritage*. Cambridge: Cambridge University Press, 1995.

Harris, David R., ed. *The Origins and Spread of Agriculture and Pastoralism in Eurasia*. London: UCL Press, 1996.

Haskins, Charles Homer. *The Rise of Universities*. Ithaca: Cornell University Press, 1957.

Hening, Martin, ed. *A Handbook of Roman Art*. Ithaca: Cornell University Press, 1983.

Henry, Donald O. *From Foraging to Agriculture*. Philadelphia: University of Pennsylvania Press, 1989.

Heurgon, Jacques. *Rome et la Méditerranée occidentale jusqu'aux guerres puniques*. 3rd ed. Paris: Presses Universitaires de France, 1993.

Higgens, Reynold. *The Archaeology of Minoan Crete*. New York: Henry Z. Walck, 1973.

—. *Greek and Roman Jewellery*, 2nd ed. Berkeley: University of California Press, 1980.

Hillman, Gordon. "Late Pleistocene Changes in Wild Plant-foods Available to Hunter-gatherers of the Northern Fertile Crescent: Possible Preludes to Cereal Cultivation." In *The Origins and Spread of Agriculture*. Edited by David R. Harris, 159-203.

Hinnells, John R. "Reflections on the Bull-slaying Scene." In *Mithraic Studies: Proceedings of the First International Congress of Mithraic Studies*. Edited by John R. Hinnells. Manchester: Manchester University Press, 1975.

Hitti, Philip K. *History of the Arabs*. Eighth Edition. London: Macmillan, 1964.

Hooker, J.T. "Linear B as a Source for Social History." In *The Greek World*. Edited by Anton Powell. London: Routledge, 1995.

Hooper, Richard. *The Priapus Poems: Erotic Epigrams from Ancient*

Rome. Urbana: University of Illinois Press, 1999.

Howell, F. Clark. "Varieties of 'Neanderthal' Man," in Fried, 1968.

Huot, Jean-Louis. *Les Sumériens.* Paris: Éditions Errance, 1989.

Hyde, Walter Woodburn. *Ancient Greek Mariners.* New York: Oxford University Press, 1947.

Jacobsen, Thorkild. "Primitive Democracy in Ancient Mesopotamia." In Kagan, *Problems in Ancient History Volume 1,* pp. 6-13.

Jaeger, Werner. *Paideia: Die Formung des Griechischen Menschen.* 1933-1947; reprint, 3 vols. in 1. Berlin: Walter de Gruyer, 1973.

Jebb, R.C. *The Attic Orators from Antiphon to Isaeos.* 2 Volumes. 1875. Reprint, New York: Russell and Russell, 1962.

Johanson, Donald; Lenora Johanson; and Blake Edgar. *Ancestors: In Search of Human Origins.* New York: Villard Books, 1994.

Jones, A.H.M. *Constantine and the Conversion of Europe.* London: The English Universities Press, 1961.

—. *The Decline of the Ancient World.* New York: Holt, Rinehart and Winston, 1966.

—. *The Later Roman Empire 284-602: A Social Economic and Administrative Survey.* 3 vols. Oxford: Basil Blackwell, 1964.

Jung, Carl. *Psychology and Religion.* New Haven: Yale University Press, 1938.

Kagan, Donald. *The Archidamian War.* Ithaca: Cornell University Press, 1974.

—. *The Fall of the Athenian Empire.* Ithaca: Cornell University Press, 1987.

—. *The Outbreak of the Peloponnesian War.* Ithaca: Cornell University Press, 1969.

—. *The Peace of Nicias and the Sicilian Expedition.* Ithaca: Cornell University Press, 1981.

—. *Pericles of Athens and the Birth of Democracy.* New York: Touchstone Books, 1991.

—. *Problems in Ancient History.* 2 Volumes. London: Macmillan, 1972.

Keuls, Eva C. *The Reign of the Phallus.* Cambridge: Harper and Row, 1985.

Kirk, G.S. and J.E. Raven. *The Presocratic Philosophers.* Cambridge: Cambridge University Press, 1966.

Koldewey, Robert. "The Walls of Babylon." In *Hands on the Past.*

Edited by W.C. Ceram.

Kramer, Samuel Noah. *History Begins at Sumer.* New York: Doubleday Anchor Books, 1959.

—. *The Sumerians.* Chicago: The University of Chicago Press, 1963.

Kuhrt, Amélie. *The Ancient Near East c. 3000-330 BC.* 2 vols. London: Routledge, 1995.

Lancel, Serge. *Carthage: A History.* London: Blackwell, 1995.

—. *Hanibal.* London: Blackwell, 1998.

Langguth, A.J. *A Noise of War: Caesar, Pompey, Octavian and the Struggle for Rome.* New York: Simon and Schuster, 1994.

Lanpo, Jia, and Huang Weiwen. *The Story of Peking Man: From Archaeology to Mystery.* Beijing: Foreign Languages Press and Hong Kong: Oxford University Press, 1990.

Lazenby, J.F. *The Defence of Greece 490-479 B.C.* Warminster, England: Aris & Phillips, 1993.

Leakey, Richard, and Alan Walker. "Homo Erectus Unearthed," *National Geographic,* 168, no. 5 (Nov. 1985) pages 625-629.

Leakey, Richard, and Roger Lewin. *Origins.* New York: E.P. Dutton, 1982.

LeGros Clark, W.E. *The Fossil Evidence for Human Evolution.* Chicago: The University of Chicago Press, 1964.

Lesky, Albin. *A History of Greek Literature.* New York: Thomas Y. Crowell, 1966.

Lévi-Strauss, Claude. *Myth and Meaning.* New York: Schocken Books, 1978.

—. *La Pensée Sauvage.* Paris: Librairie Plon, 1962.

Lieu, Samuel N.C. and Dominic Montserrat, ed. *Constantine: History, Historiorgaphy and Legend.* London: Routledge, 1998.

Lise, Giorgio. *How to Recognize Egyptian Art.* New York: Penguin Books, 1980.

MacMullen, Ramsay. *Christianizing the Roman Empire.* New Haven: Yale University Press, 1984.

—. *Constantine.* London: Weidenfeld and Nicolson, 1969.

—. *Corruption and the Decline of Rome.* New Haven: Yale University Press, 1988.

—. *Paganism in the Roman Empire.* New Haven: Yale University Press, 1981.

Marchand, Leslie A. (ed.). *Lord Byron Selected Letters and Journals.* Cambridge: Harvard University Press, 1982.

Marrou, Henri-Irénée. *L'Église de l'antiquité tardive.* Paris: Éditions de Seuil, 1985.

–. *Histoire de l'éducation dans l'antiquité.* Paris: Éditions du seuil, 1948.

McDonald, William and Carol C. Thomas. *Progress into the Past: The Rediscovery of Mycenean Civilization,* 2nd ed. Bloomington: Indiana University Press, 1990.

McEvedy, Colin. *The Penguin Atlas of Ancient History.* Harmondsworth: Penguin Books, 1967.

Meier, Christian. *Athens: A Portrait of the City in Its Golden Age.* New York: Henry Holt and Company, 1998.

–. *Caesar.* David McLintock, tr. New York: Harper Collins, 1995.

Mellars, Paul. *The Neanderthal Legacy: An Archaeological Perspective from Western Europe.* Princeton: Princeton University Press, 1996.

Metzger, Ernest, ed. *A Companion to Justinian's Institutes.* Ithaca: Cornell University Press, 1998.

Millar, Fergus, ed. *The Roman Empire and its Neighbours.* New York: Delacorte Press, 1967.

Miller, Margaret C. *Athens and Persia in the Fifth Century BC: A Study in Cultural Receptivity.* Cambridge: Cambridge University Press, 1997.

Mommsen, Theodor. *The History of Rome.* 4 vols. New York: Scribner, Armstrong, and Co., 1873.

Montagu, Ashley, ed. *Science and Creationism.* Oxford: Oxford University Press, 1984.

Montesquieu. *Considérations sur les causes de la grandeur des romains et de leur décadence.* Paris: Garnier-Flammarion, 1968.

Morby, John E. *Dynasties of the World.* Oxford: Oxford University Press, 1989.

Mumford, Louis. *The City in History.* New York: Harcourt Brace, 1961.

Murphy-Oconnor, Jerome. *Paul: A Critical Life.* Oxford: Clarendon Press, 1996.

Néraudau, Jean-Pierre. *Auguste: Le Brique et le marbre.* Paris: Les Belles Lettres, 1996.

Nicholas, Barry. *An Introduction to Roman Law.* London: at the Clarendon Press, 1962.

O'Brien, John Maxwell. *Alexander the Great: The Invisible Enemy.* London: Routledge, 1992.

O'Connor, David and Eric H. Cline, ed. *Amenhotep III; Perspectives on His Reign.* Ann Arbor: The University of Michigan Press, 1998.

Oliva, Pavel. *Sparta and her Social Problems.* Prague: Academia, 1971.

Page, Denys. *History and the Homeric Iliad.* Berkeley: University of California Press, 1966.

Pelikan, Jaroslav. *Jesus Through the Centuries.* New York: Harper and Row, 1987.

Pendlebury, J.D.S. *A Handbook to the Palace of Minos with its Dependencies.* London: Max Parrish, 1954.

Perelli, Luciano. *I Gracchi.* Rome: Salerno Editrice, 1993.

Perrin, Norman. *The New Testament: An Introduction.* New York: Harcourt Brace, 1974.

Peyrefitte, Roger. *Alexandre le Grand.* Paris: Albin Michel, 1981.

–. *La Jeunesse d'Alexandre.* Paris: Albin Michel, 1977.

–. *Les Conquêtes d'Alexandre.* Paris: Albin Michel, 1979.

Pilbeam, David R. and Simons, Elwyn L. "Some Problems of Hominid Classifications" in Fried, 1968.

Previté-Orton, C.W. *The Shorter Cambridge Medieval History.* 2 vols. Cambridge: Cambridge University Press, 1953.

Pritchard, James B. *Archeology and the Old Testament.* Princeton: Princeton University Press, 1958.

Radin, Paul. *The Trickster.* New York: Schocken Books, 1972.

Redford, Donald B. *Akhenaten the Heretic King.* Princeton: Princeton University Press, 1984.

Reiter, William. *Aemilius Paullus: Conqueror of Greece.* London: Croom Helm, 1988.

Richter, G.M.A. *A Handbook of Greek Art.* London: Phaidon Press, 1959.

Rindos, David. *The Origins of Agriculture.* San Diego: Academic Press, 1984.

Robinson, Charles Alexander. *Ancient History.* London: Macmillan, 1967.

Rogers, Elizabeth Frances, ed. *St. Thomas More: Selected Letters.* New Haven: Yale University Press, 1961.

Rostovtzeff, M. *Greece.* Oxford: Oxford University Press: 1963.

–. *Rome.* Oxford: Oxford University Press, 1960.

–. *The Social and Economic History of the Roman Empire.* Second edition. 2 vols. Oxford: At the Clarendon Press, 1963.

Runciman, Steven. *Byzantine Civilization.* Cleveland: The World

Publishing Company, 1967.

Sarton, George. *A History of Science.* 2 vols. Cambridge: Harvard University Press, 1952-1959.

Schweitzer, Albert. *Aus meinem Leben und Denken.* München: Siebenstern Taschenbuch, 1965.

—. *The Psychiatric Study of Jesus.* Boston: the Beacon Press, 1948.

—. *The Quest of the Historical Jesus.* New York: Macmillan, 1968.

Scullard, H.H. *From the Gracchi to Nero.* London: University Paperbacks, 1966.

—. *A History of the Roman World 753 to 146 BC.* Fourth edition. London: Methuen, 1980.

Seager, Robin. *Pompey: A Political Biography.* Oxford: Basil Blackwell, 1979.

Shotter, David. *The Fall of the Roman Republic.* London: Routledge, 1994.

Smith, Bruce D. *The Emergence of Agriculture.* New York: Scientific American Library, 1995.

Snowden, Frank M. *Blacks in Antiquity.* Cambridge: Harvard University Press, 1971.

Spengler, Oswald. *The Decline of the West.* 2 vols. London: George Allen, 1926.

Stockton, David. *The Gracchi.* Oxford: Clarendon Press, 1979.

Stringer, Christopher, and Clive Gamble. *In Search of the Neanderthals: Solving the Puzzle of Human Origins.* London: Thames and Hudson, 1993.

Syme, Ronald. *The Roman Revolution.* Oxford: Oxford University Press, 1960.

Tarn, W.W. *Alexander the Great.* 1948. Reprint, Chicago: Ares, 1981.

Tattersall, Ian. *The Fossil Trail: How We Know What We Think We Know about Human Evolution.* New York: Oxford University Press, 1995.

Taylor, Lily Ross. *Party Politics in the Age of Caesar.* Berkeley: University of California Press, 1971.

Tellegen-Couperus, Olga. *A Short History of Roman Law.* London: Routledge, 1993.

Thomas, Yan. "The Division of the Sexes in Roman Law." in Pauline Schmidt Panetl, ed., *A History of Women in the West: I, From Ancient Goddesses to Christian Saints.* Cambridge: The Belknap Press, 1992.

Thommen, Lukas. *Lakedaimonion Politeia: Die Enstehung der spartanischen Verfassung.* Stuttgart: Franz Steiner Verlag, 1996.

Toynbee, Arnold J. *A Study of History.* 2 volumes. ed. D.C. Somervell. New York: Oxford University Press, 1958.

Treuil, René; Pascal Darcque; Jean-Claude Poursat; and Gilles Touchais. *Les civilisations égéennes du Néolithique et de l'Age du Bronze.* Paris: Presses Universitaires de France, 1989.

Turnbull, Colin M. *The Forest People.* New York: Simon and Schuster, 1961.

Tyldesley, Joyce. *Hatchepsut: The Female Pharaoh.* London: Viking, 1996.

Ulansey, David. *The Origins of the Mithraic Mysteries.* New York: Oxford University Press, 1989.

Voltaire. *Dictionnaire philosophique.* Paris: Garnier, 1964.

Walker, C.B.F. *Cuneiform.* Berkeley: University of California Press, 1987.

Ward, Allen Mason. *Marcus Crassus and the Late Roman Republic.* Columbia: University of Missouri Press, 1977.

Watterson, Barbara. *Introducing Egyptian Hieroglyphics.* Edinburgh: Scottish Academic Press, 1981.

Weaver, Kenneth F. "The Search for our Ancestors," *National Geographic,* 168, no. 5 (Nov. 1985) pages 561-623.

Weiss, Johannes. *Jesus' Proclamation of the Kingdom of God.* Translated, edited, and with an Introduction by Richard Hyde Hiers and David Larrimore Holland. 1971. Reprint, Chico, California: Scholars Press, 1985.

Wells, Colin. *The Roman Empire.* Second Edition. Cambridge: Harvard University Press, 1992.

Wente, Edward F. "Tutankhamun and His World." In *Treastures of Tutankhamun.* New York: Ballantine Books, 1976.

White, Leslie A. *The Evolution of Culture.* New York: McGraw-Hill, 1959.

–. "The Great Man vs. the Cultural Process." In *Problems in Ancient History. Volume One: The Ancient Near East and Greece.* Edited by Donald Kagan.

Wilson, Edward O. *On Human Nature.* Cambridge: Harvard University Press, 1978.

–. *Sociobiology: The New Synthesis.* Cambridge: Harvard University Press, 1975.

Winkler, John J. *The Constraints of Desire.* New York: Routledge,

1990.

Wolff, Hans Julius. *Roman Law: An Historical Introduction*. Norman: University of Oklahoma Press, 1951.

Wooley, Leonard. *The Excavations at Ur.* London: Ernest Behn, 1955.

Index

Symbols

U

V

W

X

Z